DATE DUE

MY 20 '04			

DEMCO 38-296

Prime Time Law

Prime Time Law

Fictional Television as Legal Narrative

Edited by

Robert M. Jarvis

and

Paul R Joseph

CAROLINA ACADEMIC PRESS

Durham, North Carolina

Prime time law

For television viewers everywhere

ISBN (cloth) 0-89089-805-7
ISBN (paper) 0-89089-808-1
LCCN 98-85333

CAROLINA ACADEMIC PRESS
700 Kent Street
Durham, North Carolina 27701

Telephone (919) 489-7486
Fax (919) 493-5668
www.cap-press.com

Printed in the United States of America

On the jacket/cover (clockwise from bottom left): Richard Brooks as Paul Robinette ("Law & Order"), Jill Hennessy as Claire Kincaid ("Law & Order"), Harry Hamlin as Michael Kuzak and Susan Dey as Grace Van Owen ("L.A. Law"), Richard Dysart as Leland McKenzie ("L.A. Law"), and (center) Calista Flockhart as Ally McBeal ("Ally McBeal"). Images courtesy of Photofest.

Contents

Preface

Most of us will never meet a cowboy, or an atomic scientist, or a private detective, yet we feel that we know how such persons think and act because we have seen them, or their caricatures, in countless television shows. By the same token, most of us have only limited experience with the legal system, yet we feel we know what lawyers and judges do, and how they do it, because we have "appeared" in court with Perry Mason, "attended" a deposition with Arnie Becker, "investigated" a case with Ben Matlock, and "counseled" a client with Ally McBeal.

Television's ability to shape our view of the world in general, and the legal system in particular, makes it a powerful cultural force. More than just another form of entertainment, television serves at once as teacher, companion, and friend, influencing both what we see and how we see it.

Of course, television shows, particularly legal shows, must "look right." That is, characters and storylines must "make sense" and be "realistic," even if they do so only by reflecting earlier television shows. In this respect, the public and television occupy a symbiotic association in which neither side is able to move very far ahead of the other.

Because of this unique relationship, studying the myriad ways in which television presents lawyers and deals with legal issues provides us with an important opportunity to gauge the public's feeling about, and understanding of, the justice system. Although this can also be accomplished in other ways as well, television, as a recyclable medium, offers a vast amount of both contemporary and historical data to analyze and, as in the case of this book, write about.

Robert M. Jarvis
Paul R Joseph

Fort Lauderdale
April 1998

Foreword

CHARLES B. ROSENBERG

The stone structures of ancient Greece are mostly dust. Even the Parthenon lies in near-ruin. Greek dramatic structures, by contrast, are alive and well and living in your television set. You can see them every night on prime time: dramatic stories which feature a conflict, a prompt resolution of the conflict by story's end and what Aristotle called "denouement"—the tag scene at the very end that wraps things up emotionally for the audience.

Law is a natural stage for this type of drama. Criminal prosecutions and civil suits are conflicts by definition. At core, they are about who should win and who should lose. In dramatic terms, legal dramas heighten conflict even further by pitting protagonists one against the other in a confined space, usually a court room. Resolution arrives in the form of a verdict. The setting for denouement is ever present in court hallways, offices, jail cells, and execution chambers.

Criminal law has long been a favorite for dramatic legal stories because criminal cases have what dramatists refer to as "high stakes." If the state wins, the defendant is deprived of life or liberty. If the defendant wins, the victim's opportunity for vengeance is shattered. And win or lose, there is the ever present opportunity for wrenching self-examination, confession, and expiation.

The use of civil cases as the focus of television drama is a more recent phenomenon, as John Brigham points out in his essay on "L.A. Law." Perhaps the earlier dearth of civil legal dramas reflects the fact that during the 1950s, when dramatic television was in its formative years, civil cases had not yet become the almost blinding mirror of our social concerns that they are today. In 1954, the year *Brown v. Board of Education* was decided, the Civil Rights acts, the abortion debate, and the conflict over the right to die, among many others, were all at least a decade away. It is perhaps no accident that "The Defenders," which used social issues as its thematic material, albeit still in a criminal context, first went on the air in the Fall of 1961. The social topics explored on "The Defenders" presaged, in many ways, our long and ongoing national social debate about everything from civil rights to sexual mores. David Ray Papke explores "The Defenders" and delves deeply into its liberal social mores.

Today, television legal drama has matured to take in almost everything that is a matter of societal debate—the death penalty, gay rights, abortion, adoption, gang violence, drugs, mass murder, race relations, children's rights, sexual harassment, and disability rights, among many others. If "Perry Mason," so nicely described in this book by Norman Rosenberg, was primarily a 1950s detective dressed up to look like a lawyer, today's legal characters are, by contrast, veritable social engineers. As Douglas E. Abrams points out in his essay on "Picket Fences," during the show's run from 1992 to 1996 just about every issue in the world, civil and criminal, wandered into Judge Bone's courtroom in the fictional town of Rome, Wisconsin. My own favorite, by the way, was when the Pope was subpoenaed as a witness in connection with a domestic auto accident he had witnessed while on a trip to Wisconsin, thus bringing the concept of sovereign immunity to television viewers everywhere.

If television is a mirror of our time, however, we should not lose sight of the fact that the dramas it presents are bounded not only by ancient conventions of story telling, but by modern constraints as well. Chief among these is the very high cost of making dramatic television. The typical one-hour prime time television drama costs between one and two million dollars per episode to produce. So a season's worth (typically twenty-two episodes) costs well in excess of twenty million dollars.

Small wonder, then, that a critically well-reviewed show such as "Murder One," whose attractions as potent drama are described here by Jeffrey E. Thomas, doesn't last long if its audience isn't large. Advertisers won't usually pay big bucks to talk to small audiences, and networks want to sell their prime time ad slots for more, not less. Shows like "Rumpole of the Bailey," which, as John Denvir notes, is well into its second decade, may survive to old age, but, in my view, it's only because they run on small-audience, viewer-subsidized PBS.

The need for a very large audience in network prime time has many consequences. One consequence is the frequent triumph of character over plot. Classically, plot drives character, and character is illuminated by the way in which the protagonist resolves the issues raised by the plot. But people tend to remember character more easily than plot—they can recall Jean Valjean long after the plot of "Les Miserables" has faded. Most of us can recall the characters of Superman, Batman, Perry Mason, and Arnie Becker long after we have forgotten individual plot lines. Character is especially important in episodic drama, when viewers must be enticed to tune in week after week. Antigone might have been quite a different person had she needed to show up on television twenty-two times a year for five years straight.

As a result, many prime time television shows are at pains to create memorable characters. That is why a show like "L.A. Law," where the characters's personal lives are very much on display, tends, on average, to generate higher ratings than a more plot-driven show like "Law & Order." As Dawn Keetley points out in her essay on "Law & Order," the show has traditionally not delved much into the personal lives of its characters. Indeed, "Law & Order's" recent trend towards exploring its characters's personal lives more fully may be driven, at least in part, by a search for higher ratings.

Another consequence of the emphasis on character is the development in the last fifteen years of so-called "ensemble" casts—shows in which there is no single star, but, instead, many. If Perry Mason was clearly the star of his eponymously named show, "L.A. Law" could not easily have been called "Arnie Becker" or "Grace Van Owen" or "Victor Sifuentes." The use of many more-or-less equally featured characters in an episodic television show is thought to give maximum opportunity for viewers to identify with at least one character in the show. If interest in a character is classically generated by a viewer's feelings of sympathy ("I feel sorry for that person") or antipathy ("I hate that person") or empathy ("I feel like that person"), then empathy is clearly best because viewers who feel empathetic towards a character will tune in week after week to see what "they" themselves are doing in their other life on television. An ensemble cast maximizes this phenomenon, because there are more character-types with whom members of the audience can potentially identify.

Every rule is, of course, made to be broken. The recent success of David Kelley's "Ally McBeal," on the upstart Fox network, is a case in point. The show is a study in character rather than plot, and we have returned, in a sense, to the days of "Perry Mason," with a popular legal show named for its star.

Popularity, though, is fleeting, as the essays in this book demonstrate. Lawyer shows, like all episodic television dramas, come and go. "Matlock," "Civil Wars," and "Paper Chase" (analyzed here by, respectively, Gail Levin Richmond, Christine Alice Corcos, and Walter A. Effross) are all long gone, despite the viewers who loved them.

Given the number of such shows that come and go, many people ask a question that is essentially a question of leavings: When popular shows about lawyers are gone, what is left behind? Does television create attitudes and perceptions about lawyers or simply deliver and embellish attitudes and perceptions that already exist? Put more broadly, does television create culture or is it simply created by the culture around it?

To me, these questions, put this way, have always seemed of the begging sort. Television and culture are like waves on a beach. Over time, the beach clearly changes shape under the impact of the waves. But it is difficult to tell whether television is mostly the waves or mostly the beach—whether attitudes about lawyers and law are being changed by television or changing television. Perhaps it is some of each.

Happily, the essays in this book examine these issues in a creative rather than a didactic fashion. Whether analyzing the traditional lawyer shows, or exploring the ways in which legal culture has been represented in such far-flung areas as science fiction (Paul R Joseph), westerns (Francis M. Nevins), soap operas (Rod Carveth), and comedy (Robert M. Jarvis), the essays shed real light on the intricate and subtle interactions between popular notions of the legal system and legal television.

Charles B. Rosenberg is a shareholder in the Los Angeles office of Heller, Ehrman, White & McAuliffe. He was the credited outside legal consultant to "Paper Chase" when it ran on Showtime and to "L.A. Law" during its eight years on NBC.

Prime Time
Law

The Defenders

DAVID RAY PAPKE

Scholars are comfortable speaking of a literary work's alignment, that is, the way a work normatively expresses, explicitly or implicitly, selected experience from a recognizable point of view.[1] Sometimes, alignment is also relevant in film criticism, especially for films by recognized "auteurs" such as Bergman or Fellini among European filmmakers or Robert Altman or even Woody Allen among Americans. However, we almost never discuss television programs this way. Prime time programming is corporately produced and designed to appeal to the largest possible audience. A recognizable point of view or, horrors, political alignment is anathema among television producers and unanticipated among viewers.

"The Defenders," a one-hour dramatic series which aired on CBS from 1961-65, was an exception. The series portrayed the cases and controversies of Lawrence and Kenneth Preston, a fictional father-and-son lawyer team. Its producers strove quite consciously to present and represent "quality television." The producers wanted the series to appeal to an educated, urban audience and to counterbalance more standard prime time programming.

Most intriguingly for purposes at hand, "The Defenders's" alignment was undeniably and sometimes boldly liberal. The series was committed to equality and individual rights and to procedural guaranties. It also manifested an even more subtle liberal sensibility. Reginald Rose, the series's creator and executive producer, said "The Defenders" tried "to expand the ideals of a society that may be too tired to expand them for itself."[2] Kennedy-style, New Frontier politics stood for something similar, and "The Defenders" paralleled, reinforced, and, in a small way, prompted this liberalism.

In the years since, liberalism of this sort has been belittled by the New Left and trounced in a more sustained way by the New Right.[3] Starting in the 1970s, New Right thinkers such as Pat Buchanan, Michael Novak, and Norman Podhoretz argued that a liberal elite had taken over the foundations, the media, and the universities. During the subsequent Reagan presidency, even the ostensibly generous impulses of liberals were cast as self-serving. In his pseudopopulist attacks on Michael Dukakis in the 1988 presidential election, George Bush craftily made "liberalism" into the laughable "L-word." Even today, with a Democrat back in the White House, liberalism is almost never championed in American politics. Politicians try to shield themselves from the label. Budget-based thinking, cost-benefit analysis, and marketplace standards have, at least for now, supplanted the commitments to equality and individual rights that marked 1960s liberalism.[4]

Recalling or, better yet, viewing anew "The Defenders" might rekindle liberal politics as a viable political option.[5] More modestly, "The Defenders," with its lawyer characters and legal themes, can underscore the features of liberal legalism. The series spoke dramatically to the substantive and procedural aspects of liberal legalism and even today can inspire those receptive to its message.

A "Quality" Lawyer Show

"The Defenders" premiered on September 16, 1961 with a tense, gripping episode titled "Quality of Mercy." Employing four acts conveniently separated by commercial breaks, the episode concerned the arrest and trial of a doctor who had terminated the life of a "mongoloid" newborn. Superbly written, acted, and directed, the episode did not so much resolve guilt or innocence as it raised questions about the morality of mercy killing. The episode established a high standard for "quality" television, and the standard would remain "The Defenders's" goal throughout its four-year run.

In its quest to be a "quality" program, "The Defenders" was part of a larger trend in television programming during the early 1960s. Only one decade into the history of prime time programming, critics had begun to bemoan television's sameness and superficiality. In May 1961, a few months before "The Defenders" began broadcasting, Federal Communications Commission Chairman Newton N. Minow had described television as a "vast wasteland." *Variety* compared Minow's address to William Jennings Bryan's "Cross of Gold" speech before the 1896 Democratic National Convention and said Minow had "an army" of supporters.[6] The networks scurried to protect themselves from such criticisms.

CBS turned in particular to Reginald Rose for help. With the exception of Paddy Chayefsky, who had won much praise for his "Marty" teleplay and other works, Rose was perhaps the most respected of the television writers of the 1950s. A New Yorker and former advertising copy chief, Rose had written, among other works, the teleplay for "12 Angry Men" for Westinghouse's "Studio One." Later, he adapted this story of a jury's struggle to overcome bias and self-interest for the 1957 movie of the same name starring Henry Fonda and directed by Sidney Lumet.[7] He was also praised for "The Incredible World of Horace Ford" and "The Defender," also both for "Studio One." The latter starred Ralph Bellamy and the youthful William Shatner as father-and-son lawyers representing a sullen defendant played by Steve McQueen.

CBS thought "The Defender" could be reimagined as a "quality" series. Rose accepted the network's invitation to develop a series prospectus, and working with veteran anthology producer Herbert Brodkin and the Ashley-Steiner Agency, Rose proffered a new series to be named "The Defenders." Rose pitched the series as a drama about "intelligence rather than violence."[8] He came to his work as an artist and a writer, and he made no bones about it. "Good drama," Rose said later, "always projects a writer's moral values. A dramatic plot is always the story of a moral struggle.... I can't bear stories without plot conflict."[9]

Realizing that it had perhaps gotten a bit more than it bargained for, CBS nevertheless financed the series, and production began in early 1961. E.G. Marshall was recruited to play the senior Lawrence Preston, and no intellectual slouch himself, Marshall announced that a major purpose of the show was "to clarify the difference between morality and justice."[10] Robert Reed took the role of the junior Kenneth Preston, and New York won hands down as the production site. Production itself took place primarily in the studio, but on occasion Rose, Brodkin, and CBS utilized location shooting. The series premiered with the "Quality of Mercy" episode in the highly desirable Saturday evening time slot immediately following "Perry Mason," then in its fifth season.

To a remarkable extent, "The Defenders" achieved the "quality" for which CBS had hoped. At its peak the series attracted roughly 21 million viewers each Saturday evening, and critics were lavish in their praise. During its four-year run "The Defenders" won thirteen Emmys, a figure which dwarfed the mere four won by "Perry Mason." "The Defenders" was the most acclaimed lawyer show and one of the most acclaimed shows in general during the first quarter century of prime time television.

Holding temporarily in abeyance questions of "The Defenders's" liberal alignment, what factors explain the series's success? What led critics and viewers alike to find "The Defenders" something special? One factor was the acting. E.G. Marshall had distinguished himself not only on television but also on Broadway. His initial salary of $3,500 per episode was both remarkable for the time and also well earned; Robert Reed, by contrast, earned only $750 per episode.[11] Beyond Marshall and Reed, a bevy of superb actors appeared in one or more episodes: Mary Astor, Martin Balsam, Edward Binns, Ossie Davis, Lillian Gish, Sam Jaffe, and

James Earl Jones. Still other younger actors who would go on to stardom, such as Robert Duvall, Dustin Hoffman, Robert Redford, Martin Sheen, and Jon Voight, took featured roles in individual episodes.

Beyond the acting, the New York production base itself contributed to the quality. Mark Alvey, archivist at the Museum of Broadcast Communications in Chicago, thinks this factor was indeed crucial. As opposed to the escapist, action-packed Hollywood series, "The Defenders," like a small group of other New York productions, was realistic, character-oriented, and self-consciously urban. The series, in other words, took on a bit of the personality of its production locale.[12]

The "quality" of "The Defenders" seems also to have derived from its links to the live anthology dramas of the 1950s. Shows such as the "Alcoa-Goodyear Theater," "Armstrong Television Theater," "Kraft Television Theater," "Philco Television Playhouse," and the previously mentioned "Studio One" featured original teleplays and different casts each week. The anthologies were popular, and during 1952-53, for example, no fewer than eighteen of them aired. Critics praised them and even suggested they had helped create a "Golden Age" of television.[13]

The anthologies began to disappear in the late 1950s, and in the early 1960s filmed series fully supplanted them. However, a good number of the anthologies's best writers (Ernest Kinoy, David Shaw, Adrian Spies, and Alvin Boretz) and directors (Paul Bogard, Fielder Cook, Daniel Petrie, and Franklin Schaffner) found work on "The Defenders."[14] The work environment had undeniably grown more corporatized, but these writers and directors remained devoted to and challenged by their work. Unalienated writing and directing contributed to the series's "quality."

Particularly important was Rose himself. He authored only eleven of the series's 130 episodes, but the figure is misleading. He also originated the series, wrote the premier episode, and shaped the scripts of the other writers. "It's Reggie's mind that dominates the show," Robert Reed said. "He has a total grasp of every play that is unusual. You can feel in the writing his concern with ethics, with issues of right and wrong."[15] "The Defenders," Brodkin added, "is Reggie. He dreamed it up. He created it. He lives with it. He provides the consistent point of view."[16] This consistency was achieved only with great labor. In general, a script for a series episode went through seven drafts prior to production, with Rose usually working on the script from the fourth draft on.[17]

Hence, "The Defenders" was not only the product of excellent actors, writers, and directors, but also in many ways a single intellect or point of view, namely Rose's. This, too, sprung it from the ranks of the mediocre mainstream shows. All of them were much more fragmented in nature, created by a staff of specialists responsible for only tiny parts of the larger product. With Rose at the helm, by contrast, the acting, writing, and directing in "The Defenders" coalesced into some of the best programming television could offer.

Prime Time Liberalism

A dozen successful lawyer and courtroom shows preceded "The Defenders" during the first twelve years of prime time television, but none of them were determined to express liberal politics. Some of the very earliest shows were prepared to straddle the line between fact and fiction. "The Black Robe" (NBC, 1949-50), for example, rendered cases from New York City's Night Court. Actual witnesses and defendants sometimes played themselves, and a criminal once turned himself in after seeing a television presentation of his case. "They Stand Accused" (DuMont, 1949-52, 1954) used actors as defendants and witnesses but real-life Chicago attorney Charles Johnston as the judge. At the end of each trial "jurors" chosen from the studio audience were asked to render a verdict. "Famous Jury Trials" (DuMont, 1949-52) reenacted actual cases and then used the jury verdict to reveal which version of the events considered at trial was truly accurate.

If a blending of fact and fiction was not one's prime time preference, television in the 1950s more predictably took sides. "Mr. District Attorney" (ABC, 1951-52, 1954-55) was based roughly on the work of New York's Thomas E. Dewey and derived from a successful radio drama. Many could recite the show's opener: "Mr. District Attorney! Champion of the people! Guardian of our fundamental rights to life, liberty, and the pursuit of happiness!" On the defense side, "The Amazing Mr. Malone" (ABC, 1951-52) concerned the cases of fictional criminal attorney John J. Malone, a character in the novels of Craig Rice. "The Public Defender" (CBS, 1954-55) adapted cases from files of those defending the indigent, and each episode paid tribute to a named public defender for work beyond the call of duty.[18]

The type of early lawyer show that took the firmest hold involved the heroic, purely fictional exploits of one or more lawyers. Early examples of what would become the predominate form of programming were "The Mask" (ABC, 1954), a drama starring Gary Merrill and William Prince as sibling attorneys rooting out evil, and "Justice" (NBC, 1954-56), a more successful series featuring, strange as it might seem, the same two actors as legal aid attorneys.

When attorneys in these early shows were not cross-examining witnesses in the studio courtroom, their professional work took the form of crime-stopping and mystery-solving, two other television drama mainstays of the 1950s. The apotheosis of this type of show was "Perry Mason," which began broadcasting on September 21, 1957. The Mason character and his cases did not originate on television but rather in the novels of Erle Stanley Gardner. Himself an idiosyncratic California solo practitioner with a gold tooth and pet coyote, Gardner tired of being a lawyer and turned to writing fiction in the 1920s. The television series starred Raymond Burr in the title role and was essentially a "whodunnit." Mason excelled in the courtroom in the second half of each episode, but the denouement always came in the identification of the true murderer.[19]

Stated simply, "The Defenders" stood for none of this. The show used the law broadly understood to speak liberally. Reginald Rose was insistent that the show was not about actual cases, crime-stopping, or mystery-solving. "The Defenders" was about the law. "I felt that we could investigate, in dramatic terms, some broader and more meaningful ideas about the law in relation to individuals and society," he said in an essay for *Television Quarterly*. "I wish to emphasize that law is the *subject* of our programs...."[20]

Rose also realized that "law" allowed him to explore conflicts, morality, and human behavior, often but not exclusively in the courtroom. "The law itself is a formula," he said, "with inherent elements of conflict in all its codes of human behavior—codes that are as rich in their perplexities as life itself."[21] He then admitted that each episode carried "a point of view provocative enough to stimulate them [the audience] into discussing its implications."[22]

More so than Rose perhaps realized, the point of view was a liberal one. In the words of one co-worker, Rose stood "on the side of the angels and a little to the left."[23] This political alignment infused the fine acting, New York production, and script-writing. Herbert Brodkin said he was "a conservative Republican" in his personal life but a "reeking liberal" in his artistic life. "The Defenders," in his opinion, was "the most liberal show on the air."[24]

Substantive Liberal Legalism

The liberal legalism of "The Defenders" had both substantive and procedural features. The former, not surprisingly, involved a commitment to the two goals of early 1960s liberalism: equality and individual rights. The United States Constitution and progressive laws, it was assumed, would foster both. Intellectually speaking, equality and individual rights can of course conflict, but "The Defenders," as popular culture, looked more to the championing of equality and individual rights than to exploring the contradictions.

"The Non-Violent," an episode from the show's third season, underscored racial inequality. Written by Ernest Kinoy, the episode begins with a protest demonstration at a construction site. The demonstrators demand equal employment opportunities, and chant "Freedom, Equality, Now." When they block arriving trucks, a minister played by James Earl Jones and an eighteen-year-old white from a prominent family are arrested. In the process of defending the latter, Lawrence Preston comes to understand the needs and tactics of the Civil Rights Movement. Lest there by any doubt of the lesson he and, presumably, the audience learns, the final shot is of a jail window with bars. A light glows through the window, and a beautiful, haunting version of "We Shall Overcome" is heard outside.

Equally striking is "The Star-Spangled Ghetto" (1963). Written by Reginald Rose, the episode begins with an unsuccessful liquor store robbery which results in the arrests of a young man and woman named John Strafaci and Teresa Sullivan, symbolic representatives of the Italian and Irish New York City working class. Plagued by not only their families's disapproval of their romance but also an abject lack of economic opportunity, the couple attempted the robbery in order to get married and to buy sheets, towels, glasses and—according to Miss Sullivan—"a mixer maybe." The episode does not resolve the debate between Lawrence Preston and a prosecutor played by Ossie Davis regarding whether the defendants's grinding poverty entitles them to a break. But it is impossible to miss the call for reducing economic inequality. In his closing statement on behalf of the defendants, Lawrence Preston deplores our "materialistic society where the ownership of things is what rules our lives."

The range of individual rights championed by "The Defenders" include speech, press, religion, and, less predictably, abortion. A particularly noteworthy episode in this area is "Blacklist," which originally aired on January 18, 1964. Written by Ernest Kinoy, the episode featured Jack Klugman in the role of Joe Larch, an actor whose youthful affiliations with Communist front organizations led to his blacklisting. The episode is especially intriguing because of its willingness to scrutinize the practices of the movie and television industry, the very industry responsible for "The Defenders." One anticommunist group, it is worth remembering, published *Red Channels*, a newsletter identifying actors, writers, and directors considered communist sympathizers and urging networks and producers not to employ those identified. A so-called "blacklist" became operative.[25] Indeed, even on "The Defenders," which was to excoriate blacklisting, at least one actor felt the sting of the list.[26]

In the "Blacklist" episode itself, Larch has gone ten years without a part and is reduced to working as a shoe salesman. Finally, he is offered a role in a movie. However, the fictional Judson Kyle and the menacing National Security Vanguard League blow the whistle on Larch, and his spineless producer retracts the offer. The Prestons cannot right this wrong, much less those of the past, but Larch's philosophical dignity and the evil self-interestedness of his enemies leave no doubt regarding "The Defenders's" alignment. The denial of political and creative freedoms will cease, Larch says in the end, when Americans "start believing in what they say they're defending, when they believe in the Constitution." Hollywood thought so highly of this fictional indictment of its recent past that both Kinoy and Klugman received Emmys for their work.[27]

Other episodes such as "A Book for Burning" concerning censorship or "The Objector" concerning conscientious objection, also championed constitutional rights, but "The Benefactor" was easily the most controversial substantively liberal episode in "The Defenders's" four-year run. Aired on April 28, 1962, the show narratively advanced the argument for legalized abortion. The episode involves the arrest and trial of Dr. Montgomery, an abortionist played by Robert Simon. Driven in part by his own daughter's tragic death in a botched abortion, the doctor has performed 1,500 abortions. A much larger number of women had sought his services, but he had screened out married women who were merely "selfish," while agreeing to help rape victims and unfortunate teenagers. Dr. Montgomery, "The Benefactor" himself, also declined to charge for his services whenever a patient was needy.

At the end of the episode, the jury finds Dr. Montgomery guilty but urges leniency in sentencing, and the defendant reveals his plans to move to Africa or the Far East in order to help people. More importantly, the episode at trial and elsewhere makes the case for legalized abortion. A sociologist takes the stand to give numbers and reasons for abortion. Parents who fail to understand their daughters's plights, including one who slaps his daughter, are negatively portrayed. Kenneth Preston lividly reprimands a journalist who reveals a teenaged patient's name to the public. The unequivocal endorsement of abortion rights led the series's three regular sponsors—Brown & Williamson Tobacco, Lever Brothers, and Kimberly-Clark—to withdraw their support for the episode,[28] but CBS later reported that audience response to the episode was ninety percent positive.[29]

This type of substantive liberal legalism was eventually squeezed out by the legalism of the left and especially the right. The New Left's emphasis on participatory democracy led in various ways to the substantive gender-related demands of feminism and to the environmental stands of the greens. Branches of the right, meanwhile, looked to the market or to traditional moral codes. In the early 1960s, however, liberal legalism had its place in American political discourse, and "The Defenders" embodied it.

Procedural Liberal Legalism

Beyond substantive liberalism, "The Defenders" also endorsed the procedural liberalism so dear to the hearts of American liberals, especially those in the legal academy. The chief focal point of procedural liberalism is the courtroom trial, and using this motif, "The Defenders" underscored and endorsed those procedural guaranties which could presumably facilitate justice—the need for search warrants, the inadmissibility of some evidence, the propriety of lines of questioning. Lawrence Preston in particular was enamored with proper courtroom procedure, and he often held the line against citizens, prosecutors, and even his own son.

In more specific terms, a whole string of episodes examined and endorsed the need for an insanity defense. The 1963 "Weeping Baboon," written by Reginald Rose, features a convincing Dennis Hopper in the role of Jason Thomas, a deranged young man who kills his father and brother. At trial, Thomas jumps up to recite the Pledge of Allegiance, charges the bench, and bangs his head on the defense table. But more so than all of these antics, Thomas's tortured testimony about how he had to kill to be free convinces the judge to grant a motion for a directed verdict on the grounds of insanity. The judge at the end explains to the jurors and, presumably, to the viewing audience as well that justice is never served by punishing an individual not responsible for his acts. "The individual's responsibility to the group," the judge pontificates, "is no stronger than the group's responsibility to the individual."

Procedural justice is available not only to the insane but also to the unappealing: gangsters, psychopaths, and members of a lynch mob. In the 1962 episode "The Indelible Silence," Dennis Hopper is again in the spotlight, this time in the role of Alfred Carter, Jr., a seventeen-year-old, thoroughly offensive neo-Nazi. Charged with killing an elderly Jew outside a New York City synagogue, Carter has already been convicted in the newspapers before the Prestons come to his assistance. While Lawrence Preston dramatically quotes the Fourteenth Amendment's guaranties of due process, Kenneth Preston scours the neighborhood for a crucial defense witness, Peter Van Eck. The latter had himself been brutalized by the actual Nazis in Holland during World War II, and only with great reluctance does he take the stand. Speaking of the defendant Carter, Lawrence Preston speaks both for himself and for "The Defenders" as a television program: "I despise that boy and everything he stands for, but by defending him, I defend the system I live by."

Procedural justice in "The Defenders" even includes the possibility of reopening a conviction, a theme explored in "The Siege," a 1964 episode improbably starring Robert Redford as Gary Degan, an escaped convict who holds Lawrence Preston captive in his office. Seeking revenge against his former defense counsel á la the ex-convict in "Cape Fear" and wearing a baseball cap like the Redford character in "The Natural," Degan at first seems a disagreeable villain. As events unfold, however, it becomes clear that Degan was wrongly convicted. Lawrence Preston, always impeccably groomed as befits a man who makes his home in Scarsdale, actually takes off his suitcoat and loosens his tie once he realizes the injustice that has been done. Fortunately, a key witness from the original trial is located in a retirement home. The witness recants the earlier testimony that was crucial in Degan's conviction, and Lawrence Preston is sure he can successfully petition for retrial.

Through the twists and turns of these episodes and many others, "The Defenders's" liberal politics looked to the law. The diligent work of father-and-son lawyers, the functioning of legal institutions, and especially the give-and-take of the courtroom were ideal tropes for the expression of a liberal alignment. What's more, the law—both substantively and procedurally—showed at least the potential to respond.

Sensibility as Well as Substance and Procedure

As "The Defenders" advanced its liberal understanding of substantive law and legal procedure, the series also manifested a liberal law-related sensibility or consciousness. Substantive law and courtroom procedure are relatively easy to recognize. The substantive law takes the form of prescriptions and proscriptions backed by the state. Procedure largely involves the standards articulated under the rubric of due process. But a liberal law-related sensibility or consciousness is more subtle. It involves *how* one feels and thinks. It manifests certain of the deeper assumptions and attitudes of liberalism.

This sensibility begins with a subscription to the rule of law, and "The Defenders" proffered no shortage of pronouncements cutting in this direction. In "Quality of Mercy," the series's premier, the doctor suggests the pros and cons for mercy killing, but Lawrence Preston is quick to point out that the posited law does not concern itself with these philosophical matters. In "The Benefactor," in which the indicted doctor is an abortionist rather than a mercy-killer, Lawrence Preston again attempts to clarify what we mean by law and a rule of law. When the doctor complains about the "gap" between what the law allows and the alternatives those seeking abortions need, Lawrence Preston is sympathetic but firm.

"This country is run by laws, Doctor," he reminds his client. The way to change the law is "by legislative action."

But none of this is to say that law is always perfect and works well. "The Defenders" was formulaic to the extent that each episode began with a prologue presenting in dramatic form the legal case or issue, but the series did not tidily answer all questions in the end. Quite the contrary, in virtually all of the episodes previously discussed (and many others as well) "The Defenders" leaves heated controversies and tough questions to some extent unresolved. A point of view is coupled with open-endedness. Is mercy-killing tolerable? Might abortion be fully legalized? Should we consider socioeconomic environment in gauging degrees of criminality?

The most obvious contrast is with "Perry Mason." The latter is a primary example of what some characterize as a "closed" or "producerly" text.[30] "Perry Mason" as a series featured the classic American hero, a "Protestant American of long lineage," who can solve problems and eliminate ambiguities.[31] Everything is clear in the end. "The Defenders," on the other hand, does not close off alternative interpretations and meanings. It is, in ways noted earlier, more writerly and creative. Even though "The Defenders" foregrounds its own liberalism, it refuses to close out other alignments and positions. The Prestons lose cases, and in other instances verdicts are not rendered.

Answers to legal controversies cannot easily be looked up in the statute books, an uncertainty that leads a frustrated Kenneth Preston to declare in "Blacklist" that "The law is an ass." No, his father says, "The law is man-made and we're imperfect." We have to accept these facts and make adjustments. In Lawrence Preston's words:

> Not every story in life ends satisfactorily. Neither does the law. Sometimes everything ends up in the air. No rescue. No climax. Not even a good rousing disaster.... There are injustices in the world, and they're not always solved by some brilliant point at a dramatic moment. Things don't always work out the way you want them to.

The best lawyers can do is approach their calling honestly, use their reason instead of their emotion, and carry on. Often, Lawrence Preston, as in "Blacklist," reminds his more emotional and irascible son of just this point. Neither showed much character development in the course of the series. "The Defenders" was not like "Hill Street Blues" or the more recent "ER" and "N.Y.P.D. Blue" in tracing an arc of character development from episode to episode and from year to year. However, the older Preston's teaching of the younger is an effective pedagogical aspect of "The Defenders." As for the law's imperfection, father tells son in "Blacklist," "You'll get used to it."

Furthermore, it is healthy through all of this to engage in self-questioning. Introspection is valuable. There is a particular variety of liberalism that is too self-confident, even elitist. The enlightened liberal has all the answers. If only the less enlightened would listen, all would work out.

In the 1965 "Nobody Asks What Side You're On," one of the last and perhaps one of the best episodes of "The Defenders," this smug variety of liberalism is demolished. In the prologue a white newspaper reporter named Marla Edwards, played by actress Lee Grant, nervously traverses deserted ghetto streets in her car after investigating a police scene. When an African-American man who had concealed himself in her back seat for safety reaches out seeking her help, Edwards panics and shoots him. The man, we learn later, was an ex-junkie who had not only righted himself but also worked to help others; the reporter even knew him from her earlier philanthropic labors in the ghetto. Mounting his horse as Edwards's defense counsel, Lawrence Preston tells a prosecutor named Dan Jackson and played by Ossie Davis: "Look at her record. She's an absolutely committed liberal." Jackson is not sure that answers things, that everything is "black and white." "What's gotten into you?" Lawrence Preston asks in amazement. "The 1960s," Jackson replies, "Haven't they gotten to you? They will, Larry, they will."

As it turns out, it is Jackson rather than Preston who has a better read on things. Edwards takes the stand and admits she panicked when she saw the deceased's black hand. The color of the hand awakened fear grounded in racism. "I was the real intruder," Edwards sobs. "I don't want forgiveness. Some things should not be forgiven. I want things to change." Lawrence Preston and those viewers with a liberal law-related sensibility have learned a lesson. "Being naive," Preston says, "can be just as dangerous as being prejudiced."

Through all of this, core values of liberal legalism are manifest. Reason is prioritized. It serves us better than emotion or faith. Through reason, we can address human imperfection. Problems surround us. Narrow-mindedness, prejudice, and racism lurk. But still, through law and using our reason and good will, we can anticipate progress. Things will and must get better.[32]

Conclusion

Did "The Defenders's" successful four-year run have any ramifications? Did the show have an impact? On the first score, one must remember that its liberal legalism notwithstanding, the series remained within the economic logic of the television industry. The four "acts" in each hour grew from the advertising imperatives. Demonstrable audience loyalty and, to a lesser extent, critical acclaim were necessary for continued production.

The series's economic viability both allowed it to survive and led the networks to mount what they considered "similar shows." Other series with a liberal sensibility inspired at least in part by "The Defenders" included "East Side/West Side" (CBS, 1963-64), a drama about social workers, and "Slattery's People" (CBS, 1965), an adult narrative about a state legislator. Neither had the "quality" or the success of "The Defenders." Much worse were shows of the late 1960s such as "The Mod Squad" (ABC, 1968-73) and "Storefront Lawyers" (CBS, 1970). These, too, were adult dramas with liberal sensibility, but they lacked "The Defenders's" deeper commitments to a particular alignment. In the words of one scholar, the shows "were blatant in their exploitation of the movement of the 1960s. Their hipper-than-thou attitude and handsome stars and starlets rang false."[33]

Liberal legalism, to state it frankly, can be both expounded *and* marketed. Television producers always attempt to gauge the pulse of the viewing public. They want shows that will attract viewers and thereby facilitate the sale of advertising for as much as possible. "The Defenders" and other series which may be thought of as its descendants lived within the economic logic of the industry.

But at the same time, television and popular culture in general are not only industry products. As the television critic and scholar John Fiske has convincingly argued, television shows also have a cultural logic.[34] The successful ones find a way to interact with the interests and values of some substantial portion of the viewing public. Most fail during or after their first year of production, but those that survive provide viewers with a source of entertainment, meaning, and clarification of identity.

This "success" may fall short of impact, lasting or otherwise.[35] However, the "success" does indicate that a show has interrelated with the positions and attitudes of extant cultural discourses. In the early 1960s liberal legalism had a place in popular ideology and in more formal political and governmental dialogue. "The Defenders" represented liberal legalism in prime time television. Decades later, there is no better place to turn for illumination of the liberal legalism that once had a role in American society and politics. Might a revival be possible?

2

Hill Street Blues

Susan Beth Farmer

"Hill Street Blues," which aired on NBC from January 1981 to May 1987, was not a television show primarily about lawyers. Created and produced by Steven Bochco, Michael Kozoll, and others, it was different from the traditional crime show in form and substance. Indeed, it was initially criticized as being "too confusing, too violent, and too depressing. There were too many subplots and the main characters' personalities were too flawed."[1] All of these elements were what distinguished the show and ultimately won it a large and loyal audience. In 1985, novelist Joyce Carol Oates said it was "the only television show she watched regularly" and described it in glowing terms usually reserved for literature, saying that it "is as intellectually and emotionally provocative as a good book. In fact, from the very first, 'Hill Street Blues' struck me as Dickensian in its superb character studies, its energy, its variety; above all, its audacity."[2]

The comparison to Dickens is apt. This was no idealized, slickly photographed television version of a noble profession, with attractive, well-appointed sets, beautiful people, admirable characters, clear heroes and villains, and happy endings neatly resolved in sixty minutes. The realistic look and feel of the show, created through the use of shaky photography, raunchy language, and discussions (if not depictions) of sex, was unprecedented.[3] The series also created some fine recurring images. The most memorable is the opening sequence of every show, the morning roll call, where Sgt. Phil Esterhaus tries to call the bored and unruly group of cops to order and give them instructions and information about the work for the upcoming day. He is concerned, even paternal. The cops resemble adolescent students, gossiping, drinking coffee, complaining, joking, and paying attention sporadically. Esterhaus always ends his briefing with the phrase "let's be careful out there" and then the action begins.

The show almost never made it to the screen, premiering in January rather than the usual fall television premiere season, and when it aired, nearly failed, ranking 83rd out of a total of 97 television series.[4] But it did succeed, gained an audience, won a host of awards, and lasted for seven seasons and 142 episodes.[5] It combined the most realistic drama

shown to date on fiction television with broad comedy and the continuing stories of daytime television.

Characters for a Post-Modern Age

The show is nominally based in the Hill Street police station, a chaotic,
inefficient law enforcement agency located in an unnamed gritty urban
center. The main characters are the law enforcement officers themselves,
the administrators, and the offenders with whom they do daily battle.
They are all flawed in various ways, including by alcoholism (Detective
Johnny "J.D." LaRue, played by Kiel Martin), psychological instability
(Detective Mick Belker, played by Bruce Weitz), questionable social
habits (Sgt. Phil Esterhaus, played by Michael Conrad, who dated a high
school girl at one point during the series and had other sexual escapades
too numerous to mention), and rigid authoritarianism (Lt. Howard
Hunter, played by James B. Sikking, who was generally used for comic
relief).[6]

Several lawyers are also involved. Public Defender Joyce Davenport,
played by Veronica Hamel, is the principal legal figure as well as the love
interest of Captain Frank Furillo, played by Daniel J. Travanti. Assistant
District Attorney Irwin Bernstein, played by George Wyner, is a recurring but much less important figure. Viewers tend to remember Davenport
but have little specific recollection of Bernstein other than as the generic
prosecutor figure.

Furillo is not a hero, "neither waving weapons, screeching tires, nor
making brilliant deductions," but is instead the "dedicated middle-aged,
middle-management executive in a cheap suit" doing his best to maintain order and do his job in a difficult situation.[7] Like the show's other characters, he is a hero for a modern, or post-modern, age — more cynical
and flawed, doing a difficult and necessary job for society.[8]

A New Model of the Female Lawyer

Joyce Davenport is a new model of the female lawyer. A "professional
woman with a strength and depth that was atypical of female characters
on contemporary television,"[9] she is smart and feminine, wearing long-
styled hair and elegant suits. Well-spoken and groomed, she is clearly
upper class. Because we know that public defenders do not make large
salaries, we are meant to understand that she must come from money
and therefore from the upper class. We also understand that, because she

left behind the easy life, she has principles and is dedicated to justice. She stands out among the other characters—the law enforcement officers, the victims, and the accused—like a flower in the middle of a garbage dump. She is both sexy and a lawyer, an unprecedented combination. She receives a certain amount of grudging respect, and Furillo frequently calls her by the title "counselor." In return, she calls him "Pizza man." The episodes routinely end with Davenport and Furillo in bed.[10] However, she is typically wearing glasses, surrounded by paperwork, conscientiously doing "homework" for the next day's court appearances. Her job as a public defender is not a hobby; rather it is important and worthy of hard work and long hours.

Davenport is also no pushover.[11] Nevertheless, she occasionally fails and experiences frustration and does not always succeed in her job.[12] Although rarely shown in the courtroom, she is frequently shown arguing with Furillo about a client. She vigorously and competently upholds the Constitution[13] and acts in the best interests of her clients.[14] She does not always win these arguments but there is no sense of ridicule in the depiction.

Realism and Ethics

The show is about characters, and generally does not attempt to accurately depict the lives and work of public defenders.[15] Some realistic touches surface, however, including a threatened strike by the public defenders. Joyce Davenport is portrayed as being caught in the middle of a no-win situation, trying to defend her clients while dealing with her colleagues on the labor issue.[16]

But realism is not the point. The requirements of the drama demand unrealistic stories, including, for example, the shooting death of Pam Gilliam, another public defender.[17] While the audience is meant to understand that Davenport believes in her job and does it well, her job is more a shorthand description of her character than a lesson about the work of public defenders. Indeed, the stories routinely gloss over ethical issues in the relationship between Furillo and Davenport. They are seen discussing clients[18] and cases and she frequently has a cooperative relationship with the officers that may not be realistic.[19] Moreover, Davenport occasionally comes off as naive[20] and unprofessional.[21]

The most unrealistic and ethically troubling story line came during the fifth season in 1984. In January, Davenport resigns from her job, becomes an Assistant District Attorney,[22] and promptly begins to prosecute cases.[23] By the end of the season, however, she has re-joined the Public Defender's office.[24]

Conclusion

The lawyers on "Hill Street Blues," primarily Public Defender Joyce Davenport, are depicted as relatively powerful and respected people. This probably exaggerates the actual status and power of public defenders. They are also shown as virtuous, trying to do their jobs as well as possible despite difficult working conditions and frustration. They are even heroic, according to the norms of the time. Davenport does not always win, but the portrayal of the character is respectful, even admiring. She is a hero with modern upper middle class values, defending the Constitution and enjoying a sexual relationship outside of marriage.[25] Female lawyers are portrayed as real women, but also as competent professionals.

3

L.A. Law

JOHN BRIGHAM

"L.A. Law," which was produced by Steven Bochco (who also did "Hill Street Blues" and "N.Y.P.D. Blue") and Terry Louise Fisher and featured music by Michael Post, raised important questions about television's influence on law in America. This influence included the rise in law school applications during its run on NBC from 1986-94 and the subsequent drop in law school applications after "L.A. Law" went off the air. The popularity of the show and the sophistication of its writers make it an apt vehicle for understanding tensions between parts of the legal culture — like the legal profession — and the whole.

In a cleverly-titled article by Stephen Gillers, "Taking L.A. Law More Seriously,"[1] the author argued that the show is important because it operates like a good law school class. That is, it made legal ideas the central focus and eschewed easy or pat answers. While acknowledging that the show, with its headline stealing cases and lack of legal drudgery, is as much Hollywood as law, Gillers praises the show and encourages the legal profession not to write it off.

Against what has often been essentially a pluralist tradition, this essay draws on a constitutive theory of law in order to document the authoritative nature of culture, especially when it is constructed in marble or concrete.[2] Rather than simply treating the court in a television show as a set to be put up and taken down at will, the structure of the courtroom on television becomes one of the enduring symbols of justice in America. Increasingly, these are also the symbols being exported to cultures that consume American video. The courtroom in "L.A. Law" will be compared with courtrooms in other television dramas as representations of the culture of place and of law.

Because "L.A. Law" is not primarily a courtroom drama, the courtroom scenes will be set against a number of other special qualities, such as an emphasis on civil rather than criminal law, the prominence of the boardroom at the beginning of each show, and lawyers's offices and restaurants as places where law operates. Like police and detective shows, "L.A. Law" situates most legal work, and hence the law, outside the courtroom. This recentering of the law has important effects on the significance of the courtroom. While it has changed little in appearance, the courtroom as a legal icon has diminished in significance.

The Law in Architecture

The attic portico, the architectural feature where columns hold up a triangulated pediment that outlines the front of a traditional roof, emerged in American court architecture during the Greek revival of the 1820s. The shape, appearing in vernacular architecture without the columns, also outlines the ordinary attic.[3] Through its place in the home, the attic is a familiar repository for the stuff of memory and, inevitably, this is the stuff of community. Although the portico has faded from new court architecture[4] in response to modernism and the sleek functional lines of the international style, the classical form lives in contemporary jurisprudential images. The most important example is the United States Supreme Court building in Washington, D.C., ubiquitous as a symbol of justice. The classical forms that gave us the attic now exist in memory and video more commonly than in stone.

Architectural Jurisprudence

Though relatively simple in comparison to some of the architectural styles that preceded and followed the western adaptation of Greek ideas, there seemed always to be room for ornamentation in the classical style. On the Supreme Court, the facade of the pediment arrays the great lawgivers and behind the columns huge bronze doors depict stories in the life of the law. Between column and pediment the words "Equal Justice Under the Law" are etched in stone. Today, the Supreme Court bears a heavy burden of legal semiotics. Both because local courts have not sought to achieve such symbolic grandeur and because the Court itself has been employed as a symbol of the law, the actual physical manifestation of the attic has been exchanged for a virtual reality.

In her recent book,[5] Magali Larson depicts the rich social context in which architecture is made. Any piece of architecture, she says, draws various aspects of the community—the funders, the builders, and the neighbors—into its web. Architecture, in her sociological presentation, is public art, and as such it is a social phenomenon. Legal architecture has at least as many masters. It has the social interests and capacities of those who identify a need and those who propose and fund buildings. It has the aesthetic interests behind it of architecture and of engineering, which give form to the interests and capacities we imagine to be primary sources for the built world. Legal architecture also has the special needs of the legal community, particularly the judges, for whom the security of the building is as important a consideration in many cases as aesthetics. Thus, buildings are linked to jurisprudence in a multifaceted way that reflects the link between law and society generally.

With a few notable exceptions,[6] there is little scholarly work on courthouse design. Much of it remains local, with historical societies recording the courthouses of particular states and professional groups issuing specific suggestions and code requirements for the construction of court buildings. The grand contributions, like those by the American Bar Association in conjunction with the American Institute of Architects, have tended, at least in more general circulation books, to focus on the outside of the buildings rather than the interiors.[7] This is in part due to the expectation that the interiors are less distinctive than the structures within which they are arrayed.

Innovation in courtroom design has come from foundation support and academic interest as much as from the professional builders and the practicing bar. The round "courtroom of the future" at McGeorge School of Law in Sacramento has for twenty years been a model ("show car") for courtroom innovation, featuring "up-to-date technology including: concealed television cameras; monitors on the bench, witness box, counsel and jury tables; a lectern which can recess into the floor; an x-ray viewing panel; and a screen which can descend from the ceiling for the viewing of overhead transparencies or slides."[8] Similarly, albeit on a more practical and operational scale, the courtroom of the Midtown Community Court in Manhattan has suggested new ways of organizing the work process with the intensive use of video monitors in a converted police court building.

Scholars such as Richard Mohr and David Tait have recently contributed to how we understand the social dynamics of courtrooms with their combination of post-modern theory, semiotics, and social science. Mohr has focused on such things as the relative height of the judicial bench in modern courts and what the height of the bench says about the authority of the judge. Tait has looked at small claims courts with attention to the manner in which judicial authority is maintained where there is little in the way of professional distance. My own work, beginning with *The Cult of the Court* in 1987, addressed the symbolism of the Supreme Court building from outside and in. The Supreme Court chamber remains a video-resistant space that has changed very little over the years. Its iconography, from the purple curtain behind the bench to the constant flow of traffic in (and almost immediately out) the back door, contribute to a sense of its considerable authority. Other courtrooms come into the public consciousness only when they have been featured in the news (which seldom includes pictures unless there is a video presence), in a television or movie drama (which is common), or in literature (which probably only matters if it makes it to film or video).

A period of virtual reality does not move from these constraints entirely. "Court TV" employs a stylized representation of the Supreme Court as its logo, as do many of the networks when they cover legal stories. The most significant development in the architecture of law or architectural jurisprudence is the role of television in constructing spaces where the law resides. Thus, where in the past the elevated bench of the judge was meant to instill awe, the box for the jury was a place to gather a group so that they might perform a civic duty, and a bar or rail continues to separate the public from the court (as it has for hundreds of years), today the lawyers's news conference, the celebrity legal commentators, video images of testimony (and video testimony), and the orchestration from the anchor desk are the forms through which law is transmitted to most of us. It is through these latter forms, not the halls and walls of justice, that black and white Americans formed their divergent opinions of the O.J. Simpson case. Given this shift, the fictionalized presentations of the halls of justice take on special significance.

Screening Rooms

In the case of television, a number of considerations apply to the construction of the place where law happens. In the first instance, "L.A. Law" courts are court*rooms* rather than buildings. The architecture of law on the show is almost always interior space. "L.A. Law" differs from the police precinct, with its storefronts and alleys, and from the sheriff's posse galloping over the western hills. Shows with this focus give more attention to buildings or landscape as backdrop than does "L.A. Law," once it lets you know it is in Los Angeles. Westerns and contemporary action dramas, like the "Die Hard" movies, use entire structures as the set: blowing them up, shooting from them, dying on and in front of them. Indeed, the prominence of law themes in the Western genre, generally taking place outside, has a man rather than a structure as the embodiment of the law. The architectural fact for "L.A. Law" is that the law is depicted as taking place within buildings and not around them. If the show was about a firm of architects we would get to see buildings on sites as objects of struggle, but as mentioned, the law in "L.A. Law" is about ideas.

Other rooms have been important to the representation of the legal process: the precinct house, the prison cell, the judge's chamber, the lawyer's office. In one of America's most compelling legal dramas, Sidney Lumet's 1957 movie "12 Angry Men" (the source of the story was a television play), the jury room is the focus of the action. In police dramas, of course, it is often the station house or, in the case of "N.Y.P.D. Blue," the interview room that takes center stage. In series like "L.A. Law" and "Murder One," the lawyer's office or the firm's suite of offices becomes the center of attention. But by most accounts, television has not totally shifted cultural attention from the courtroom as the center of the legal enterprise. In "Law & Order," the courtroom is the finale. Even where, as in "L.A. Law," it is not the actual center of the action in most episodes, the courtroom remains a place of distinctly legal drama and of climax. While "L.A. Law" makes bargaining more prominent than its predecessors, the courtroom brings structure and finality. And, although it is more expensive to produce than a conversation, the limited, familiar space of a courtroom is relatively easy to capture on television.

In this regard, the courtroom represents some of the more recent cultural descriptions of the penetration of law in the culture as something situated in the interior relations of our mental and emotional lives. Rather than standing "bone white" on a hill behind the Capitol as the Supreme Court does, the courtrooms of television are places we enter from the holding cell or approach as from the litigants's table or view from the jury box. All angles reflect the constituted points of view the law defines for us. While the Supreme Court or one's local court are seen from cultural spaces not generally defined in law—streets, parks, parking lots— the spaces of television courtrooms are constituted inside the law. In her 1996 book *Imagining Crime*, Alison Young draws our attention to what she calls "the trauma of the visible" in discussing the case of two-year-old James Bulger who was killed by a group of young boys near Liverpool in 1993. The boys were caught on video as they left a mall. Because the trial was not televised, the video image was of an aspect of the crime rather than the response of the law. A video of the beating of Rodney King bore a similar relation to the trial that would follow and situated monitor (and camera) as the central feature of the case. With its decentering of the courtroom, "L.A. Law" is part of the shift from such structures to the authority of the video.

The internal expression of the law in the courtroom is necessarily on a more human scale than is the case when dealing with the external architecture of the law. This reflects the popular understanding of television as a "hot" rather than a "cold" medium, like radio. Instead of massive bronze doors, larger than life statuary, and the aspirational scale of Olympian (or Victorian) motifs, the inside of the courtroom has always been limited in the forms of jurisprudential expression. Inside, we have the elevated bench, the positioning of opposing counsel side by side with the prosecution nearest the jury, who are themselves set apart from the rest and close to one another. And the gallery is present and separate. In "L.A.

Law," the center aisle, the judge's bench, and the witness stand become the focal points. This is a lawyers's show, not a judge show (like "Night Court"), and the lawyers interact with each other at the crucial juncture where the center aisle crosses the bar of the counsel tables. Witnesses and defendants are necessary for the interaction between the lawyers which goes on before, during, and after the trial. Like "Perry Mason," "L.A. Law" featured important players in the prosecuting role and while they would initially be outside the firm, on more than one occasion they would later be brought into the private sector (which on this show seemed bigger and certainly more substantial than the public sector).

Like court buildings themselves, television courtrooms are reflective of time and place. This is not simply the time and place of the trial, but of the architecture. The Supreme Court's chamber, though built during the Depression, reflects a Victorian grandeur that was more stylish at least fifty years prior to when it was built. Architecturally, and now with enduring significance, the Victorian is a familiar expression of law. Like the quill pen and the flower script in which the Declaration of Independence was drafted, the Victorian courtroom has a traditional place in the iconography of law. But the contemporary courtrooms to which we have had so much video access of late are not the Victorian courtrooms of law's traditional shrines. Not surprisingly, they are the more austere, functional courtrooms of our newer cities. In a fascinating twist on the old double institutionalization thesis, the courtrooms of the modern cities are getting a special place in the cultural iconography because, at least in part, they have offered more ready access to the video camera. The shyness displayed by denizens of our Victorian courtrooms, particularly the Supreme Court, when it comes to video access has been amply compensated for through the access provided in California and Florida to television.

The courtrooms of "L.A. Law," on the other hand, are inevitably Los Angeles courtrooms. That is, they are in the style of the public spaces of modern American buildings, particularly of the sunbelt variety. The courtroom is without ornamentation, it is small, it is efficient. It is not the Los Angeles of Malibu or "Baywatch" with their sense of the promised land of sun, surf, and beautiful bodies. Nor is it the Los Angeles of swimming pools and opulent vehicles. The courtroom is from a pared-down Los Angeles, a society where the public has had much less attention than the private and the societal far less cache than the personal. Rather than the Victorian architecture of public buildings, which, even in California, reflected the grandeur of collective aspirations and ruling classes, the court buildings of Los Angeles represent the sense that the courts deal with others and for the most part there is nothing particularly grand about their business or how it is handled.

On television, Los Angeles interiors run to glitz while the built environment in the East (New York, Boston, and Philadelphia) are places of grit and grunge. This is somewhat paradoxical because in popular culture and even on the big screen, Los Angeles and its neighborhoods are often depicted as places of riots, gangs, and drive-by shootings. Before and after "L.A. Law," Steven Bochco hung out in the graffiti-covered precincts of New York, while David Kelley, a Boston lawyer who went to Hollywood to write for "L.A. Law," recently created "The Practice," which has been described by *U.S. News and World Report* as "a grunge update" of "L.A. Law." In "The Practice" a newer legal realism continues to rely on the penetrations of society in the East and updates the package within which Hollywood presents the law.[9]

On the episode of "L.A. Law" titled "Wattsamatter," which aired in 1990, a courtroom becomes the focus for a segment of the show and the place of the room in society is a matter for comment. The episode opens with a judge looking at his courtroom after it has been trashed by a Watts-type riot. The judge observes, "The American courtroom is a reflection of American society and society is a reflection of it." Presumably this comment is meant for the law as much as for the courtroom. Anyone who has visited an American courtroom can see that is it hardly representative of America, with its over-inclusion of people of color and relative absence of people of means. We know, of course, that the courtroom is not representative of the law, at least not in the sense that most or even representative cases go to court or that disputes decided in court are decided the same way most cases are decided. Still, the courtroom does represent a public perception of the law and on "L.A. Law" at least a few of the attorneys return to the court for their legal reality check.

After the Law

For many students of law in society, the law has been treated as an alien realm difficult to penetrate by the average citizen. The authors of the text *Before the Law: An Introduction to the Legal Process* take their title from the Czech novelist and lawyer Franz Kafka. They begin the presentation of materials with excepts from *The Trial*, Kafka's famous 1937 novel:

> Before the law stands a doorkeeper on guard. To this doorkeeper there comes a man from the country who begs for admittance to the Law. But the doorkeeper says that he cannot admit the man at the moment.

While elements of the Kafkaesque scene of standing before the law are present in the television courtroom where the judge is the law, for the most part the fact of being in the presence of a judge with a hope for justice, as opposed to Joseph K.'s odyssey in the darkened halls and forbidding architectural landscape of *The Trial*, sets the television courtroom apart. It is not the alienated vision of the great Czech writer and influential visionary for a generation of law's critics.

The courtrooms in "L.A. Law" served for both criminal and civil cases, like the firm itself; indeed, like "the law." Because the firm was primarily a civil law operation, its handling of criminal cases was generally connected to the client base: an errant child of a wealthy corporate executive, or a divorce client who takes retribution too literally. Here the reality of the show does run against convention. Where the great television and most of the movie dramas have been crime dramas, "L.A. Law" shifted our attention to the law that we are used to seeing in the headlines or that we learn about in the liberal arts curriculum in college. This is the law of divorce, personnel, and corporate power. It is also the law of "The People's Court," the Thomas and Bork Senate confirmation hearings, and now, *Jones v. Clinton*. This is the law of Ann Kelsey's feminism and Arnie Becker's divorces, as well as Douglas Brackman's bottom line and Leland McKenzie's corporate stewardship. This picture is only somewhat more representative of the full range of the law or of social life but the show clearly indicates the constitutive power of television. The presentation of this slice of life in the law caused us to see the law differently, culturally. Indeed, the show made the law more interesting than a visit to Uncle Joe's or Aunt Mary's law office.

Recent commentary on television has problematized reality at the same time that it has heralded the significance of the medium for serious students of culture. John Fiske says a television show is "'realistic' not because it reproduces reality, which it clearly does not, but because it reproduces the dominant sense of reality."[10] Driven by markets to touch base with more than a few senses of reality, television refines, incorporates, and spins reality according to a subset of forces in the society. For Fiske, television realism is middle class-focused but it also "incorporates" cultural change such as respect for diversity with regard to race and gender.[11] This incorporation is inevitably a moderating force in society because it is incorporation "into" something that is dominant. While the dominant form changes somewhat, the incorporated form necessarily changes more. "L.A. Law" was clearly a vehicle for this sort of incorporation and the courtroom was just one of the places where it happened.

Video Jurisprudence

Realism is part of law's expansion from the courtroom to the boardroom. As Christine Harrington and I have said before, "Realism is the new paradigm for legal authority." We seek to bring familiarity to this form of authority much as Realists did in founding new authority on a foundation of legal formalism. In the tradition of Foucault we see the penetration of the law through its familiarity. The traditional forms by which law expresses itself, the Temples of Justice, are expressions of a society able to rely on class relations. The authority of those relations is expressed in art and architecture. In this sense, the modern corporation rules through expressions of bureaucracy and process instead of the traditional symbols of power.

Law in Society

In matters of law, like in other social forms such as entertainment and education, patterns of behavior are shared across professional boundaries. Ways of doing things in one area are often reflected in others. In this sense, some of the law on television becomes the law in our lives. Indeed, like Martin Shapiro's notion that the public policy of one generation is the political theory of the previous generation, it may be that the video jurisprudence of one season is the legal practice of the next. Recent commentary in *The New York Times* concludes that post-O.J. trials are responding not to the law made in the traditional hierarchical fashion but to the law made by the commentators and reactions to the verdicts from the public. And *U.S. News and World Report*, in discussing the prospects for "The Practice," suggests that in the wake of the O.J. verdict it is daring to ask the audience to identify with a defense lawyer (presumably the magazine was worried about the reactions of its white audience).

Commenting on the relationship of form in law to form in another area of social life, David Bordwell, Janet Staiger, and Kristin Thompson describe the psychotherapeutic films of the 1940s, such as "Spellbound" and "Shadow of a Doubt," as vulgarizations of Freudian theory because they copy the traditions of the crime drama with their interrogations and often spontaneous revelations on the witness stand.[12] In "L.A. Law" those revelations have for the most part been replaced by characterizations in which the power of law is less apt to provide the basis for a therapeutic catharsis. The show tends more often to affirm struggles over status within a plastic culture that heralds identity formation as a transcendent social project. Thus, we get emotional presentations from Ann Kelsey on her value to the firm when she is demanding to become a partner and clever remarks about not becoming the "Mexican gardener picking up the snails" when Victor Sifuentes initially resists entreaties from the firm to become an associate.

On "L.A. Law" nearly every episode juxtaposed the courtroom, lacking in artifice, spare, and businesslike in character, with the relative opulence of the law offices and the luncheon venues to which the attorneys were inevitably drawn. In the second part of the premier episode, the firm takes Sifuentes to a very expensive lunch where much is made of the restaurant's grandeur as an inducement to come to the firm. In another early episode, Arnie Becker goes to an expensive lunch with a beautiful and rich potential client to instruct her as to the realities of the divorce process. Though he picks up the tab for the meal it is clear to all but the client that it will eventually be billed to her. To some extent this positioning links the activity in the courtrooms with the law's traditional venues and distinguishes them from the more integrated spaces of the new legal practice where law is done between golf swings, bits of salad, or while getting the car out of valet parking.

The courtroom in "L.A. Law" is subordinate to the boardroom. Recurring in the opening of each episode, the long table around which attorneys gather to discuss business becomes the unifying frame for the show. This form is more common on "L.A. Law" than the courtroom and it serves as a prominent and realistic expression of the corporate core of modern law. In the boardroom, like the courtroom, participants have places that relate to status. In one show, Ann Kelsey fights with a new attorney over the senior lawyer's traditional place at the table. Of course, Leland McKenzie, the head of the firm, is at the head of the table. With its glass walls, the boardroom still looks out to the firm where the staff can see but not hear and the special place of those allowed to participate is affirmed. This affirmation is through the transparency of the walls and it works as well as any leather-covered courthouse doors did in the past. Against this manifestation of realism, the courtroom is a formal setting downtown that allows the contemporary authority of the boardroom to be embedded in a social realism where viewers think they have become part of the action.

Realism

Representation of the television courtroom has shifted. The traditional style that held sway from at least "Matlock," if not "Perry Mason," to "L.A. Law" is no longer dominant. Instead, there has been a shift from process-based conception to hyper-realism. This shift plays out in the arts, influenced by MTV and video styles, which in turn influences jurisprudence. An aspect of this shift is a shift in scene. The move from East to West means a move away from a darker, more ethnically-charged arena. From "Hill Street Blues" to "L.A. Law," the same creator, Steven Bochco, changed the context for his treatment of diversity issues and other aspects of social life. These issues appear to stand out in more analytical ways in the "L.A. Law" set than they do in the gritty precinct house of either "Hill Street Blues" or, later, in "N.Y.P.D. Blue."

It is difficult to discuss jurisprudence without considering realism and video jurisprudence provides ample opportunity to examine the expressions of the realist form. In her discussion of law in soap operas, Dianne L. Brooks distinguishes between the realism where "the trial proceedings, the mise-en-scene etc. is seemingly true-to-life," and the "legal realist" movement.[13] Perhaps there is a relationship. Realism on television does not much come from law. Other successful television shows are a major influence. Presently the prominence of the richly-detailed emergency room in "ER" has some impact on representations across shows and across professions.[14] An aspect of this realism may derive from the expansion of the soap opera form into prime time television. Though not a direct appropriation, the sweaty details of the soaps seem to be appearing on the evening courtroom dramas. Although characterized by melodrama, soap operas also feature greater reality in some respects than do traditional prime time television shows, especially the pervasive situation comedy.[15] For instance, in soaps the extreme closeup is a feature, showing the details of struggle in the faces of the actors (emotion as well as high drama, of course, are staples of this genre). Brooks points out the significance of legal narratives, often highlighting both the melodrama and the emotional intimacy of the form. She mentions rape, domestic violence, incest, pornography, and the killing of prostitutes. The most obvious thing for the analysis of the presentation of the courtroom is the close-up. Although the close-up in the case of the soaps is usually human, with an often stagy background, in the case of "Law & Order"[16] and "The Practice," although not "L.A. Law," there is a sense that this space can stand a more complete picture.

The realism on television tells us something about realism in law. As television law visits the constructions of law in society, the familiar courtroom of the popular television show becomes the even more familiar courtroom of the actual O.J. Simpson trial. Certainly at an aesthetic level we were prepared for the meting out of justice in the O.J. trial by the work of Grace Van Owen and her colleagues. And it is safe to say that the relatively young female prosecutor of "L.A. Law" influenced how we saw Marcia Clark in her role as O.J. Simpson's prosecutor. Likewise, the image of the court building has taken the place formerly occupied by the writings on earlier courts. It is a referent displayed as part of the semiotic presentation in the primary frame, the electronic monitor.

Perhaps the greater clarity in the television situation allows us to understand what has generally been difficult with regard to realism. This is the capacity of an allegedly critical position to achieve hegemony in a large and complex system and maintain its hold for generations. In its television form, law is increasingly depicted in harsh closeups that give us a sense that we are participants and knowledgeable. Certainly we can appreciate that Americans and viewers around the world have learned a great deal of both civil and criminal procedure from the tube. On television we get the incorporation of our aspirations into a dominant framework as part of law's more general incorporationist propensity.

Conclusion

Like the police drama "Cagney & Lacey," which ran at about the same time, "L.A. Law" infused its texts with social commentary and followed a political agenda. Perhaps this agenda was not as consistent as the one on "Cagney & Lacey," but it was identifiable nonetheless.

On the surface, the agenda of "L.A. Law" was one of liberal reform. Racial tolerance is good, racism is bad. Gender equality is good, old inequalities are bad. People that merely want money are silly and shallow, although they may be attractive and appear fortunate. Some of these political stands are part of the realist presentation characteristic of the show in that they connect with a dominant conception of reality as facing the issues. But where the traditional courtroom drama, in its focus on disputes, was a perfect vehicle for facing such issues, "L.A. Law" offered a mixed bag. At times, however, the multiple story lines enabled the show to transcend the form of the courtroom drama and become a showcase for law.

4

Law & Order

DAWN KEETLEY

In a 1995 episode of "Law & Order" entitled "Rage," a wildly successful Wall Street trader kills his employer. The trader is black and his employer is white, and, evincing its trademark moral ambiguity, "Law & Order" puts an apparently clear-cut premeditated murder into doubt with the trader's defense of "black rage": he was, according to his attorney, insane at the time of the killing because a relentlessly racist society triggered a psychotic episode. "The kettle boiled over," his lawyer claims. Outraged at what he believes to be a spurious defense, Assistant District Attorney Jack McCoy (Sam Waterston) insists that the defendant is nothing but a thief and a murderer. After he wins his conviction, however, and as the episode ends, a taxi driver ignores a black man who has been standing on a corner vainly trying to flag down a cab, and pulls up beside McCoy, who is white.

Like most episodes of NBC's critically-acclaimed "Law & Order," "Rage" leaves its viewers with more questions than answers: Does racism still determine the lives of black men in America? Was McCoy misled by his own privileged status? Did the law or its inevitably biased practitioners dictate that the trader committed murder when he may not, in fact, have been completely responsible? To what extent does and should the world beyond the legal system—the racism of the streets of New York, for instance—affect what happens inside the courtroom?

This essay examines two of the most distinctive characteristics of "Law & Order," both of which "Rage" exemplifies. First, the show is rightly praised for its moral complexity. As producer Dick Wolf has said: "The perfect 'Law & Order' episode will be when all six characters are on six sides of a single issue—and they're all right."[1] Secondly, at least one television critic has pointed out that the real protagonist of "Law & Order" is not its characters but the law itself. Writing in the *Kansas City Star*, Aaron Barnhart argues: "roles are dictated more by process than personality.... The real star of 'Law & Order,'" he continues, "is the criminal justice system.... Here process is king and woe to those naive enough to think they have some control over its mysterious ways."[2] Certainly the show's increasing popularity *despite* an unprecedented number of cast changes, as well as its signature refusal to feature the private lives of its characters, appears to confirm that the show puts the law on center stage.[3]

I begin by arguing that the ambiguity of "Law & Order" derives from the show's persistent unsettling of the notion of "crime," as it puts into play the two primary elements of a crime—*actus reus* (guilty act) and *mens rea* (guilty mind). The show repeatedly asks the audience to consider not only "who did it?" but "were the defendant's actions actually criminal?" Even if it is clear that the defendant did commit the crime, his or her state of mind and thus his or her criminal responsibility are often put in doubt.

As questions proliferate during a typical episode, both in terms of whether a crime occurred at all and, if it did, whether the person who committed it was culpable, a new issue inevitably arises: who or what is most instrumental in actually determining who the criminal is—the law or the lawyer? In the second part of the essay, I argue that when the ambiguity is, in part at least, resolved by a verdict, "Law & Order" represents the lawyer and *not* the law as the primary agent, first, in defining what the crime is, and then in assigning responsibility for it. Contrary to Barnhart's claim that the show puts the mystifying processes of the law at center-stage, I argue that the law is subject to the moral vision of its agents. This is clear, for instance, in McCoy's moral outrage at the Wall Street trader and his self-serving defense: "You disgust me," McCoy proclaims; his efforts to define the trader's actions as first-degree murder are driven by this outrage. The prior moral vision of the lawyers, then, drives the legal processes of indictment, trial, and conviction, as defendants are regularly made to take responsibility for their actions by the prosecutors— despite the excuses that the law might allow.

The preeminence of the moral outlook that motivates the prosecutors on "Law & Order" to seek conviction and to hold people culpable may well account for its success, perhaps even more so than the show's moral complexity. At a time when often notorious insanity defenses are proliferating—many, like the "twinkie defense," provoking widespread condemnation—and when acquittals on the grounds of legal technicalities are sure to make the headlines, "Law & Order" fulfills a societal desire to hold people accountable. The show also works to forge a bond between a skeptical American audience and the legal profession, revealing the lawyer to have deeply-held moral convictions about guilt and insisting that the amoral technicalities of the legal system do not always triumph over common sense ideas of fairness. "Law & Order" rehabilitates the law as an efficacious and just system during a decade when both scrutiny of and pessimism about the legal system is perhaps at its most intense; furthermore it rehabilitates lawyers, who are shown to put probity before both legal rules and before either personal or political advancement.

Lastly, I turn to the ways in which "Law & Order" shows the possibilities for justice to be ultimately bounded by one particular blind spot of both the law and of lawyers: the presumption that *individuals* commit crimes as free, rational, and purposeful actors. While the show is often very expansive in its ascriptions of blame—reaching back to the remote causes of crime rather than seeing only its immediate causes, its lawyers finally find *an individual* to blame rather than larger cultural, social, and economic forces and systems. In their unexamined propensity to attribute responsibility only to a single person, and in their dismissal of defenses that recognize contextual reasons for crime (such as the black rage defense), both the lawyers and the law they blindly serve obscure the impersonal and institutional causes of harm.

"Six Sides of a Single Issue"

One hallmark of "Law & Order" is its equal division of time between the police investigation and the prosecution—between apprehending a suspect and proving his or her guilt. Producer Dick Wolf has claimed that, "'The first half is a murder mystery. The second half is a moral mystery.'"[4] Indeed, the first half of "Law & Order" is a conventional murder mystery, as the police officers track the "clues" that take them inexorably from the initial crime (almost always a homicide committed off-stage) to one guilty individual. Conventionally linear, this initial plot of investigation and arrest is a typical "whodunnit," and the narrative interest derives from watching a field of suspects narrow to one. At the midpoint of each episode, it appears that the culprit has been apprehended and all that remains is for the district attorney's office to "prosecute the offender," as the voice-over intones at the start of each episode. The second half of the narrative is less conventional, however, as the trajectory is less a movement toward a guilty individual than a movement *away* from sure guilt. The lawyers struggle not merely to convict their suspect in a court of law but often to convince themselves and each other, as the clarity of the defendant's guilt dissolves or gets deferred to other still more guilty parties. As one critic puts it: "Nothing has ever been what it seems on 'Law & Order'....Murderers turn out to be victims, victims to be accomplices. Motives are morally murky. The show's regular characters are often fallible, misguided or just plain wrong."[5] Trying a case that is suddenly far from clear-cut, the lawyers in particular often end up taking different positions on who is guilty, of what, and why.

The principal source of the show's famed ambiguity derives from the recurrent concept of responsibility. While the first half of each episode (the "murder mystery") tries, like most other crime dramas, to ascertain who *committed* the crime, the second half of each episode investigates the slightly different question: who is *responsible for* the crime? (or what Dick Wolf calls the "moral mystery"). So rather than being simply about apprehending a person, "Law & Order" ends up being about the process of apprehending an irreducibly complex legal and moral abstraction—accountability. Typically, one of two plot devices places the concept of culpability at center-stage: first, the defendant's lawyer raises some kind of legal excuse or mitigation for what his or her client did—and the prosecutors then enter into a debate not only with the defense but also among themselves about the validity of the defense claims; second, the blame gets shifted from the original suspect to a more remote, less immediately obvious participant in the crime—someone who may appear to be beyond the purview of the criminal law but whom the prosecutors work creatively to convict.

In putting the concept of responsibility both on center-stage and in contention, "Law & Order" also puts the very idea of "crime" into dynamic play—refusing to take crime for granted or to lend it the self-evidence that so many other crime dramas do.[6] As opposed to prosecuting a clearly intentional murder, "Law & Order" consistently asks: What *is* the crime here? This question is mobilized by the fact that the two defining elements of a crime become a matter to be determined and not a matter already determined: the *mens rea* (guilty mind) and *actus reus* (guilty act) are both rendered highly visible sites of conflict and are not left as the invisible foundations of easy attributions of blame and of simple answers to the problems of crime. The audience of "Law & Order" is never allowed to rest comfortably in the belief that the defendant (if it becomes clear that he or she did in fact commit the homicide) is either legally or morally blameworthy, that he or she intended to kill or was possessed of the capacity to form intent. The audience is rarely allowed any effortless preconceptions about whether, where, and by whom a crime was actually committed.

In its explorations of the mental state of the person who committed the crime, "Law & Order" draws liberally from those high-profile defenses that Alan Dershowitz has recently popularized as the "abuse excuse." The show has explored, among others, the defenses of black rage, abuse, fan obsession syndrome, genetics (the claim that XYY males are predisposed to violence), and involuntary intoxication.[7] Discussion of a specific episode of "Law & Order" entitled "Trust" (1992) illuminates the ways in which the show attempts to keep the state of mind and thus the guilt of the perpetrator of a homicide permanently uncertain. Much of that doubt persists even through those stages of the judicial process— arrest, indictment, and conviction—that presumably give closure to a crime; in fact, in "Trust," not one but two verdicts ultimately fail to settle the issue of the defendant's culpability.

Early in the episode, it becomes clear to the two detectives, Mike Logan (Chris Noth) and Phil Cerreta (Paul Sorvino) that 15-year old Jamie Maser shot one of his schoolmates, and they focus their investigation on whether the death was accidental, as Jamie claims. Jamie insists: "I didn't mean it, you know. . . . [The gun] just went off," but Logan and Cerreta uncover a previous incident, two years prior to this shooting, in which Jamie killed another boy and also claimed it was an accident. In fact, he gave exactly the same excuse—that he thought he had to cock the hammer on the gun manually before it would fire. The detective who investigated the earlier crime tells Logan and Cerreta that even the first shooting was "an accident asking to happen" and the second crime certainly appears still less of an accident—so Jamie is arrested.

As the prosecutors take over the case, the question of Jamie's responsibility is complicated further by the difficulty of *proving* the intent of which the detectives are now so sure. Even though the facts of the case seem to point to a settled guilt, the strictures of the law immediately intervene to unsettle that guilt, staging a recurrent gap between "common sense" (mostly represented by the police) and the law. As Cerreta says, "He pointed the gun at someone before. He pulled the trigger before. He knew the consequences." And Logan asks incredulously, "That's not enough to prove intent?" The lead prosecutor, Ben Stone (Michael Moriarty), answers that while there is enough evidence of intent for everyone in the room, there may not be enough to prove it in a court of law. Consequently, the lawyers indict Jamie for murder in the second degree; "depraved indifference to human life—no need to prove intent," explains Assistant District Attorney Paul Robinette (Richard Brooks). The law intervenes still further to complicate Jamie's guilt when his defense lawyer enters the picture with the claim that Jamie was "involuntarily intoxicated" when he committed the crime—that his capacity for murder was diminished by the "powerful psychotropic drug" that he was taking, because it "affected his ability to appreciate the consequences of his actions." As is typical in those "Law & Order" episodes that invoke legal excuses for crime, the prosecuting attorneys give the "involuntary intoxication" excuse relatively short shrift. Ben Stone passionately decries the proliferation of legal excuses: "Nobody's responsible anymore. You kill somebody, it's not your fault. You're addicted to sugar or the wrong medication, and someone should pay you a million dollars for *your* suffering."

In addressing the ambiguities of criminal intent, however, "Law & Order" frequently goes beyond the differing opinions of police officers and lawyers and beyond competing defense and prosecution narratives— both conflicts that are expected, even unavoidable, in a legal drama. As Jamie and his state of mind are put on trial, the prosecuting attorneys open up *within their own case* still another ambiguous moral terrain between Jamie's guilt and his innocence. Part of the prosecution's strategy is to show that while Jamie does not suffer from "involuntary intoxication," he has been psychologically abused by his father—abused enough to cause him to kill, as he repeatedly enacts the inner conflict created by his abuse and takes on the position of the powerful abuser rather than the powerless victim. The prosecutors argue, of course, that this abuse does not excuse his actions, and they finally get a guilty verdict in a second trial. But their own strategy for rebutting the excuse mounted by the defense initiates a persistent ambiguity that renders the guilty verdict as inadequate as the earlier not guilty verdict. Jamie *was* psychologically abused by his father, after all, and although this explanation works to negate the "involuntary intoxication" defense and to ensure Jamie's conviction, it also mitigates his crimes by displacing much of the moral responsibility onto his father. Even Ben Stone says near the end of the episode, in what appears to be a contradiction of his earlier denunciation of Jamie for not taking responsibility, that he holds Jamie's father ethically, if not legally, responsible for the deaths of both boys shot by Jamie.

This episode is typical in its palimpsestic design, as one contested script about culpability gives way to an underlying and equally contested one: (1) did Jamie shoot the boys accidentally or intentionally?; (2) was he involuntarily intoxicated and thus not aware of the consequences of what he did—or was he very aware, as his having the presence of mind to lie to the detectives suggests?; and, (3) was Jamie's responsibility for the crime in any way mitigated by his father's abuse and his general failure to inculcate any moral values in his son? In its investigations of state-of-mind, "Law & Order" refuses to rest on any one question to drive its plot, clearing up one dilemma (e.g., it was not an accident), only to reveal a deeper, still more troubling and unanswerable question. As in "Trust," the bottom layer of these contested scripts often turns out to be the question of how responsible parents are for the behavior of their children—a question which is mostly both chronologically and causally beyond the reach of the criminal law but which, the show insists, is often at the very root of crime.

In its unsettling of the second element of crime, *actus reus*, the arena of the show's exploration is often precisely the culpability of parents. When do questionable parenting practices become a crime? When do parents warrant indictment? There are two broad categories of plot that implicate parents in crimes: in some episodes, as in "Trust," the show simply asserts the moral responsibility of typically despicable parents, who have literally created killers but who are beyond the reach of the law in that they do not directly commit a crime. In other episodes the prosecutors manage to find ways to prove that not-so-clearly reprehensible parents did cause the death of their child, even though they too appear at first to be beyond the law's grasp. In cases in which a parent harms their child, the police and then the prosecuting attorneys take what appears to be a non-criminal death and trace its causes beyond the most immediate cause to find an *actus reus*. Out of an apparently accidental, random, or suicidal act—even out of a parent's conviction that they were raising their child correctly, the lawyers create a crime. While such shows begin with characters reiterating—"What's the crime here?" or "There's no crime here"—the ostensibly innocent behavior is peeled away to reveal a guilty act.

In "God Bless the Child" (1991), Ben Stone convicts the Driscolls of manslaughter in the death of their young daughter from a very treatable viral infection, even though their religion specifically forbids seeking medical help for any illness. Stone proclaims that while they can martyr themselves for their religious convictions, they "don't have the right to martyr their child." Since the state cannot prosecute someone for their religious beliefs, the prosecutors must make their case about the Driscolls's criminality by proving that they slipped from their faith. If they had any doubts about prayer and spiritual healing working, they are guilty of letting their child die. Thus the fact that Nancy Driscoll drank coffee and bourbon (both prohibited by her church) and, more damningly, that Ted Driscoll called 911 in a fleeting moment of despair, become the tenuous markers of criminal guilt. This upsets, of course, common sense notions about what constitutes a crime in that not only religious beliefs but also habitual acts like drinking coffee and seemingly law-abiding acts like calling 911 become the signs of a guilty act. As the episode takes its audience, then, from an apparently "natural" death to the innocuous sites of private lives, it first destabilizes and then redefines what constitutes a criminal act.

In another episode, "Aria" (1991), the prosecutors likewise convert an ostensible non-crime into a criminal act committed by a parent—thus, again, creatively re-shaping what we call a "crime." Mrs. Blaine is convicted of manslaughter in the apparent suicide of her daughter, Priscilla Blaine. Priscilla had taken an overdose of pills and died repeating the words, "I didn't want to do it." "It" turns out to be starring in a pornographic film, a business her mother has forced her into in her obsession to make her daughter a celebrated actress—a clear displacement of her own thwarted desire to act. There appears to be no prosecutable crime here: a nineteen-year-old woman kills herself. But Stone and Robinette charge the mother with second-degree murder—a depraved indifference to human life, which was, they argue, the proximate cause of Priscilla's suicide. Unlike in "God Bless the Child," this time there is overt dissent among the principal characters about whether there is a crime. The police captain, Donald Cragen (Dann Florek), says of Mrs. Blaine: "Guilty?

Of being a rotten mother, yes. But there has to be a line. Kid goes out and robs a bank, you put the parents in jail?" "Maybe," Robinette responds, "if there was cause and effect." Cragen objects, however, that Priscilla "was nineteen; she could have left home. She did not have to kill herself." "Maybe she did," Ceretta adds, marking out the line of strict causality between the mother's obsession and her daughter's suicide that the attorneys will need to prove in court.

In the end, however, Mrs. Blaine's actions *as mother* in coercing her daughter into pornography fail to bear the burden of the murder charge—fail, in other words, as a site of criminal action. In a plot twist the episode backs away from the suggestion that parents who obsessively drive their children are potentially criminals. Instead, the prosecutors charge Mrs. Blaine with procuring the drugs for Priscilla in what they now decide is an "accidental" overdose. In a plea bargain, Mrs. Blaine is sentenced for second-degree manslaughter. The episode flinches from its unconventional location of crime in overbearing and self-centered parenting and finds the *actus reus*, finally, in the more conventional and unambiguously criminal act of pushing drugs. The limitations of the law are the source of this flinching, because it is very difficult to prove the necessary direct and proximate causation between one person's actions and another person's suicide. However, the law nevertheless serves as the means to punish the person who is truly at fault. And while the *law* may only allow conviction for drug-peddling, the *episode* itself, around the edges of the system at its center, reinforces the "true" crime—the mother's coercion of her daughter from the moment she was born. The last lines are spoken by Stone, outside of the courtroom: "The mother looked at her daughter and saw herself." *That* is what "Law & Order" defines as Mrs. Blaine's real crime—even though the law cannot.

As these often multi-layered conflicts over *mens rea* and *actus reus* demonstrate, the show's shifting attributions of responsibility for crime account for much of its celebrated ambiguity, as it puts the concepts of both responsibility and crime into contestation. In its self-conscious rehearsal of the many sides of a single issue, "Law & Order" self-consciously broadcasts its representations as ideology rather than abstract, universal truth—as, in the words of cultural critic Mimi White, "an arena of representational practice (and therefore a site of struggle and contestation) rather than a fixed set of beliefs."[8] "Law & Order" reveals the struggle to create the meanings of crime, in other words, rather than taking them as found. But while "Law & Order" the television show foregrounds its own textuality and openness—its own making of meaning—the question arises, does it broadcast its *subject*, the law, as ideology? In its explorations of the potential ambiguity of the law itself, "Law & Order," I argue, focuses on the relation between law and lawyer. In particular it asks whether the law is an independent and closed set of already-defined positions which the lawyers merely enact and which determines their character and their choices, or whether it is open and subject to their values?

Lawyers and the Shaping of the Law

There certainly are moments in "Law & Order" when the law seems to precede and define the perspective of the lawyers and thus limits at the most fundamental level the ways in which they can even conceive of a crime, let alone attribute responsibility and blame. The process by which the law establishes itself as the determinative measure of crime and responsibility has been called by sociologist Pierre Bourdieu "rationalization"—a constant increase in the "separation between judgments based upon the law and naive intuitions of fairness."[9] The law's process of "rationalization" is exemplified in the moment in "Trust" when Ceretta voices precisely such a "naive intuition of fairness"—"he pointed the gun at someone before. He pulled the trigger before. He knew the consequences"—and Stone retorts that such logic does not necessarily constitute intent in a court of law. The law is not only separated from common sense attributions of criminality but is revealed to be the *dominant* arbiter, subjecting common sense to its own specific rules of judgment. As the District Attorney, Adam Schiff (Steven Hill) snaps at his assistant, who is arguing that common sense should prevail in a legal situation: "Common sense has nothing to do with it."

When television critic Aaron Barnhart writes that "process is king" on "Law & Order," he is essentially arguing that the show evinces the law's self-referential rationalizing process and its exclusion of "common sense" morality. It is precisely this process of rationalization—by which the law creates itself as independent of lay definitions of crime and justice— that has fostered much of the popular cynicism about the law and lawyers. In the public conception, lawyers and the human values they potentially *could* represent are seen instead as subject to a mystifying system that baffles simple conceptions of who is blameworthy and who should be punished. Barnhart has summed up such attitudes toward the legal system: "TV news started bringing us new images of the judicial system, this time from real life: murderers getting off scot-free, hoodlums back on the street only hours after being picked up, convictions rendered moot on technicalities."[10] In news story after news story, the legal system seems to be at odds not only with morality but also with the justice with which it is supposed to be synonymous.

I argue, however, that far from demonstrating the triumph of the law's mystifying rationalizing processes over common sense morality, "Law &

Order" consistently *bridges* this gap—showing that the law does serve morality. It does so, first, by separating the lawyer from the law, rather than subsuming him or her to it, and then by showing that the lawyer's independent moral vision shapes the legal process, and that the lawyer can actually use the law as an instrument to effect social justice and to hold the guilty responsible. Ben Stone, Jack McCoy, Claire Kincaid (Jill Hennessy), and Jamie Ross (Carey Lowell), in particular, consistently express their own views of the morality of the people they try, and while sometimes the realities of the law defeat their attempts to convict those they consider guilty, more often they are able to negotiate (sometimes very inventively) the tangled web of laws in order to punish those whom they have *already decided* are guilty. On "Law & Order," the beliefs and values of the lawyers take precedence over the abstractions of the law—and it is those beliefs and values, *not* law as an autonomous system, that are most often instrumental in assigning criminal responsibility. The legal system on "Law & Order," then, is not a closed system, in which only limited and predetermined perspectives are available, but a system that is constituted by the moral views of lawyers. Lawyers, in other words, attribute blame by using the law as opposed to its using them.

As "Law & Order" consistently puts the very definition of a "crime" into play, and as the exact crime to be prosecuted remains in flux, the driving force behind the final crystallization of the prosecutable offense and of a guilty offender is the team of prosecutors and, more specifically, the moral sense of one or another of them. Adam Schiff, the District Attorney, is frequently the voice of moderation—the touchstone directing what crimes are politically and legally prosecutable, but the prosecutors who work for him are consistently portrayed as impassioned moralists who often decide to prosecute on the basis of a personal conviction of injustice as much as—or sometimes more than—a clearly transgressed law. Finally even the District Attorney, who is most closely allied to "the law," typically assents to the moral agenda of his team and confirms the moral trajectory of the show. This acquiescence continually re-enacts the subordination of legal process to common sense morality and fairness.

In a fascinating episode entitled "Misconception" (1991), a young couple, Chris and Amy, entrap Amy's wealthy employer into an affair with her. The initial plan was for them to tell the employer the baby was his in order to blackmail him, but when that fails they stage an assault on Amy that causes her to miscarry so that they can frame him for the assault and then sue him for civil damages. The prosecutors, particularly Ben Stone, are incensed when they finally uncover this plot, and Stone decides to try Chris and Amy for the attempted murder of their own fetus. The problem for the prosecutors is that according to a New York statute, a fetus can only be murdered after twenty-four weeks of gestation—and

Chris and Amy's unborn child, it turns out, was only twenty-two weeks old. Voicing his disgust at the arbitrariness of the statute, police officer Mike Logan comments: "Lawyers decide if you're alive enough to be murdered." Prosecutor Robinette retorts, "You expect me to tell you the law makes sense." In the way he frames his protest, Logan presumes an already-existent life: "Lawyers decide if *you're* alive enough to be murdered." An Irish-Catholic, Logan's objection implicitly registers a pro-life stance, but any political divide around the issue of abortion and beliefs about when life begins is immediately displaced to the objection that *lawyers* are deciding when life begins. As Logan condemns the law's attempt to define life, even the lawyer Robinette agrees with him and validates the law's distance from common sense. Early in the episode, then, a conflict emerges between the common sense view of both life and murder and the power of the law to distort as it capriciously defines both terms.

The law is only fleetingly allowed to define Chris and Amy's act as an innocent one, however, as Stone decides to prosecute even though they are not legally guilty of attempted murder. Chris, a disbarred lawyer, knew the New York statute, knew how old the fetus was, and thus knew he was not attempting murder when he and Amy staged the assault. Schiff, adopting his role as principled guardian of the law, reiterates Chris's legal innocence to Stone: "If you fire an unloaded gun at me, it's intent. If you know the gun isn't loaded, it's nothing." Chris, Schiff insists, knew "the gun wasn't loaded." Stone, though, explains that in order to prove his knowledge of relatively arcane law, Chris will have to get on the witness-stand and testify — giving the jury the chance to see how despicable he is and to "do the right thing." A conversation ensues that effectively stages the tension between the law and what Stone sees as "the right thing":

> Schiff: You want the jury to ignore the evidence.
> Stone: Chris and Amy want the jury to look at the law. I'll get the jury to look at Chris and Amy.
> Schiff: The law's supposed to be a shield not a sword. They're despicable, yes, but by the letter of the law, they're not guilty.
> Stone: The legislature could never have conceived of anything like this. Wrong should not win by technicalities. You know that yourself.
> Schiff: Get these bastards off the street.

In this case, Stone is, as Schiff puts it, using the law as a "sword" to punish what he believes to be an immoral act that is quite unambiguously *not* a crime. But the speed with which Schiff, the upholder of the law, comes to agree with him — revealing his own vehement distaste for the "bastards" — epitomizes the show's persistent privileging of a private sense of justice over law when the two conflict. In fact, the show persistently stages that very conflict simply to re-enact, over and over, the triumph of justice and the defeat of legal technicalities.

Reading Schiff as representative of the "law," his sudden capitulation to Stone's technical misuse of the law dissolves the conflict between law and morality by suggesting that he has agreed with Stone all along and thus that the law and morality have been in tandem all along. This reading, which conjoins law and morality beneath an only superficial conflict, is bolstered by the fact that Stone does, after all, use the legal system, specifically the jury, to hand Chris and Amy their just deserts. As an integral part of the system, yet at the same time as a body composed of twelve lay people, the jury represents the synthesis of law and basic human morality. They arrive, appropriately, at a guilty verdict that is paradoxically legal despite its having ignored the law. It is based, as Robinette says, on the jurors's "horror" at Chris and Amy rather than on a New York statute. Not only, then, does "Law & Order" stage a conflict in which justice triumphs over the law, but it retroactively negates the conflict and shows the law to be moral—when, of course, it is in the hands of fair and principled attorneys. While the agency of Stone's moral vision in shaping the law is clear throughout, it is most fully realized in his last words about Amy, who has been rendered incapable of conceiving another child by the attack she and Chris staged: "There's another piece of justice," he says to Robinette. "She'll never reproduce." Stone's use of the word "justice" in this instance clearly invokes a non-legal justice. Whether one calls it natural, poetic, or divine, it shows how, for Stone, the concept is not defined solely by the letter of the law but, rather, that his view of the law is shaped by a justice that both surpasses its limits and that challenges and extends them.

The show's instrumental view of the law as a tool to be wielded by principled attorneys is only sharpened by its negative depictions of defense attorneys who do not subordinate the law to their own moral vision. Defense attorneys are almost always presented as devotees of the letter of the law, practitioners who justify defending clearly guilty offenders on the grounds that the law entitles everyone to a defense. "Law & Order" routinely parades a string of defenders who irresponsibly fabricate exculpatory narratives that misrepresent truth and defy morality, all in the name of doing their job—that is, the law's job.

That adhering to the letter of the law and ignoring justice is the mark of lawyerly anti-heroism is evidenced in a 1996 episode. As Jack McCoy and Claire Kincaid investigate the death of a baby, they become convinced that the English au pair poisoned him with pesticide. The au pair's attorney decides to construct reasonable doubt by attacking the baby's mother, and by persuading the jury that she was irresponsible and was thus, in a remote way, responsible for her baby's death. In the courtroom, the defense attorney excoriates the mother for not checking into the agency that sent her the au pair, for knowing virtually nothing about her baby, for taking frequent business trips—and even for having a career at all, because her husband makes enough money for both of them. After the trial, Claire Kincaid and the defense attorney meet for a drink and Kincaid expresses her outrage that her colleague is single-handedly setting feminism back fifty years by playing on the benighted misconception of the jury that women should not combine family and career. The defense attorney, of course, tells Kincaid that she should not proscribe a legitimate defense in order to further her political views—and that while she herself is a working mother, she will not subordinate the law to her private view of what is right and wrong. If her defense, even of an unpleasant and possibly criminal young woman, involves relying on and even instigating the jury's sexism—so be it. The law, she claims, is more important than personal politics and morality. Ironically, the defense lawyer is partially justified in her position, as the au pair is proved innocent, but in a final twist, the killer turns out to be the father's teenage son by his first wife, a boy who felt abandoned when his father left. That a *father's* absence from his family, due to his absorption in not only his career but also a new family, can be the remote cause of a crime is a truth investigators and jurors may be blinded to, the episode suggests, if they see only the disingenuous and sexist narrative condemning working *mothers* spun by the defense lawyer in her attempt to exonerate her client.

Sometimes, however, the legal system does triumph over the prosecutors's moral vision. Sometimes the law really does appear to be a tangle of mysterious rules that are essentially uncontrollable—that take on a force and an agency of their own, subordinating lawyers, morality, and common sense. A 1995 episode, for instance, concerns McCoy's and Kincaid's prosecution of a young man, abused by his mother as a child, who kills two people thinking they are his parents while in a state of drunkenness. Despite very persuasive arguments from psychiatrists—even the prosecutors's own specialist—that the defendant believed he was a little boy again and thought he was acting in self-defense, the prosecutors convict him. At the end of the episode, Kincaid expresses her doubts that the young man belongs in jail for twenty-five years. McCoy replies, "Do you want him on the street?" and Kincaid answers, "That's not what I meant." "The law," McCoy explains, "only gave us two choices."

This representation of an autonomous judicial system—a kind of monster come back to wreak vengeance on its creators—is not presented as an inevitable and essential attribute of the law, however. The law is more often than not represented as an instrument in prosecutors's moral hands. Most of the time, the prosecutors are far from being coerced into one of only two predetermined and absolute choices, as they typically create their own options within the loose, as opposed to the fixed, limitations of the law. Thus, the overall intent of "Law & Order" is not to represent the law as a machine, independent of its wielder's basic morality. So when the occasional episode *does* present the law as autonomous, it seems to be for purposes of a relatively self-conscious critique of that autonomy rather than to reinforce it. When "the law" as an impenetrable entity triumphs over the prosecutors's best efforts, for instance, they always indicate their awareness of that triumph; they recognize that they have become momentarily tangled in the machine. This recognition signals that the lawyers, while fleetingly entrapped, are nevertheless at least free enough to acknowledge their entrapment, and thus that they occupy a position partially beyond the boundaries of the law, from which they can challenge it. McCoy's and Kincaid's closing dialogue about the law's offering them only two options is part of a consistent narrative strategy: episodes often end not in court but with a subsequent exchange *outside* the courtroom about the end result of the lawyers's prosecution. Significantly, the lawyers are often walking, outdoors, or on the thresholds of offices — about to leave. They are, in other words, in liminal spaces — between and not firmly inside of the static and closed spaces of the legal system, such as courthouses and offices. When Kincaid expresses her doubt about convicting the abused man, she has her hand on the door of McCoy's office, symbolizing her freedom from being defined and circumscribed by the system that office represents.

What the critical awareness and the symbolic liminality of the lawyers does is to demystify the law, since its workings are, after all, understood and thus do not encompass and define the lawyers at a level prior to their conscious awareness. It also creates a space for change, because the lawyers, already constituted by the show as moral beings in their understanding of and objection to what the law has wrought, provide a standpoint beyond its boundaries — a potential leverage point — from which to effect transformation. In fact, it is necessary to the show's predominant presentation of its protagonists's essential morality that they occasionally lose to the ineffable authority of the law. If they did not, their private morality might risk becoming too closely identified with the law itself. The occasional triumph of the law reinforces the separate sense of justice of the lawyers — and they are thus represented as people who can not only use the law, but as people who can potentially also change it when it causes injustice.

In an episode called "Seed" (1995), Jack McCoy and Claire Kincaid fail to convict a villainous doctor, but at every lost chance to prosecute, their indignation serves to condemn a legal system that thwarts their efforts. The episode begins with a woman forcing her way into the bank where her husband works and screaming that he killed her baby; when she pulls out a gun and fires at him, a security guard kills her. Through a series of the show's hallmark plot twists, the blame for the woman's death finally lands on a fertility specialist—although he is never tried for this or any other crime. Dr. Gilbert's moral sins, as the prosecutors piece them together, include lying to patients about their being pregnant and using his own sperm to inseminate at least twenty-five women, who are under the misconception that the sperm is from an anonymous donor. That these practices are not crimes becomes a refrain. As Lieutenant Anita Van Buren (S. Epatha Merkerson) says: "Lying's not a crime." And as Kincaid tries to convince a judge that Gilbert defrauded his client, he barks, "Is there a crime here?" In a different court, when the prosecutors raise the fact that Gilbert inseminated twenty-five women, the judge insists that "he hasn't done anything that even smells criminal." The District Attorney, Schiff, agrees: "What Gilbert did is disgusting, but there's nothing in the penal code that says he can't do it."

Finally, the prosecutors find out that Gilbert inseminated a woman, Mrs. Brock, who had contracted with him to be inseminated by her husband; in fact, the Brocks were only having a child in order to provide a potential bone marrow donor for their first child. McCoy and Kincaid finally, then, light on the idea of indicting Gilbert for second-degree murder in the death of the Brocks's daughter from leukemia, since his lying to them about whose sperm he was using significantly lowered the chances of their new baby being a match with their daughter, and thus he showed a reckless disregard for human life. However, despite the prosecutors's consistent denunciations of Gilbert—especially in a monologue by McCoy, in which he accuses Gilbert of "trying to populate the world by himself," of causing the deaths of a woman and of the Brocks's daughter, and of "gall or ego or complete disregard for human decency"—the law fails, this time, to provide the lawyers with a means to match legal and moral justice, to match their private convictions with public conviction. But at each discrepancy between the lawyers's moral condemnation and legal recourse, "Law & Order" opens a space for a critique of the law and for change—especially marked in "Seed" because the area of reproductive technologies is relatively new. That it is not illegal for a doctor to inseminate twenty-five women with his own sperm is clearly a fault in the law the show suggests; it is, moreover, an easily fixed fault, and not an underlying and fundamental or systematic problem. It is something as-yet overlooked rather than an entrenched and structural blind-spot.

Blind Spots

Thus far I have elaborated on the show's representations of the malleability and openness of the law—its enactment of the indeterminacy of the elements of a crime (*actus reus* and *mens rea*) and, furthermore, how what constitutes a crime is contingent primarily on the potentially infinite array of lawyers's moral perspectives. However, in this last section, I want to discuss how that openness has limits — and where, exactly, those limits are drawn (again as "Law & Order" attributes responsibility for crime).

While at one level "Law & Order" represents both crime and responsibility as complex and multivalent, an obvious point that gets lost precisely because it is, perhaps, in plain view is that "Law & Order" is about lawyers who work for the Manhattan District Attorney's office, and in most cases they try *and* convict *someone*. Unlike the predominance of private-practice and defense lawyers on other legal shows ("Perry Mason," "Matlock," "L.A. Law," "Civil Wars," "Murder One," "The Client," and "The Practice"), the lawyers in "Law & Order" "prosecute the offender," as the beginning voice-over proclaims, almost always holding someone responsible for the crime that initiates the episode. The fact that the opening voice-over defines the show as about the stories of the attorneys who "prosecute the offender" suggests two things: first, that the prosecutors presume that there is *an "offender"* somewhere — even before they try him or her; and, second, that the offender will be singular — will be *the* offender — an *individual* who caused harm. The ambiguity of "Law & Order," the proliferation of its interpretations of crime and guilt, is finally bounded, then, by the limitations of both law and lawyers, as the latter finally acquiesce in perhaps the most fundamental structural bias of the criminal law — its bias toward holding some*one* guilty for the harms of life, its bias toward presuming that an individual is the final and intentional cause of harm.

In "Seed," for example, McCoy and Kincaid blame Gilbert for the death of a woman who came to him so desperate to have a baby that she became momentarily insane when she miscarried and tried to kill her husband. While Gilbert certainly deserves a great deal of blame, the lawyers never ask themselves *why* women might wait so long to try to get pregnant, and *why* they might then need to have a baby so badly that they become criminally insane when they cannot. The only broader vision — and it is fleeting — happens in an exchange between the investigating officers, Mike Logan and Lennie Briscoe (Jerry Orbach). They are reading Gilbert's patient files looking at the ages of the women who came to see him, who were mostly in their forties. Briscoe comments, "Talk about leaving it to the last minute." Logan responds, "Maybe they had something better to do. Women are allowed to have other priorities." One of the women herself, in a later scene, says that she had been dedicated to succeeding in her demanding career — and had no time for a family until it was too late. What these fleeting scenes suggest is that the real "culprit" in "Seed" may be the contradictory, even impossible, societal expectations placed on women: succeed in corporate America; have a family; never let your family interfere with your drive to the top. That the lawyers never discuss this issue is in large part because the law cannot, of course, put societal expectation and gender roles in a courtroom and try them. Thus both the legal system and its participants inevitably pursue only one link in the chain of causality — without, in this case at least, self-consciously acknowledging that Gilbert *is* only a small part of the cause of this particular harm.

In "Seed," the seeds of a larger cultural, social, and economic responsibility for crime are planted, but are not allowed to grow into a comprehensive indictment of those ineffable forces. As the episode progresses, more is revealed about Gilbert; he is given more and more agency by the episode as its protagonists pursue him. His quite deliberate insemination of twenty-five women — what McCoy calls his attempt to populate the world by himself — serves as a potent symbol of individual agency, as Gilbert becomes not only the literal source of twenty-five new lives but the symbolic source of as many potential crimes. The symbolic power of Gilbert's originary status as criminal is so great that it elides any suggestion that some of the causes of harm lie beyond Gilbert. While "Law & Order" presents multiple views of the causes of crime and criminal responsibility, then, the trajectory of each episode clearly narrows to privilege the individual over the societal cause. This is perhaps inevitable because the show's wholesale focus on the legal process in the second-half of the show necessarily ties its vision to that of the law — as the camera invariably moves from one courtroom and legal office to another, mostly confined to the closed spaces of the justice system. While the law's narrow view of intentionalism may be fleetingly challenged, often earlier in each episode, it invariably takes over through the trial process and excludes other possibilities from the narrative.

One episode, which aired in 1994, dramatizes particularly effectively the coercive power of the law's underlying presumption that harm is caused by an intentional actor, and how this presumption works as an entropic force — pulling lawyers from difficult and dissenting positions into its impetus to "prosecute *the* offender." In this episode, McCoy and Kincaid are prosecuting a woman, Susan Forrest, who was involved in an armed robbery in which one of her cohorts, now dead, shot and killed a policeman. The twist is that the robbery happened in 1971 and Forrest, then a student at Columbia University and an anti-war protester, was stealing the money to further the cause of ending the bloodshed in Vietnam. After living for several years underground, Forrest re-invented herself as the wealthy suburban wife of an accountant. She has become a different person, and both her changed identity and her former status as an anti-war protester become potentially mitigating issues in her prosecution. Lennie Briscoe, the older of the two detectives, and McCoy, the older of the two principal prosecutors, are particularly unsure about whether they should prosecute. Both repeat to their colleagues the refrain: "You had to be there." You had to live through the 1960s to be able to understand what Susan Forrest did. In two separate conversations with the younger Claire Kincaid, McCoy expresses his misgivings about Forrest being a criminal at all.

> Kincaid: She killed a policeman.
> McCoy: She was a college kid who was angry about the war.
> Kincaid: I never heard you make excuses for a criminal before.
> McCoy: It's not an excuse. It's the way things were.

Later on, Kincaid and McCoy have a similar conversation that ends, however, with McCoy's abrupt transformation, as he utterly discards "the way things were" and anger over Vietnam as any kind of excuse for Forrest's actions.

> Kincaid: If it had happened in the fifties, you wouldn't hesitate to prosecute the murder.
> McCoy: I'm sure you've listened to all the Doors albums, but you just don't have any idea what it was like back then.
> Kincaid: I can't prosecute Susan Forrest because I wasn't at Woodstock?
> McCoy: Everyone was breaking the law, including the government. Young people felt like they were a force in history.
> Kincaid: How many cops did you kill, Jack?

Just moments later, McCoy decides to prosecute Susan Forrest for first-degree murder, even though she did not even pull the trigger. His change of heart is due in large part to Kincaid's insistence that he consider the individual ("How many cops did *you* kill, Jack?") rather than the environment ("what it was like back then"). Quite startlingly, given his earlier awareness of the complex circumstances surrounding and shaping Forrest's "crime," McCoy later comes close to lying to a witness in order to persuade her that Forrest has betrayed the cause and that she should testify against her former friend. Forrest is tried and convicted — and the only voice that is raised in the remainder of the episode is not McCoy's, since he has undergone as complete a transformation as Forrest herself, but another former 1960s radical who asks: "Why are you doing this to us? The real criminals killed 50,000 American boys and over a million Vietnamese, and they've never been in a courtroom." Her protest now goes unheard by all the lawyers in their drive to locate the sins of the 1960s in the body of one anti-war protester and to ignore the radical redefinition of crime presented by another protestor. While the episode has certainly raised objections and alternatives to this very narrow construction of guilt, the *lawyers* become wholly identified with the law's unspoken ideology of intentionalism: killing millions in the course of war is not a prosecutable crime; being involved in the death of one person during anti-war activism is. While "Law & Order" fleetingly recognizes the injustice of this, it also shows that the law cannot.

The most consistent way that "Law & Order" dramatizes the law's presumption that individuals commit crimes and commit them with clear intent and knowledge of the consequences, and thus with the full burden of responsibility, is the short shrift the prosecutors give to what Alan Dershowitz has called "the abuse excuse"—causes of crime that mitigate or excuse a defendant's criminal responsibility. In a recent review of Dershowitz's *The Abuse Excuse*, Susan Rutberg argues that Dershowitz's ridicule of "psychiatric or other context-based evidence as a defense in a criminal case... has effectively dumbed down any serious discussion of the causes of crime."[11] Like Ben Stone's tirade on "Trust"—"Nobody's responsible anymore"—various prosecutorial outbursts on "Law & Order" about what they deem irrelevant ploys by corrupt defense attorneys serve the same unfortunate purpose—reinforcing a blinkered view of crime and disallowing a more complex societal and institutional causality.

Conclusion

I want to end with the episode that opened this essay and that directly addresses an "abuse excuse"; rather, it shows how the prosecutors do *not* address the institutional causes of crime that the "abuse excuse" embodies. "Rage" is based on the real case of Lonnie Gilchrist, a stockbroker for Merrill Lynch in Boston, who, in 1988, shot and killed the vice-president of his firm who had fired him the previous day. "Law & Order" makes a couple of salient changes to the Gilchrist case, both of which function to legitimate Jack McCoy's consistent belief that race is irrelevant to the murder and that "this is about convicting one man of homicide."[12]

First of all, the crime of Bud Greer in "Rage" is represented as much more premeditated than that of Lonnie Gilchrist. Gilchrist shot his former boss in his office, in the middle of the work day, and in full view of numerous Merrill Lynch employees. He shot him, moreover, five times and also beat him with his gun—shouting: "No billionaire is going to ruin my life." On the other hand, Bud Greer on "Law & Order" killed his boss in the latter's home and was careful to make it look like a suicide. As the coroner comments: "the entire scene was staged." Far from any appearance of having ever lost control, and far from being apparently unconcerned about the consequences of his actions, Greer made every effort to conceal what he had done and to direct suspicion elsewhere.

Furthermore, the only evidence about Gilchrist's motive pertained to his obsession with being exploited and discriminated against by whites. Witness after witness at his trial told of his belief that "'the white man was going to kill all blacks.'"[13] In the show's representation of the case, however, Bud Greer has been engaging in phantom trading and claiming millions of dollars's worth of phony profit. His boss found out about the fake trades just two days before Greer killed him—and the prosecutors maintain that Greer had a completely explicable motive in wanting to murder his employer, before he ruined Greer's reputation and career. What allows McCoy to claim that race had nothing to do with the crime is the fact that the victim "was about to pull the plug on a billion dollar scam." The very personal motives of Greer translate for the prosecutors into a very personal murder—and they will not see Greer as one of many de-personalized victims of a racist society.

By far the most significant change that "Law & Order" makes to the Gilchrist case is that Greer's lawyer explicitly argues a "black rage" defense, whereas Gilchrist's lawyers simply pled insanity. As *The Boston Globe* reported it, psychiatrists testifying for the defense claimed that Gilchrist "suffered from a longstanding personality disorder that led him to harbor irrational beliefs that he was being persecuted because he is black. The stress of being fired, combined with his irrational beliefs... triggered a temporary psychosis that left Gilchrist unable to control his behavior."[14] Gilchrist's defense consistently argued that Gilchrist's longstanding paranoia about racial injustice was *irrational*—a sign of clinical insanity, but in "Rage," on the other hand, Greer's lawyer argues that Greer's act, his eruption of rage against white oppression, was an *understandable consequence* of having grown up a black man in the United States. The expert witness in "Rage" is not a psychiatrist testifying to Greer's specific condition but a doctor who discusses the generalized and historical alienation of all black men in America—from slavery through lynching and segregation to contemporary racism. The black man is alienated, the witness says, because of history—and she echoes the words of Greer's lawyer who has told McCoy that "this country is still one big plantation." In "Rage" *the black man* is defended against the violence he may commit, unlike in the case of Lonnie Gilchrist where only one man's unstable mental state was on trial.

"Law & Order" goes beyond what the law has done in depicting a "black rage" defense (no actual lawyer has yet used it), and by doing so, the show registers the complex institutional and systemic roots of crime. But at the same time, its protagonists refuse to acknowledge that the defense has any validity: for McCoy, race is not just tangential but "entirely irrelevant," and Greer is not just a deliberate killer but a "disgusting" thief and murderer. As much as the episode points toward racism as an explanation (in Greer's defense, and in the ending scene of the black man unable to get a cab), it pulls just as much in the opposite direction. In fact, the show is itself pulled, I would suggest, by the constraints of the law that is at its center; it is pulled toward the view that is perfectly framed by McCoy's words: "This is about convicting one man of homicide."

5

Matlock

GAIL LEVIN RICHMOND

What makes a television series memorable? If it fails to be cited by *TV Guide*, should we relegate it to the nostalgia trash heap?[1] In the case of "Matlock," this is no rhetorical question. Despite enjoying considerable commercial success, it failed to make the *Guide's* "100 Greatest Episodes of All Time."[2] Other attorney shows made the list: "L.A. Law" contributed number 91; "Law & Order," number 79; "Murder One," number 60; and "Perry Mason," number 51. Other detective and crime shows also produced winners: "Columbo," "Wiseguy," "The Fugitive," "Homicide: Life on the Street," "N.Y.P.D. Blue," "Alfred Hitchcock Presents," "Hill Street Blues," "Dragnet," "Miami Vice," "The Mod Squad," "The Untouchables," and even "Batman." Andy Griffith himself made the list for "The Andy Griffith Show," which produced number 24. So where is Ben Matlock?

Although no single episode was sufficiently memorable for the *TV Guide* list, "Matlock" clearly attracted a following. It ran for nine years on network television and has since flourished in syndication.[3] Ben himself returned during the 1996–97 television season for a two-episode stint on "Diagnosis Murder."[4]

History and Cast

Following a successful pilot, which appeared in March 1986, "Matlock" began its run on NBC in September 1986. Its initial cast included three continuing character types: the main character, Ben Matlock, played by Andy Griffith; a second attorney; and an investigator.

Several actors filled the last two roles during the show's run. Linda Purl played the second attorney, Matlock's daughter Charlene, during the first season. Between 1987 and 1992, the second attorney was Michelle Thomas, played by Nancy Stafford. Another Matlock daughter, Leanne, became the second attorney for the show's last two seasons; Brynn Thayer played this role.[5] Kene Holliday spent three seasons as investigator Tyler Hudson. He was followed for the next four seasons by Clarence Gilyard,

Jr., playing Conrad McMaster. Two other characters of note were opposing attorney Julie March and neighbor Les Calhoun, played by Julie Sommars and Don Knotts.

NBC canceled "Matlock" after the 1990–91 season, despite its being a Top 20 show, but brought it back in the fall of 1991 to shore up sagging network ratings. Although it succeeded in that mission, "Matlock's" return was brief; NBC canceled it again at the end of the season. "Matlock" moved to ABC in 1992 and completed its first-run episodes during 1994–95.[6]

Matlock's Appeal

"Matlock" endured for as long as it did by appealing to a variety of viewers. Despite popular disdain for lawyers, television shows featuring them attracted, and continued to attract, audiences. Mystery and crime shows are a television staple. Amateur detectives such as Ben Matlock boast loyal followings, in part because they solve crimes and in part because they are amateurs. Because Ben Matlock was a "good" lawyer, audiences who disliked attorneys could watch him without guilt.

Other factors contributed to "Matlock's" popularity. Several cast members enjoyed audience recognition. The Southern locale may have attracted some. Still others may have been comforted by the characters's ages or the general lack of violence. Even its schedule may have played a role.[7] The remainder of this essay weaves several of these themes together.

Genre Television

Lawyers on Television

"Perry Mason" was a Top 20 series in 1958–59, its second year, and remained on the list for three more years. "The Defenders" joined the Top 20 in 1962–63, its second season, but never repeated that feat. "Crazy Like a Fox" cracked the Top 20 in 1984–85 but remained there for just one year.[8] From the end of "Perry Mason" until the advent of "L.A. Law" and "Matlock," lawyer series achieved more critical acclaim than commercial success.[9]

Although most attorney dramas never attained a Top 20 ranking or earned a major Emmy award, networks continued to schedule them. Representative listings for various periods include "They Stand Accused" (1940s); "Court of Last Resort," "On Trial," and "Traffic Court" (1950s); "Court Martial," "Courtroom U.S.A.," "The Defenders," "For the People," and "Judd for the Defense" (1960s); "Hawkins,"[10] "Kate McShane,"

"Kaz," "Men at Law," and "Owen Marshall, Counselor at Law" (1970s). Dramas that began their run in the 1980s achieved the most sustained commercial success, at least as judged by ratings. "Matlock" ranked in Nielsen's Top 20 in every season from 1986–87 through 1990–91. The more famous "L.A. Law" was a Top 20 show for three seasons (1987–88 through 1989–90). Although not ranked in the Top 20, "Jake and the Fatman" ran five seasons. "Night Court" and "Amen," comedy series featuring lawyers and judges, also ranked highly during "Matlock's" first two years, although "Amen" rarely focused on Sherman Hemsley's lawyering duties.[11]

During 1994–95, "Matlock's" final year, no series focusing on lawyers, whether comedy or drama, ranked in the overall Top 10. The police drama "N.Y.P.D. Blue" and "Murder, She Wrote" both ranked in the Top 10. "Law & Order" ranked highest among lawyer shows, at thirty-ninth. Although ratings have clearly fallen from their 1990–91 levels,[12] networks continue to purchase lawyer dramas. "Ally McBeal," "The Client," "Courthouse," "Feds," "JAG," "Michael Hayes," "Murder One," and "The Practice" have all debuted since then.[13] Of these, the two-season "Murder One" was closest to the Ben Matlock/Perry Mason model.[14]

Detectives on Television

Detective stories have a large following. Children who followed Nancy Drew and the Hardy Boys grew up to read or watch their adult successors.[15] Mainstream bookstores allot significant shelf space to the genre; specialty bookstores devoted to the subject exist in many cities; and a mystery book club provides access to a wide array of authors.

Detective series have been more numerous, and probably more successful, than lawyer series.[16] One factor explaining the significant number of dramas featuring police officers or private investigators is the audience's desire to solve the puzzle. Perhaps more important, however, is its belief that detectives are trying to serve justice by unmasking wrongdoers. The public does not always believe lawyers serve that function. Finally, detective shows often involve more action than do courtroom dramas; as a result they may appeal to a younger audience. Highly-rated dramas in this genre include "Dragnet," "Man Against Crime," "Martin Kane, Private Eye," "Peter Gunn," and "77 Sunset Strip" (1950s); "The F.B.I.," "Hawaii Five-0," and "Ironside" (1960s); "Adam 12," "Baretta," "Barnaby Jones," "Cannon," "Charlie's Angels," "CHiPs," "Kojak," "Mannix," "The Mod Squad," "The NBC Mystery Movie," "The Rockford Files," and "Starsky and Hutch" (1970s); "Cagney & Lacey," "Hunter," "In the Heat of the Night," "Magnum, P.I.," "Moonlighting," "Riptide," "Simon & Simon," and "Unsolved Mysteries" (1980s); and "N.Y.P.D. Blue" (1990s). Surprisingly, "Hill Street Blues," which ran for seven seasons and earned Emmy awards in each of its first five, never finished a season in the Nielsen Top 20.

When the detectives are amateurs, their appeal increases. Audiences read or watch them to enjoy the interplay as the amateur solves the case before the professional does and to put themselves into the amateur's shoes and solve it themselves. Amateurs who captured the public's interest were featured in a variety of series, including "Ellery Queen," "Hart to Hart," "Murder, She Wrote," "Mr. and Mrs. North," and "The Thin Man."[17] Producers even invited the television audience to solve the crime on "Armchair Detective" (1949), "Ellery Queen" (1950), and "Public Prosecutor" (1951 version).

Lawyers as Amateur Detectives

Both "Matlock" and "Perry Mason" featured lawyers who solved crimes. They were amateurs, at least as compared to the police and private investigators. Their ability to solve cases before the professionals did and complete judicial proceedings in a one-hour time block never tested our powers of belief.[18] In combining genres, they entertained us and we continued watching.

Audience Expectations: Risks and Rewards

Viewers liked Andy Griffith and welcomed him into their homes. He shares audience favor with several actors whose popularity allows them to work regularly in a profession not known for job security. When one series ends its run, these actors move on to another. To some extent, the same is true for programs that draw sufficient audience goodwill. They may generate spin-offs to develop other storylines and clones to capitalize on a particular genre's current popularity. The results, predictably, are mixed. Subsequent series, whether a spin-off with the original actors, a spin-off with new actors, or a new series with a familiar actor, may be as successful as their predecessors but often fail miserably. Efforts to reincarnate a successful series many years later also usually fare poorly.[19]

Actors and Their Roles

Certain actors seem so perfect in particular roles that audiences forget their less memorable performances. Dennis Franz, for example, successfully portrayed police officers on "Hill Street Blues" and "N.Y.P.D. Blue," while Sam Waterston was an attorney on both "I'll Fly Away" and "Law & Order."[20] Still other actors play a type that cuts across career lines: Katherine Helmond personifies ditziness.[21] We know what to expect and these actors rarely disappoint us.

Although actors may become associated with a particular genre, others easily switch between comedy and drama. Bob Newhart, Harry Anderson, Tony Danza, and Rhea Perlman are comedy performers; Mark Harmon and Barbara Bosson appear in dramatic series. Patrick Duffy, Robert Reed, and Cybill Shepherd do both.

An actor's popularity may be a mixed blessing when he attempts a role or genre switch, as audience expectations may doom the later outing. Andy Griffith attained his popularity portraying small-town Southerners, first on the dramatization of "No Time for Sergeants" and then on "The Andy Griffith Show." When he moved to offerings such as "Headmaster" (set in California, 1970–71), "Great Roads of America" (documentary, 1973), and "Salvage 1" (adventure series, 1979), his audience stayed behind.[22]

Spin-offs, Cast Changes, and Clones

Sometimes a new series continues the actor's original role. Spin-offs such as "The Jeffersons," "Maude," and "Joanie Loves Chachi" exemplify this format.[23] In other cases, the actor retains an occupation but in a different role. As noted earlier, Dennis Franz played police officers on both "Hill Street Blues" and "N.Y.P.D. Blue." When necessary, a series replaces an actor who left with another actor playing that same role. Both Dick York/Dick Sargent in "Bewitched" and Pamela Sue Martin/Emma Samms in "Dynasty" exemplify this sort of change.[24] "The Perry Mason Mysteries" replaced Paul Drake with Paul Drake, Jr., thus playing on a familial connection.[25]

Clones appear in clusters, capitalizing on a particular genre's popularity. At one time or another, Westerns, rustics, and single parents were in vogue. Numerous police and detective dramas appear interchangeable. As noted elsewhere in this essay, "Matlock" and "Perry Mason" share many common features. Some clones surpass the original in popularity; others crash and burn almost immediately.

Unlike the original "The Andy Griffith Show," "Matlock" produced no spin-offs.[26] Likewise, "Matlock" is not spun off from Griffith's earlier success. However, that earlier success may have influenced several viewers to give "Matlock" a try.[27] Griffith was popular enough to attract viewers even as he crossed several genres, going from comedy to drama and from small-town family life to working as an amateur detective.

You Can't Go Home Again

Television's attempts to reincarnate old series rarely succeed. Events that made the old show successful may have changed. Nostalgia for the old show may not extend to the new show when staged with different actors. "Perry Mason" is one example of this problem. The original series, with Raymond Burr, Barbara Hale, and William Hopper, ran from 1957 through 1966. "The New Perry Mason," a 1973 version with Monte Markham, Sharon Acker, and Albert Stratton, lasted less than one season. When NBC brought back Burr and Hale in 1985, "The Perry Mason Mysteries" again became popular. Other failures include "The New Odd Couple," "The New Dragnet," and "The New Monkees." Not surprisingly, a 1964 attempt to serialize "No Time for Sergeants" without Griffith also failed.

An Actor Can Change Genre

Despite his initial inability to launch a noteworthy second series, Andy Griffith ultimately joined the group of successful genre switchers. His move from Sheriff Andy Taylor to attorney Ben Matlock echoes switches made by Tom Bosley, Jack Klugman, and Dick Van Dyke.[28] Each had long-running half-hour comedy series. Each later played an amateur who solved crimes in a one-hour dramatic format. Each made the switch in middle age.[29]

None plays a police officer or prosecutor in the later series, although Jack Klugman's Quincy is a coroner and Dick Van Dyke's Dr. Mark Sloan is the father of a policeman.[30] With the exception of Quincy, whose "clients" are dead, each of these professionals must follow a code of conduct that requires confidentiality (attorney-client, doctor-patient, priest-penitent). Because of the manner in which they stumble on their "cases," they rarely discuss potentially significant ethical issues.

Griffith's change is slightly different, as he played a law enforcement officer in his first series. This is another point of similarity between him and Raymond Burr, who starred as Police Chief Robert Ironside between his "Perry Mason" stints.

If They Like You, They Will Watch

In "Matlock's" early seasons, several supporting cast members were also reasonably well-known to potential viewers. Linda Purl, best known for her two roles on "Happy Days," also had appeared in "Beacon Hill" and "What Really Happened to the Class of '65?" Nancy Stafford, her replacement, had worked on "St. Elsewhere" and "Sidekicks." Kene Holliday had a role in "Carter Country," also set in Georgia and far more Southern than "Matlock," and Julie Sommars had appeared in "The Governor and J.J." The most inspired, or hokey (depending on one's point of view), casting occurred in "Matlock's" third season, when Don Knotts joined the cast as Ben's neighbor Les Calhoun. Knotts won five Emmy awards portraying Deputy Barney Fife on "The Andy Griffith Show," and his association with Griffith actually went further back. Knotts played a role in the 1958 movie version of "No Time for Sergeants," in which Griffith reprised the role of Will Stockdale.[31]

In addition to being familiar, the supporting players provided interesting subplots. Although parent-child relationships and adult romance never intruded on Ben's zealous advocacy, they did allow viewers to identify with him as a human being who happened to be a lawyer rather than as a lawyer who, like those portrayed on "L.A. Law," had his values backwards.

Matlock in the South

Why set "Matlock" in Atlanta? This really involves two questions. Why select a Southern city in the first place? And why Atlanta instead of Charlotte, Nashville, or numerous other venues? All are growing, as the region enjoys the economic and population growth[32] that yield that ultimate American prize, a professional sports franchise.[33]

Although "Matlock" is set in the South, it is not a Southern lawyer show. Most of the characters, both continuing and guest stars, are decidedly non-Southern. There are no Southern themes.[34] Certainly Andy Griffith's accent identifies him as a Southerner, but his daughters don't share that characteristic. Ben Matlock could just as easily have been a Southern lawyer practicing in New York or Los Angeles as in Atlanta.

Setting "Matlock" in the South may have appealed to viewers nostalgic for Mayberry, the city Griffith served as sheriff on "The Andy Griffith Show." A market existed for rural (and predominantly Southern) locales during the 1960s when shows such as "The Andy Griffith Show," "The Beverly Hillbillies," "Green Acres," "Hee Haw," "Mayberry, R.F.D.," and "Petticoat Junction" threatened to displace Westerns from their prime time dominance. When Ben Matlock appeared in 1986, he may have awakened our nostalgia for the shows of our youth.[35]

The Southern locale allowed "Matlock" to avoid one potential trap: Ben did not have to contend with Northern stereotypes of Southern race relations and overall educational achievement. Rather than being a rube in hostile territory, he fought for his clients's freedom on his own turf.[36]

Atlanta and the "New South"

Setting a series in the South in 1986 probably required setting it in Atlanta. Miami's image was too violent, epitomized by "Miami Vice"; depending on one's frame of reference, the rest of Florida was Spring Break, Anita Bryant, college football, or Disney. Mississippi warranted shows such as "In the Heat of the Night" or even "I'll Fly Away." North Carolina was still "Mayberry, R.F.D." Tennessee combined Elvis and the Grand Ole Opry.

Atlanta, on the other hand, symbolized the "New South." It boasted one of the world's busiest airports, numerous universities (several of which enjoy prestigious reputations), important corporations, a large metropolitan population base,[37] and significant in-migration. The last two features are particularly significant. Matlock, known for high fees, could not prosper without a large and wealthy client base. In addition, in-migration explains why so few of his clients had southern accents. Finally, Atlanta is the state capital. Matlock could try cases and, if necessary, appeal them without leaving home.

Matlock's Cast and the New South

Throughout its first seven seasons, "Matlock's" office included a black investigator and a female attorney. Both casting decisions characterize, albeit stereotypically,[38] the end to discrimination in the New South. Casting a woman as the second attorney involves some degree of irony. Women of the Old South were expected to live up to "precious notions of modesty and decorous behavior."[39] Well into the 1990s, Southern institutions such as Virginia Military Institute and The Citadel admitted only males because women were believed incapable of enduring the physical rigor involved.[40] The first major judicial ruling dealing with gender discrimination in law firm partnership decisions involved an Atlanta firm.[41]

Matlock and Mason: Two "Good" Lawyers

In common with Perry Mason, Ben Matlock freed his clients without upsetting the law-and-order contingent. Because he unmasked the real miscreants, Matlock's clients received "not guilty" verdicts that really meant "innocent." He gave police and prosecutors enough evidence to proceed against the real malefactor. In addition, he didn't treat police and prosecutors as evil, a characterization employed occasionally on both "Murder One" and "The Practice."

Was "Matlock" different because it was based in the South? That question needs a frame of reference: different from what? As noted earlier, "Matlock" was not a series about a Southern lawyer; it was a series about a lawyer who happened to be Southern. Yes, there were some regional differences. His suits were lighter in color than those worn by attorneys in the North.[42] He occasionally strummed the banjo and sang; he even cooked fried chicken.[43] And, as is important in the South, he had family and other relationships.[44] These included the two daughters who joined his law practice, prosecutor Julie March, and an assortment of relatives and old friends who appeared in a two-hour episode in October 1991.

When viewers discuss courtroom dramas, they invariably mention "Perry Mason" as one of their examples. If the two series were too similar, viewer nostalgia for the original "Perry Mason" could have doomed "Matlock."[45] Perhaps the Southern connection provided sufficient differentiation for some viewers. One Southern mystery writer humorously notes: "Until the Late Unpleasantness, the South thrived on the devaluation of human life; nowadays we've modified our approach to avoid indictments whenever possible. Maybe this is why we're a sight fonder of Mr. Matlock than of Mr. Mason. There's something innately comforting about an affable lawyer in a rumpled white suit, sitting on the bench outside the barbershop and swapping jokes with the likes of Atticus and Clarence."[46]

Ben and Perry did have much in common. Both were courtroom lawyers who handled criminal cases. Both invariably proved their client's innocence and unmasked the guilty party. Both employed a regular investigator. Both had unresolved personal relationships, Matlock with prosecutor Julie March and Mason with secretary/office manager Della Street. Both employed memorable theme songs.[47] "Matlock" and "The Perry Mason Mysteries" even shared Fred Silverman and Dean Hargrove as producers.[48]

Matlock was by no means a Perry Mason clone, however. For one thing, he had been married and had reasonably congenial relations with his daughters, each of whom practiced law with him. In addition, his un-resolved relationship with prosecutor Julie March was never as enigmatic as Perry Mason's with Della Street. Adversarial in court but close at other times, the Matlock-March relationship is a comfortable throwback to that enjoyed by Spencer Tracy and Katharine Hepburn in "Adam's Rib" or Veronica Hammel and Daniel J. Travanti in "Hill Street Blues." Thus humanized, Matlock attracted viewers who followed relationships as well as those who enjoyed detective stories and lawyer shows.[49] At the same time, the relationship never became a running story line, which might have interfered with the mystery genre aspects. "Matlock" never at-tempted to emulate "The Thin Man" or "Mr. and Mrs. North."[50]

The courtroom setting provided several advantages for both "Mat-lock" and "Perry Mason." Time spent in court reduced producers's location costs and outlays for stunt doubles.[51] Audiences could view conflict with-out savagery (an important factor for parents concerned about excessive television violence), learn how circumstantial evidence could ensnare in-nocent people, and try to solve the case themselves. A well-written court-room mystery is a win-win situation.

Conclusion

"Matlock" retains its appeal in syndication because it offers likeable characters, recognizable actors, and a comfortable format. Do viewers cluster around the water cooler discussing the most recent "Matlock" episode? Probably not—the stories are appealing but not overwhelming in their impact. Had "Matlock" crusaded for social justice, instead of for an individual defendant, the result may have been different. But given a choice between a marketable format and a listing in the *TV Guide 100*, most producers would opt for the former. It's difficult to argue with com-mercial success in an industry noted for early failure.

6

Murder One

JEFFREY E. THOMAS

After months of watching a murder trial unfold in painstaking detail, millions of Americans tuned-in for the verdict. But it wasn't the O.J. Simpson case. It was *People v. Avedon*, a fictional case portrayed in the ABC television drama "Murder One." Unlike previous television dramas that focused on *stories* from legal cases, "Murder One" focused instead on the legal *process* of a single murder case over its entire first season.[1] As one reviewer put it, "it's clear even after the first episode that the real subject of Murder One is process: how the murder is investigated, how the police decide to arrest a suspect, how that suspect is prosecuted and defended, and all the various social politics that figure in every one of these stages."[2] Steven Bochco, the creator of the show, reflected: "Murder One was a show for people who like process, who get caught up in following the convolutions of a murder trial."[3] "Murder One" therefore represents a unique, if short-lived,[4] contribution to the genre.

This bold experiment in television programming[5] was inspired by the public's fascination with real-life cases such as the O.J. Simpson case.[6] Bochco explained that those cases "introduced people to the intricacies of the law, the procedures, the impact of the media. So for the first time we [could] roll the dice creatively. We [took] the one case and really [ran] it, in all of its intricacies."[7]

What does "Murder One" tell us about the intricacies of the legal system? In the wake of several high-profile acquittals and hung juries, the American justice system has come under increased criticism. The real-life cases have left many with the feeling that "slick defense attorneys [are] using their wily ways to bamboozle unsuspecting jurors into letting 'obviously guilty' persons — the Menendez brothers, O.J. Simpson, Lorena Bobbitt — go free."[8] "Murder One" does not directly contradict this image. It recognizes that juries may reach unjust verdicts in specific cases, but at the same time it shows that the legal *process* relating to the jury is basically fair.

The jury is at the center of the legal process. It holds the ultimate power and responsibility of determining the accused's guilt or innocence. When the O.J. Simpson jury reached its verdict, some 80% of Americans, and many other millions of people throughout the world, tuned in to see it announced.[9] That verdict, like those in other high-profile cases, set off a storm of controversy about the jury system.[10]

The essential premise of many criticisms of the legal system is that juries have reached the wrong result.[11] The jury in "Murder One" also reached what turned out to be an incorrect result. Notwithstanding that error, however, the show developed the evidence in such a way that the jury reasonably could have gone either way. This, of course, added to the dramatic tension leading up to the verdict. But the process relating to the jury, although imperfect, was generally balanced and fair.

The Evidence

In order to analyze the depiction of the legal process, we need to begin with the evidentiary context of the case. The main case during the first season of "Murder One" arose out of the rape and murder of the beautiful fifteen-year-old Jessica Costello. The first suspect arrested was Richard Cross (played by Stanley Tucci), a multimillionaire philanthropist and businessman. Cross owned the apartment where Jessica was staying, and he was caught on a security videotape the night of Jessica's murder entering the apartment. When initially interviewed by the police, he lied about not being there the night of the murder.[12] Cross was represented by attorney Theodore Hoffman, the main character of the show, played by Daniel Benzali.

The charges against Cross were dropped when the woman with whom he was "clubbing" came forward and provided an alibi. She claimed that she hadn't come forward earlier because she was afraid that her violent husband would beat her if he learned she had been out with Cross. After Cross was released, the second suspect, Neil Avedon (played by Jason Gedrick), was charged with the murder. At the insistence of Cross, and with Cross's waiver of any conflict of interest, Hoffman agreed to represent Avedon.[13]

Neil Avedon was a young, rising Hollywood star with alcohol and cocaine abuse problems. He had some previous minor skirmishes with the law, including an incident where he strangled a swan at a wedding. Hoffman represented Avedon in connection with that incident and managed to get the charges reduced to a misdemeanor to which Avedon pleaded no contest in the first episode.[14] Avedon was suspected because he had dated Jessica Costello, and his DNA, obtained from a test in an unrelated paternity suit, matched the semen found in Jessica's body.[15]

As the investigation continued, evidence against Avedon began to accumulate. A former lover of Avedon's came forward with a videotape showing him choking her during sex.[16] The D.A.'s office theorized that the same thing might have happened to Jessica. The prosecution also uncovered evidence of Avedon's violent tendencies during encounters in his drug rehabilitation therapy,[17] and a witness to Avedon threatening and choking Jessica prior to her murder.[18]

The most compelling evidence, however, was Avedon's purported confession to his psychiatrist, Dr. Graham Lester, the night of the murder. Lester's secretary testified that Avedon called the Zephyr House clinic in an agitated state the night of the murder at 1:45 a.m. When confronted by Hoffman outside the courtroom, Lester told him that Avedon came to the clinic around 2:15 a.m., was sobbing and confused, and confessed to killing Jessica.[19] Lester initially refused to testify about the confession because of the doctor-patient privilege, even though ordered to do so by the court, but after a few days in jail gave in and testified about the purported confession.[20]

This evidence made the prosecution's case pretty compelling. However, Hoffman, the expert defense lawyer, exposed the weaknesses in the evidence and argued that Neil was the subject of a conspiracy to frame him. The key to that conspiracy was Richard Cross. Cross's alibi was revealed after he was arrested because the woman providing the alibi allegedly feared she would be beaten by her jealous husband. The defense uncovered a videotape, however, that showed the woman and her husband having sex in front of Richard Cross.[21] In addition, the defense called Roger Garfield, the District Attorney, as a witness to show that Cross was a major contributor to his campaign for governor, and to imply complicity on the part of Garfield in having the charges against Cross dropped.[22]

Cross was also tied to other men who might have a motive to kill Jessica. Cross introduced a number of influential men in Hollywood to her. Jessica kept a diary that reported her sexual encounters with these men, and portions from the diary were entered into evidence as business records. These men, including Gary Blondo, the producer who was promoting Avedon's soon-to-be-released motion picture, were examined about these diary entries in court.[23]

The defense also presented evidence connecting Cross to Dr. Lester's secretary, Susan Dominick. Although she denied receiving anything of benefit from Cross, her brother was called to testify that Cross provided him with $300,000 of annual medical treatment for AIDS. The defense contended that this gave her a motive to lie, and that she re-wrote the telephone log not because of a coffee spill on it, but to change the record to reflect a 1:45 a.m. call from Avedon.[24]

The only connection the defense can prove between Dr. Lester himself and Cross is that they were friends,[25] but the defense investigator uncovered a different source of impeachment of Lester. Several women tes-

tified that they were raped by Dr. Lester after he had given them tran-
quilizers as part of drug rehabilitation therapy at Zephyr House.[26]

The defense rounded out its case with character evidence about Avedon and with his taking the stand to deny committing the crime. Avedon's mother testified that he ran away from home when he was fifteen
because of his father's abuse, but that he still provided financial support
for her.[27] Jessica's "Cocaine Anonymous" sponsor testified that Avedon
was a loving boyfriend to Jessica and supported her in her efforts to quit
using drugs.[28]

Although Hoffman advised against it, Avedon insisted that he should
take the stand in his own defense. In the course of his testimony, he recounted the abuse he received from his father, admitted that cocaine made
him abusive and violent, and provided some additional connections to
Richard Cross. Cross and Avedon were friends, and Cross referred Avedon to Lester and introduced Avedon to Jessica. Avedon described his relationship with Jessica this way: "One minute we'd be curled up in each
other's arms, you know, reading or watching TV or talking, and the next
minute she'd be hitting me on the head with a telephone or throwing my
clothes out the window, or we'd get high together. Um, as crazy as we
both were, we understood each other and as much as I've loved anyone,
I loved her."[29]

As to the specifics on the night of the murder, he testified: "I was staying at Chris Docknovich's house. I left there around 10:00 to go over and
see Jessica. I got a pizza, a gram of coke. We ate, we got high. We put
'Two-Lane Blacktop' on the VCR. We made love while we watched it
and I left around midnight." He specifically denied having raped or murdered Jessica.[30]

On cross-examination, the lead prosecutor, Miriam Grasso (played by
Barbara Bosson), emphasized the main themes of the prosecution's case.
She brought out that Avedon had strangled a swan and choked a girlfriend during sex, that he was accustomed to his bad behavior being tol-
erated because of his celebrity status, that he was ten years older than
Jessica, and that he was essentially accusing several prosecution witnesses
of lying. She also got Avedon to admit that he had experienced some
memory loss, and therefore that it was possible that he raped and murdered Jessica in the course of a drug-induced blackout.[31]

The Closing Arguments

Each side was given the opportunity to put its own "spin" on the conflicting evidence during closing arguments. Prosecutor Grasso gave this interpretation of the facts:

Who committed this brutal crime? The facts support only one conclusion. He [indicating Avedon] did. The defendant, Neil Avedon. By his
own testimony, he admits he was at her apartment that evening and had
sex with her. Well, what could he say? Doctor Gafore identified his semen
inside Jessica. Said it was one in a billion that it could be someone else.
But Mr. Avedon claims he merely went over to her apartment, had sex with
her and left. Allowing some mystery man to enter her apartment and kill
her after he was gone? Is that the truth?

Not according to Susan Dominick. Ms. Dominick testified that the
defendant called Zephyr House at 1:45 a.m. on the night of the murder.
She knew his voice. She talked with him. And when the phone company
traced the call, where did it come from? Jessica's apartment. That puts
Neil Avedon at the scene of the murder between the time that Jessica
made a frightened, frantic call to Richard Cross at 1:15 and Mr. Cross's
discovery of her body forty-five minutes later. Right in the middle of the
time-frame established by the medical examiner.

Now, is this a coincidence? Just bad timing that put Neil Avedon at
the scene of a crime he didn't commit? Well, that's what he says. He says
he never could have killed Jessica. He loved her. But what are the facts?
Again, by his own testimony, he admits he was prone to violence. He
admits he suffered blackouts during which he forgot entire evenings. He
admits he had sex with Jessica Costello and supplied her with cocaine.
A fifteen-year-old girl.

So what does Mr. Hoffman do? Mr. Hoffman parades in front of you
a line-up of manufactured suspects. Ah, Richard Cross did it! Oh, Gary
Blondo did it. Her dentist did it. Anyone but Neil Avedon. Neil Avedon
the drug-abuser. Neil Avedon, the man who got his kicks videotaping
himself strangling women during sex. Neil Avedon, the actor, who gave
his finest performance when he got up on this stand and said, "Pay no attention to the facts. Damn the facts. Believe the role I'm playing."

And what did he say to Dr. Graham Lester on the night of the crime?
"I did it. I killed Jessica Costello." Oh, of course he denies saying that now.
Despite the drugs and the blackouts, he's certain he didn't say that. And
in fact, Dr. Lester must have some sinister motive for saying such a thing.
What are the facts? Neil Avedon can't remember. So, Mr. Hoffman drags
up four very confused young ladies who accuse Dr. Lester, a respected
board-certified psychiatrist, of raping them. But when they called Julie
Costello, Jessica Costello's older sister to the stand to confirm this wild
story, what did she say? "It never happened."

Why did he do it? Why did Neil Avedon murder Jessica Costello?
Simple, really. Because she rejected him. She was tired of the parties and
the drugs and the lifestyle Neil had introduced her to. She wanted out.
But no one had ever denied Neil. Not since he had become a star they
hadn't. So he goes over to her apartment, furious at his rejection and he
rapes her. And as she desperately struggled, in order to have a bigger
kick, a bigger orgasm, he choked the life out of her. Because she dared to
say no to him.[32]

Defense counsel Theodore Hoffman, of course, put the evidence in a different light:

> [W]hen you look at this case critically, as the law requires you must, you see that it rests on the credibility of three witnesses: Susan Dominick, Graham Lester and Richard Cross. If any one of them is lying, Ms. Grasso's case falls apart.
>
> Susan Dominick says that Neil called Dr. Lester's clinic at 1:45. Ms. Grasso says that this places Neil inside Jessica's apartment at the time of her death. Putting aside the medical examiner's testimony, that the murder could have occurred as much as three hours later, you're still left with this: Neil was only there if Susan Dominick is telling the truth. You remember the phone log? The one that purports to document Neil's call? Ms. Dominick says she had to copy it over, not because she had to enter a call from Neil which never occurred, but because she spilled coffee on it. Accidents happen, she says. Well, maybe they do. But when she was asked if she knew Richard Cross, why was she evasive? Why did she conveniently forget that he was paying hundreds of thousands of dollars for her brother's medical treatment? Ask yourselves, was Susan Dominick telling the truth?
>
> Graham Lester. He says that Neil confessed to him. What can be more conclusive than that, Ms. Grasso says. Well, nothing, unless Dr. Lester was lying for his good friend, Richard Cross. Four women took the stand and described how Dr. Lester drugged and raped them, how he violated every canon of medical ethics. Ms. Grasso says these women were confused. There were too out of it on drugs to know what happened. Angela Scalese was not confused. She stopped taking her medication. And when Dr. Lester entered her room and attempted to rape her, she knew exactly what he was doing. Ask yourselves, was Dr. Graham Lester telling the truth?
>
> Richard Cross. He says he found Jessica's body at 2:00 a.m. and that he was concerned about the reputation of a woman who made her living as a prostitute. Who only surfaced after Mr. Cross himself was arrested for Jessica's murder. Who didn't Richard Cross know in this case? He introduced Jessica to the men in her diary. He married her sister Julie to keep her from testifying against him. He was one of the biggest contributors to the campaign of Roger Garfield who personally ordered his release from jail. Richard Cross was in Jessica's apartment that night. Did he kill Jessica? Did he make that call to Zephyr House at 1:45 so that he could conspire with Graham Lester and Susan Dominick to set up Neil? From all you know about him, ask yourselves, was Richard Cross telling the truth?
>
> Susan Dominick, Graham Lester and Richard Cross. Ms. Grasso's case rests on the rotting foundation of their testimony. To confuse you she tells you that we're trying to make Neil the victim, to put Jessica on trial. I assure you, we are not. When we put the men from Jessica's diary on the stand we did so to show you the dangerous lifestyle she was leading.

We let Neil's mother and his friends speak to you so that you could see another side of him, the side the prosecution doesn't want you to see. Neil Avedon and Jessica Costello were two lost souls who found each other and fell in love. That's why no one grieves more for Jessica's death than Neil Avedon. That's why nothing could compound Jessica's tragedy more than to convict Neil Avedon of her murder.

Did Richard Cross kill Jessica? I can't tell you. I can tell you this: Listen to your doubts, your very reasonable doubts about Ms. Grasso's unholy three. Then you'll know Neil Avedon did not kill Jessica Costello. Neil Avedon is an innocent man.[33]

The summary of the evidence and the closing arguments show that each side was given a fair opportunity to present its case. Both sides were give some significant evidentiary latitude, admittedly in part for dramatic effect. The prosecution was allowed to show the videotape of Avedon choking a girlfriend during sex, and Dr. Lester was compelled to testify about Avedon's purported confession. On the other hand, the defense was allowed to show the videotape of Cross's alibi having sex with her husband in front of Cross, and was permitted to have four different women testify as a form of impeachment about Lester's raping them. In the final analysis, each side had a believable theory supported by credible evidence. It was simply up to the jury to decide whom it would believe.

The Verdict: Was Justice Done?

The jury returned a verdict of "guilty," apparently believing the witnesses that supported the prosecution's interpretation of the evidence.[34] Thus, unlike the O.J. Simpson case and other high-profile, real-life cases, the defense failed. One might therefore view "Murder One" as having a more positive result than real-life high-profile cases. The jury finally got it right.

As the last two episodes revealed, however, this verdict was incorrect and unjust. Neil Avedon *was* innocent.[35] Richard Cross had installed a video camera in Jessica's apartment so he could record her sexual activities, and her murder had been recorded by that camera. The tape revealed that the real killer was Roberto Portalegre (played by Miguel Sandoval). Richard Cross was in business with Portalegre to launder drug money. On the night of the murder Cross had arranged for Portalegre to be with Jessica, but when she changed her mind, Portalegre raped and strangled her. After discovering Jessica's body, Cross feared that he would be killed if he turned the videotape over to the police, so he called Dr. Lester from Jessica's apartment and concocted the plan to frame Avedon.[36]

Even though the jury convicted an innocent man, this case does not necessarily represent a failure of the legal system. There was substantial evidence supporting the verdict against Avedon, including a confession. The case turned on a decision about the credibility of the witnesses, and the jury (through the writers, of course) simply believed Cross, Dominick, and Lester, more than they did Avedon.

Although a jury would make such a choice in real life based on an assessment of demeanor, which is quite difficult to portray on television, there was a logical basis for the jury's decision on credibility. Avedon had every reason to lie because his life was in the balance. In contrast, there was no apparent reason for Cross to conspire against him. In fact, Cross seemed to be on Avedon's side. He waived the conflict of interest so Hoffman could represent Avedon,[37] he posted one million dollars for Avedon's bail bond,[38] and he brought Jessica's diary to Hoffman for use in the defense.[39] During cross-examination, the prosecution brought out that Cross was a friend of Avedon, had posted his bail, had cooperated with the defense, and even had his own private investigators working on Avedon's behalf.[40]

As a general matter, the few empirical investigations that have been done show that juries reach what appears to be the correct result in the vast majority of cases. For instance, in one of the first major studies on jury decisionmaking, judges were surveyed to see if they agreed with the result reached by the jury. In some 75% of the cases, the judges responded that they agreed with the verdict of the jury.[41] Similarly, in "Murder One" the judge, Beth Bornstein (played by Linda Carlson) agreed with the decision reached by jury. During the sentencing phase of the trial Avedon persisted in his claim of innocence, and she responded:

> Mr. Avedon, rarely have I seen such a stubborn refusal to accept the truth. In your statements to probation and to this court today, you continue to profess innocence in the face of overwhelming evidence of your guilt. You have shown absolutely no remorse for the heinous crime. You're a violent young man and a danger to our community. Therefore I see it is my duty to sentence you to life in prison, without the possibility of parole.[42]

Even though both the judge and the jury were wrong, this still does not necessarily represent a failure of the legal system because those responsible for an innocent man being convicted were outside the system. It was Cross and Lester, because of the threats of Portalegre, who were to blame for the miscarriage of justice, not the lawyers, judge, or jury.

On the other hand, if a jury can be so easily manipulated, perhaps it is inappropriate for the legal system to rely on that institution. The jury apparently can be manipulated into letting the guilty go free *and* the innocent being convicted.

In addition, the only way to correct the erroneous verdict against Avedon was to operate outside, and contrary to the guidelines of, the legal system. To get the proof of Avedon's innocence the defense team broke into Jessica's apartment to look for a hidden video camera and VCR, thereby committing a felony. The police discovered the crime, but looked the other way. Even after finding the camera, the defense team had to appeal to the moral conscience of Richard Cross, the architect of the frame-up, to turn over the tape and authenticate it.[43] If Cross hadn't been on his death bed, it seems likely that Avedon would not have been freed.

The Importance of Process Over Outcomes

The failure of the system in an individual case, however, does not, in and of itself, indict the legal system as a whole. The Avedon case, the O.J. Simpson case, and other high-profile cases are the exceptions to the usual criminal trial. And even though one may disagree with the outcome in a particular case, no one can be absolutely certain of the "truth" in that case. As a result, what is crucial is that the *process* be just. So long as the process is fair, the results from that process should be considered just.

This process-oriented moral philosophy is illustrated in a secondary, "B" story in the third episode of "Murder One."[44] In that case the firm represented an investment advisor, Charles Galbraith, who had embezzled $4.7 million from the elderly and lost it gambling. Two of the associates, Lisa Gillespie (played by Grace Phillips) and Arnold Spivak (played by J.C. MacKenzie), handled the case. They negotiated a court-approved plea agreement for probation, house arrest, and restitution so Galbraith could take a market analyst position paying $300,000 per year.

After the court approved the plea agreement, Galbraith, Spivak, and Gillespie were confronted by Sam Carter, one of Galbraith's victims, who felt that justice had not been done. Carter's wife had died from a heart attack after learning that their savings had been wiped out by Galbraith's actions. Pointing a gun at Gillespie and his lawyers, Carter said: "I brought this with me every day thinking if justice was not done in that courtroom I'd handle it myself. Well, justice was not done."[45] Carter ultimately decided not to use the gun because it wasn't "worth ruining the good name [he] took a lifetime to earn."[46]

The incident caused Spivak and Gillespie to consider the morality of their work. Spivak reflected:

> When I see contempt in an old man's eyes when he looks at me, I don't like feeling he's right.... I got to be careful about being so goal-oriented

and task-oriented that it takes an old man with herring breath and a broken heart to remind me that my actions have consequences.[47]

Both Spivak and Gillespie acknowledged feelings of remorse. Hoffman, upon hearing of their feelings, offered this advice:

> Don't get addicted to remorse. It is contemptible in a lawyer. The world does not revolve around you. Your behavior is not its moral center. Someday someone may sit in judgment on this legal system and say it could have been fairer or more compassionate or more responsive to social need. Maybe it'll be me, but not while I'm a criminal defense lawyer. While I'm a lawyer I'm going to defend my clients because it's the job I chose. And I choose to believe, which may be self-deceiving, that the only system worse than this one is every other one I've ever studied. What I'm not going to do is be a lawyer by day and then scratch the scabs on my conscience by pretending to be a moral pathfinder by night. I don't know if Charles Galbraith got what's coming to him. If he didn't maybe he'll get prostate cancer and that'll even the score. I don't know if this kid I'm defending is guilty or innocent. And I don't need to know to do my job. That's all we are here to do. And if we do it right, that's enough....Make yourselves a promise. Every time you want to have one of these conversations, find a defendant who can't afford us. Work for him pro bono. That's electricity I don't mind paying for.[48]

Thus, the moral act of the lawyer is to do the job assigned by the legal system, and to let the process determine the morally appropriate outcome.

This reliance on the process, a hallmark of the American legal system, has some social benefit in and of itself. It requires that the criminally accused be treated fairly and with some level of dignity by the justice system, even if the specific outcome of that process is not what some of us might prefer. For instance, even if O.J. Simpson was guilty of murdering his ex-wife Nicole Brown Simpson and Ron Goldman, the jury may have found that police misconduct required them to acquit him.[49] Ted Hoffman explained this social benefit in response to an accusation that he had fewer "scruples" than "hookers on Sunset."

> My friend, do you think anyone in this bar believes you've got a head of hair? We all know that's a comb-over. But till you get so obnoxious you forfeit your right to civil treatment, no one in here points it out. Think of the trial system like that. We know accused people aren't always innocent. Maybe not even usually innocent....And even though we know that, we treat people like they're innocent until they've had their shot in court because it make us better people. It civilizes us to treat them that way. Civility's important. That's why no one in here called you a self-deceiving fool until you opened your drunken mouth.[50]

The Process Is Fair

This reliance on the legal process to generate moral outcomes, and as an end in itself, is only justified if the process is fair. To many observers, the process is not fair because it results in outcomes with which they disagree. "Murder One," which focuses on the process more than outcomes, concedes that some outcomes are unjust, but that, on the whole, the process tends to be fair and balanced.

One of the most commonly criticized weaknesses of the legal system is the jury selection process. Jurors are selected at random from a pool of prospective jurors, and then lawyers are permitted during voir dire to have people disqualified for cause or can use a certain number of pre-emptory challenges to eliminate jurors from the pool. Some people believe that the outcome of a case can be determined simply by who is on the jury. For example, one prominent defense attorney explained the O.J. Simpson verdict this way: "They lost this case in jury selection."[51]

The Jury Cannot Be "Rigged" by Using Jury Experts

"Murder One" categorically rejects this simplistic view, although it recognizes that jury selection can make a difference. This is reflected in the defense team's decision about which jury consultants to retain. It is becoming increasingly common for defense lawyers to hire social science consultants to help with jury selection.[52] These consultants collect and analyze data, assist in the preparation of voir dire questions, and interpret juror responses to help identify bias and to select the most favorable jury possible.[53]

"Murder One's" focus on the trial process allowed it to consider the use of jury consultants in more depth than any other show in this genre. It showed Hoffman and one of his associates, Justine Appleton (played by Mary McCormack), interviewing two potential jury consultants before the trial began. The first consultant took the more aggressive position on the importance of jury selection and his "scientific" advice.

> Consultant: I'm not going to insult you by pretending what I do is an exact science. What you buy when you buy me is a strong statistical probability that the jurors I recommend will look favorably on our arguments.
> Appleton: And if they don't?
> Consultant: I'd recommend you change your argument.
> Appleton: You don't think that's the tail wagging the dog?
> Consultant: What's the difference as long as you get the client off?

Hoffman: I assume you use questionnaires? The Meyers-Biggs profiles?

Consultant: Everybody does. What you pay for is my experience in interpreting the data.

Appleton: What's your record in court?

Consultant: 16 wins and 1 defeat.

Appleton: Tell us about the loss.

Consultant: Well, I suggested a defense, the attorney ignored it. Against my better judgment, I stayed on, formulated a shadow jury. Not that I didn't know the outcome. His client paid the penalty.

Hoffman: So what you're saying is you had nothing to do with the case going south.

Consultant: You hire me for the truth — good, bad or indifferent. The truth is the attorney blew it.[54]

Hoffman rejected this consultant. Although that decision might reflect a rejection of the character's arrogance, or perhaps a desire on the part of the lawyers to maintain control of the case, it seems more likely to reflect a rejection of the premise behind the pitch — that jury selection is the key to victory, and that as long as you have the right jury and the right arguments, you will win regardless of the evidence.[55] Hoffman's rejection of the premise is supported by comparing that exchange with his conversation with the second jury consultant. The second consultant articulated the more moderate view of the role of the consultant in jury selection.

Consultant: Everyone has two sets of biases. Those they present to the world; those they live by but can't admit to, even to themselves.

Appleton: I'm assuming that's where you come in?

Consultant: I can pinpoint those secondary biases by working off of focus groups and interviews. But you have to understand my results can go out the window once a jury is seated.

Appleton: You didn't mention that on the phone.

Consultant: It could go out the window with any consultant. People change in relation to other people. A jury's dynamic is always fluid.

Hoffman: We appreciate your candor, but then what can you bring to the table for my client?

Consultant: I've worked up a method of predicting to a degree how each juror will alter their behavior and opinions once they're impaneled. I've also had some success in predicting the election of the foreman and I can gather data on how sequestration will further change the jury. With the intense media coverage this case has already received, there's a good chance the prosecution will go for sequestration.

Appleton: Your record is 28 wins, 4 losses?

[The Consultant nods.]

Hoffman: Explain the losses.

Consultant: Three of them occurred early in my career. I learned more from them than from any of my wins.

Hoffman: And the fourth?

Consultant: I made a mistake and misread the jury.
Hoffman: How soon can you start?[56]

The second consultant recognized the uncertainties involved in predicting how a jury will behave, especially when the interaction between jurors is taken into account. This is consistent with what studies have shown regarding jury behavior. As one commentator put it, "we have no reason to think, from jury studies, that any selection system can guarantee or even make especially likely a 'winning' jury."[57]

The Jury Selection Process Can Eliminate Potential Bias

Even though the jury selection process cannot be used to "rig" the jury to guarantee a win, it can eliminate some prejudiced jurors and jurors who have already made up their minds.[58] "Murder One," with its emphasis on process, took more time than any other show of this genre to explore the details and implications of jury selection. Where other shows might spend a few minutes on jury selection, "Murder One" devoted a substantial portion of two episodes to jury selection for the Avedon trial.[59] These episodes showed that the selection process is generally fair and balanced. During jury selection, the lawyers can make a motion to disqualify a prospective juror for cause, or can use one of a limited number of preemptory challenges. For the juror to be disqualified for cause, the judge must find bias or prejudice on the part of the juror. If the judge chooses not to disqualify a juror for cause, the lawyers can use a preemptory challenge to eliminate that person from the jury so long as the lawyer is not motivated by an improper purpose such as race, ethnicity, or gender.[60] "Murder One" depicted both kinds of challenges.

The challenge for cause eliminates those individuals most obviously disqualified from serving on the jury because of bias or prejudice. An example of an appropriate challenge for cause was seen when prospective juror number 11 was disqualified from the Avedon trial.

No. 11: My money says there's going to be a new suspect, one to free Avedon up, and I bet Richard Cross has something to do with it.
Judge: Sir, have you followed this court's admonition since jury selection not to watch or read anything about the Costello case?
No. 11: Yes I have, your Honor. Why?
Judge: Because the court needed clarification. Please proceed.
No. 11: Like I said, Richard Cross'll have something to do with Avedon getting out.
Grasso: And you base this theory on what?

No. 11: Cross put up his bail, didn't he? Follow the money. What's Forbes say Cross is worth? 400 million? All in multinational corporations. Now, look at Avedon's new movie. Could it be any clearer?

Grasso: I'm afraid, sir, it could.

No. 11: Avedon's new movie was partly financed by a Dutch company, shot in Canada, to be distributed by a French corporation. Follow the money.

Grasso: Mm-hmm.

No. 11: Multinationals — Eurodollars — the erasure of economic boundaries? Cross and Avedon are Freemasons.

Grasso: You're referring to the fraternal organization?

No. 11: I am referring, ma'am, to the secret organization whose goal is a one-bank, one-government world. Cross and Avedon are active members. That's why Avedon slips out— 'cause they don't have time for your little trial.

Grasso: Oh. Now I get it. Your honor?

Judge: Uh, the court appreciates your insights, sir. Thank you, you're excused.

No. 11: Oh. I'm dismissed, is that it?

Judge: That's it. The Bailiff will see you out.

No. 11: Fine. The conspiracy continues.[61]

Although this scene includes the ironic twist that number 11's theory turned out to be correct, he was properly disqualified from the jury. He had already formed beliefs about those involved in the trial that were based on rumored associations and conjectured conspiracies. Those beliefs showed a willingness to reach conclusions without the presentation of any direct evidence. Such a person should not be permitted to serve on the jury because they seem unlikely to fairly and objectively weigh the evidence.

Sometimes, however, a prospective juror's bias or predisposition is not so obvious, and that is when a lawyer may choose to use a preemptory challenge. The use of preemptory challenges has come under attack in recent years.[62] Some feel that preemptory challenges allow lawyers to manipulate the selection process and to load the jury with those who tend to support one side or the other.

"Murder One" portrays the use of preemptory challenges as a mechanism that is consistent with the fair and balanced administration of justice. It allows lawyers to eliminate jurors that may be biased against one side or the other, but where there is not sufficient evidence of bias to convince the judge to excuse the juror for cause. A good example of this use of the preemptory challenge was in the ninth episode.[63] Initial questioning of prospective juror number 5, whose name was Milligan, seemed to show that she would be reasonably objective. Although she admitted that she wouldn't approve of someone having sex with a girl as young as her daughter, she said she thought she could decide the case on the facts. She also admitted that it bothered her when people were late and didn't pay their bills, "because it's wrong," but agreed that "there are instances where people's actions cannot be viewed in black and white terms, that things which appear one way on the surface in fact may not be what they appear."[64]

During a court recess, Hoffman and his associate Chris Docknovich (played by Michael Hayden) discussed the prospective jurors with the jury consultant, Lorraine Vitalli,[65] who pointed out some concerns she had with Milligan.

> Vitalli: Now the one I'd definitely pass on is Milligan.
>
> Docknovich: The one who makes time for her kids and works for a shrink?
>
> Hoffman: I have to say, Lorraine, I liked her. She's patient, maternal, willing to weigh the evidence.
>
> Vitalli: All true. But when I look at her demeanor, her body language, I see trouble.
>
> Docknovich: If you're bothered by the crucifix she had on,[66] my sixteen-year-old sister has one just like it. And a navel ring.
>
> Vitalli: Wear it one day, it's a fashion statement. Wear it three days in a row as this woman has and it's who you are. Whenever sex is mentioned she shifts in her seat or folds her arms. What I see is a judgmental, moralistic woman who, as soon as she gets the chance, is going to drop the hammer on Neil.
>
> Hoffman: At this point I don't want to use a preemptory because we don't like this woman's wardrobe choices.
>
> Vitalli: Ask her if she thinks she'll be unduly influenced by Neil's celebrity. She'll dispute the notion that Neil is a celebrity in the first place. Ask her about Neil's history with drugs and alcohol. She'll say substance abuse is a failure of character. Watch.
>
> [Back in court, voir dire resumes.]
>
> Hoffman: Do you think Mr. Avedon's celebrity status will influence your ability to remain impartial?
>
> Milligan: The fact that he was in a TV show doesn't make any difference to me one way or the other.
>
> Hoffman: So if he were to take the stand in this trial, your ability to objectively evaluate his testimony wouldn't be affected by his being famous?
>
> Milligan: Jonas Salk was famous, Mr. Hoffman. Susan B. Anthony was famous. He's just someone who gets his picture in a lot of magazines.
>
> Hoffman: In those magazines, have you read about Mr. Avedon's struggle with drugs and alcohol?
>
> Milligan: Yes.
>
> Hoffman: In your opinion, is it more or less likely Mr. Avedon committed the crime with which he is charged because he suffers from the disease of alcoholism?

Milligan: Hmm. One's got nothing to do with the other, but I don't buy this disease business. If you get drunk or take drugs, it's because you want to. It's not a disease, it's a failure of character.

Hoffman: Nothing further. Your Honor, the defense thanks and excuses Ms. Milligan.[67]

This scene shows that some predispositions are below the surface and may be subconscious. A jury consultant sometimes can identify non-verbal cues that can assist in identifying those predispositions. Once the predisposition is identified, the lawyer can make a judgment as to whether the use of a preemptory challenge is warranted. It is possible that Ms. Milligan's moralistic beliefs would not interfere with her ability to be objective, but the risk that it might is sufficient to warrant giving the defense lawyers the right to eliminate a limited number of such potential jurors from the jury.[68]

The use of preemptory challenges might be unfair if one side is able to learn information about a prospective juror that is not available to the other side. For instance, one of the prospective jurors in "Murder One," Wayne Cormier, was a retired police officer. Normally, defense lawyers would assume that a person with connections to the police would tend to favor the prosecution.[69] But the defense team learned that Cormier was disgruntled about the way the police department handled his disability and that he had worked with David Blalock (Kevin Tighe), the investigator for the defense team that had been murdered during investigation of the case. As a result, they believed Cormier would be likely to favor the defense.[70]

This information, however, was equally available to both the prosecution and the defense, so any advantage to the defense was not unfair. As it turned out, the prosecution discovered this information during the voir dire of Cormier and moved to disqualify him for cause. After the judge learned that Cormier and Blalock were acquainted, but not friends, she denied the motion and the prosecution used a preemptory challenge to eliminate Cormier from the jury.[71]

Jurors Are Not Unduly Influenced by Improper Considerations

Another common criticism of the jury system is that jurors are improperly influenced to make decisions on grounds other than the evidence in the case.[72] In the O.J. Simpson case, for instance, many have suggested that the jury's decision to acquit was motivated by concerns about race.[73] Although race was not an issue in the Avedon trial portrayed in "Murder One," there were other examples of attempts to use emotion to influence the jury. For instance, the defense called Avedon's mother as a witness to provide a "more sympathetic portrait" of him. A survey by the jury consultant showed that the jury probably did not have a very sympathetic image of him. Of the people surveyed, 59% thought Avedon was guilty after the government's case, and 47% thought he was the type of person to commit the crime.[74]

Avedon's mother then recounted that he was a good son who was abused by his father, that he ran away from home when he was fifteen to seek his fortunes in Hollywood, but that he sent money home and paid off her mortgage when he was home to do a photo-shoot about where he had grown up. On cross-examination, the Assistant District Attorney implied that the defense was using the "abuse excuse," and that she had "concocted this entire story to play on the jury's sympathies." This line of questioning reduced Avedon's mother to tears and elicited this reply:

> The crime is mine, Mr. Washington. For twenty years I've lived with the guilt of what I allowed Neil's father to do to him. I've seen my son's bitterness, the anger in his eyes when he looks at me. If I could take his place right now, I'd do it. I'd do it. Maybe then he wouldn't hate me for my weakness, for the terrible way I've failed him. I'm sorry, Neil. I'm so sorry. Pease forgive me.[75]

This strategy worked in part. It engendered sufficient sympathy that it brought some of the jury to tears. But sympathy alone generally will not overcome the evidence. Research has shown that juries tend to base their verdicts on the strength of the evidence.[76] Despite whatever sympathy the jury may have felt for Avedon, they still returned a guilty verdict against him. Likewise, even though there may be reason to believe that race played a part in the O.J. Simpson case, the verdict might have been justified because of evidentiary weaknesses.

Moreover, the fact that there is some opportunity to interject sympathy into the jury's consideration does not make the decision unjust. It may be appropriate for the harshness of the law and the legal system to be tempered by more equitable considerations of equity.[77] In addition, both sides have the opportunity to interject emotional matters into the fray. In the Avedon trial, for example, the prosecution sought to emotionally influence the jury by showing pictures of the crime scene at the beginning of their closing argument, and by showing the videotape during their rebuttal argument of Avedon choking an ex-lover during sex.[78]

Limitations of the System

On the whole, the first season of "Murder One" shows that the process of the legal system is generally fair and balanced. But that does not mean it is perfect. On the contrary, the show demonstrates that the outcome of an individual case may be unjust. The convolutions of the Avedon trial, with the conspiracies, the lying, and the cover-up, shows how the system is subject to possible manipulation.

Wealthy Defendants Receive Greater Protection

"Murder One" implicitly recognized that there is a difference between justice for the rich and for the poor, which is an important criticism of the legal system raised in the wake of the O.J. Simpson trial.[79] Pamela Anagnos Liabakis, the president of the Association of Trial Lawyers of America, makes the point this way:

> O.J. Simpson is a unique individual—a wealthy celebrity capable of as-sembling his own "dream team" of defense lawyers and with the re-sources to find an obscure screenwriter in North Carolina who possessed the proof that the prosecution's key witness was a perjurer. A man with the money to hire the foremost pathologists in the country to challenge the mountain of evidence introduced by the state. How much justice could the average American afford if his or her freedom were placed in similar jeopardy?
>
> In the criminal courts, the accused is often limited to the amount of justice that he or she can afford.[80]

Hoffman and his associates, like O.J.'s "dream team," were expen-sive. Hoffman was making enough money to pay $427,000 a year in al-imony and child support, and to split other assets worth $2,000,000.[81] Hoffman's clients, of course, considered him to be worth every penny. When Avedon was first charged with murdering Jessica, Hoffman in-formed him that he would have to get another lawyer because Hoffman's earlier representation of Cross in the same case had created a conflict of interest. Avedon virtually begged him to stay on the case: "Look, another lawyer takes this case and he biffs it because he's not as good....I'm the dead guy, Ted. I am the dead guy. Teddy, please. Please!?"[82]

Even the villain, Roberto Portalegre, was cognizant of Hoffman's abil-ities. After Portalegre was arrested for Jessica's murder, he offered Hoff-man $20 million to defend him.

> Portalegre: I must applaud your skills, Mr. Hoffman. To get a murder conviction overturned is truly remarkable. Unfortunately, it has resulted in my arrest....Now that you're responsibilities to Mr. Avedon are con-cluded, I am prepared to offer you twenty million dollars to represent me.
>
> Hoffman: And what makes you think I would take it?
>
> Portalegre: Besides the money? You are a man who is drawn to the bat-

tle, Mr. Hoffman. And once the joy of your victory has passed, you will require a new challenge — one that will test you to the utmost. I am that challenge.

Hoffman: You brutally strangled a fifteen-year-old girl and you were perfectly prepared to see an innocent man go to prison for it. There's no amount of money on earth that will convince me to represent you. Good day, Mr. Portalegre.[83]

Portalegre recognized that Hoffman could expose weaknesses in even the most formidable case. Like O.J. Simpson's "dream team," Hoffman would explore every defense and scrutinize every piece of the prosecution's evidence. In the Avedon case, Hoffman provided the jury with numerous alternative suspects and theories. Using the accounts of Jessica's sexual escapades from her diary, the defense team showed that many other men might have had a motive to murder her.[84] And the defense team impeached each of the prosecution's key witnesses. With the assistance of their able investigator, the defense located a videotape of Cross watching another couple having sex, found several women who accused Dr. Lester of raping them, and discovered that Cross was spending $300,000 a year to provide medical assistance to Susan Dominick's brother. Between the impeachment evidence and the diary, the defense was able to make what would have been an air-tight case a close call.

Another "B" storyline from "Murder One" provided a contrast with the high-profile Avedon case. In the second episode, Daryl Jackson, the African-American boyfriend of the law firm's receptionist, was falsely charged with assaulting a woman by ramming her car with his truck. Jackson's defense lawyer, who was recommended by a friend, required a $10,000 retainer and advised Jackson to plead guilty to stay out of jail. One of Hoffman's associates, Justine Appleton, came to Jackson's rescue. She took over the case for free and obtained an acquittal by convincing a jury that the charges had been trumped-up to support a frivolous civil suit.[85] But had Appleton stayed out of the case, an innocent man would likely have gone to jail because the best representation he could afford advised him that was his best option.

Media Coverage May Affect the Process

Another potential limitation of the legal system, one that has been highlighted by prosecutions like the O.J. Simpson case, is the influence of the modern media. Many are concerned that intense television coverage can influence the jury. "Murder One," which evolved in part out of television coverage of criminal trials, showed many of the challenges created by intense media coverage. For instance, the lawyers, defendants, and witnesses were constantly plagued by inquiries from the media. In addition to traditional news coverage, a cable-television network devoted to legal affairs — "LawTV" — carried detailed summaries and critiques of daily developments. This intense interest and scrutiny resulted in confidential information being leaked to the media, sometimes to influence public opinion, and sometimes in return for favors or money.

Although these challenges made the handling of the Avedon case more difficult, they did not seem to affect the outcome. There was plenty of evidence to support the jury's conclusion that Avedon was guilty. It therefore seems likely that the jury's decision was based on the evidence rather than the influence of the media. This is consistent with some studies finding that juries "are able and willing to put aside extraneous information and base their decisions on the evidence."[86]

On the other hand, the storyline of "Murder One" shows that Avedon was innocent, and it is possible that the jury's error was influenced in some part by the media coverage. Studies of pretrial publicity have shown that media reports historically favor the prosecution, and that such information often comes from the police or the prosecutor's office.[87] As a result, public opinion tends to align with the prosecution,[88] which may increase the chances of a conviction.[89] "Murder One" followed this pattern. An opinion poll before the trial began found that 67% of the public believed Avedon was guilty.[90]

"Murder One," however, also shows that the present media environment may give the defense a chance to respond to unfavorable reports. For instance, after the tabloid news program "Deadline America" aired the videotape showing Avdeon choking a girlfriend during sex, Hoffman was a guest on the program and explained that the tape could have been doctored and that in any event the activities were consensual.[91]

An even more aggressive tactic was when the defense let Avedon be interviewed on live television before the trial began. O.J. Simpson had a similar opportunity, but his defense counsel decided the risks were too great,[92] and, in light of the way the civil case came out, they were probably right.[93] Avedon's defense team, working with their jury consultants, recognized the risks and potential benefits of such an appearance.

> Hoffman: Is there anything in your data that indicates there would be an upside to Neil doing an interview with Felicia Norell tomorrow night?
> Stratton: A venue like that puts him in America's living room with one of the most respected women alive. The visual association alone with Felicia Norell helps humanize him.
> Docknovich: Plus he's charming, charismatic, knows how to play the camera.
> Hoffman: When he's acting. This is the real deal, live, no take two.
> Docknovich: What's the downside?

> Vitalli: Even if he says all the right things, he'll be under a microscope. Everybody's going to be looking for guilty behavior. In his body language, his eyes, his affect.
>
> Stratton: People tend to believe their televisions tell them the truth. If he comes off badly.... [94]

Although Avedon was ultimately convicted, this media tactic seemed to improve the public's perception of him. Hoffman's wife Annie reacted positively.

> Hoffman: Well, what do you think?
>
> Annie: He's beautiful, boyish, sensitive, tragic. Now every woman in American wants to mother him.
>
> Hoffman: Do you?
>
> Annie: I don't know. He's an actor so I can't tell if I'm being manipulated or if I've just watched an innocent man pour out his soul. I know that in concept I've been allergic to him up to this point, but for the first time I'm beginning to wonder if Neil Avedon is really capable of murder.
>
> Hoffman: Give me twelve jurors who feel the same way you do, and I've got a shot at getting him off. [95]

Conclusion

"Murder One" portrays the legal system as far from perfect. The outcomes are sometimes unjust, the wealthy have an advantage, and the media might be an inappropriate influence. But "Murder One" also shows that the *process* of the legal system, which was its real focus, generally advances the interests of justice. It shows, for instance, that the use of preemptory challenges cannot "rig" the jury, but can eliminate potentially biased jurors. Moreover, "Murder One" shows that the *process* is fair in that it gives equal opportunities to the prosecution and the defense. Each side has the same chance to affect the make-up of the jury and to present its side of the case. Therefore, "Murder One" counters the arguments that the jury system is inherently flawed. Although we cannot be sure of the cultural significance of its representation of the legal system, on the whole it is a positive one that reflects some level of confidence in the legal system, and may also, in some small measure, improve the public's perceptions of legal process.

7

N.Y.P.D. *Blue*

Richard Clark Sterne

The only television show Joyce Carol Oates watched regularly in the mid-1980s was "Hill Street Blues," which she found as intellectually and emotionally provocative as a good book. "In fact," she said, "from the very first, 'Hill Street Blues' struck me as Dickensian in its superb character studies, its energy, its variety; above all, its audacity."[1] Nevertheless, Todd Gitlin commented in his searching *Inside Prime Time* that this "literate, intelligent, ensemble police series" — broadcast by the same network that put "The Brady Brides" and "Sheriff Lobo" on the air — had such low Nielsen ratings at the end of its first year that it was renewed by NBC only on the condition that its creators, Steven Bochco and Michael Kozoll, "build each episode around a single story line, complete with beginning, middle, and end."[2] For the show had given a modern, high-velocity twist to the 19th century novelistic technique of intertwining multiple plots, and one network programming official, speaking for who knows how many of his confreres, complained, "My wife is confused, and she is a smart broad."[3]

Despite "Hill Street Blues's" impressive merits in the world of commercial television, Gitlin also noted that the series restricted itself to the world view of "decent, dogged, local police." And he agreed essentially with Kozoll's elegiac observation that doing episodic television "is like raising a retarded child."

> By which he meant that there are only so many things it will ever learn to do, no matter how much you love the child.... It will never shine....[4]

Although this appears to be a bit overstated, it is true that the commercial preoccupations governing the creation of television drama make it extremely difficult to evoke the startled recognition of human truths that a movie like "Nashville" or a play such as "Long Day's Journey Into Night" can elicit from us. While the makers of the best plays and films think and compose with the freedom that art demands, the writers and producers of network television series — however high their intelligence, however cultivated their sensibilities — are prisoners of the ratings, the periodic "sweeps," and the perpetual fear that their extremely expensive shows will be canceled.[5] News about the number of households tuned into a particular television program does more to concentrate the minds of network executives than the program's quality can, and high Nielsen ratings mean high advertising revenues, the lifeblood of the industry.[6] So a goalie's anxiety at the penalty shot is serenity in comparison with the worrying among the upper echelons and writer-producers that a particular television police or legal drama will not prove enough of a hit with the public and the sponsors to be renewed for another year (something which even the most astute minds in the industry are unable to foretell).[7]

Detective Clark and the Real N.Y.P.D. Blue

It was against this backdrop of low expectations that work began on "N.Y.P.D. Blue," the highly successful episodic police show that garnered twenty-six Emmy Award nominations for its first season (1993–94) and was recently renewed by ABC for a sixth season. In his book about the show, David Milch, the show's co-producer (with Steven Bochco), conveys the impression that its being based on "real" stories supplied by Bill Clark, a former New York City detective who became the program's professional adviser, has much to do with the series's success.[8] Clark has been scornful about shows like "Law & Order" and "Homicide: Life on the Street," because the members of their police forces work "too much by the book"—

> there's always a search warrant, a suspect is usually read his rights and then the lawyers are involved, and there's no conviction.[9]

Real detectives, Clark had clearly indicated in conversation with Milch, sometimes use violent means of coercing confessions.[10] So, taking their cue from Clark, the creators of "N.Y.P.D. Blue" could confidently claim that the laying of hands by police on people in custody was "realistic." Bobby Simone (played by Jimmy Smits), though in general more "humane" than his multi-bigoted detective partner Andy Sipowicz (Dennis Franz), sometimes resorts to graphic threats against detained "scumbags" or "assholes,"[11] and in one 1996–97 episode, after removing an informant's glasses, shakes and slaps him repeatedly in order to elicit the name of a "perp." In another episode, Greg Medavoy (Gordon Clapp) resorts to an unusual kind of "directory assistance" by whacking a suspect's head with a telephone book; and in a different scene, Medavoy and his partner James Martinez (Nicholas Turturro) slam a suspect's face against an automobile hood. Such use of force, and threats of force, may well have helped "N.Y.P.D. Blue" win its high audience ratings. It is not news that a large segment of the American public goes for violence on both the large and the small screen, especially the violence of "good" guys against "bad" ones.

The violence in "N.Y.P.D. Blue" is regularly presented from the perspective of "decent, dogged, local police"—and it's worth noting that this cop show, unlike "Hill Street Blues," has no Public Defender who would want members of the police force to go, as Bill Clark disdainfully put it, "by the book" on civil liberties.[12] It's true that when Bobby Simone scornfully tells a middle-aged homosexual man who has hired a lawyer to defend one of his young companions against a prospective murder charge that "All that ACLU stuff is out the window," any member of the audience can reject the detective's apparent contempt for civil liberties. But that we ought to reject it is suggested neither by what the camera shows us, nor by the context of the many "N.Y.P.D. Blue" episodes in which it's implied that if a suspect in custody has to be manhandled in order to get at the truth, then so be it. I can't recall seeing an episode that presented criticism of police violence in a form stronger than the expression of regret by the person who had used it, but a regret pragmatically inspired, as by fear of a lawsuit. (Medavoy admits to Martinez that he'd lost control of himself in the telephone book incident, but at the same time he takes pride in having gotten results.)

The Amnesty International 1996 Report

If, however, seized with an extraordinary fit of courage, ABC were to broadcast a couple of "N.Y.P.D. Blue" episodes based on the material presented in the Amnesty International 1996 report on police brutality and excessive force in the New York City Police Department, an aspect of reality heretofore ignored by the series might be given its due. The meticulously sober document issued by Amnesty International "acknowledges that a number of reforms have taken place within the NYPD during the past three years, partly in response to a commission of inquiry into police corruption which was appointed in 1992."[13]

The report also "recognizes that the police are permitted—even obliged—to use force in certain situations," and that the New York City police "have a difficult and often dangerous job and that most encounters between officers and members of the public do not result in allegations of misconduct."[14] Nevertheless, having collected information on "more than 90 cases of alleged ill-treatment, or excessive use of force resulting in ill-treatment or death, by New York city police officers dating from the late 1980s to early 1996," Amnesty International concluded that "police brutality and unjustifiable force is... a widespread problem."[15] In many of the cases examined, the report found that "international standards as well as US law and police guidelines prohibiting torture or other cruel, inhuman or degrading treatment appear to have been violated with impunity."[16] The following passages in the report seem to me particularly relevant to the question of the extent of "N.Y.P.D. Blue" realism:

> In most of the cases examined police officers were not disciplined or received only minor sanctions. The "code of silence" in which police officers refuse to testify against their colleagues appears to have contributed to immunity in many cases....
> More than two-thirds of the victims in the cases examined were African-Americans or Latin and most, though not all, of the victims in the cases of deaths in custody (including shootings) reviewed by Amnesty International were members of racial minorities.[17]

The "code of silence" referred to in the first of these passages could be said to be at least implicitly recognized on "N.Y.P.D. Blue" — we don't hear of police officers testifying against their colleagues — but I've never seen what could be a grippingly realistic episode, in which a detective is torn between loyalty to a buddy and a feeling that the buddy can't be allowed to get away with an act of torture. As for the reference in the second passage to "deaths in custody (including shootings)," this goes well beyond any "N.Y.P.D. Blue" "reality" I can recall watching: suspects are hit, shoved, and shaken, but apparently never shot, as the document issued by the Nobel Prize-winning Amnesty International tells us, citing specific cases, they sometimes are.

The report observes that although "as a result of out-of-court settlements in civil actions," damages — according to statistics supplied by the City Comptroller's Office — "have been awarded to victims of police misconduct in between 100–400 cases annually since 1988," and although the money "paid out by the city in damages to alleged victims of police misconduct has risen from around $7m in 1988 to more than $24m in 1994," some city counsel and police officials have suggested that lawsuits are being filed "in frivolous cases" by "opportunistic lawyers" in "an increasingly litigious society." Replying to this charge, the report states:

> Attorneys and civil rights groups repeatedly told Amnesty International that many cases of ill-treatment did not result in lawsuits; these included cases where there were no independent witnesses; or the alleged victim was convicted of an offense arising out of the incident, and had little chance of prevailing against the testimony of police officers, or the

injuries were not severe enough to justify the costs involved in pursuing litigation....[18]

This report should make us want in television police shows — because they'll obviously continue to be popular — something more deeply true to reality than the kind of "realism" of which David Milch is so proud. To cite the 1927 standard for broadcasters, a concern for "the public interest, convenience, or necessity" should give one of the networks an incentive to probe in either a police or a legal drama the problem of the use of violence by detectives and uniformed cops. The long history of commercial broadcasting, however, indicates that violence pure and simple sells too well to permit its being closely examined on the tube.[19]

Close examination seems to have been limited, as far as television dramas are concerned, to their vetting by advertisers for "dangerous" content. Thus, on "Man Against Crime" (which premiered in 1949), one crime only was forbidden by the show's sponsor, Camel cigarettes, to be used as a plot element: arson, because it might remind viewers of fires caused by cigarettes. The sponsor could also be said to have "criminalized" a phenomenon never before treated as an offense: coughing was verboten on all episodes of "Man Against Crime."[20] As the playwright August Strindberg put it, "There are crimes and crimes."[21]

The Wall Street Journal as Corporate Crime Reporter

Because week after week police shows and legal dramas depict felonies — usually one of the infinite variants of homicide — that we tend to equate with "crime" pure and simple, it's useful to recall that lawbreaking by large corporations involves social costs often greater than those of the bloodiest murders on the street. Although the format of the police show obviously couldn't accommodate "crime in the suites" (the legal drama can, and on rare occasions, does), the dialogue of a cop series could demonstrate an awareness that not all wrongdoing is done by the "scumbags" treated with such contempt on "N.Y.P.D. Blue."

Inspired by Ralph Nader's remark that *The Wall Street Journal* "is the main reporter in our country of corporate crime," Robert Sherrill read "a year's supply" of the paper and then recounted what he'd found.[22] We quickly learn from his piece a key difference between the usual consequences of corporate malfeasance and of the crimes to whose scenes the police speed, both in reality and in police and legal dramas:

Although three executives were sentenced to spend a few months in prison (for fraud resulting in ten deaths) and a couple of others seem

destined to land in jail eventually, the kindly manner in which most business chieftains were treated solidly underscores the fact that in the United
States a prison sentence is rarely looked upon as the proper fate of corporate villains.[23]

The naive reader of Sherrill's article might expect to learn at least of
painful civil penalties inflicted on the big business perps. He would be
disappointed: "Don't be impressed by the seemingly hefty fines and resti-
tution paid by some corporations. They were a minor inconvenience, for
1996 was a banner year for corporate profits."[24]

Under the sub-head "Jim Lehrer's Fallen Angel," Sherrill details the
malfeasance, as reported in *The Wall Street Journal*, of the food giant
Archer Daniels Midland, a sponsor of PBS's "Newshour with Jim Lehrer."
ADM was involved in the most publicized corporate crime of 1996:

> Caught in a sting by Justice Department investigators, A.D.M., the
> planet's largest grain processor, pleaded guilty to charges of conspiring
> to fix prices for two products: lysine, a feed supplement for livestock,
> and citric acid, used in soft drinks and detergents. A.D.M., which was fined
> $100 million, and its Asian co-conspirators also agreed to pay more than
> $100 million to settle civil lawsuits brought by shareholders and cus-
> tomers. More lawsuits lie ahead.

Again, lest we suppose that such fines amount to real money, Sherrill
disabuses us. Archer Daniels's stock price "actually jumped, because Wall
Street judged the settlements and fines to be bargains"—the experts cal-
culate that the company cheated its lysine customers alone out of over
$170 million.

> Although the $100 million is seven times larger than the largest an-
> titrust penalty ever before levied by the Justice Department, it's (you'll par-
> don the expression) chicken feed for A.D.M., which in the last fiscal year
> had revenues of $13.6 billion from its agricultural products, most of
> which were heavily subsidized by the U.S. taxpayer.[25]

The one case Sherrill found reported in *The Wall Street Journal* that resulted in criminal prosecution involved three Kentucky coal executives
who had lied to federal prosecutors in an investigation into a 1989 gas explosion in a Pyro Mining Company shaft. The explosion caused the deaths
of ten workers, the lying concerned the existence of the mine's hazardous
conditions, and the executives "drew sentences ranging from five months
(and a fine of $375) to eighteen months (and a $3,000 fine—or $300 per
victim)." According to the *Journal*, which used Federal Mine and Safety
Administration data, these sentences were unusually long in cases filed
in behalf of the agency: most criminal complaints "result in no prison

time," and the agency estimates "that only about 40 people have gone to jail since 1991 because of criminal safety violations at mines."[26]

My final selection from Sherrill's culling of *The Wall Street Journal* crime reports concerns the disregard by many employers of the minimum wage law. According to the *Journal*, Alan Krueger (a Princeton University labor economist) estimates that "as many as 3 million workers are paid less than the minimum wage." Violation of the minimum wage law has, in Krueger's words, "a certain economic logic to it because an employer, if caught, usually has to pay only the back wages that were due. Penalties are generally levied only on repeat or extreme violators."[27]

Violations of the minimum wage law would strike nobody as the stuff of television drama. Still, "N.Y.P.D. Blue" could conceivably recognize (as "Hill Street Blues" occasionally did, especially in its earlier days), the economic and social setting in which felonies are committed. One of the informers used by the detectives of the 15th Precinct might, for example, be a formerly law-abiding man turned thief when cheated by an employer of the wages he'd earned.

"N.Y.P.D. Blue's" Perspective on Crime and Community

Contrasting with the detectives's verbal and physical abuse of adult perps are the occasional efforts of officers like Martinez, Kirkendall, Fancy, and even Sipowicz (the most complex character in the series) to change the direction of a young delinquent's life through encouragement or by getting him or her into a drug rehabilitation program. But the show doesn't extend to the community in which the 15th Precinct is situated the generous understanding of flaws and problems with which it treats the detectives themselves. Greg Medavoy's various insecurities, Sipowicz's concern about his son's future, and Diane Russell's struggle with emotional problems apparently due to her having been sexually abused by her father—all help to "humanize" the defenders of law and order. But I kept wanting to see an attempt to do justice to the diversity of their "neighborhood," in which there must be more decency and more resistance to sinister temptations than the writers indicate. "Reality" isn't well served by a series which, except when it evokes the personal lives of the cops, focuses almost exclusively on the pursuit and arrest of homicide suspects, frequently African-American or Hispanic.

There was a time, it's true, when television dramas distorted reality in a different way. In the early 1980s entertainment reviewer Ben Stein remarked that in the thousands of hours he'd spent watching adventure shows, he had "never seen a major crime committed by a poor, teenage black, Mexican, or Puerto Rican youth, even though they account for a high percentage of violent crime."[28]

"Conservative" slice-of-life realism, however, now distorts social reality as badly as "liberal" evasions of truth once did. The influence of the mass media, sociologists Paul F. Lazarsfeld and Robert K. Merton have noted, stems "not only from what is said, but more significantly from what is not said.... [T]hese media ... fail to raise essential questions about the structure of society."[29]

I suggested earlier that "N.Y.P.D. Blue" would be more truthful about the police if it probed rather than evasively touching on their use of force. The program would also be more truthful about urban blacks and latinos if its way of being "fair" to them were not the usual cliche of including several members of these groups among the detectives and other employees at the 15th Precinct station. If the writers and executives responsible for the series were willing to slow its hectic pace, the camera could enter and linger in some of the homes, schools, bars, and churches of neighborhood people without much money, with hopes rarely fulfilled, but with a few successes along with their disappointments and grief. If the audience were to get to know a community activist before, not after, he became a DOA, or if we were occasionally to meet a member of a minority group with something of the quality of a Sandra Cisneros, a Muhammad Ali, a Maya Angelou, or a Jose Torres, the racial and ethnic bias that "N.Y.P.D. Blue" currently encourages in the name of a factitious realism would be reduced, if only to a small degree.

Watching Episodes of "N.Y.P.D. Blue"

A suspect speaking a street jargon to the detective questioning him during an episode will occasionally be told to speak more plainly. I myself often find it hard to follow not only some of the detainees's stories, but parts of the detectives's conversation with each other. This is due less to their use of police jargon than to a convention that seems increasingly to have been adhered to in both movie and television dramas since the late 1960s: the velocity of speech (and of action) must be so great that the audience, instead of "following" it, is immersed in it. In fact, the increase since as recently as the 1980s in the devaluation of articulate speech can be measured by comparing an "N.Y.P.D. Blue" episode with one of the early "Hill Street Blues" episodes. While the writers on "Hill Street Blues" deliberately created confusion, even chaos, in crossing one or more conversations with others, they did so to communicate something, such as the way a hostage-holding situation can develop and be defused or how one cop, such as Buntz (played by Dennis Franz), can be framed by another.

"N.Y.P.D. Blue," on the other hand, appears to be less interested in communicating with its audience than with arousing feelings, which are often inchoate. The flashing urban montage images in the show's introduction, accompanied by Mike Post's pounding, percussive music (quite different from his bittersweet "Hill Street Blues" theme), are meant—like the more phantasmagoric images that introduce "Homicide: Life on the Street"—to impinge on our nervous systems, and they do. The generally visceral stimuli of "N.Y.P.D. Blue" thin the line between the segments of the show and the numerous commercials; and a viewer soon gets used to hearing the voice of Dennis Franz (or is it, Pirandellianly, Sipowicz himself?) telling us at the middle commercial that "N.Y.P.D. Blue will be right back, on ABC."

Some Memorable "N.Y.P.D. Blue" Episodes

Despite my criticism of the series for its constricted realism—its failure to face up to police brutality as an issue, its narrow view of what constitutes crime, its virtual ignoring of what must be the variegated nature of the community in which the 15th Precinct is situated—I have found a number of episode narratives extremely affecting and (as is characteristic of the series as a whole) well-acted.

One of the most arresting programs was especially distinguished by the performance of a guest actor, Michael MacRae, as Drucker, a quondam good cop who's gone bad. Under surveillance by Internal Affairs, Drucker is assigned at the beginning of the episode to the 15th Precinct, and Bobby Simone is told by his superior, Lieutenant Fancy (James McDaniel), to keep an eye on him. Simone teams up with Drucker to investigate a complaint by a man who claims, with his young son's coerced cooperation, that the boy has been molested by Markham, an apartment house neighbor. Bobby, letting Drucker take the lead in questioning the accused man, rapidly concludes that Markham (movingly interpreted by Albert Henderson) is honest in asserting his innocence, and that the accuser, Mario Generro (played by Nicholas Mele with savage energy), is maliciously lying. Drucker, however, bungles the end of the interview by gratuitously instructing Markham, even though there's no charge against him, to keep his "robe closed." Drucker then compounds this blunder in Simone's mind by dragging him to the Bronx on a 911 call from his Colombian girlfriend, who's evidently involved in the drug trade. Bobby later blames Drucker, as well as Markham's vicious accuser, for the tragic outcome of the false "morals" charge. Ill and depressed, Markham has killed himself.

MacRae makes Drucker a kind of seedy Graham Greene character whose deterioration is apparently related to his failed marriage and his involvement with the Colombian woman, with whom he wants to go away to Barbados. But there's also a darkness in the man: he eventually seems to invite his own death by refusing to give up his gun to the detectives at the station house and by attempting to escape. The detectives shoot him dead, then feel low about what they've done to a man once one of their own. (Variations on the theme of the strayed "brother" often crop up on police shows—this version, however, was compelling.) Jimmy Smits convincingly conveys Simone's bitter anger at both the slanderer and the negligent, destructive Drucker.

Drugs, frequently involved in the felonies that the series dramatizes, are important in another well-conceived episode, in which the African-American Lieutenant Fancy gets one of his few opportunities to play more than a formal part in the precinct's activities. With his former foster son, Maceo, having been arrested for distributing drugs, Fancy's desire to persuade the boy to change his life dovetails with his duty as a detective to arrest perps. He makes a deal with a sergeant from another precinct with whom he and his own precinct haven't been on good terms: in return for Fancy's help, and Maceo's, in breaking the gang that has commissioned the boy to make a drug drop on the street, the sergeant will ask the United States Attorney to give Maceo a break. Maceo's part in the deal is to make the drop and get arrested along with his contact so that the gang won't suspect what he's done. Whether the bitter Maceo, who doesn't like his role, completely trusts Fancy at this point isn't clear, and as he is being arrested he and the lieutenant exchange ambiguous glances.

Maceo subsequently learns that he'll have to testify against his own mother, who has angrily been told by Fancy in a conversation Maceo was allowed to listen in on that, in order to stay high, she's had the boy running smack. In return for his testimony—pitifully, Maceo asks Fancy if he can talk to his mother, but is turned down—and for the help he's already given the police, he'll be sent to a "boot camp" to learn a trade; the judge may credit his probationary time against a two-year term. In the story's final scene, Fancy invites Maceo to come home with him for dinner with "Lillian and the girls," and reminds him that the boy's life has not been all bleak: he hasn't had good parents, but he once spent time with people who loved him. Maceo (skillfully played by Alex Bass, who modulates well from sullenness toward Fancy, to an expression of torn feelings over his drug-dealing mother, to a reciprocal response to the lieutenant's kindness), we feel, may be able to follow Fancy's advice to use the future to repair the past. James McDaniel maintains throughout the episode a delicate balance of sternness and affection toward Maceo.

Similar to Fancy's treatment of Maceo is Detective James Martinez's behavior in another episode toward Marco, a youth who after being arrested for shoplifting tells Martinez he knows the whereabouts of a corpse. This information leads to the discovery of a man who has died of a fractured skull and a hematoma and to the arrest of two felons. Martinez has grilled Marco about his drug-taking and sexual behavior, but in a way that shows he's concerned that the boy may contract AIDS. Later in the story line, Martinez encourages Marco—over the objections of the boy's father, who has been beating him—to take home from the station some comic books that the detective had let him read there. Martinez also plans to get Marco into a drug rehabilitation program, and warns the father to stop the beatings.

The conversations of Fancy with Maceo, and of Martinez with Marco, afford welcome respites from the cops-and-killers action at the heart of "N.Y.P.D. Blue." Without ceasing to be detectives, Fancy and Martinez take on the symbolic role of father or older brother in efforts to prevent two youths from falling irretrievably into crime. For me, these efforts symbolize the commitment we need to make as a nation to change the numerous environments of poverty in which drug-selling can be more attractive than honest work and drug-taking can serve as a way from despair to oblivion.

In the same episode as the Martinez-Marco encounter is another story-line whose hair-raising pragmatism in the pursuit of "justice" I find memorable in a very different way. Here, Bobby Simone, in love with Detective Diane Russell (Kim Delaney) and jealously angry at her for taking an undercover assignment to trap James Liery (who's apparently linked to "organized crime") by rekindling his old attraction to her, seizes a chance to question him about an alleged felony. Visiting Liery, evidently without a search warrant, Simone finds an AK-47 in his apartment (to Simone's sardonic question, "You in the Russian military?," Liery answers "Da"), arrests him, but is soon told by Fancy that he can't be charged and must be released.

Simone and Sipowicz then concoct a plan to get rid of Liery (played with restrained menace by Christopher Meloni), a vicious character whom in a previous episode we've seen surreptitiously drug Russell in a bar in order to carry her to his place and rape her. The two detectives visit the bartender, and without disclosing their identities tell him that Liery had given them his name when questioned about the AK-47. Soon afterward, Liery is found murdered. Simone and Sipowicz's end-justifies-the-means method of dealing with him corresponds exactly to the Soviet Communist Party's methods that Arthur Koestler's protagonist, Rubashov, in the

penetrating novel *Darkness at Noon*, is eventually revolted by. He reflects, shortly before his execution following a show trial, that "Perhaps
it did not suit mankind to sail without [ethical] ballast."[30]

Interestingly, in an early, Emmy-winning "Hill Street Blues" episode
written by David Milch, Public Defender Joyce Davenport accuses Captain Furillo—hardly the worst of cops—of having "perverted the law" with
"the oldest excuse in the world: the end justifies the means." At the end of
the episode we see Furillo in church saying at confession, "Bless me, Father, for I have sinned." (A winning aspect of "Hill Street Blues," it should
be noted, was its occasionally giving voice to the notion of justice as an ideal
that the defenders of the law should do their damndest to uphold.)

Black and Latino Civilians on "N.Y.P.D. Blue"

I want now to take a closer look at the depiction in the series of blacks
and latinos who do not, like Fancy and Martinez, belong to the police
force. As in actual life, more arrests are made among these than among
other groups, and the image of white (in most instances) detectives ver-
bally and sometimes physically assaulting African-Americans or Hispanics in custody is bound to be vivid in the mind of anyone who has
watched many "N.Y.P.D. Blue" episodes. Not all interaction, however,
between the police and members of these minority groups occurs in the
precinct's interrogation rooms. The predominant impressions one gets
from those encounters that take place elsewhere are of black and latino
men who either perpetrate or suffer violence, and of black and latino
women who are disturbed by but incapable of changing their men's law-
less behavior, or are freely or by coercion involved in it.

One of the pertinent story lines concerns the results of an appeal by a
distraught young black man, Aries Mitchell (Perry Moore), who fears
for his life, to the white detective Jill Kirkendall. Aries's fear is a reaction
to his girlfriend's brother Bernard's threat to kill him unless he marries
Brenda (Monique Ridge): Bernard alleges, though Aries denies, that he has
fathered Brenda's baby.

Although Kirkendall (well acted, with unsentimental sympathy, by Andrea Thompson) tells him there's little she can do about the threat itself,
her keen observations during a visit to Bernard and Brenda's apartment
make her suspect that the baby the young woman is uncomfortably holding in her arms is not hers. Kirkendall's further investigations reveal that
a woman is missing who'd given birth at the same hospital where Brenda
supposedly has had her child. Brenda eventually confesses that Bernard,

in order to get Aries to marry her, had offered to pay $500 to a woman who'd come out of the hospital with a baby. After the woman had turned him down, he had strangled her in an alley and taken the infant home to his sister. Simone and Sipowicz now arrest a glowering Bernard (effectively played by Amani Gethers) on the charge, recently made by Aries, that Bernard has tried to choke him—but clearly he will be grilled about the woman's murder. The motherless, homeless infant is fetched at the police station by a white social services representative.

The Bernard-Brenda aspect of this story would tend to confirm in the minds of many audience members a preconception of the brutal African-American male and the feckless black woman. Even more troubling, however, because of the dramatic use it makes of what many ignorant whites have claimed to be a "black" trait, is another "N.Y.P.D. Blue" narrative concerning the decapitation of a gay, white New York University professor by an African-American former student who has become psychotic. After murdering Professor Reese, Rodney Wellstone has driven off in the dead man's car, which he claims, during a taped confession at the police station, the professor had wanted him to have. Suddenly, he asks Bobby Simone if he is "smelling" him. When Simone indicates he doesn't know what Wellstone means, Rodney says, "Are you reacting to the way I smell?" Later in the episode, the professor's mother—who upon hearing the hideous news of his death had withdrawn (and this is a fine psychological touch) into an intense preoccupation with the whereabouts of the car that she and he had been paying for together—enters the police station crying that the car is ruined, that someone's "body odor is there." She adds, "I taught my son cleanliness," then cries, "That's the smell... the murderer... I smell him." And we see, at the end of the corridor, Rodney, whom Mrs. Reese has evidently never seen before.

There is superior acting in this story. Monti Sharp plays Rodney chillingly as a profoundly deranged man who sometimes deviates into sense. As the murdered man's mother, Anne Haney, speaking with a cultivated Southern accent, effectively gives the impression of trying to keep her nerves under control. But what is troubling is not only, once again, the narrative's confirmation of the stereotype of the brutal black male, who is here especially frightening in his irrationality, but the reinforcement of a notion which is part of racist folklore: that of a distinctively "black" body odor. Rodney Wellstone, depicted as hating his own "negritude" (just as some members of other highly visible minority groups hate their ethnic identities) projects on Simone his own fear of emitting a racial odor. And Mrs. Reese, with her "That's the smell... the murderer... I smell him," speaks words that make a sinister emotional appeal to those members of the audience who, complacently biased, know nothing about African-Americans or American history.[31] This story, for all the skill with which it is written and performed, comes closer than any other police narrative I've seen to espousing the attitude of anti-black racism.

As far as the presentation of Hispanics is concerned, the series partly inoculates itself against the charge of bias both by giving an earnest, like-able detective the name Martinez, and by depicting him as attracted to and protective of the appealing Gina Colon (played by Lourdes Benedicto). Nevertheless, not far from their desks are the interrogation rooms where, like Simone and Sipowicz, Martinez and Medavoy team up to question suspects, a substantial number of whom are latinos. Mendonca is the name of the recipient of the telephone book whack I mentioned earlier. Cowed by that forceful gesture, Mendonca names "Ugaldi" as the shooter from a bus of a woman and a child. It is when arresting Ugaldi that Me-davoy and Martinez slam his face, for no clear reason, against the car's hood. And back at the police station, Medavoy punches Ugaldi hard for giving Martinez the finger after being photographed. Then, losing control of himself during the interview, Greg picks up Ugaldi's Spanish word "puta" (whore), and repeatedly throws it back at him, calling him a "stu-pid puta." Consequently, Martinez later tells Medavoy that he "blew it," but neither detective has qualms of an ethical sort about the day's activ-ities: Medavoy ruefully remarks that nobody seems to be bothered when Sipowicz "breaks back"; James replies that the difference is that Andy "gets a statement."

Lopez is the name of the suspect, in another narrative, whose "balls," the detective Vince Vitelli tells Sipowicz, he's "beaten off." Because Vitelli wonders whether Lopez intends to sue, Andy gives his colleague a help-ing hand: he threatens Lopez with a jail term for selling drugs, promises to "beat your balls off," and without explicitly telling him to "escape" from custody, encourages him to do so. At one level, Sipowicz's loyalty to Vitelli wins my respect; but it's also, obviously, an illustration of what, in the largest sense, the Amnesty International report calls "the code of silence."

By winking at this complicity; by so frequently showing latinos and blacks (unless they're members of the 15th Precinct station) in the roles of suspects or perps; and by praising itself for a fidelity to reality that flouts the *Miranda* decision in particular and civil liberties in general, "N.Y.P.D. Blue" evinces disdain for the common good of our society.[32]

An Episode Sui Generis of "Homicide: Life on the Street"

Based on David Simon's *Homicide: A Year on the Killing Streets* (1991), the NBC police drama "Homicide: Life on the Street" sometimes treats with greater complexity than "N.Y.P.D. Blue" the relationships between African-Americans and a precinct station. One episode in particular — "Three Men and Adeena" (1993), which I found remarkably well conceived, written, and performed — evokes with an insight rare in television fiction mutual tensions and distrust in such relationships that can militate against the establishment of "the facts" in a police interrogation.[33]

The interrogation which comprises virtually all of "Three Men and Adeena" follows two earlier grillings that have failed to break the resistance of a late-middle-aged African-American, Ridley Tucker (Moses Gunn, in one of the finest television performances I've ever seen) to the charge by black detective Frank Pembleton (Andre Braugher) and his white partner Tim Bayliss (Kyle Secor) that he has disemboweled and strangled an eleven-year-old girl named Adeena. Now the detectives are under pressure from their Chief either to get results or release the "Araber" — whose nickname, Ridley explains, derives from his traveling about Baltimore like a nomad, with horse and wagon, selling fruits and vegetables. The girl, Ridley tells them, had worked for him, cleaning the horse's mane. But in general the Araber responds briefly and vaguely to questions during the earlier part of the episode.

To his remark that at a certain point there was "no more job" for Adeena, Tim sternly replies that the girl's mother had been afraid to let her continue to work with Ridley. And the white detective goes on to enumerate discrepancies in statements the Araber has made about when he'd last seen the girl. Frank, playing the "good cop" (but it's one of the merits of this ambiguous episode that we can't be sure Frank is not at moments sincere) gently insists to Ridley that he's an alcoholic. "I'm a Baptist," the Araber responds. He tells them that the girl had been in his apartment a couple of times, and that they'd watched television together. "Say her name!" Tim demands, showing Ridley a picture. "Adeena!" is his defiant answer.

Tim seems to score an important point by asking why Ridley has said he wasn't at the church for the girl's funeral, despite photos that show him there. (Might one imagine him to have some obstinate reason of his own for denying what sounds like an incontrovertible fact?) Soon after the Araber expresses willingness to take a polygraph test, there is a flare-up, either spontaneous or contrived, between the two detectives, triggered by Frank's suggestion that somebody else may have killed the girl. Bayliss spits on the table, grabs Ridley's head, and shakes it. Whereupon the Araber declares that he'll look him "straight in the eye," and say "all night" that he "didn't kill her."

Frank, now taking over, ignores Ridley's plea that he needs sleep, points out to him that he's used the phrase "I don't remember" more than any other, and asks if alcoholism has impaired the Araber's memory. Pembleton then asserts that the Araber's former fiancee has told the detectives that she knew Ridley didn't really love her. Failing to evoke a reaction to this jab, Frank asks the Araber to trust him — "We're in this together, just you and me" — and asks if he "had a drink that night." Ridley retorts that he's been sober for sixteen months. During a brief pause in the interrogation, the chief warns Tim that within four hours, if no confession is extracted, they'll have to release the Araber. But a moment later a triumphant Tim tells Ridley that the results of the polygraph test (which he'd willingly taken) show him to be a liar. Ridley's response that he knows they can't use the polygraph in court makes us swerve to the detectives's side as they hound him with the question, "Why? Why?" Suddenly they ask about statutory rape charges against him fourteen years earlier, but the Araber calmly says they'd been dropped. With contempt, he's told that his rule for girls is, "If you cry, you die." Startlingly, when Ridley is asked if he's positive "right now, that you didn't do it," he appears to doom himself by saying in a subdued voice, "Not right now."

Time has passed before the next scene begins. The table at which the three men sit is littered with empty coffee cups and other paper debris. To a weary Tim, whose tie hangs around his shirt, Ridley once again denies having killed Adeena. Suddenly the Araber launches a verbal attack on Pembleton: he resembles, Ridley says scornfully, the proud, successful, rich colored folk he, the Araber, had once met in New York — like the maitre d' he'd fought with, causing his own girlfriend to leave him. More impassioned than he's been at any time during the questioning, Ridley turns to Bayliss and asserts that he knows him too: a native Baltimorean related to slave owners who'd raped slaves. "You've got your dark side," he says. Then suddenly affirming his very soul against the men who've tormented and exhausted him, he gives his long, drawn-out street cry: "S-T-R-A-W-B-E-R-R-I-E-S, R-A-S-P-B-E-R-R-I-E-S!" A change in the power relationship — as in a Pinter play — occurs between the suspect and his interrogators. Ridley speaks out for the first time about Adeena. He recalls her having tied a bow, a red ribbon, around his horse Magdalene's tail; remembers her having wanted to be a dancer: "She could've been," and he continues, "I never touched her. . . . I didn't hurt her. I didn't kill her. I loved her. . . . I've got to live with that the rest of my life — the one great love of my life was an eleven year old girl."

After a pause, Tim says, "Time's up," and Frank is shaking his head as they all emerge from the interrogation room. He tells Ridley to relax, that a car will take him home. But in conversation a little later with the chief, while the Araber awaits the car, Frank says, "He killed Adeena." Tim, shaken, admits he's "not so sure any more."

The episode is remarkable both for its pacing and for its structure: that of a contest in which Frank and Tim build an evidentiary case that seems overwhelming, until the Araber, after admitting — out of sheer weariness? — that he wasn't sure "right now" that he hadn't killed Adeena, speaks of her with what sounds like great tenderness, and finally confesses with apparently pure shame that an eleven-year-old girl was the one great love of his life. We don't know whether Frank's ultimate assertion of Ridley's guilt is unconsciously the result to some degree of resentment against the Araber's telling him he's like snootily rich New York colored folks. Nor do we know whether Tim's change of heart is brought about in any measure by Ridley's opening in him a hidden "decent Southern white" guilt-wound over slavery and its heritage. In any case, what Frank ultimately reacts to as a con job, Tim thinks may be the honest passion of a man falsely accused.

Conclusion

That an episode as intellectually and emotionally intense as "Three Men and Adeena" could appear on a network police show suggests that almost nothing is impossible, even in commercial television. On the other hand, nothing I've seen this year on any cop show or legal drama matches "Three Men and Adeena's" probing, rather than just touching on, the problem of attaining "truth" in a criminal investigation, and the complex tensions evoked by likenesses and differences of class and race between a suspect and his interrogators.

Just as only people in pain arrive at hospital emergency rooms, in reality and on television, only people who are presumed to be criminals, or are witnesses to crimes, or informants about criminals, go to or get dragged to police stations. What this means is that the boundaries of the police show genre must be trampled if a "realistic" series is to be other than a succession of narratives in which, with exceptions like the Maceo and Marco and Drucker stories, the forces of law and order seek and grill and bash perps. When such questions as, "How do I know what the truth is?" and "What biases and preconceptions of mine may be influencing me?" enter a detective's mind, we're no longer in the realm of the cop show, but of classic drama. And classic drama is among the many fine things that don't survive on commercial television.

What's unfortunate about "N.Y.P.D. Blue" is that so many talented people are confined within the borders of a purported fidelity to fact that actually tends to distort reality: by not facing up to the issues like the ones raised in the Amnesty International 1996 report; by implying that "crime" is definable in terms of what the police drama presents as crime; by helping to perpetuate—again with the excuse of "realism"—stereotypes about African-Americans and Hispanics among an audience largely unaware of the history and social reality of people unlike themselves.

Still, given the vacuity of most of what appears on television, it's understandable that many intelligent viewers like and respect "N.Y.P.D. Blue." The writers exhibit a wry, if at times macabre, sense of humor, the terrific velocity of the program—which alienates me—evidently fascinates others, and the acting is frequently superb. I suspect, however, that the series's marked popularity is largely due to its appeal to people fearful for their own physical safety, glad to see presumed "perps" treated roughly, and tranquil about the program's scornful attitude toward civil liberties. Probably only a general perception in the United States that the incidence of violent crime had significantly decreased would cause "N.Y.P.D. Blue" to lose its Medusa-like glamour.

8

Paper Chase

WALTER A. EFFROSS

You teach yourselves the law, and I train your minds. You come in here with a skull full of mush, and I send you out thinking like a lawyer.
—Professor Charles W. Kingsfield

Early in Paddy Chayefsky's 1976 movie "Network," a television executive rejected out of hand a proposal for a series "set in a large Eastern law school, presumably Harvard.... The running characters are a crusty but benign ex-Supreme Court Justice, presumably Oliver Wendell Holmes by way of Dr. Zorba. There's a beautiful girl graduate student and the local district attorney, who's brilliant and sometimes cuts corners."

Two years later, though, CBS aired the television series "Paper Chase," which was based on the 1971 book by John Jay Osborn, Jr. and the 1973 movie of the same name. Although the show ran on CBS for only one season, new episodes produced for the Showtime cable channel from April 1983 through August 1986 continued the adventures of the law students on a prestigious but unnamed Massachusetts campus. However, district attorneys, former Supreme Court justices, and even law firms played limited roles in the series.

In fact, by focusing on the formal and informal processes of legal education as opposed to the graduates's actual practice of law, "Paper Chase" resembled an expanded version of the memorable "temple" flashbacks in the 1972-75 ABC series "Kung Fu." Replacing the Shaolin monks who trained disciple Kwai Chang Caine in the martial, mystic, and meditative arts, John Houseman's "crusty but benign" and supremely logical Professor Charles W. Kingsfield awakened in James T. Hart (played by James Stephens) and his classmates the ability to analyze and argue laws and their limits. However, though Caine's televised quest centered on his adventures in a land far from his monastery, Hart's chronicles conclude with his graduation and imminent departure from campus. The final episode does not even reveal which of two options (a judicial clerkship or a position as an associate with a large law firm) he will pursue.

Learning the Law

Like Caine's masters, who often taught philosophical principles by referring to the behavior of plants, insects, and animals, Kingsfield relies on more than his blackboard, casebook, and lecture notes to convey the practicality and pervasiveness of contract law. In one episode, he deliberately fails to appear for a class to be taught before an examination, thus forcing the students to teach each other the material set for discussion that day: namely, whether his absence constitutes a partial breach of his contract to teach them the law and thus excuses their own obligation to take his examination. Not only are the students forced to examine the material in a practical context, but they must collaborate in arriving at their answer. Shortly after the professor reveals to a colleague that "my absence was meant as an academic maneuver, to instruct the students," Hart realizes that "Kingsfield may have done us a real favor when he put us under so much time pressure we had to cooperate." Upon his return to class, Kingsfield sternly advises a student who protests this unorthodox method, "Lecturing is only one way of teaching. Sometimes other approaches are equally effective.... The question is not where *I* was, but what *you* were doing."

On another occasion, Kingsfield angers his dean and colleagues by requiring the students to conduct an intellectual scavenger hunt through all the different libraries of the university. Searching in the medical library for an answer to a legal question, Hart deduces that "Kingsfield's trying to tell us that the law is everywhere." Once again, though, the lesson involves not only context but collaboration: in order to pass the exam by submitting the required number of correct answers, the various teams of exhausted scholars are forced to trade information, and thus to draft fair contracts, with each other. "The law of contracts," Kingsfield concludes triumphantly, "does not reside in the flimsy pages of books. It grows naturally out of the interactions of people as they try to do tasks which no single person alone could accomplish. Contract law describes the human condition.... The purpose of this assignment was to show you that contract law surrounds you in every facet of your daily lives. The purpose of this assignment was to lift your eyes from the printed page to the natural order of life."

Over and over again, "Paper Chase" portrays the law, like life, as a dynamic process rather than a static collection of facts and rules. A third-year student counsels a first-year, "You can't worry about not studying enough, because it's impossible to study enough. Concepts, that's the key—how concepts apply in different situations." As in the movie on which the series was based, academic difficulty befalls a student who has a photographic memory but little capacity to analyze the reasoning of the assigned cases. Kingsfield himself advises hyper-organized student Rita Harriman (Clare Kirkconnell) that her written work is deficient because "research is the realm of clerks and librarians. You've compiled and organized, not synthesized, drawn your conclusions. Step outside well-worn paths; think for yourself." Selecting his replacement as editor-in-chief of the school's law review, third-year student Gerald Golden (Michael Tucci) elevates Hart over the acknowledged "logical choice," the super-efficient Harriman, because Hart built the routine assignment of analyzing a new judicial decision into a perceptive paper on the judge's philosophy of law. Golden explains, "I want someone to explore, be creative, take risks—to see the art in the law, as well as the craft."

The Importance of the Socratic Method

Central to cultivating the student's appreciation of the law's complexity, and prominently featured in many episodes, is the famed "Socratic dialogue," in which a professor bombards a student with questions on how a law would apply to various real and hypothetical situations. Defending the law school's grading methods against a disappointed student's lawsuit for breach of contract, Kingsfield reminds the judge that "through training in the Socratic method a lawyer's mind comes into being.... Law grows and changes like a living being. We never know what the law is, only that we have the proper tools to study it."

Elsewhere, Kingsfield initiates his students into the Socratic secret: "Why don't I just give you a lecture? Because through this method you learn to teach yourselves. You may at times think you have reached a correct and final answer. I assure you this is a delusion on your part. You will never in my classroom reach the final, correct, and ultimate answer. In my classroom, there is always another question. There is always a question to follow your answer."

Thus, with the help of his students, Kingsfield can defeat a computer programmed by the university's engineering students to apply contract law to various factual situations. Although the computer's responses cite more caselaw than do Kingsfield's, its circuits short out when Kingsfield submits to it the same hypothetical questions that he poses to his classes; its limited logic can't handle the gaps, conflicts, and ambiguities that the classroom dialogue is designed to highlight.

Because the Socratic process demands the student's active engagement with the material, Kingsfield is (almost) unforgiving of those who are unprepared for class. In the first episode of the series the professor (apparently following the example of at least one real Harvard law professor of generations past) "shrouds" with an imaginary sheet the hapless Hart, who was unaware that there was a reading assignment posted for his very first law school class. Although many students might be overjoyed by the gesture's implication — that Kingsfield will never call on Hart again — a distraught Hart pleads his way past the professor's secretary and into Kingsfield's office, where he implores, "I have to have a true Socratic dialogue with you." Kingsfield, who professes not even to recognize Hart, warns him, "It is my obligation to prepare my students to exist in the most competitive of all worlds, where there is no room for error." (Kingsfield relents only when Hart appears in class covered with a real sheet, but completely prepared to discuss the material.)

In a later episode, the professor states as he distributes an examination, "You may have noticed I don't subscribe to the permissive school of learning. Some day you may be defending a human life. You must be prepared." And to a student who offers to resubmit a written assignment because she "was pressed for time" in completing it, Kingsfield frowns, "You occupy a privileged position and are expected to put forth your best effort. Precious few second chances are given in life. In my class there are none."

Law as a Jealous Mistress

Law school's intensity, its insistence on both accuracy and timeliness, and the commitments and sacrifices that it requires enable "Paper Chase" to illustrate the differences among mere motivation, actual enthusiasm, and true passion for the process. Taking an involved legal project with him on a trip home to his family's farm in Minnesota, Hart finds himself telephonically tethered to the law school, turning the kitchen table into his desk as he tells his disappointed friends and relatives, "I gave Kingsfield my word — don't you know what that means?. . . There's some people on the other end of the phone counting on me. I can't let them down."

Many of the show's major characters appear to have submerged their artistic talents and ambitions: at a pre-graduation costume party, Hart arrives as a rodeo clown, his roommate Franklin Ford III (Tom Fitzsimmons) as a novelist, and others as Dolly Parton, Rocky Balboa, a ballet dancer, and a punk rocker. (Harriman appears as "The Woman Who Has It All": both the Presidency and a family.) In the same episode, a first-year student struggles with the competing demands of Kingsfield's class and an art class that rewards her with more freedom and appreciation.

For some students, however, the tradeoff is only tragic. A member of Hart's study group, soon to leave the school after cheating on an exam, tells Hart, "I envy you. You know exactly where you're going, and you know why. I never wanted to be a lawyer—my father-in-law, parents, brother want me to be a lawyer. I'm here to please everyone else—I've been doing that my whole life." Kingsfield, sadly shaking the student's hand, acknowledges, "[w]e never do well in things that we're not interested in. Now find what you wish to do in the world and do well in it." In another episode, a father investigating his musically-talented son's suicide at the law school realizes that he pressured the student too much. One classmate recalls that the student found true happiness playing the guitar and that "[h]e just didn't want law that badly." Hart remembers advising the discouraged young man that "I could distinguish cars when I was a kid, because I loved the cars. If you care, you'll know the difference" between different elements of the law.

Even students who are properly motivated occasionally succumb to overwork, fatigue, an addiction to performance-enhancing drugs, and, in one instance, to the temptation to punch a professor who refuses to extend a deadline. In this sense, the Eagles's contemporary rock hit, "Life in the Fast Lane," dimly heard in the background of the first episode, is a much more appropriate theme than the gentler Seals and Crofts song "Years of Our Lives," which played over the title and end credits of the CBS episodes. Yet as Hart concludes after the scavenger hunt, "the whole purpose of this assignment is to learn that we can't make it alone. We have to honor the relationships we make with one another. And we make it through law school by relying on one another." At the costume party, he marvels, "There are people here that I know better than my own family."

In fact, the tone of the series softened somewhat over time, as the students changed from a coldly maneuvering group of grade grubbers, among whom Hart stood out for his compassion and humanity, to a generally supportive team that would go out of its way to provide legal and emotional support to a student whose husband had just filed for divorce. However, the classmates's study groups retained their exquisite balance between collaboration and competition, as their members shared insights and outlines yet shunned those who couldn't carry their academic weight or who, near exam period, showed symptoms of a possibly-communicable flu. On another level, the law review united an elite group of students in producing and editing high-level legal analysis but also occasioned its own internal power struggles.

In this hermetic environment, the students frequently subordinate personal relationships to pre-professional ones. The series consistently captures this element through the classmates's preferred form of address: abbreviating their professors's calling on "Mr. X" and "Miss Y," most students, even roommates and best friends, address each other by last name. Only in rare situations, such as when they help a study group member who has accused a professor of sexual harassment, do the students use each other's first names. In the first episode, as students are settling into study groups and dividing up outlining duties, one student brusquely demands of those in her own group, "Don't call me Linda—call me O'-Connor." In a later episode, an editor of the law review, suspecting an attempt to curry favor, insists that the usually-imperious Harriman use only his last name because "you're rude, overbearing and smug—let's keep it that way."

The students's depersonalization (or Platonicization) reaches its climax, so to speak, after Harriman, just rejected by her long-time boyfriend as not "spontaneous" enough, spends the night with Hart. The next morning, Hart confides to Ford, "I just got carried away by the moment." He regrets not the intimacy itself, but the effect that it might have on their professional relationship: "How am I going to keep working with her [on the law review]? I want this to end before it goes any farther." Ironically, Hart only realizes the extent of his affection for Harriman when she seems even more eager than he is to forget the incident and its implications.

In fact, love and other emotional issues most often enter the world of "Paper Chase" as inconvenient intrusions or impertinent interruptions of the serious business of study, schedules, and cite-checking. During the scavenger hunt, Ford refuses to pursue a budding relationship with a classmate's sister, spurning her impulsive suggestion that they take off to visit Europe together: "I can't just run away—can't you see how much I've got invested here?" Nor can love's riddles be vanquished by the lawyer's analytic arts. Perhaps aware of Hart's and Harriman's short-lived liaison, Kingsfield, for once at a loss, counsels Hart that "there are no correct answers, only unfortunate ones, when you struggle with personal issues in your professional life. I appreciate the complications that arise when one finds oneself struggling with personal feelings in a professional situation. It's a condition that one continues to come up against for the rest of one's life. And I regret to say that there are no correct answers, Mr. Hart, only unfortunate ones."

On another occasion, Kingsfield seems almost fatherly as Golden is torn between accepting the offer of a prestigious judicial clerkship or immediately pursuing his true love—litigation—as an associate at a law firm. "I spend my life trying to get students to grapple with the problems in a logical way," Kingsfield acknowledges. "However, logic is a mere tool, used only when one has all the facts. Emotional facts, personal facts, are far more difficult to uncover and it is here the great god logic is often reduced to impotence." (At the end of this conversation, Kingsfield pays Golden the supreme compliment of addressing him by his first name.)

Kingsfield as the Law's Embodiment

Despite his eminence, his spacious sanctum, and his telephonic connections with Supreme Court justices and other legal luminaries, the illustrious Professor Kingsfield appears to be a lonely man. Isolated from the students by his separate entrance to the lecture hall, his scheduling secretary, and his own forbidding manner, he seems no less removed from his own emotions. Rare is the occasion on which he even raises his voice; often, his pained facial expressions and deliberate manner of speech imply that he would rather not respond at all to a particularly aggravating situation. If Kingsfield does love, it is a gruff mixture of appreciation and respect for his students as a group and for some, like Hart, in particular. Defending the school's grading policies from the breach-of-contract suit, he testifies, "In any law school, we are still family. My students's relationships to me and mine to them is a country of its own, a hallowed ground into which the law must not intrude." And in fact he ultimately writes the student-plaintiff a letter of recommendation that lands the student a sought-after job with a large firm. (Such attitudes do not go unrequited. Investigating Kingsfield's possible improprieties in a decades-old litigation, Hart informs Ford that "I have to find out [the truth]. I love this man. I respect him tremendously." What if Kingsfield did "throw" the case in exchange for a bribe?, Ford asks. "I'd still feel the same," Hart admits.)

Yet Kingsfield never stops reminding his students of their responsibility for themselves and their actions. The students are not only his intellectual charges but in some way his colleagues, and it is to them that his generation will pass the custodianship of both the law and the school. Despite his seeming embodiment of legal tradition, Kingsfield works both overtly and subtly to reflect changes in the law and to direct changes in the school.

On the most obvious level, his approval restores confidence to students cowed by the majesty of the law and Kingsfield himself. After Hart, as an intern in the public defender's office, has helped to acquit the mugger who brutally attacked Kingsfield and stole his watch, Kingsfield reassures his doubtful student that the experience was "time well spent.... You didn't free [him], the court did. You skillfully pointed out [flaws in the prosecution's case]—no more or no less than a good lawyer. These questions you're asking, these doubts and suspicions, do you credit....Perhaps you'll have a part in resetting [the law]."

On another occasion, Kingsfield suggests that as the new president of the law review Hart devote an article in an upcoming issue to a specific court's decision on gift taxation. Ultimately concluding that he would rather pursue the unusual approach (for television's law reviews, at least) of focusing on larger trends in the law, Hart nervously declines to follow the professor's advice. To his surprise, Kingsfield compliments him: "as President, you chose the theme and not to wander—I congratulate you on your decision." As Hart leaves Kingsfield's office, the professor indulges in a rare smile. Further endorsing Hart, Kingsfield visits the law review office to hand Hart the first printed copy of the issue— "Since it's an historical fact that the Supreme Court shifts... I congratulate you on a very exceptional first edition."

On a more indirect level, Kingsfield personifies the school and its systems, as both a first recourse and a last resort. He demands of Professor Tyler (Diana Douglas)—one of his few featured female colleagues and one whom he personally encouraged to join the faculty upon her leaving the Securities and Exchange Commission—that she not allow a student without the proper course prerequisites to take her Securities Regulation seminar, because "we can't have haphazard standards." Yet when the student is admitted to the class on a probationary basis even Kingsfield is impressed at his synthesizing from work in other courses an original contribution to the discussion. Smiling at both the class and her colleague, Tyler notes, "One can't resist a progressive idea forever."

When alerted by students to problems at the school, Kingsfield typically dismisses their concerns peremptorily but quietly acts to preserve the institution. For instance, when a student approaches him in support of the tenure candidacy of an associate professor who is an especially inspiring teacher, Kingsfield gravely notes that just as students aren't allowed to grade their own papers they aren't invited to contribute to the tenure process. However, he then seeks out and counsels the candidate on improving his chances.

Similarly, when students respectfully inform Kingsfield that an older professor's mind is wandering during lectures, Kingsfield sternly reminds them of his colleague's outstanding qualifications and impugns their ability to assess faculty teaching. Yet despite his seeming unresponsiveness he diplomatically approaches the faculty member, discreetly assesses his mental competence (over a game of chess), and gently convinces him to retire from the classroom.

Finally, when student Elizabeth Logan (Francine Tacker) complains to Kingsfield that another professor (played by Robert Reed) is sexually harassing her, Kingsfield bluntly accuses her of "los[ing] control of yourself because of low grades—and you're striking back like a hysterical child, heedless of the consequences to [him]." Nonetheless, as Hart and the other members of Logan's study group attempt to find other women whom Professor Howard allegedly harassed (one of whom admits privately that "it's like one of Kingsfield's contracts. I cooperated and he gave me decent grades."), Kingsfield delicately reminds Howard, over drinks at the faculty club, of a previous student who'd brought similar accusations. After he is convinced that Howard is harassing his students, Kingsfield extracts from him a promise to leave the school.

Conclusion

Kingsfield's last televised contribution to the law and the school (and one which might still provoke debates among members of appointments committees) appears in the final episode of "Paper Chase," in which Professor Tyler invites Hart to submit his name for a faculty position. Many viewers no doubt anticipated an ideal ending for the series: the outstanding student would become a teacher, and a new cycle of education would begin. Yet despite his colleagues's enthusiasm for Hart, Kingsfield ultimately torpedoes his application. Assuring the faculty that he has the highest respect for Hart's analytic abilities, Kingsfield opposes the candidacy on the grounds that Hart has not been seasoned by real-world practice and that he should not be teaching what he has not yet fully learned. If Hart is upset by this development, he doesn't show it; on receiving his diploma he warmly embraces his professor.

Thus, the series's final lesson: the law, like life, is not a circle to be closed but a spiral expanding with every new experience. In the first episode of "Kung Fu," Master Kan informed the young Caine, "[w]hen you can take the pebble from my hand, it will be time for you to leave" the sheltered monastery. But in the last episode of "Paper Chase," the burden has shifted: Hart can return to the school to help prepare the next generation of students only when he, like the stone he has to offer them, is well-worn by weather and the world.

9

Perry Mason

NORMAN ROSENBERG

Prime time television's great lawyers never die; they just retire to syndication. Perry Mason, Erle Stanley Gardner's immortal super lawyer, established the pattern, and others, such as Ben Matlock, have followed it. Matlock, in fact, took over in 1996 Mason's mid-morning legal practice on Ted Turner's WTBS. But Mason (as portrayed by Raymond Burr) remains active, through the syndication market, on cable outlets, and on local stations throughout the country. As the current number of Web sites devoted to "Perry Mason" confirm, the classic show—which ran on CBS from 1957 to 1966—retains a corps of loyal viewers. They lovingly post the titles of all 271 episodes; summarize the plot of each of them; and list every actor, from Burt Reynolds to Lee Miller, ever to receive a screen credit for appearing in "Perry Mason."[1]

As a result of his longevity, Perry Mason has practiced law before successive generations of television fans. This trans-generational audience likely means that the program continues to take on new meanings. Although no one has ever carefully analyzed the issue, my own informal survey suggests that today's viewers of the classic "Perry Mason" series may not be seeing the same program in the same ways that viewers of the 1950s and 1960s saw it.

Consider the following two examples: "Perry Mason" as "nostalgia" and as "camp." More seasoned "Perry Mason" fans, who can remember the show from its run on CBS and from its earliest round of reruns, can now watch Mason's courtroom performances through nostalgic eyes. In a post-Watergate, "Court TV"-era, "Perry Mason" may well reassure many of these viewers that the legal practices with which they grew up remain viable, or at least can seem so whenever Perry Mason (re)enters the courtroom. But to the contemporary college student, part of a generation that is definitely post-Watergate and very much immersed in such "Court TV" spectacles as the O.J. Simpson trial, "Perry Mason" may now offer what scholars of mass culture call "camp."[2]

Camp is a slippery concept. I use the term here to denote a cultural product that, through the passage of time, has become so anachronistic that it begins to take on, at least for some people, humorous meanings that were not part of the expected response when it was first produced. To qualify as camp, a television program or motion picture should have become, at least for certain viewing tastes, so "bad" that it has also become "good." My unscientific sample suggests that this has happened with "Perry Mason." "I used to watch 'Perry Mason' reruns with my family," one student told me, "they really still identified with it, but I liked it because it seemed so 'campy.'"

Why might students of the 1990s now see a super lawyer from the 1950s, much like they view Rock Hudson (the "great straight hope" of the same decade), within the framework of camp? Most obvious to anyone who has learned about the law from watching television programs and motion pictures of recent vintage is the fact that the classic "Perry Mason" episodes show little trace of the constitutional revolution, particularly in the protection of the rights of criminal defendants, that was initiated, ironically, while the series itself was running in prime time. To a generation which sometimes appear to have been born knowing its *Miranda* rights, "Perry Mason's" mode of lawyering, which shows little concern for fundamental constitutional principles or broad social causes, can appear dated. Mason's clients rarely include civil rights or anti-war activists.

In addition, the ways in which the mass media represents "heroes" have changed. To a generation whose "legal heroes" might include Bruce Willis or Jackie Chan — modern-day warriors who use an automatic weapon or the martial arts — an overweight attorney whose heroism depends on legal words and phrases might, unless refurbished in other ways, seem a quaint relic from television's version of ancient history.

Finally, there is the somewhat strange, stolid solemnity with which Raymond Burr, the actor, portrayed Perry Mason. The image of Mason may now seem very much at odds with the ways in which today's television lawyers — and virtually everyone else on television in the age of "Seinfeld" — are represented. For many people who were born in the late 1970s or early 1980s, the absence of any trace of self-reflexive humor in "Perry Mason" might mark his demeanor as resembling that of "The Simpsons's" Lionel Hutz, who pursues minimum wage babysitting jobs as seriously as he chases ambulances. The tightly-wound attorneys on "The Practice" might keep Perry Mason around to be "of counsel," but they would not likely assign him an important case. Younger viewers, in other words, are likely to watch the classic "Perry Mason" with very different sensibilities and through equally different ideological frameworks from older fans of the show.

The "Perry Mason" Formula

It is necessary to begin by foregrounding this diversity of perspective because this essay will look at "Perry Mason" within a very specific, historically-grounded framework. It seeks to reimagine how the show, when it first debuted in the 1950s, tried to offer both fictive entertainment and a "realistic" view of the law. In an era before "Court TV" or "CNN," the classic "Perry Mason" series provided the dominant television form of what might be called "jurisprudence for the millions."[3] Then, as now, most people receive their primary, if not their only, view of law and its operations from watching mass-mediated, generally fictive, representations. In 1957, "Perry Mason" seemed, for many viewers, to be the "next best thing" to "the real thing."

This dual assignment, to provide both entertainment and what would pass as television's version of "realism," posed a serious dilemma for the creators of "Perry Mason." If the "Perry Mason" series, and Burr's Perry Mason, were to look as legal and lawyer-like as possible, they could not, at the same time, risk appearing too legalistic or too lawyer-like. Why should "Perry Mason" want to look "real" but not "too real?"

An answer to this question best begins with a brief tour through popular legal history. For a number of years, students of American mass culture have been exploring the vast number of popular texts that express a deep distrust of the legal system and of the lawyers whom it shelters. Criticism of law and lawyers in the United States can be traced back to the early nineteenth century novels of James Fenimore Cooper; into the pulp fiction of the nineteenth and early twentieth centuries; through Hollywood motion pictures, especially those of the 1930s and 1940s; and, then, to television. Recently, the World Wide Web has emerged as an important site from which to criticize the law and the legal profession.

Two of our culture's most popular heroes—the classic western gunfighter and the hard-boiled detective—have helped to focus this kind of criticism. These heroic figures rarely worry about the law and even more rarely deal, in any respectful way at least, with lawyers. Both dismiss legal forms as silly and burdensome; they solve disputes with their guns and according to their own "higher-law" codes of justice. Thus Shane, Sam Spade, and Mike Hammer (all of whom were Perry Mason's contemporaries in pulp fiction and in the visual media) can generally go about their violent business without worrying about—or even in direct opposition to—law and lawyers. But Perry Mason, as an attorney, cannot so openly embrace this brand of higher-law justice. If "Perry Mason" were to succeed as a television show that represented legal issues during the 1950s, in short, it would have to do so in competition with programs, particularly westerns, that could articulate critical discourses that would be unavailable to a show that featured a prominent attorney.

In fact, during the time in which Erle Stanley Gardner and his collaborators were trying to bring "Perry Mason" to television, the western genre had become the most popular form, at least on television, of jurisprudence for the millions. The sagebrush saga had no close rival on prime time television during the late 1950s. During the 1959–60 television season, more than thirty westerns were being produced either for the three networks or, like Ronald Reagan's "Death Valley Days," for syndication. In "Have Gun Will Travel," for example, a cynical soldier-of-fortune named Paladin (played by the sinister-looking Richard Boone) brought order and dispensed justice from the end of his "fast gun-for-hire." The black-clad Paladin pointedly showed how people who were devoted to black-letter legalisms failed to appreciate how "real" law "actually" operated.

Perhaps the most powerful example of the western genre's approach to law and lawyers during the era of "Perry Mason" was John Ford's "The Man Who Shot Liberty Valance" (1962). The first western to co-star James Stewart and John Wayne, "Liberty Valance" consistently compared, in an invidious way, the competing kinds of law championed by Wayne's gunfighter hero and Stewart's idealistic attorney. Stewart's brand of by-the-book-law is not only inadequate to the task of achieving order and justice, but Ransom Stoddard, the lawyer character whom Stewart plays, seems a pompous, self-important windbag, especially when compared to Wayne's Tom Doniphon, the "toughest" man in the territory.

By the late 1950s, John Wayne, especially as his image was represented in John Ford's westerns, had become a highly evocative symbol of the idea that the man with a gun represented the highest form of law. There was simply no competing visual representation — or counter-icon — to celebrate the legal system or the public-minded attorney. In order to become a successful, prime time television show then, "Perry Mason" needed to negotiate the deep-seated, historically-rooted suspicion of law and legal practitioners that still dominated the representations in mass commercial culture.

Worse, Erle Stanley Gardner had been disappointed by an earlier effort to translate his novels into visual images. Shortly after Gardner published the fourth in his series of "Perry Mason" books, he and Warner Brothers signed a film deal. Perry Mason seemed about to embark on a long film career, but his celluloid law practice disbanded after only six cases. Why did the filmic Perry Mason disappear so quickly?

Mason came to the silver screen at a time when Hollywood invariably portrayed attorneys through the "mouthpiece" or "shyster" genre. At worst, Hollywood's shyster cynically manipulated the legal system in the interest of a corrupt client, generally a ruthless gangster; at best, the mouthpiece—the archetypal portrayal came in a film by the same name, "The Mouthpiece" (1932), starring Warren William—displayed a raffish charm but ignored legal ethics and cut procedural corners. The Perry Mason who emerged from Gardner's earliest novels could not fairly be called a shyster, but he was as tough and as hard-boiled as any pulp-fiction detective. (In fact, if the early "Perry Mason" formula had been subjected to a precise cultural analysis, the result would likely have revealed at least two parts detective for every one part lawyer.) Equally as important, Gardner's books presented Perry Mason as the kind of attorney who, in the interest of seeing justice done, might casually ignore the distinction between a fair and a foul legal tactic. Warner Brothers, in fact, selected the original mouthpiece, Warren William, to star in its first Perry Mason film, "The Case of the Howling Dog" (1934).[4]

Trying to look back at the "Perry Mason" films of the 1930s through a lens that inevitably becomes colored by Raymond Burr's portrayal is difficult. Yet Warren William, even if one cannot entirely forget Burr, should still be, especially on the basis of his performance in "The Mouthpiece," an appealing Perry Mason. Moreover, he had earlier replaced William Powell as the super sleuth Philo Vance, a role which would seem to have prepared him for the detective side of the Perry Mason character. And before William fell victim both to changing ideas about how Hollywood would represent its romantic leading men and to personal problems, he seemed poised to translate his resemblance to John Barrymore into stardom in "A"-quality films.

But while "The Case of the Howling Dog" was in production—and while two follow-up Perry Mason films were taking shape—studio heads at Warner Brothers suddenly decreed that the Perry Mason series should add another element. They wanted the breezy banter, borrowed from the earliest screwball comedies, that had proved so successful with William Powell and Myrna Loy in "The Thin Man" (1934). Even if Warren William could have managed to recall William Powell playing Dashiell Hammet's Nick Charles, the studio never supplied a co-star with either the name recognition or the talent of Myrna Loy. When Bette Davis preferred being suspended for breach of contract rather than accepting the role of Della Street, Mason's secretary, Warner Brothers assigned an obscure contract player to play the character.[5]

Gardner disliked the four films that starred Warren William as well as the two other "Perry Mason" pictures that followed. If none of these six films, all of which were budgeted and then produced as "B" pictures, could be called flops, they did not qualify as smash hits either. These films of the 1930s seem most striking for too often allowing Perry Mason to stray from his home turf, the courtroom. In "The Case of the Howling Dog,"

for instance, Mason breaks down the murderer in a drawing room, a setting more appropriate for a detective than an attorney, rather than in a
courtroom. As a result, the classic Perry Mason technique of "discovery-
through-interrogation" loses much of its force. A drawing room, for all
kinds of reasons, hardly evokes the cinematic aura of a courtroom.

In any event, the "Perry Mason" film series lasted only several years.
When Warner Brothers, largely as result of a desire to cut costs, let Warren William leave for another studio, Ricardo Cortez assumed his role
as Perry Mason. Cortez, a veteran of the silent screen, gives the Perry
Mason character a dignity and solemnity—and sense of courtroom gen-
eralship—that anticipate Burr's later portrayal. For the next Perry Mason
film, however, the studio slashed costs again and replaced Cortez with a
capable, but colorless, contract player, Donald Woods. Then, after Woods
starred in "The Case of the Stuttering Bishop" (1937), it canceled its deal
with Gardner. For the next twenty years Perry Mason limited his practice
to pulp novels and a long-running radio series.

Why did the Perry Mason films prove disappointing? Although film
historians can point to a number of "defects" in individual films, Perry
Mason simply came to Hollywood at the wrong time. Taken together,
the six-film series of the 1930s never emerged as a credible alternative to
the shyster genre. But it was not alone in failing to supplant the mouthpiece film with another frame within which to portray a defense lawyer.
Only a relatively few American films made between 1930 and 1960, the
heyday of classic Hollywood, offered what might be considered "positive" representations of a criminal defense attorney such as Perry Mason.

The closest Hollywood came to portraying a criminal lawyer in the
Mason-mold during the 1930s was in John Ford's "Young Mr. Lincoln"
(1939). This film concludes with a Mason-like sequence in which Abra-
ham Lincoln (played by Henry Fonda) literally pulls the evidence that
will acquit his clients out of his top hat and then mercilessly breaks down
the real murderer on (or, to be technical, near) the witness stand. It now
seems difficult to view "Young Mr. Lincoln" without seeing its representation of the intrepid defense lawyer paralleling the depiction of Perry
Mason in the classic "Perry Mason" television series.

"Young Mr. Lincoln," more successfully than the earlier "Perry Mason"
films, manages to transcend the shyster genre. Most obvious, of course,
any film about the life of the Great Emancipator (especially when played
by another American icon, Henry Fonda), even when he is practicing law,
can draw on a vast stock of historical and cultural capital. Even so, the
film takes no chances. It portrays the reel-life Lincoln (as opposed to the
real-life one) as an attorney who doesn't know very much about law; it
shows him to be a person who generally settles disputes through com-
monsense solutions, not complicated legal forms. He prefers what would

now be called "dispute resolution" to litigation. And the film depicts Lincoln merely passing through Springfield, and his legal career, and never settling down to become (as did the real-life Lincoln) an important member of the city's legal community. Lincoln rides into Springfield from screen left. After saving his wrongly accused clients, he walks out of the film's frame, screen right, and into a thunder storm, a somewhat obvious symbol for the Civil War. "Young Mr. Lincoln," in other words, constantly works to represent its heroic lawyer as someone who can, when necessary, work *within* the law to achieve justice but also as someone who resists ever becoming a *permanent* part of the legal machinery itself.[6]

Most other film portrayals of defense lawyers during the 1940s and early 1950s continued to follow the broad outlines of the shyster genre. Anthony Chase correctly argues that Hollywood did begin to film examples of what he calls "the positive image of the virtuous attorney"; but for every portrayal in this mode, I would estimate, there are two or three that remain closer to the mouthpiece model. Especially in the film noir cycle, which became the most important cinematic form in which to do law-and-lawyer pictures, attorneys rarely appear as either a "positive" force for social change or as a "virtuous" individual.[7] Even Raymond Burr, as the astute student of "Perry Mason" lore knows, began his legal-reelist career playing noir villains, most notably the spouse-killing Lars Thorwald in Alfred Hitchcock's "Rear Window" (1954); he was recruited to the "Perry Mason" television project as a possible Hamilton Burger, the ambitious District Attorney. In short, when Erle Stanley Gardner began trying to bring Perry Mason back into view during the 1950s, he needed to construct an appealing televisual framework in which to portray his lawyer-hero.

This task proved to be a challenging—and sometimes frustrating—one. Gardner always feared that his television series, in retaining the lawyer-detective mix, risked becoming "an Alice-in-Wonderland farce out of Never-Never land," especially if writers became tempted to resurrect the Warren William model and to turn Mason into a "smart aleck." Gardner wanted Mason to "be the equivalent of the knight on a white charger riding to the rescue of damsels in distress" but not to seem invincible. Viewers were savvy enough, he believed, to know that Mason was not going to get disbarred and that his client was not going to be convicted. In order to inject greater dramatic tension into the show, he urged that Mason's character, somehow, become more apprehensive about the outcome of his cases and that the scripts try to make the courtroom showdown less of a one-sided battle.[8]

The need for additional dramatic tension in the series, however, could help to exacerbate the problem of developing a television format show that could plausibly claim to reflect actual legal practice, at least in the eyes of viewers who were not lawyers. But Gardner, who himself had been a lawyer before turning to writing, and Eugene Wang, another writer-attorney who became the story editor of the television series, feared that good lawyering would make for bad television.

Eventually, the creators of "Perry Mason" hit upon a stable, yet flexible, formula for mixing a credible (at least in the eyes of most television viewers) vision of legal practice with the generic demands of the dramatic crime show series. The result, in terms of American legal culture, draws from popular images of law and from the conventions of television drama to create a hybrid form in which the lawyer-hero was *above* but not *beyond* the law.

The policing and criminal justice systems, as the detective element in the "Perry Mason" formula required, could not effectively guarantee that they would produce justice. The police and the prosecutor's offices — most memorably represented in the "Perry Mason" series by Lieutenant Arthur Tragg (Ray Collins) and Hamilton Burger (William Tallman) — are not corrupt, uncaring, or even absurdly inept. Once they know what they are supposed to do, their sense of professionalism will carry them through. Their problem, rather, is that they themselves, and the legal machinery they command, consistently head in the wrong direction and thereby rush to judgment. Tragg *always* corrals, and Burger *always* prosecutes, the "wrong" suspect. But in contrast to Alfred Hitchcock's chilling noir thriller, "The Wrong Man" (1956), in which sheer chance rather than brilliant defense lawyering saves a person wrongly accused of a crime, the narrative structure of "Perry Mason" undercuts its own noirish representations and empowers someone who is a member of the legal system to set things right. Here, then, is another way in which the "Perry Mason" formula parallels the narrative structure used, nearly twenty years earlier, in "Young Mr. Lincoln."

The lawyer-turned-film-critic who still insists that "reel-life" law is supposed to — or even can — mirror "real-life" law will always find fault with both Ford's film and Gardner's television series. A view that is more attuned to the nature of visual representation in mass commercial culture, however, suggests a very different way of judging Lincoln's and Mason's fidelity to legal norms. Both Abe Lincoln's and Perry Mason's method of slowing the legal engine and putting it back on the tracks, while unorthodox in terms of real-life standards, never openly conflicts or goes beyond the legal process when judged by legal-reelist norms. As David Ray Papke has suggested, "inaccuracies" in legal-reelist texts generally serve a "purpose."[9] Mason, in particular, remains within the bounds of the legal process at least as those boundaries are represented, through conventions that have now been used in film and television for more than fifty years, in the cultural products that provide jurisprudence for the millions.

In contrast to the western hero, the private detective, and even "Young Mr. Lincoln," Perry Mason never, for example, challenges the legitimacy of, or the necessity for, a complex legal system. In this sense, he resembles the archetypal "organization man" of the 1950s. He is not only loyal to his calling but can effectively manage his own team, Paul Drake (William Hopper) and Della Street (Barbara Hale). And in contrast to Sir Arthur Conan Doyle's Sherlock Holmes or Mickey Spillane's Mike Hammer, Erle Stanley Gardner's legal hero rarely exhibits condescension or contempt for legal insiders. In this important sense, Perry Mason can operate "above" the law without going "beyond" it. Moreover, the legal system—as long as lawyers such as Perry Mason can work *within* the law without being *entirely of the law*—can appear to be a self-correcting mechanism.

In articulating this vision, the classic "Perry Mason," as the media scholar Dennis Bounds has recently suggested, relies on a complex, ten-part narrative structure.[10] In order to consider how the classic "Perry Mason" episodes might work as a set of legal texts, three elements in this narrative formula seem particularly crucial: 1) a client who is not simply wrongly accused of a crime but who can, in fact, be shown to be innocent; 2) a faulty, though seemingly reasonable, view of the case by the criminal justice system; and, 3) Mason's discovery, through the process of adversarial, lawyer-like interrogation, of the correct resolution. Moreover, each individual episode must offer just enough variation to prevent the formula from getting stale or overly predictable.

Perry Mason as Super Lawyer

In order to consider, more precisely, how the "Perry Mason" formula works to create legal texts, I want to look at several episodes (selected at random) from a time period—the early 1960s—in which Perry Mason's law practice had settled into a familiar routine. These episodes, representing the very best of formulaic television, manage to be pretty much the same but, also, pretty much different.

Each episode begins with an opening sequence that features the names of the regular cast members, the haunting "Perry Mason" theme music, and a shot of Perry himself in a court room. The sequence for both "The Case of the Envious Editor" (1961) and "The Case of the Tarnished Trademark" (1962) later became the standard opener for the "Perry Mason" reruns on WTBS. Mason approaches the judge's bench; he picks up a file; he glances quickly at its contents; his face breaks into a look that seems a cross between a knowing smile and an outright smirk; his filmic image turns into a graphic one; and when the camera pulls back, this graphic image now appears in the sword being held by Lady Justice.

Then, the camera immediately cuts to the beginning of the case that Mason will, about fifty minutes later, conclusively resolve.

"The Case of the Prankish Professor," from the 1963 season, begins with a different opening sequence in which Mason is sitting alone, in an otherwise empty court room, reading a case file. The camera, which is initially positioned above Mason, swoops down until it stops at a medium close-up; Mason glances up, pondering what he has just read; he then reprises the smile-to-smirk routine which was used in the 1961 and 1962 sequences; the camera pulls back and up, providing an overhead shot of Mason returning to his file, until it reaches the jury box; finally, just as we, the viewers, are positioned as an imaginary jury, the picture immediately cuts to the story.

These openings are as much a part of the "Perry Mason" formula as the interactions with Hamilton Burger or the discovery-through-interrogation sequence. They instantly reaffirm the fact that Perry Mason is still defending the innocent and that he is, as always, prepared to produce the proper piece of evidence at precisely the right time. In the 1961 and 1962 opener, Mason is symbolically subordinated to the cause of justice: His superior legal talent, the opening graphic might reassure viewers, is merely an instrument that serves the clients whom he represents. His own powerful presence, the graphic further suggests, pales in comparison to the awesome symbol of the legal system itself.

The 1963 opener works, though in a different way, to contain Mason's super lawyer within a larger legal order. When the camera is finally positioned behind the jury box, it symbolically designates ordinary people, including the television viewer at home, as the ultimate legal decision-makers. This same idea, and the camera placement that represents it, is repeated in nearly every "Perry Mason" segment. During the show's initial season, Mason resolved his case before a jury which appeared in the film frame; thereafter, however, no jury was shown. Instead, during the crucial discovery-through-interrogation sequence, the camera is generally placed to one side, so that the television audience is symbolically placed — students of film would use the term "sutured" — into the courtroom scene at the point where the members of a jury would be expected to sit.

The rapid cinematic cut from the opening sequence to the first "facts" of the case serves several purposes. First, it immediately brings the viewer into what will be a crisp, straight-forward narrative. Here, the original "Perry Mason" series, by telling its stories in a simple, linear fashion, without any flashbacks, breaks with the pattern often used in Hollywood's law noirs. It produces a storyline that is complicated enough to create tension but not so tangled that even a Perry Mason might fail to straighten it out.[11] In addition, this narrative structure eliminates any suggestion that Mason aggressively seeks out cases — a charge that Tragg and Burger sometimes level against him. It also underscores the claim, which has become the standard story in legal history, that the common law court system is essentially a "passive" institution; it responds to the disputes that come to its doors, but it does not aggressively seek cases or try to "meddle" in people's lives. In this traditional view, the role of an attorney, even a Perry Mason, is merely to deal with the legal consequences of people's individual actions.

Following the initial scene, each of the three cases I have chosen to study proceeds toward a crime. In "The Case of the Envious Editor," Alyce Aitken (Sara Shane), the wife of the respected but stodgy magazine publisher Edmund Aitken (Philip Abbott), is accused of killing Donald Fletcher (James Coburn). Fletcher has pushed Aitken aside and plans to inject liberal doses of sex, scandal, and sleaze into all of Aitken Publications's magazines in order to boost their circulation figures. Outraged, Aitken begins a counterplan to oust Fletcher, but he finds Fletcher to be so devious that he has already obtained the proxy from Aitken's own wife. When Fletcher is found shot, Tragg arrests Alyce Aitken for murder. The prosecution's theory is that she killed him in revenge for his having obtained her proxy through blackmail.

Of course, viewers immediately recognize that Alyce cannot be guilty, because Mason is her attorney. Thus, attention turns to several other potential suspects: Aitken himself; the cynical editor of a small poetry journal, whom Alyce jilted in order to marry Aitken; Alyce's weird, manipulative sister, Millie Nash; Aitken Publications's business manager, whom Fletcher has been blackmailing; and Lori Stoner (Barbara Lawrence), Fletcher's personal secretary and long-time lover. Alyce, of course, must remain a credible suspect. Tragg has found her fingerprints on a LP record at Fletcher's apartment. A neighbor testifies that he heard this LP playing *after* the time of Fletcher's shooting and saw a woman, who fits Alyce's general description, running from Fletcher's apartment house. Alyce finally admits to Mason that she had gone to see Fletcher and had touched the record but swears that he was still alive when she left.

"The Case of the Tarnished Trademark" has a very similar narrative structure to that of "The Case of the Envious Editor." Another legitimate business — a Danish furniture company owned by Axel Norstad (Karl Swenson) — is sold to the sleazy Martin Summers (Dennis Patrick) who plans to exploit its respected trademark by marketing a line of cheaply made knockoffs with the Norstad logo. The storyline about the factory is paralleled by another in which Norstad, an aging bachelor, becomes infatuated with the younger Edy Morrow (Marie Windsor), a glamorous public relations expert who has promised to help him raise money to build a children's hospital on land adjacent to the furniture factory. After

Summers is found murdered, Axel is eventually arrested. The evidence against Axel, including his bloodstained trousers, continues to mount, and Hamilton Burger suddenly shows up to prosecute the case. Perry Mason becomes Axel's attorney, only to find that his client is withholding information from him because he fears that Edy Morrow may have killed Summers.

"The Case of the Prankish Professor" makes only slight alterations in the "Perry Mason" formula. Here, the supposedly respectable institution, which the narrative quickly reveals to be the site of hidden corruption, is a college campus. The episode begins with an apparent act of senseless violence. Ronald Hewes (Barry Atwater), a creative writing teacher, is gunned down before his horrified class by a suspicious-looking man. It turns out, however, that the "shooting" was a classroom stunt; the professor merely wants to demonstrate the gap between what students have just seen and what they are able to remember when they are asked to write a paper about the incident. But the faux gunman tells Hewes that, after the first blank, the gun contained a clip of live ammunition and that only dumb luck saved him. Professor Hewes is later murdered—by a letter opener rather than a gun—and his ex-wife Laura (Patricia Breslin) is arrested for the crime. Mason steps forward to defend her and, once again, runs up against a client who refuses to tell him all that she knows about the dark corners of the case. Fortunately, though, envy only begins the list of sins with which Hewes might be connected. He turns out to be such a scoundrel that a surplus of alternative suspects soon step forward.

Mason wins all three cases in a similar manner. In each instance, investigator Paul Drake skillfully pursues witnesses, potential perpetrators, and concealed information. Mason carefully sorts through Drake's findings and applies his own trained legal mind to the legal puzzle. Della Street is loyal and supportive. The prosecution is sincere but misguided. The judge (who is likely privy to Mason's win-loss record—and to that of his prosecutorial opponents) remains wise and patient.

Most important, Mason's discovery-through-interrogation skills unmask the real killers. In "The Case of the Envious Editor," Mason demonstrates in court that, contrary to Tragg's claim, someone could have played the LP record without leaving any fingerprints. As the sound of the record fills the courtroom, the camera pans over the face of each of the other suspects, all of whom have already testified, and the astute judge asks Mason whom he wants to recall. Without formally recalling Lori Stoner, the secretary, he accuses her of having killed Fletcher. Standing up in the audience, she breaks down and confesses that she did shoot him—out of jealousy. "Yes, I killed Donald Fletcher, and it was the best thing I ever did in my life." During the final "wrap-up" segment of the narrative,

Mason explains that the neighbor had testified to having heard a "clattering" sound while he saw a woman with blond hair flee Fletcher's apartment, but his client had told him that she had removed her shoes, so as not to alert the neighbor, before she left. A detective's logic—and a lawyer's presumption of a client's innocence—decreed that the killer must be another woman impersonating Alyce.

"The Case of the Tarnished Trademark" offers fewer suspects but compensates for this by adding the Axel-Edy love angle. This storyline heightens the suspense because Marie Windsor, one of the most sinister femme fatales ever to appear in the film noir cycle, brings a strong aura of duplicity to her role as Edy Morrow. Moreover, her role is scripted, and then played, so that it plausibly misdirects the viewer: It appears highly possible that Axel, whom the "Perry Mason" formula requires to be innocent, may be willing to take the fall for Edy, whom he fears is the real killer. But Mason's discovery-through-interrogation routine works so well in this case that it not only unmasks the real killer, a real estate agent who is every bit as shady as Summers, but reveals that Edy just looks—and acts—like a femme fatale. Surprisingly, Marie Windsor has been playing against type; her character genuinely loves Axel! Meanwhile, the real estate agent, true to the "Perry Mason" formula, confesses his guilt. With no hidden clues to be explained, the "wrap-up" can turn on the comical (at least for this series) contrast between Edy and Axel, who are off on a honeymoon, and Street and Mason, whose "affair" remains as platonic as ever.

"The Case of the Prankish Professor" employs the same multitude-of-suspects strategy as the "The Case of the Envious Editor." Was the raunchy academic killed by the student who blames him for the death of his own former girlfriend? Is the killer his dead girlfriend's sister, who has discovered that Professor Hewes secretly turned a paper that she had once ghostwritten for her sibling into a best-selling pulp novel? If this trashy book is ever connected to the professor, scandal would engulf the dead girl's family and nearly everyone still connected with the campus. Might not, then, the killer be Esther Metcalfe (Constance Towers), the wife of the head of the English Department, who is a recovering alcoholic and a person whose sordid past is hidden within the plagiarized book? Or is it the distinguished Dr. Metcalfe himself (Kent Smith)? He might have killed his own colleague in order to protect his wife's now-fragile sobriety and her reputation.

Once again, Mason correctly sorts out the suspects and elicits a courtroom confession from Esther Metcalfe, the professor's wife. She stabbed Professor Hewes, she sobs, as an act of self-defense, after he tried to extort money from her and then assaulted her. She was ready to step forward, she claims, whenever it appeared as if Mrs. Hewes might actually be convicted of the crime. The "wrap-up" to this episode serves to cast additional aspersions on the character of the dead professor and to indicate that Perry Mason himself will represent Esther Metcalfe and enter a plea of self-defense at her trial. It appears doubtful, though, that this case—in which a defendant is not entirely "innocent"—will make it on to television.

Conclusion

In wrapping up one's own episode on "Perry Mason" as a legal text, it is appropriate to stress two central elements in the formula that dictated the shape of almost all of the 271 original episodes. First, the issue is never whether the legal system will convict an innocent person—Perry Mason would never let that happen—but on *how* the great attorney will rise *above* the day-to-day legal processes, while not straying *beyond* the legal system, in order to see that justice prevails. Mason's virtuoso performance provides reassurance that the legal system, at least when a heroic attorney is on the case, really does serve the citizenry.

Second, when viewing a "Perry Mason" episode as a legal text, it is important to remember that the formula also requires a full, unequivocal confession by the guilty party. There can be no O.J. Simpson (or Esther Metcalfe) cases on "Perry Mason." This vital element in the formula operates, once again, in a reassuring manner. Mason's awesome legal powers can seem to be limited by the requirement that they be used to induce people—both his clients who wish to reveal only parts of what they know and the guilty party who wants to conceal virtually all of what they know—to break their silence and speak truthfully.

Mason cannot be accused, in other words, of coercing confessions out of people who become confused or overwhelmed by his powerful legal performances. This formula provided the means by which "Perry Mason" could offer both dramatic entertainment and a "realistic" view of the legal system. It also permitted the show's super-hero to appear above but not beyond the law. Throughout the series, then, Perry Mason is acting as the agent of a higher power—perhaps the secular legal system, perhaps a higher law, perhaps both—that demands not simply justice but THE TRUTH.

10

Picket Fences

Douglas E. Abrams

"Scarcely any political question arises in the United States that is not resolved, sooner or later, into a judicial question."[1] So wrote Alexis de Tocqueville more than a century and a half ago in his classic study of American institutions. A modern de Tocqueville would feel right at home in Rome, Wisconsin, the fictional town whose courtroom dominated "Picket Fences" on CBS from 1992 to 1996.

Rome was not your typical small midwestern town because week in and week out, prosecutions and civil lawsuits implicated nearly all the decade's hot-button social issues. Only a narrow threshold separated real-life headlines from the drama that unfolded in Rome's Hogan County courthouse.

Trials explored such vexing education issues as school desegregation, separation of church and state, and drugs and violence in the public schools. Also on the docket were family issues, including surrogate parenthood, child abuse, children's right to divorce their parents, and parental rights in custody battles against non-parent relatives.

Medical litigation explored issues ranging from physician-assisted suicide, euthanasia, and the rights of HIV-infected persons to fathers's rights in prenatal decisionmaking, the right to life and the right to die, fetal tissue experimentation on patients with Parkinson's disease, cryonics, and religious rights to refuse medical treatment.

"Picket Fences" also focused the spotlight on Native American sacred burial ground rights, homelessness, federal sentencing guidelines, sexual abuse notification statutes, sexual harassment, drunk driving, domestic violence, vigilantism, police misconduct, animal rights, date rape, and lawyers's ethics.

Once viewers suspended any disbelief about how so many divisive issues kept finding their way into one small-town court with such regularity, they were treated to creative screenplay, superb acting, and some of the best television drama in recent memory. For lawyers and others loyal to syndicated reruns, "Picket Fences" will remain a mirror reflecting the profound issues that have moved our generation.

A Strong Cast

A strong cast was a necessary foundation.[2] In one way or another, most of the courtroom proceedings embroiled the Brock family. Sheriff Jimmy Brock (Tom Skerritt) enforced many of the challenged laws and arrested many of the defendants. His wife, surgeon Jill Brock (Kathy Baker), was at the center of medical controversies. Their three children, Kimberly, Matthew, and Zachary, found themselves as parties or witnesses in more lawsuits than your average 9-to-16-year-olds. Kimberly also spent her high school senior year working as a part-time legal assistant to Douglas Wambaugh, Rome's leading defense attorney. Sheriff Brock's top deputies, Kenny Lacos and Maxine Stewart (Costas Mandylor and Lauren Holly), were central players in the legal drama. If all this were not enough, the legal process also dogged the coroner and Rome's succession of mayors, which included Academy Award winner Marlee Matlin.

Then there were the imposing courtroom protagonists. The lawyers appearing before Judge Henry Bone (Ray Walston) demonstrated once again that in a quality television drama series, criminal and civil litigation can emerge as an art form. The best episodes culminated with defense attorney Wambaugh (Fyvush Finkel) in a trial that placed the week's social issue squarely in Judge Bone's lap. Wambaugh's most formidable adversary was District Attorney John Littleton (Don Cheadle).

For Walston, as he approached the age of eighty, "Picket Fences" climaxed more than a half century of dramatic and comedy roles on stage, screen, and television. In the 1950s, he starred on stage and screen in "South Pacific" and "Damn Yankees" (winning the 1956 Tony Award for best actor in a musical as the devil Mr. Applegate). The 1960s saw him star as the lovable alien in "My Favorite Martian," the situation comedy that aired on CBS from 1963 to 1966. In the 1970s and 1980s, he appeared in such films as "The Sting" (1973) and "Fast Times at Ridgemont High" (1982).

A child actor in New York's Yiddish theater more than six decades ago, Finkel spent a dozen years on stage in "Fiddler on the Roof," and more recently had film roles in "Brighton Beach Memoirs" (1986), "Seize the Day" (1986), "Q & A" (1990), and "Nixon" (1995). Cheadle's resume recites more than a dozen film roles, plus television guest appearances on "China Beach" and "Hill Street Blues."

A National Civics Lesson

Judge Bone and the lawyers left an indelible mark on courtroom drama because their trials were national civics lessons. Testimony appeared only in small doses, no more than a few questions at a time. Most fact development occurred outside the courthouse because television tends to avoid prolonged testimony, which appears tedious on screen, as it frequently does in real life. "Picket Fences" reserved testimony for specific purposes, usually to permit observation of witnesses wrestling with their consciences, to snare witnesses in inconsistencies, or to enable them to make an identification or other crucial disclosure.

With testimony truncated, the "Picket Fences" civics lessons emerged during counsel's opening statements and closing arguments. To maintain the show's dramatic cadence, these addresses minimized the customary previewing or marshaling of evidence. Counsel concentrated on advocating their contrary positions, freely mixing public policy pleas with legal argument. Each side had fair opportunity to present its points, without evident favoritism from the show's writers.

Given Americans's passion for so many of the issues the show tackled, many viewers doubtlessly began the hour with strong opinions and perhaps with their minds made up. The lawyers's eloquence challenged us to pause and think, perhaps even to reevaluate our opinions, but at least to grant the contrary position a respectful hearing.

With some viewers likely inching toward intellectual limbo after closing arguments, Judge Bone would usually render his decision or his comment on the jury verdict from the bench. Sometimes he made his views known only afterwards in chambers. In either event, he would review the opposing arguments, discuss the issues's intractability, and offer perspectives on the underlying legal and policy questions, often candidly acknowledging that the trial's lingering moral issues were incapable of ready resolution.

The beauty of the screenplay was that the lawyers gave partisans of conflicting viewpoints such potent intellectual ammunition that viewers could freely disagree with Judge Bone (and with the show's writers, if you happened to believe they occasionally articulated their own policy preferences by speaking through the judge). Like any worthwhile lesson about law and social policy, the lessons crafted by Judge Bone and the lawyers invited the audience to think by presenting the opposing arguments without dictating which conclusion to reach.

The Genius of "Picket Fences"

Why did "Picket Fences" win such critical acclaim, including Emmy Awards for outstanding drama series in its first two seasons?[3] One reason was the stellar cast, which garnered the lion's share of the show's other twelve Emmys. Setting the pace were Kathy Baker with three Emmys for outstanding lead actress in a drama series, Ray Walston with two for outstanding supporting actor, and Tom Skerritt and Fyvush Finkel with one each for outstanding lead actor and outstanding supporting actor respectively. In 1992–93, "Picket Fences" became only the third show to win Emmys for outstanding drama series, outstanding lead actor, and outstanding lead actress in the same season. (The earlier shows to accomplish this feat were "The Waltons" in 1972–73 and "Hill Street Blues" in 1980–81.)

Another reason for the critical acclaim showered on "Picket Fences" was the inherent excitement of courtroom drama on the small screen. Never mind that trials are actually relatively rare events in our legal system, which disposes of about 90% of civil and criminal filings by settlement, plea bargain, dismissal, or other informal adjustment.[4] For decades, trials have gripped the television audience because they are the civilized equivalent of combat. The courtroom is the arena. Lawyers are the combatants, armed with ideas rather than swords, battling with intellect rather than physical prowess.

Neither a strong cast nor the courtroom, however, guarantees critical acclaim. This volume chronicles television's best courtroom dramas, but numerous other courtroom dramas (including ones graced with talented acting) have quickly fallen by the wayside, unable to make the grade.

Courtroom drama succeeds best on television when talented acting complements screenplays that reflect the contemporary circumstance. Television is preeminently a medium of mass entertainment, but "Picket Fences" succeeded in the early 1990s because its courtroom format did more than merely entertain. In a time of strident national debate about divisive social issues, "Picket Fences" challenged viewers to examine their beliefs about these issues. The national civics lessons presented by Rome's judge and lawyers were distinctive, almost embracing an interactive format that invited viewers to empathize with the cast's struggle to resolve the legal and moral uncertainties emerging from the courtroom. At the end of an episode's entertainment, it was mighty difficult just to go about your business or switch channels to lighter fare. The lingering uncertainties did not let go of you quite that easily.

"Picket Fences's" gifted creator was David E. Kelley, a former Boston lawyer who penned many of "L.A. Law's" most memorable episodes, including ones that presaged "Picket Fences" by grappling with a variety of public policy issues. Kelley deftly used Rome's Hogan County courthouse as something more than a vehicle for producing drama, though the drama was unrivaled. "Picket Fences" barely survived its fourth season, when new writers replaced Kelley and largely abandoned the issue-oriented courtroom format to plumb the cast members's personalities. But even in the show's twilight, the periodic issue-oriented courtroom episodes remained among television's best offerings.

The next section provides a glimpse of "Picket Fences" through highlights of selected episodes. The final section uses these episodes to discuss the impact of Judge Bone and Rome's lawyers on popular perceptions of American law.

A "Picket Fences" Legal Sampler

Education and Family Issues

Does violence in the media adversely affect children's behavior?[5] Will civil liberties be an early casualty of the battle against violent juvenile crime?[6] Both questions react to soaring violent juvenile crime arrest rates and to dire forecasts of an even grimmer short-term future. After more than a decade of relative stability, the rate of juvenile arrests for violent crimes increased more than 50% between 1988 and 1994 before declining slightly in 1995 and 1996.[7] One leading criminologist has warned that the United States is in "the lull before the crime storm" because the crime-prone male 14-to-17-year-old population will increase by 23% by the year 2005.[8]

Lawmakers and a majority of the American people have concluded that pervasive media violence affects the behavior of some juveniles.[9] To enable parents to block television programming they deem too violent for their children, congressional legislation requires installation of the V-chip in all televisions manufactured beginning in 1998. To help inform parents about program content, the television industry has instituted a rating system amid pressure from a Congress seemingly ready to mandate such a system.[10]

States and localities have sought to combat juvenile crime with such measures as curfews, school uniforms, and random drug testing of elementary and secondary students.[11] President Clinton has even suggested that teenagers be required to submit to drug testing as a condition for securing a driver's license.[12] The likely efficacy of these measures has produced spirited public debate, while courts are left to determine their impact on civil liberties.

Judge Bone confronted the media violence and civil liberties questions in two 1994 episodes entitled "Guns 'R Us" and "Remote Control." The episodes opened with thirteen-year-old Timmy Hendricks shooting classmate Matthew Brock in the chest with a .38 caliber revolver from ten feet away in the junior high hallway. The assault left Matthew temporarily paralyzed and initiated a chain of events that threatened to cost Jimmy Brock his position as Sheriff.

The shooting climaxed a feud that began when a group of high school kids entered the boys's restroom by an open window and, through the haze of cigarette smoke, singled out Matthew, roughed him up, and dunked him head-first in a toilet. The high school troublemakers included Jason Hendricks, Timmy's older brother.

To get even a few days later, Matthew and younger brother Zach hid in the bushes alongside an icy winter road and shot a potato spud gun at Jason's blue Camaro as he drove home from wrestling practice. The Brock boys meant only to dent the vehicle. Instead, the potato shattered the windshield, and Jason suffered two broken lumbar vertebrae when he lost control, flipped the car over into a ditch, and remained pinned inside until Dr. Jill Brock and paramedics extricated him from the upended vehicle.

Timmy retaliated by taking his parents's revolver from their locked safe, whose combination he and his older brother knew. Concealing the weapon in his book bag, he confronted Matthew in the hallway after school and fired a single shot that lodged a half centimeter from Matthew's spine, leaving him paralyzed from the abdomen down with doctors uncertain about the permanence of the damage. With growing numbers of public school students bringing guns or other weapons to school, and with about 70% of Americans identifying drugs and violence as problems in the public schools, this televised shooting was grounded in realism, even though the scene was a small town in middle America.[13]

After a hastily arranged search of junior high and high school lockers uncovered a cache of firearms, Rome's mayor Rachel Harris responded. Some of her initiatives, well beyond those tested in localities throughout the nation, were obviously extreme. Newly-enacted Rome town ordinances, for example, banned handguns except for the police and required citizens to be fingerprinted. Random highway checkpoints would make criminals "think twice" about entering Rome.

Several of the mayor's initiatives, however, sounded strikingly familiar to viewers who follow the headlines. Metal detectors would be installed at all junior high and high school entrances, and school lockers would be searched weekly. The school library would be purged of books deemed violent, such as John Steinbeck's *Of Mice and Men*. Using the threat of franchise non-renewal as leverage, the town began pressuring the local cable company to scramble images of "all television shows that we think are too violent," including "N.Y.P.D. Blue" and (as the stammering Mayor Harris put it during a news conference) "Beaver and Butt-face."

The divided Brock family debated the civil liberties concerns that have accompanied efforts to combat juvenile crime. While his son lay paralyzed in Memorial Hospital, Sheriff Brock asserted that the fingerprinting and highway checkpoint ordinances were unconstitutional and refused to enforce them. "What about basic civil rights?," he demanded of Mayor Harris. "Safety first," she tersely responded.

Jill Brock also remained skeptical of her husband's defiance. "Maybe we have more freedom than we know what to do with.... So we fingerprint? So we stop a few cars, and we search for guns? What's the worst that can happen? A few less people get shot? A few less criminals get away, maybe?"

With Judge Bone sitting as a juvenile court judge, Timmy pleaded to attempted murder and proceeded to the dispositional hearing the next day. The court also heard criminal charges lodged against Sheriff Brock for refusing to surrender his badge after the mayor fired him for insubordination.

The juvenile dispositional hearing was a primer on the effects of media violence on children. As expert witnesses summarized existing studies, Wambaugh's effort to establish mitigating circumstances resembled the "television intoxication" defense unsuccessfully advanced in a celebrated 1977 Florida prosecution of a fifteen-year-old who shot his 83-year-old neighbor to death during a failed burglary and fled in her car to Disney World.[14]

"Video mayhem," Wambaugh began his closing argument, "is out of control," exposing children to "brainwashing" from violence brought daily "right into the living room." "On morning cartoons," he continued, "a child witnesses twenty violent acts per hour. Video games at the mall are called Total Carnage and Captain Destroyer." Violent stimuli transcend popular entertainment. "Our heroes like Clint Eastwood cock the trigger and say 'make my day,' a quote later used and glorified by President Reagan. President Bush and President Clinton, why, their popularity in the polls soared when they sent men to battle in Iraq and Somalia." "We love to fight. We love to kill," Wambaugh concluded. "It's the American way."

Wambaugh acknowledged that his young client shot Matthew Brock, but he asserted that "we all have to take responsibility." Evoking an African proverb that provided the title of Hillary Rodham Clinton's best-selling book shortly after the "Picket Fences" episodes aired, Wambaugh argued that "it takes a whole village to raise a child," and that the village fails when popular entertainment exposes children to incessant violence.[15]

District Attorney Littleton resisted the defense's effort to try the media. "[I]f we want to use television and movies as a scapegoat for all the mayhem in our country," he argued, "then our society is diseased beyond repair." He urged the court to examine other industrialized societies. "Toronto," he began, "gets the same television, the same movies, the same video games as Chicago. In Chicago there are a thousand handgun murders a year. In Toronto, fifteen. Television programs in Japan are ten times more violent than American programs, yet violent crimes in that country are almost nonexistent."[16]

The district attorney concluded with a plea for personal responsibility: "Yes, video violence may desensitize our kids. But if you really want to desensitize them,... [s]end [Timmy Hendricks] back to the playground and let the sociologists debate the influence of Ninja Turtles.... Society's problem, yes, no question, but he is guilty of attempted murder."

With Jason Hendricks and Matthew Brock each on the road to recovery, Judge Bone sentenced Timmy to indefinite confinement in a juvenile facility. After dismissing the criminal charges against Sheriff Brock, the judge assumed his role as Rome's conscience. "You want to go home and blame television for what transpired here, feel free," he challenged the adults assembled in the courtroom, "but don't forget to condemn yourselves in the process." "Mr. Wambaugh is right," he lectured from the bench, "it takes an entire village to raise a child. And this village is failing horribly." "I don't know how to fix it, but the answer can't be in the obliteration of civil rights.... We can't be exalting fear and retribution at a time we need vision and education.... [A] government has to respect and trust its citizenry."

Medical Issues

What ethical limits constrain a person's right to donate organs? In a gripping 1994 episode entitled "Abominable Snowman" that also examined the rights of a homeless, mentally-ill Vietnam veteran named Frank Teacher, the court explored this question when Kevin Buss, a forty-year-old widower with three young children, suffered a massive coronary brought on by previously undiagnosed congenital heart disease. With the nation's homeless population continuing to grow,[17] and with advancing medical technology raising ethical dilemmas unanticipated even a generation ago, viewers confronted issues that are likely to hold the nation's attention in the coming years.

After determining that Kevin would live only two or three weeks without a new heart, Jill put him on the emergency list for a transplant. Because the nationwide shortage of available donor hearts left the outlook bleak, Kevin's seventy-year-old father, Howard, pressed his wish to donate his heart to his son. The elder Buss suffered from Alzheimer's disease diagnosed by Jill a year earlier. "My brain is rotting away," he implored her, adding that he wished to die "with some dignity" and "give my son life."

Howard's request tested the frontiers of medical ethics. Where living persons have wished to be donors, the organ involved has been a kidney or some other organ that would not necessarily result in the donor's death. Courts have not yet been called on to decide whether persons, in effect, may commit physician-assisted suicide through organ donation.[18]

At the same time, Rome authorities sought to banish Teacher, who lived huddled in a nearby cave during Wisconsin's harsh winter. After the sheriff's office tracked him down with dogs and apprehended him at gunpoint, Deputy Stewart told him he could not lawfully live in Rome. "There's a town ordinance against sleeping on public property. That means if you sleep in Rome, you're committing a crime.... If you're on someone's land uninvited, you're trespassing."

Rome had no homeless shelter. Mayor Harris refused to build one to care for "such a minuscule minority," explaining that Rome could not afford the cost and did not wish to risk attracting homeless people. After Judge Bone refused to dismiss Teacher's suit to compel the town to provide housing, however, the anxious mayor had a change of heart. She and the town counsel offered Teacher a confidential $8,000 cash settlement to leave Rome and agree never to return.[19] With his counsel Wambaugh at his side, Teacher rejected the offer.

Fearing the specter of murder charges, Thayer Hospital refused to permit the proposed Buss transplant surgery without a court order. Appearing before Judge Bone, the hospital's counsel likened the surgery not to physician-assisted suicide, but to the difficult life-and-death decisions physicians make "every single day in every hospital across this country." Doctors decide whether to transplant a vital organ into one candidate or another, whether to separate Siamese twins who share vital organs, or whether to end a vegetative patient's life support. These and similar decisions determine who will live and who will die. With Howard Buss beyond help and his son capable of cure, the hospital assailed any conception of public policy that would say "it is better to let a forty-year-old man die of heart failure while forcing his seventy-year-old father to suffer the lingering torture of having his mind and his dignity destroyed by Alzheimer's."

To the special state attorney, however, the dispositive issue was "the meaning of life." He argued that the Buss transplant surgery would empower doctors to make "subjective determinations about whose life has more merit," an Alzheimer's patient or a cancer patient, for example, or an apparently healthy person. "Do we really want to start heading down that slope?" In the end, Judge Bone refused to authorize the transplant of Howard Buss's heart. "I will not sit up here as a judge and deem your life worthy of termination. That job belongs to a much higher power."

The court, however, found in Teacher's favor. "There's nothing in our federal or state constitutions that guarantees shelter," Judge Bone reasoned. "We can guarantee a person's right not to be searched in his dwelling. We just can't provide the dwelling. We make people work for it. They have to earn a house."

Because Frank Teacher was a mentally-ill Vietnam veteran, however, the court found his case different and ordered the town to provide housing: "We took these kids at the age of eighteen, mortgaged their future, and put them in a war. They came back psychologically battered, many to the point where they were not really employable." Now that the Vietnam War's devastating effect on its veterans has been acknowledged even by most of the nation's leaders who waged it, Judge Bone's novel legal determination invited viewers to engage in collective soul-searching. "An implied social contract was formed between government and these men," he ruled. "The consideration should be mutual."

As it turned out, Wambaugh never had an opportunity to enforce the judgment. After Teacher failed to appear for the court's ruling, Deputy Stewart searched his cave and found him frozen inside. When Jill pronounced him dead of hypothermia minutes later at the hospital, she noticed an organ donor card in his wallet. In a dramatic turnabout, a surgical team immediately transplanted his heart into Kevin. "This donor had a good heart," a team member remarked as the organ began beating strongly. "*Very* good," Jill echoed, remembering the man the entire town had scorned in life a few decades after he had served his country in battle.

Legal Ethics

What measures may a criminal defense lawyer ethically take to free a defendant the lawyer knows or suspects is guilty of the acts charged?[20] Even before fear of crime gripped the nation in the 1990s, the defense bar had endured scathing criticism for helping set criminals free by securing acquittals or dismissals of charges, sometimes assertedly by resort to sharp tactics. Criticism only increased as television brought one celebrity trial after another into our living rooms, often with high-priced counsel appearing for defendants whose guilt the public had determined before the presentation of evidence in open court.

Rome tested the constraints of advocacy when Wambaugh defended Brian Latham, a young drifter charged with the grizzly murder of Susan Engrams, a sixteen-year-old who had disappeared after an angry argument with her parents at home. In five episodes that aired in the fall of 1994 — "Survival of the Fittest," "Systematic Abuse," "Rebels With Causes," "May It Please the Court," and "For Whom the Wind Blows" — the evidence against Latham was entirely circumstantial, a conundrum commonly faced by criminal juries throughout the nation.

Defense counsel Wambaugh instructed the sheriff's office not to speak to the accused in jail. With the office stymied in its effort to find the girl's body or direct physical evidence incriminating Latham, Deputy Kenny Lacos ignored these instructions and initiated a conversation with the prisoner in the cellblock. Latham reasserted his innocence but, after Lacos prevailed on the prisoner's religious beliefs, indicated that the deputy might search a local pond. The sheriff's office found the girl's body, wrapped and weighted down, at the bottom of the pond with eleven stab wounds.

Despite United States Supreme Court decisions indicating that Lacos's jailhouse conversation violated Latham's constitutional rights, Judge Bone denied the motion to suppress the conversation and evidence arising from it. The circumstantial case appeared strong even with no murder weapon, no eyewitness, and no blood found on Latham or his belongings. The jury heard that Latham was last seen with the victim, that his footprints were at the pond, that he directed Deputy Lacos to the pond, and that he had a felony record for breaking and entering. (District Attorney Littleton also said a teenage girl was ready to testify that Latham had threatened her at knifepoint two years earlier, but this testimony would be admissible only if the defendant put his own character into evidence.)

Taking the stand in his own defense, Latham admitted that he and Susan had been together in her car shortly before she disappeared and that they began wrestling when he tried having sex, but he testified that he backed off and left in his truck when she refused. Hair and fibers found in the car all belonged to the victim, her family, or the defendant. Wambaugh charged that the sheriff's office had rushed to judgment, arresting Latham without investigating possible involvement by the Engrams family.

Wambaugh raised eyebrows with his dogged defense of the man already adjudged guilty in the court of public opinion. Sixteen-year-old Kimberly Brock, a friend of the dead girl, offered her dubious nine-year-old brother Zach a textbook rationale for the defense counsel's role on behalf of unpopular clients. "The state has to prove guilt before they can lock somebody up. The defense attorneys have to make sure that the burden of proof is met in every case. It's all about protecting our system of justice. So when defense attorneys represent guilty people, they're nevertheless protecting the system. And by doing that, the innocent are served." Zach insisted he still did not understand. "You will when you're old enough," his sister reassured him. "He killed somebody, and you're helping him," Zach replied. "How old do I have to get?"

Zach was not the only one who left the bedroom conversation unconvinced. Wambaugh provided a much different answer the next day when Kimberly questioned her boss about why "it's proper procedure for lawyers to navigate around the truth." Defense counsel was frank with his legal assistant. "The system of justice... doesn't always mean that the players should act justly.... [T]he truth is supposed to be a product of the adversary process. So yes, that means both sides try to win at all costs." "Even when it means we're trying to free a guilty killer?," Kimberly persisted. "I try not to ask myself such tricky questions," Wambaugh conceded.

Rome cheered Latham's first-degree murder conviction, and the appeal proceeded to the United States Supreme Court, which heard oral argument from Wambaugh and Littleton. Wambaugh lost when the justices (nine look-alike actors who conducted an oral argument uncanny in its realism) swiftly overruled precedent and upheld the conviction.

With lingering doubt about an earlier rush to judgment, Sheriff Brock's office reopened the investigation. Susan's mother confessed to the stabbing at the pond, where she and her husband had encountered the girl after she left Latham following the family quarrel. Wambaugh's dogged defense of an innocent man had come full circle, from the Hogan County courthouse to the highest court in the land and back again.

The "Picket Fences" Legacy

In this volume devoted to scholarly analysis of television's effects on American law, I cannot resist the threshold temptation to say simply that watching "Picket Fences" was just plain fun. The show provided a steady menu of charismatic acting, creative storylines, and heady unpredictability. All this drama without descending to the depths of gratuitous violence that has infected so much entertainment programming in recent years.

Violence was part of some "Picket Fences" episodes, as Matthew Brock's shooting and the aftermath of Susan Engrams's stabbing demonstrate. A drama featuring law enforcement officers and lawyers must necessarily feature crime, including violent crime. But "Picket Fences" never exalted violence, and never resorted to it as a cheap substitute for thoughtful writing and acting. Indeed, Timmy Hendricks's juvenile confinement and the belated arrest of Susan Engrams's mother illustrate the stern condemnation and eventual sanction that awaited purveyors of violent acts in Rome. Television critics had much basis for advancing "Picket Fences" as the sort of quality dramatic series that might suffer if self-censorship accompanied the V-chip or the incipient rating system.[21]

What impact have the "Picket Fences" lawyers had on America? In the short term, they have drawn renewed attention to the ambivalence many Americans feel for the legal profession. On the one hand, polls have reported a low public regard for the profession. In a 1995 *U.S. News and World Report* poll, for example, 69% of respondents said lawyers are only sometimes honest or not usually honest, and 56% said lawyers use the system to protect the powerful and enrich themselves.[22] Lawyer jokes were by no means unknown in earlier generations, but their contemporary popularity seems rooted in a core antipathy because humor disparaging an insular group persists only when it reflects perceptions of the target held by sizeable segments of the public.

On the other hand, "Picket Fences" continued the trend that has seen the courtroom captivate dramatic television audiences,[23] with lawyers portrayed as positive role models in the vast majority of episodes. One recent study found that the ratio of positive-to-negative portrayals of television lawyers was 2 to 1 from the mid-1950s to the mid-1960s, 6 to 1 from the mid-1970s to the late 1980s, and a hefty 10 to 1 in the first month of the 1992–93 prime time season.[24] With Neilsen ratings closely watched by network executives and advertisers alike, we can postulate that screenwriters endeavor to provide the sort of entertainment they believe the audience desires.

If audience desires are the touchstone, perhaps quality courtroom dramas like "Picket Fences" remain popular at least partly because their generally positive portrayal of lawyers comports with a sometimes unarticulated respect television viewers hold for the legal profession. Judge Bone's strength of character was the indispensable glue that helped hold Rome together. Wambaugh and his adversaries were articulate and thoughtful even in defeat. Wambaugh himself was cantankerous and obstinate at times, but he also had a good mind and a good heart, marked by passion for his clients and concern for his friends and the Rome community. He may have openly sought out retainers, but he never turned his back on people like Frank Teacher and Brian Latham, who obviously could not pay for his representation.

Most Americans never hire a lawyer except to write a will, and never set foot in a courtroom unless they happen to serve briefly as a juror. Their most lasting visual impressions of the legal process come from television. All in all, proceedings in the Hogan County courthouse helped polish the legal profession's image. As the judge and lawyers grappled with fundamental social issues, their thoughtful devotion reassured viewers that the nation is governed by the rule of law, even as law remains an essentially fallible human institution needing ongoing reflection and reform.

Courtroom drama also remains popular on television because Americans are fascinated by what lawyers do, or at least by what dramatic programming generally has portrayed them doing. The portrayal has not been, and could not be, thoroughly faithful to the realities of contemporary law practice.

Law books lined the shelves of Douglas Wambaugh's office and Judge Bone's chambers, but no one ever reported cracking a *Shepards* volume or otherwise engaging in legal research. In one episode, a murder trial began one day after the crime. Judge Bone frequently decided ultimate issues from the bench after taking matters under advisement for little more than a few hours.

In the Brian Latham prosecution and other matters alike, Judge Bone and the lawyers knew relevant case law and statutes, thanks to a lawyer-screenwriter who had done his homework.[25] Because the players were so evidently articulate and well-prepared, the implication was that they too had done their homework. But for all we could see, Rome's lawyers spent barely any late nights on trial preparation, never entered a law library to research points of law, and never filed briefs or engaged in formal pretrial discovery. Nor was it apparent whether the judge ever wrote orders or opinions.

As a general matter, this dramatic license is perfectly acceptable because television endeavors to entertain, not to provide career counseling for viewers wishing to learn how real-world professionals spend their days. Law practice necessarily bears little resemblance to the unstinting adrenaline rushes that have dominated television drama for decades because tedium and petty annoyances pass unseen when days, weeks, or even months are compressed into an hour on the screen. Most viewers would not want or expect it any other way.

Dramatic license is particularly acceptable with a show like "Picket Fences," whose courtroom drama achieved a lofty purpose that transcended mere entertainment. The most enduring legacy of Rome's judge and lawyers was their graceful use of the judicial forum as a medium for creative national civics lessons that thoughtfully examined fundamental social issues. The midwestern small-town setting inevitably left some pressing urban issues largely unexplored, much as the urban settings of many other courtroom dramas have not provided ready forums for exploring essentially small-town issues. But "Picket Fences" established a new nationwide standard because no courtroom drama series had ever immersed itself so regularly, and so effectively, in such a broad range of public policy questions.[26]

The "Picket Fences" touch did not stop at public policy. In the 1996 episode "Winner Takes All," for example, the father coaching Zach's youth basketball team suffered a mild heart attack on the sidelines during a game while berating his young charges and baiting the referee. When Jill stepped in as coach for the balance of the season, her attitude swiftly changed from "we're going to have fun" to "win at all costs."

Fed up with parents and coaches who were taking the fun out of the game and regularly benching less talented players in favor of the talented few, Zach and his teammates and virtually all the league's other 100 players formed an association called "Save Our Sports." SOS engaged Wambaugh, who successfully sued to enjoin Jill and the other parents from coaching or attending games for the remaining two months of the season. After Judge Bone decried "the ridiculous importance we attach to winning," the kids managed their own league, emphasizing fun through wholesome competition while fairly allocating playing time. As a youth ice hockey coach for the past thirty years, I welcomed the dramatic use of civil litigation to highlight the impact of overly-aggressive parents and coaches, a persistent problem infecting youth leagues throughout the nation even though it does not intrude on public policy.[27]

Professor Bernard J. Ward called judges "the indispensable teachers of the American people," conducting seminars "every day from the classrooms of [their] courtrooms."[28] Other scholars have also found education compatible with judging, particularly in the Supreme Court but also below.[29]

For his part, Chief Justice William H. Rehnquist has rejected educative decisionmaking on the ground that judges hold authority only to resolve disputes between adverse parties, a constitutional role he believes is at least sometimes incompatible with judicial pedagogy.[30] We need not take sides in a jurisprudential debate, however, to relish television drama that uses the judicial process to invite, and indeed challenge, viewers to draw their own lessons about provocative public issues.

Television has become a significant source of information for Americans of all ages, and a significant influence on the way we perceive the world around us.[31] Ninety-eight percent of American households own at least one set, more than the number of households that have indoor plumbing.[32] The average American adult spends about thirty hours a week — a quarter of all waking hours — watching television.[33] The average child or adolescent watches between 21 and 23 hours a week, spending more time in front of the screen than in any other out-of-school activity except sleep.[34] Newton N. Minow, a former chairman of the Federal Communications Commission, has lamented that many children spend more time with television than with their parents, and that many parents spend more time with television than with their children.[35] By the time the average American child reaches the age of 70, he or she will have spent the equivalent of about seven to ten years watching television.[36]

For better or worse, our attitudes about public policy may be influenced not only by the newscasts, political interview shows, and magazine shows that occupy our time, but also by weekly comedy and dramatic programming, the occasional dramatic miniseries, and even the sometimes seamy "tabloid" talk shows. For four years, "Picket Fences" demonstrated that a courtroom drama series can assume a meaningful place in the public discourse, reaching citizens whose knowledge of the law comes primarily from the media rather than from judicial opinions, statutory codes, or other primary sources.

The eloquent arguments of defense counsel Wambaugh and his adversaries, and Judge Bone's equally eloquent decisions and commentary, presented countervailing policy positions as well as (and perhaps better than) anchors or guests would likely do in a talk show or news panel format. If one were seeking a concise-yet-balanced expression of opposing positions on the effects of media violence on children, for example, an hour of television could provide no better resource than the episodes that treated Matthew Brock's near-fatal shooting and the ensuing juvenile proceeding.

Conclusion

By the time Rome, Wisconsin left our television screens in June 1996, "Picket Fences" had helped to illuminate both the extent and the limits of the roles judges and lawyers play in resolving provocative social questions—the extent, because the judicial role in our national experience has largely remained true to de Tocqueville's perception, despite ongoing debate about the virtues and vices of "judicial activism"; the limits, because the quest for answers to these social questions frequently outlasts efforts at judicial resolution. Virtually all the social questions argued before Judge Bone have been argued before federal or state courts throughout our nation, but these questions remain grist for great television drama precisely because judicial decisions have not put them to rest.

If the record from these past several decades is an accurate barometer, the courtroom will continue as a mainstay of dramatic network programming because the public wants it that way. New social issues will inevitably emerge, as will new perspectives on existing issues. If at least some quality courtroom dramas follow the example set by "Picket Fences," their creative treatment of profound social issues will continue fashioning a worthwhile chapter in the story of television lawyers and their effect on American life.

11

Rumpole of the Bailey

John Denvir

The Rumpole Society of Northern California recently held its annual picnic. The guests played a few rounds of SWMBO ("She Who Must Be Obeyed") bingo, held a treasure hunt featuring clues from various "Rumpole of the Bailey" episodes, and, of course, consumed generous allotments of Horace Rumpole's favorite beverage, "Chateau Thames Embankment."

As it is now almost two decades since PBS started to import "Rumpole of the Bailey" from the BBC, it is worth asking what it is about Horace Rumpole, a portly, bulbous-nosed barrister, that inspires the "Rumpolians" (as the Society members call themselves) to continue to celebrate him as we move towards the 21st century.

One answer is that they enjoy the half-hour (later expanded to one hour) comedy, but that seems too simple. Rumpole appears to play a role in their lives greater than the normal amusing sitcom. A more persuasive answer is that they find in Rumpole a fictional incarnation of the "good lawyer," a practicing lawyer whom they can admire both on a professional and a personal level. But this really only raises the deeper issue of what makes Rumpole a "good lawyer."

I think the answer to that question is important not just because it solves the riddle of Rumpole's continuing popularity, but also because it tells us a good deal about how lawyers perceive their role in society. My thesis is that Rumpole attracts lawyer admirers because he represents a tension the lawyer viewer experiences in his own life, and simultaneously resolves that tension at an imaginative or mythical level.[1]

The Dilemma of the "Good" Life

The tension in Rumpole's case is the dilemma over how a lawyer can live a "good" life practicing law in a manifestly unjust society.[2] Rumpole lives a "good" life in two senses of the term: on a professional level, he fights the "good fight" on behalf of the poor criminal defendant; on a personal level, he enjoys himself, drinking wine, telling stories, and reciting poetry.

My thesis about the "mythical" function of "legal heroes" is not limited to "Rumpole"; it extends to the function that "legal hero" fiction in general plays in our profession's imaginative life. Therefore, I would like to extend my discussion to include another famous fictional legal hero, Atticus Finch of "To Kill A Mockingbird." My strategy is to show first how different Atticus and Rumpole are on a variety of measures, but then to show that they play the same imaginative function of resolving the "good lawyer" dilemma.

Comparing Rumpole and Atticus

Both Rumpole and Atticus are attempting to be good lawyers in both a professional and personal sense. Unfortunately, this often involves a conflict because what must be done professionally may detract from the quality of a lawyer's personal life. Fiction's resolution of this contradiction is accomplished by somehow eluding one (or both) horns of the dilemma as we face it in real life. Therefore, I will attempt to unravel the imaginative resolutions in both "Rumpole of the Bailey" and "To Kill A Mockingbird" in order to allow us to better contemplate the ethical dilemmas they conceal.

Just picturing the short, squat Rumpole (played by Leo McKern) next to the tall, slender, movie-star handsome Atticus (played by Gregory Peck) makes one smile. Could any two lawyers be less physically alike than these two? Yet physical appearance is by no means the only striking contrast between the two.

One obvious difference is the type of legal practice they pursue. Atticus is a country lawyer in a small Southern town with a general practice; his neighbor brags that he can write a will that no one can "break." But it is not as a probate lawyer that he figures in "To Kill a Mockingbird." Rather, it is his decision to accept an appointment by the local judge to represent Tom Robinson, an indigent black man accused of raping a white girl.

Rumpole, of course, is a London barrister who specializes in criminal law. Almost his entire practice revolves around the lower echelons of the British justice system. When the crime trade is slack, he reluctantly takes on a divorce, but it is difficult to imagine him volunteering to write someone's will.

A less obvious difference is their attitude towards law. Atticus is very much a man of the "law." Even his conversations with his six-year-old daughter Scout reek of the law library. For instance, when she asks him what "compromise" means, he replies by saying that it is "an agreement by mutual concession." Atticus usually sounds like his lines are cribbed from *Williston on Contracts*. But Atticus's faith in the law is more than rhetorical; he sees "law" as the institutionalization of reason, society's only refuge in a world of violence.

Rumpole, on the other hand, has little interest in law and less in legal principles. A poor law student, he readily admits that "although I only feel truly alive and happy in Law Courts, I have a singular distaste for the law." In fact, he reminds his young associate Phyllida Trandt that "being a lawyer's got almost nothing to do with knowing the law."

Rumpole has little faith in the law, but much in facts. Even his wife Hilda ("SWMBO") concedes that "Rumpole is very good with blood stains" and Horace himself continually relives his glory in the "Great Brighton Benefit Club Forgery" case where he displayed his great knowledge of typewriters. In fact, in "Rumpole and the Married Lady," it is this typewriter expertise that allows him to trip up the ten-year-old culprit, who has been forging rude notes so as to stoke the fires of marital discord between his parents.

Another area of contrast is that of motivation. Atticus's motivation in taking the Robinson case is clearly duty; someone has to do it and (as he tells Scout) if he refused "he couldn't hold his head up." Clearly he will pay a financial as well as a social price for defending such an unpopular client, but he sees that as a necessary price to maintain his self-respect. Note that he doesn't claim that he is motivated by outrage at the injustice the Southern justice system is about to inflict upon an innocent black man.

Rumpole never claims such lofty motivations. He continually assures us that his primary motivation is financial. As he tells his son Nick's fiancee in "Rumpole and the Honourable Member," "Money, if it wasn't for the Legal Aid check, I tell you, Rumpole would be quiet as a tomb."

The viewer never quite fully believes Rumpole on this point. It is true that for Rumpole it is important that "Legal Aid brings us quite a drinkable claret," but one suspects that his prime motivation is the pure joy in performance. In fact, in "Rumpole and the Showfolk," his client, a leading lady, pays him the ultimate compliment. "You're a marvelous performer, Mr. Rumpole. Don't let anyone tell you different." For Rumpole, performing in court is like a drug. "Once you're a lawyer you're addicted. It's like smoking, or any other habit-forming drug. You get hooked on cross-examination...." Unlike most lawyers, who spend sleepless nights in anticipation of a court appearance, Rumpole looks forward to trials as a forum for self-expression.

Atticus is very much an "officer of the court." The local judge who asks him to represent Tom Robinson clearly sees Atticus as the local lawyer best able to handle this controversial matter with discretion. We sense that Atticus is a very important member of the local elite in Maycomb County; he has represented his neighbors for many years as a member of the state legislature. We can easily imagine him becoming the local judge when the current judge retires. Earnest, polite, fair, morally principled but staunchly loyal to the Southern social system into which he was born, Atticus is the quintessential "insider."

Rumpole is clearly an "outsider." At the age of 67 he is still a "junior" barrister. He has been passed over as head of chambers in favor of the unctuous Guthrie Featherstone, M.P., Q.C., although he is by far the more senior and better lawyer. In "Rumpole and the Age of Retirement," he discovers that his chambers's mates are trying to push him into retirement in order to make room for a well-connected young barrister. And Rumpole is not the type of barrister who will be rewarded with a judgeship at the end of a long career. But that is fine with Horace, to whom the very idea of Rumpole as judge is anathema. As he so aptly puts it, "I don't judge, I defend."

Atticus is by nature an aristocrat. His courtly charm when dealing with poor people (of whatever race) does not disguise his recognition of strict class distinctions. Within Maycomb society there are four classes of people: gentry like Atticus and his children; poor white farmers like the Cunninghams, who pay Atticus's fee by periodic delivery of fruits and vegetables from their fields; poor black folks like Calpurnia, Atticus's maid, and Tom Robinson, who are portrayed as simple, hard-working religious folk; and white "trash" like Bob Ewall, the man who alleges that Robinson raped his daughter.[3] Atticus is very much aware of the appropriate way in which to deal with members of each group.

And while Atticus abhors the racism which motivates many of his neighbors, he knows how strong a force it is in their lives. Although he makes an impassioned plea to the jury to rise above their prejudice to find Tom Robinson innocent, he later makes clear that he never expected an acquittal, but was only setting the stage at trial for a hopefully-successful appeal, an appeal to be heard by the state supreme court, a "jury" of his "class" peers where he hopes law and reason may prevail.

Rumpole is much more the democrat. He strongly identifies with his clients, whom he likes to picture as small scale entrepreneurs much like himself. In "Rumpole and the Younger Generation," he meditates on the parallels between his hopes that his son Nick will follow him to the criminal bar and those of the Timson family training their son Jim to take over the family burglary trade. Socially, he has little use for the high-flying Featherstone or the priggish Claude Erskine-Brown, preferring to rehash old "war stories" with Albert, the chambers's working class clerk.

As a "family" man, Atticus excels. We only get a glimpse of a photo of his deceased wife, but the inference is clear that they were a loving couple. I think Atticus the lawyer is only part of the reason why "To Kill A Mockingbird" is such an important film to lawyers. The other part is

Atticus the father. Whether we are listening to his philosophical chats with Scout or his attempts to rein in her rambunctious older brother Jem, we can't help envy them their luck in having such a father. Unlike many contemporary lawyers, Atticus seems to experience no stress in honoring his professional and family responsibilities; he finds time for each. At the end of the movie, when the voice-over tells us that Atticus will spend the night with his unconscious son Jem so that the boy will see him when he awakes, we leave the theater secure in the knowledge that Atticus will do just that.

Rumpole is less successful as a "family" man. It is clear that his marriage to Hilda began as one of convenience from both sides (she was the spinster daughter of the head of chambers) and has gone down hill since. They are clearly not a couple made in heaven; at best they live a long-term domestic cease-fire. Horace professes great love for his son Nick, and we have little reason to doubt him. But there is evidence that he was not the world's most involved father. In "Rumpole and the Younger Generation," Rumpole nostalgically reminds Nick of the good times they used to have walking through Hyde Park playing Holmes and Watson. Nick tellingly replies, "I remember one walk." Between the Times's crossword, the drama of his work, and socializing at Pommeroy's Wine Bar, it is easy to see that Rumpole wouldn't have had much time for interacting with a young child.

But despite all his principles and virtues (or is it because of them?), Atticus strikes us as melancholy. I can't remember a smile on his lips during the entire two hour film, much less a hearty laugh. He is very sweet with his children, but it's a sad sweetness. We might attribute this to the premature death of his wife just four years before, but it seems to extend beyond that. I suspect that it's the downside of being a morally sensitive "insider"; you have to spend a lot of time running the system, recognizing its shortcomings, and your own reluctance to confront them.

Rumpole is by nature ebullient. I think that this joy which permeates all aspects of his life is certainly one reason why they are still holding picnics in his honor in Northern California. We don't hear about many happy lawyers these days. But whether he is grilling a reluctant witness on cross, or muttering disrespectful comments under his breath to a pompous judge, reliving old glories at Pommeroy's Wine Bar, or carving the Sunday roast, Rumpole exudes a joy in life. Even his daily run-ins with Hilda seem less genuine arguments than opportunities for him to thwart her by quoting at length from the *Oxford Book of English Verse*.

Yet despite all these contrasts, there is a similarity between Atticus Finch and Horace Rumpole which I think explains their great popularity with lawyers.[4] Both Rumpole and Atticus are lawyers attempting to achieve justice for their clients within a system they know to be morally flawed.

In Atticus's case, this is easy to see because we react viscerally to the manifest injustice in Tom Robinson's case: an innocent black man convicted on clearly perjured evidence by a white jury. It is interesting to note that the author Harper Lee did not make up this fact pattern; the Robinson case closely parallels the famous Scottsboro case in which innocent young black men were convicted on incredible evidence by a rural Southern white jury for allegedly raping a white woman.[5]

The traditional view of Atticus's defense of Tom Robinson calls him a hero, accepting a case of a classically "unpopular client" and litigating it with competence despite the social opprobrium and physical danger to himself and his family. And while Atticus is unsuccessful in his defense of Robinson, this is easily seen as the result of his neighbors's racism, not any professional incompetence or moral failure on Atticus's part. This traditional view sees Atticus as a tragic figure, a victim of a racism which he personally abhors. And the fact that he knows that there will be a time of reckoning for the sins of his community only makes him more tragic and more admirable. As he tells his children: "Don't fool yourselves — it's all adding up and one of these days we're going to pay the bill for it. I hope it's not in you children's time."

No wonder the poor guy seems a little melancholy. But the fact that Atticus cannot singlehandedly defeat racism in no way detracts from his hero status. You might say that his attempt and failure legitimizes the work of all decent lawyers in today's America who, despite their best efforts, are not able to squeeze justice from a social and legal system racked with racial and class inequities. In this sense he serves, in Professor Michael Asimow's words, as a "patron saint" to today's lawyers, "everything we lawyers wish we were and hope we will become."[6]

It is easy to see Rumpole as playing a similarly heroic role. He is defending mostly poor people accused of crime in Margaret Thatcher's United Kingdom. Here too injustice is rampant. Not only are there gross economic and social inequalities, but also a police force which ignores procedures to attain convictions and a class-based judiciary prone to prejudge poor defendants who are usually represented by barristers like Featherstone with a singular distaste for defendants from the lower classes. Like Atticus, Rumpole fights the good fight, placing all his eloquence on the side of the underdog. And if he often loses, we no more blame him than we do Atticus; after all, he is not responsible for the British class system.

Like Atticus, Horace fights for the underdog, but unlike Atticus his attitude is anything but tragic. Rumpole adopts an ironic view toward law. He makes a joke out of the whole system. He tells us he has found "British justice a life-long subject of harmless fun." And much of Rumpole's time is spent lampooning the absurdities of the English class system as it plays out in the criminal courts. Even when Rumpole doesn't win the case, he does make the point that laughter is the best revenge. It is little wonder that American lawyers caught in an equally unjust and even more bureaucratic legal system than that of the United Kingdom should find comfort in this iconoclast's capacity to merrily ridicule the system within which he struggles.

Taking a Second Look at Rumpole and Atticus

In recent years, Atticus Finch's hero status has been challenged.[7] A revisionist view has surfaced which claims that rather than confronting the racism of the Southern legal system, Atticus succumbed to it, refraining from giving Tom Robinson the "zealous" defense he deserved. If Atticus knew he couldn't win before an all white jury, why didn't he challenge the exclusion of blacks from the jury? While we should be leery of judging a lawyer in the 1930s by the standards of the 1990s, the historical fact is that lawyers in the Scottsboro case did challenge the exclusion of black jurors. Why didn't Atticus?

Suddenly Atticus becomes a more complex character. To defend a black man against the testimony of white "trash" was an affront to Southern mores, but one which still allowed him to keep his "insider" status. For instance, we are told in the book that the November after the trial Atticus was re-elected without opposition to the state legislature. To challenge exclusion of blacks from the jury would be to squarely confront segregation, a direct repudiation of the whole Southern social system. The defense lawyers in the Scottsboro case were from New York; they could accept the consequences of such a challenge. One suspects that Atticus could not.

He knew his neighbors were wrong on segregation, but they were still "his" people, and he refused to condemn them. For instance, listen to his comment on a member of a lynch mob which threatened to kill him the night before: "Mr. Cunningham is basically a good man. He just has blind spots along with the rest of us." Atticus doesn't approve of his neighbors's racism, but he accepts it as part of their common heritage. And he warns his children never to forget that these racists are their friends. "But remember this, no matter how bitter things get, they're still our friends and this is still our home."

I personally think that this conflict between his instinctual affection for the "Old South" and his intellectual belief in "equality before the law" makes Atticus a more tragic and more interesting figure than the old "hero" motif. And it underlines a dilemma which lawyers still face today: No matter how much you do, more must be done. There is no "natural" point of equipoise between our professional duty to achieve justice and our duty to ourselves.[8] It's impossible to condone Atticus's failure as a lawyer, but more difficult to condemn him as a man and father.

So we can see that Harper Lee was able to reconcile Atticus's duty to client and duty to self and community by suppressing one real, albeit painful, legal option open to him—challenge the exclusion of blacks from the jury which tried Tom Robinson. Can a similar "revisionist" case be made against Rumpole? Has John Mortimer suppressed factors which would make Rumpole a less heroic character?

I think so. First, he has trivialized the problem of crime by giving Rumpole only sympathetic (or at least non-violent) clients. The typical Rumpole clients are the Timsons, a family Rumpole has defended for decades in their chronic interactions with the law for non-violent offenses like burglary and fencing. In "Rumpole and the Alternative Society," Rumpole defends a beautiful young hippie who has sold cannabis to an undercover policeman in hopes of freeing her brother, who has been jailed on drug charges in Turkey. In "Rumpole and the Learned Friends," Rumpole defends a man who is accused of blowing a safe, but actually has been framed by the police. In "Rumpole and the Man of God," his client is a charmingly naive Anglican minister who is found innocent of the crime of shoplifting. And so the list goes on. We can share Rumpole's sympathy for these clients and still wonder how typical they are of "real" criminal defendants in contemporary London. And would we have the same warm reaction if the Timson family business was dealing crack cocaine to inner-city teens? Defending innocent people is the narrative form of shooting fish in a barrel. Of course, I share my profession's belief that even crack dealers deserve a zealous defense, but I must admit to some ambivalence when their lawyers are called "heroes."

Rumpole also seems to place a premium on performance values, sometimes to his client's detriment. Enjoying one's work is of course a loveable trait, but sometimes Rumpole seems to be having too much fun. For instance, in "Rumpole and the Fascist Beast," he makes a very persuasive argument to the jury that his client, a neo-fascist, is in truth a ludicrous and harmless eccentric more worthy of pity than punishment. The client is found not guilty, but his only comment to Rumpole is, "May God forgive you Mr. Rumpole. I certainly shan't." The client's wishes (and self-respect) were an obstacle to Rumpole's performance, and therefore had to be removed.

And emphasis on courtroom performance may downgrade the need for other types of legal skills. Clearly Rumpole excels in cross-examination, but there is more to a trial than cross-examination. If you will accept a golf metaphor, good golfers who drive the ball long distances spend much of their time practicing putting, a different but no less necessary skill. Really good courtroom lawyers do likewise, putting extra time in on the technical questions of law which, although less dramatic, can be crucial to success. If I were accused of a serious crime in the United Kingdom and forced to choose a barrister from British fiction to defend me, I think I would prefer the workaholic Gareth Peirce (Emma Thompson) in "In the Name of the Father" to Rumpole.[9]

Rumpole also often seems so obsessed with the courtroom that he ignores other fora where the fight for justice must also be waged. Rumpole subscribes to what he calls the "pour sand in the gearbox of justice" school of jurisprudence, what in America we might call poking a stick in the spokes of the authoritarian state. And, of course, that is what we ask of criminal defense lawyers as a profession: make the prosecution prove its case. But while not all lawyers need be political philosophers, it seems fair to ask that a "good lawyer" have at least some inchoate idea of how his professional activities impact the community as a whole. Is he or she making society a better, more just place to live? While Rumpole's cry of "never plead guilty" may (or may not) be an intelligent strategy in handling criminal cases, it certainly falls short of a political theory — unless we see it as an underdeveloped anarchism. And Horace, the *petit* bourgeois raconteur, seems an unlikely candidate for political anarchism.

Rumpole appears to have nothing but contempt for the political system, cheerfully noting that his nemesis Featherstone has wasted his time at another all-night session in the House of Commons on "the East Sudsbury Water Main Bill." Can a lawyer interested in justice afford to ignore the legislative system? This would seem to be especially perilous in the United Kingdom, where there is no written constitution to constrain the legislative drafting of criminal rules of procedure.

Actually Rumpole seems to have contempt for most of the people he meets other than those like the Timsons, whom he chooses to romanticize. The police are crooked, the judges are sadistic bores, opposing counsel are unctuous sycophants, and most of his colleagues are avaricious snobs. Standing against them is Rumpole, armed only with his eloquence and wit. Even "sympathetic" characters are not spared the barbs of Rumpole's (or Mortimer's) irony. For instance, Phyllida Trandt, the young leftist feminist, never seems able to practice her principles, and even marries the prig Erskine-Brown. And Rumpole's Pakistani "pupil" Ali Khan, who one expects to be sensitive to social injustice, turns out to have social views far to the right of Margaret Thatcher.

Irony is of course a valuable rhetorical resource; it keeps us aware of the hypocrisy which makes up much of our professional lives. But while it is a quite appropriate stance for an artist, it is a dangerous one for a lawyer. Irony can be a refuge from engagement — an attitude which not only laughs at current social conditions, but accepts its resistance to change. In this vein, irony becomes a mask concealing despair, the acceptance of the invincibility of injustice and our impotence to defeat it. Laughter becomes a substitute for justice.

The danger is that Rumpole's irony can play the same function for contemporary lawyers as Atticus's "tragic" efforts to save Tom Robinson; it allows lawyers to focus on the lawyer's drama rather than the client's. Just as we focus less on Tom Robinson than Atticus's gallant defense, we start to forget about the effect of the justice system on the lives of real defendants and concentrate more on style. How good a performance did Rumpole give? Did he enjoy himself? There's more to being a "good lawyer" than style.

Conclusion

If my analysis of Atticus and Rumpole appears negative, I don't mean it as an artistic criticism of either "To Kill A Mockingbird" or "Rumpole of the Bailey." Quite the opposite, it is a mark of good fiction that we can value it on more than one level. On first viewing, "Rumpole" is a very amusing comedy, but the fact that we continue to watch it almost twenty years later shows the Rumpole character to be much more than only that. Like Atticus, he incarnates a problem which all lawyers should be aware of—how to be a "good lawyer" in a not-so-good society.

We each have to decide how well he resolves the "good lawyer" dilemma we all face. It's a discussion our profession should have more often, and one that might even fit in well at next year's picnic.

12

Science Fiction

PAUL R JOSEPH

The huge black starship materialized without warning only 50,000 parsecs from the Terran stronghold. Base commander Buck Zeal had been expecting just such a move. Ever since the Zambrosian incursion, he knew that the ultimate confrontation was inevitable. Smoothly, without betraying a hint of the nervousness that even a battle-hardened warrior would feel at such a moment, Captain Zeal punched the button on his tactical display and issued the command. "Call the lawyers!," he barked. "We have some tough negotiating to do."[1]

What is wrong with this passage? It would be easy to say that lawyers, and by extension, law, have no place in science fiction. The very name "science fiction" could imply that the genre is narrowly concerned only with "gee whiz" scientific creations, not with the deeper cultural implications of those creations. Phaser weapons, space ships, and matter transformers may seem to be the stuff of high adventure, not of law.

But the "science" in science fiction does not — and cannot — exist in a vacuum. We have seen that major technological advances have profound cultural effects. Airplanes, telephones, space exploration, and "wonder" drugs have changed patterns of living. More than that, they have forced us to face profound questions.[2]

Cloning, for example, is not just a technical achievement, but an ethical quagmire. Should parents be able to create a genetic "replica" of a deceased child? How about growing a genetically compatible fetus to supply a needed organ for transplantation? The answers to these and other cloning-related questions have the potential to alter the way we view the very nature of what it means to be human and the relation between each individual human creature and humanity in the aggregate. While issues such as cloning will be debated by religious leaders, philosophers, and politicians, if the issue is to be decided in a way which is enforceable, rather than merely left to the conscience of the individual, the arena for decision will eventually have to shift to law. Uniquely in our society, it is the law which claims proper authority to compel obedience to its dictates by bringing to bear the force of the state in the name of us all.

Some of the best science fiction examines not only scientific advances but their social and cultural context. As "Babylon 5" creator J. Michael Straczynski argues:

> Part of what has screwed up so much of SF-TV is this sense that you must utterly divorce yourself from current issues, from current problems, from taking on issues of today and extrapolating them into the future, by way of aliens of SF constructs. And that is *precisely* why so much of contemporary SF-TV is barren and lifeless and irrelevant.[3]

Much of the very best science fiction *speculates* not only about scientific advances but about the social, religious, moral, and cultural consequences of those advances. In fact, "science fiction" has also been called "speculative fiction,"[4] in recognition of its focus not only on science but on the effect that science and technology have on society as a whole. This sort of speculation leads to a consideration of political and public policy issues where law often plays a central role.

Law but No Lawyers?

In print media, it does not take an exhaustive search to find lawyers, judicial decisions, court procedures, and legal issues in science fiction. In fact, when teaching a course in law and science fiction some years ago, I quickly had more than I could use. A few examples will suffice to make the point.

> A down-on-his-luck lawyer wages a legal battle to defeat the corporation which controls the monopoly on decent housing in a grim future world where the difference between the good life and destitution is a precious employment-at-will contract and the high-tech house which comes with it.[5]
>
> The President plans to use a newly-created federal court to reign in the independence aspirations of off-earth colonists, but the plan hits a snag when his choice for judge refuses to be a political tool of an evil administration.[6]
>
> The concept of "right to life" is applied to protect the rights of single-celled organisms, and later to hold them responsible for the injuries they cause.[7]
>
> A retired lawyer finds new meaning in his life when he is recruited to sit on an intergalactic tribunal.[8]
>
> The "right to bear arms" becomes the duty to do so in a fanciful review of future history.[9]
>
> The legalization of torture to extract confessions is reluctantly approved in a crime-ridden future.[10]

Unfortunate experiments with a matter transmitter result in its in-
ventor and several heads of state being declared legally dead.[11]

The picture is somewhat different on television.[12] While a number of
science fiction television shows have explored legal *issues*, there are far
fewer portrayals of *lawyers*. There is, I believe, one primary reason for this,
which has less to do with science fiction than with the nature of television.

In television—especially television drama—conflict involving the main
(recurring) characters is central. The audience tunes in week after week
to follow the stars with whom an emotional bond has been established.
Thus, it is no wonder that "lawyer shows" will find it easier to feature
lawyers than shows where legal issues arise only sporadically.

In a show like "Law & Order," some of the main characters are lawyers
and the show focuses primarily on their professional role within a legal
setting. Even in a show such as "L.A. Law," where we were permitted to
learn more about the personal lives of the principal characters, much of
the show involved their work as lawyers.

By contrast, science fiction shows are not primarily about law. Legal
issues are likely to be involved in only a few episodes of a particular series.[13] The shows's creators may not see the need for a regular legal character, and, because only a minority of shows will involve legal issues,
there is the problem of what to do with the character until a legal issue
shows up. Also, the main characters are unlikely to be identified as
lawyers because such a role could be seen to conflict with other, more central ones, such as "starship captain," "science officer," or "chief engineer."[14]

This raises a dilemma for writers of science fiction shows. If the central conflict in an episode involves, for example, a trial with lawyers and
judges, the main characters are likely to be reduced to peripheral roles. This
is flatly unacceptable in a series format.

Therefore, where legal issues are to be explored in an ongoing science
fiction series, a way must be found to allow the principal characters to
step into some or all of the legal roles. And indeed, this is exactly what
we find. While lawyers are included from time to time in particular episodes
of science fiction television series,[15] where legal issues are to be explored,
often a way will be found to have the principal characters assume the
legal roles.[16]

An example can be seen in the "Star Trek: The Next Generation"
episode entitled "The Drumhead," in which an investigation of possible
sabotage leads to a McCarthy-like witch hunt conducted by an obsessed
admiral. As the circle of suspicion threatens to engulf a hapless young
crewman, he is offered a lawyer but opts, instead, to be represented by a
fellow officer, series regular Commander Riker (Jonathan Frakes).

The same device is used in "Murder on the Rising Star," an episode of "Battlestar Galactica," in which a trial is held. The accused asks to be defended by a friend (a series regular), and this desire is honored.

In "Overview," an episode of "Babylon 5," aliens refuse to allow their child to undergo a life-saving operation because of their religious beliefs. It is series regular Dr. Franklin (Richard Briggs) who makes the case for the operation and series regular Station Commander Sinclair (Michael O'Hare) who decides the question.[17]

Thus far, I have argued that there is nothing intrinsic to science fiction which would preclude the inclusion of legal issues and characters. Yet, the focus on the recurring characters who are unlikely to be lawyers means that lawyers are likely to appear only sporadically and in single episodes as supporting players. Further, where legal settings and issues do arise, there may be some tendency to find ways to have the focus remain on the series regulars. These devices may mean that non-lawyer series regulars will step in and fulfill roles similar to judge or lawyer which would more properly be filled by characters identified as lawyers in other television shows.

Whoever plays the legal role, the more basic question is whether science fiction can portray legal issues well, and what makes a good rather than a bad inclusion of law in science fiction television. It is to these questions that I now turn.

Doing Law Well in Science Fiction

The law is not like a block of granite or another aspect of the physical world. Granite comes into being without human agency and its properties exist independently of human desires. Thus, one would not expect a block of granite to be materially different whether portrayed on television in a western, a modern crime drama, or a science fiction program.[18]

Law, however, is different. Law is a human construct. We invent it— we "make it up" to serve our needs.[19] I do not mean that law is whimsical or capricious. I do not mean even that the growth and change of law is always, or even mostly, conscious, although sometimes it certainly is.[20] Because the law serves deeply felt values, such as justice, fairness, and finality, its practices and content are established and change in response to evolving societal understandings of such concepts. Those needs can also be products of deeper and more hidden social forces.[21]

Thus, where a science fiction setting is radically different from our own, we would not want law in that setting to slavishly follow that which we know in contemporary United States[22] society, or even that portrayed in western genre television set one hundred or more years ago. The law in science fiction television should reflect the time, place, culture, and species portrayed in the show.

It should be expected that alien races, with their own history, cultural development, and values, would have their own legal system which would reflect their differences. Even where a science fiction show focuses on humans, where a socially transforming event or history is postulated, the law on the show should reflect law which is consistent with the transforming event.

Presenting the Law and Legal Systems of Aliens

If an alien race with a significantly different social organization and value structure is portrayed on a science fiction television series, it would be expected that its legal system would likely have developed differently than our own. A good portrayal of the aliens's law, therefore, should reflect their particular values and cultural development as presented to us by the show's creators. A poor portrayal of their law would embody the unexamined assumption that an alien history, culture, and value system would have somehow combined to produce a legal system which looks like that in 20th century America.

For example, consider the Ferengi, a race of trader-thieves portrayed in "Star Trek: Deep Space Nine." The cultural values of the Ferengi can be summed up by quoting one of their guiding ethical principles from their most revered (almost holy) source, the "Rules of Acquisition." The rule states, "once you have their money never give it back." Thus, it can be seen that the "sharp" practice and the "shady" deal are considered admirable and moral in Ferengi culture. Shouldn't that be reflected in their legal system?

What their legal system would look like could be the subject of both serious and humorous speculation. The one thing which is certain, however, is that it is unlikely to look like ours.

> The Ferengi legal system would have to include a heavy component of bargaining and deal-making, or it would be unlikely to garner respect within Ferengi society. A number of possibilities present themselves. Perhaps judges compete to be selected by the litigants to hear the case. Perhaps witness testimony must be "purchased" in order to be presented. That is, perhaps a Ferengi litigant must risk his assets in order to proceed. One vision of such a system might have the look of a high-stakes poker game combined with the haggling common to flea markets or bazaars.[23]

An excellent example of an interesting alternate legal system which fits the alien culture in which it is set can be seen in an episode of "Star Trek: Deep Space Nine" called "Tribunal." In this episode, Chief of Operations O'Brien (Colm Meaney) is kidnaped and taken to Cardassia to stand trial for weapons smuggling. At the time of the episode, Cardassia is an expansionist military oligarchy in which obedience of the population is maintained not only through coercion but through propaganda mixing messages of Cardassian superiority and the infallibility of the leadership.[24]

Our notions of adversarial criminal trials have no place on Cardassia. The idea of a trial, in which the individual contests the judgment of the state, would undermine the central articles of Cardassian political faith. Instead, criminal investigation is the "trial" in the sense that we would understand that term. The administrative process, functioning in secret, determines after investigation whether a person is guilty of a crime. Only if the determination of guilt is made is a public "trial" held. The purpose of the trial is not to determine guilt or innocence but rather to demonstrate the means by which the infallible government uncovered the wrongdoer, and to give the guilty party an opportunity to admit his guilt publicly. For me, this episode has always been an example of a television series taking a portrayal of law seriously. The writers constructed a legal system which mirrored the goals and style of the broader alien culture.

Contrasted to this might be the previously discussed episode of "Battlestar Galactica" known as "Murder on the Rising Star" in which a murder leads to a trial. With the exception of the names of the legal roles, the trial looks like nothing so much as an episode of "Perry Mason," right down to the device of getting the "real" killer to confess under questioning. Such an unimaginative use of law wastes the potential for a melding of law and science fiction.

The Law of Humans: Seeing Ourselves and Our Future

When presenting human culture, the basic rule is the same as with that of aliens: Be consistent with the rest of what is presented.

It is, perhaps, not surprising that science fiction produced in the United States often adopts what might be termed an "Amero-Centric" point of view. The base culture to which the science fiction element is added needs to be familiar enough so that changes due to the science fiction can be recognized and understood. Thus, even where a plotline postulates a future "united earth," the unity may have a distinctly American cast to it.

This is a criticism of television science fiction generally (and maybe of television generally) and is beyond the scope of this essay. For our purposes, what can be said is that legal portrayals should be consistent with the rest of what is shown. Therefore, when law is included in an "Amero-Centric" science fiction show, the law should tend to follow that pattern. It should not surprise us to find that "human" law will often look like some version of the American legal system. If the culture is reasonably contemporary with our present and the science fiction element of the show has not radically altered the culture, then a legal form which mirrors ours makes sense.

Even when the time is different, for example, the 21st century, the law, or at least the basics of the legal system, would probably be easily recognizable. The situation would not be very different from a western set in the 19th century. Some aspects of law will be different,[25] but the broad outlines will be much the same.

Even where a show is set very far in the future, the legal system could be recognizable in form although somewhat different in content, to take into account the resolution of new problems over the centuries. The key question is always whether the law fits the rest of what is presented.

"Babylon 5," for example, is set in the early part of the 23rd century. The assumption is that capitalism is still the basic system.[26] Although earth people are now galactic players who have to cope with new technology and alien races, the people themselves are not so different from ourselves. Even the show's technology of deep space travel came from an alien race rather than being the original product of earth advances. While their laws have developed to deal with new issues and while the realities of their situation have dictated some modifications of legal procedure,[27] much of it is recognizable.

Even with our legal system as the baseline for portrayals of human law in television science fiction, there is room for innovation. Where a show is set very far in the future, for example, an evolution of the legal system would be expected. Where the show posits a radically different culture, perhaps due to some cataclysmic or transformative event, the legal system should reflect these differences.

An example of a transformed human culture can be seen in "Star Trek: The Next Generation." The series is set in our future, the 24th century. The back story indicates that on earth scarcity of resources has been solved through technology and money has been abolished. Much of the conflict which seems so central to our time, including racial and gender conflicts, has faded away. Further, within the Federation (a multiple world and race alliance led by earth) and particularly within the peacekeeping and exploration force of the Federation, "Star Fleet," people are more able to trust each other and to work together for the common good.

Our legal system is structured to assure multiple levels of procedural checks and balances. It is a system built on conflict and distrust. Such a system would make no sense in the culture postulated in "Star Trek: The Next Generation." Happily, the series's creators managed to craft a legal system which fit the culture they portrayed and which would not merely echo our 20th century.

A number of episodes of "Star Trek: The Next Generation" have focused on legal themes and it has been argued that consistent differences between their system and ours exist.[28] Much of the formalistic procedure of our day has fallen into disuse in the 24th century because it is no longer perceived as necessary to achieve a fair outcome. Informal decisional process and a fluid response to objections raised by contesting parties are the rule. A number of episodes demonstrate the relaxed nature of procedure in that setting.

Yet, "Star Trek: The Next Generation" retains roots in the procedure of our day. Some anachronistic procedures and formalities are preserved. This is not surprising. In our own century, English judges still wear wigs. More importantly, formal procedures from earlier times exist in the background for those few occasions when more informal decisional processes break down. The key seems to be that a party must conclude that informal procedures are not working fairly and must specifically ask for more formal procedures. Thus, there are episodes in which a party has special reason to distrust the normal informal procedures or in which those procedures have broken down for one reason or the other. In those situations, older, more formalistic rules of procedure exist and can be invoked.

The legal system of the Federation has been labeled "dual tracked,"[29] in which a system of procedural safeguards and formal rights existed as a sort of last resort safety net which could be invoked when more informal processes went wrong. Absent such a claim by one of the disputants, more informal forms are the norm in the series. The system of law portrayed in "Star Trek: The Next Generation" is appropriate because it fits the culture portrayed on the show while also demonstrating a continuity with our own 20th century system out of which it supposedly grew.

The construction of this legal system appears not to have been conscious. That is, the writers didn't sit down and create a legal system. Instead, they did something better. They resolved legal problems on an ad hoc basis by relying on their understanding of the culture and history which is at the center of "Star Trek: The Next Generation." This is science fiction at its best.

It is certainly not required that science fiction make law the centerpiece of its story telling. Legal issues can be inserted as secondary stories and can be effective when their use is believable and consistent with the rest of the structure of the society which is portrayed.

The less successful uses of law occur when legal issues are raised but then ignored in favor of an "action" resolution starring the continuing characters or when legal verbiage seems to be thrown in for no apparent reason. Also less than satisfying are situations in which law is introduced to explain a science fiction setting in which problems can be resolved in essentially non-legal ways.[30] For example:

> In the *Battlestar Galactica* episode, "Murder on the Rising Star," Lieutenant Starbuck is charged with the murder of a man named Ortega. For many years, the two had been rivals in love, life, and sports, and in a particularly violent game of Triad, Starbuck is heard threatening to kill Ortega. Starbuck is put on trial before a panel led by Commander Adama. Starbuck is entitled to a defender known as a "protector." Finding synonyms for current legal terms seems to be the extent of the show's creative spin on future lawyers.[31]

Legal Issues Through a Science Fiction Lens

Legal issues can be depicted in science fiction series. Assuming that writers are sensitive to the nature of law as a human construct and strive to be as inventive and consistent in the portrayal of law as in other parts of the show, law can even be depicted well. But there are plenty of "lawyer shows" around, as this book demonstrates. Assuming that we are unlikely to see "Buck Zeal: Space Lawyer" any time soon, why *should* science fiction shows tackle legal themes?

One answer might be that science fiction, which portrays a rich and well-textured setting, will be unable to avoid doing so. Law is too much woven into the fabric of organized society to be wholly absent. It is instructive that Gene Roddenberry, the creator of "Star Trek," wanted to believe that there were no lawyers in the "Star Trek" setting, but then found it impossible to keep them out. As "Star Trek: The Next Generation" developed, legal issues from treaties to trials became ever more evident. In fact, a study of the law in "Star Trek: The Next Generation" found that episodes repeatedly examined issues such as the right to privacy, sexual orientation and gender, and criminal justice.[32]

The second reason to include legal issues, however, has more to do with the possibilities of science fiction. It is the ability of science fiction to focus on a contemporary issue in an altered form and thereby to shed new perspective on it.

One of the most disheartening aspects of our current "culture wars" is the all-too-obvious fact that nobody is really listening to anybody else. When the news presents yet one more scene of pro-choice and right-to-life advocates screaming at each other across barricades outside some abortion clinic, the overwhelming feeling I am left with is that it has all been screamed before and will be again and that neither side is listening. The point-counterpoint interviews on CNN or MSNBC tend to be dreary precisely because any halfway intelligent person knows exactly what each guest will say even before they open their mouth.

Television drama in general—as with other forms of fiction—can present powerful human stories which serve to illuminate an issue in a more personal way. Novels which immediately come to mind include Victor Hugo's *Les Miserables*, Upton Sinclair's *The Jungle*, and John Steinbeck's *The Grapes of Wrath*. They are but three examples of works which, through fictional characters and settings, nonetheless throw powerful spotlights on the reality of social conditions. Films such as Steven Spielberg's "Schindler's List," Jonathan Demme's "Philadelphia," and Alan Parker's "Mississippi Burning" achieve similar effects. Television drama also has focused light on contemporary issues. Racism has been powerfully portrayed on "Homicide: Life on the Street." "N.Y.P.D. Blue" has shocked viewers with its images of police violence. "Law & Order" and "Picket Fences" have been almost "issue of the week" shows, grappling with nearly every major social and legal issue.

One refreshing thing that science fiction can do is to transpose a contemporary issue out of its contemporary setting. It can identify the essence of an issue and give it a different spin. It can ask us to look at an issue with new eyes.

For example, instead of doing a "gay rights" show about sexual orientation, the episode "Outcast" on "Star Trek: The Next Generation" asked us to imagine a world where *any* expression of gender whatsoever is banned. The sexless and androgynous cultural mandate, rigidly enforced by the power of the state, provides a context in which to think through our own assumptions and views.

In "Up the Long Ladder," another "Star Trek: The Next Generation" episode, skin grafts are stolen and used to grow clones of two Enterprise crew members. "I have a right to control my own body," says one of them as he destroys the partially-grown clone. This isn't a show "about" abortion, but it raises the same difficult questions in another way.

Other alterations of our reality have targeted lawyers and the legal system. In "Sliders," a show in which the regulars "slide" to an alternate San Francisco in each episode, we have been treated to a world where lawyers use guns to settle disputes ("The Good, the Bad, and the Wealthy"), another where over 80% of the population are law school graduates, making even minor everyday transactions fraught with the danger of litigation ("Greatfellas"), and another in which lawyers have been abolished and criminal trials are now conducted as game shows ("Dead Man Sliding").

Criminal law and justice have often been the grist for the television science fiction mill. An episode of "Sliders," entitled "Obsession," presents a world in which police are allowed to arrest future law breakers on the word of a psychic. In another episode, "The King is Back," the desire for law and order has led to the "Instant Justice Initiative," where appeals are immediately denied and even minor crimes carry the death penalty.[33] In "A Matter of Perspective," "Star Trek: The Next Generation" presented an extradition hearing where Captain Picard (Patrick Stewart) had to decide whether to send Commander Riker to stand trial on a world where defendants are guilty until proven innocent.

In our own age, we debate the proper balance between our desire to have criminals brought to justice and our belief in privacy rights. The law of search and seizure has been given a new twist on science fiction television with the question of whether telepaths can be used to gather information against possible defendants. Here again, the issue is familiar to us but the context—mind reading—is enhanced by the science fiction context.

"Babylon 5" has the best developed answer to the question. Telepaths are not permitted to "scan" anyone without their permission or a lawful order to do so. Telepaths cannot scan a criminal defendant to determine guilt or innocence because that violates due process. A crime victim may be scanned but, unless the information is corroborated, the scan is inadmissible in court.[34]

> [T]he accused cannot ask for a psi to validate his or her innocence; the trial can ONLY proceed on the basis of evidence. This is to prevent abuse, trials where a Psi [sic] looks at you and determines your guilt. When a life is at stake, you can't risk the possibility of some hidden agenda on the part of the telepath. You'd have to use a telepath to verify the first telepath's scan, and on and on. Best simply to exclude them from that aspect of the law.[35]

By contrast, "Star Trek: The Next Generation" does not present a clear answer. Betazoid telepaths are used in various capacities and it seems that the individual commander has a great deal of discretion in deciding when to use them and to what degree. In "The Drumhead," an obsessed admiral leads a destructive witch hunt among Starfleet personnel looking for spies. When Picard objects to the use of a telepath by the admiral, she points out that Picard's use of the half-Betazoid Counselor Troi (Mariana Sirtis) hardly puts him in a position to object. Picard's expressed ambivalence, that perhaps he should re-think his use, is not convincing. The series does, however, present some harmful telepathic probing as criminal in an episode called "Violations," in which the conduct is analogized to rape.

One of the most moving episodes of "Star Trek: The Next Generation," entitled "The Measure of a Man," focused on another issue, the question of whether the android officer Data (Brent Spiner), was a rights bearing creature or merely a machine. The outcome of that question would determine whether Data could refuse an order to allow himself to be disassembled to study how he worked. Captain Picard's closing argument in Data's defense is an excellent example of a powerful legal presentation in a science fiction setting.

> Your honor, a courtroom is a crucible. In it we burn away irrelevances, until we're left with a pure product—the truth—for all time. Now, sooner or later this man or others like him will succeed in replicating Commander Data. The decision you reach here today will determine how we will regard this creation of our genius. It will reveal the kind of a people *we* are, what he is destined to be. It will reach far beyond this courtroom and this one android. It could significantly redefine the boundaries of personal liberty and freedom, expanding them for some, savagely curtailing them for others. Are you prepared to condemn him and all who come after him to servitude and slavery? Your honor, Starfleet was founded to seek out *new life*. Well, there it sits... waiting. You wanted a chance to make law, well here it is. Make it a good one.

Conclusion

The foregoing demonstrates that there is nothing intrinsic about science fiction television which precludes the inclusion of lawyers and legal issues. Especially where a series presents a well thought out historical and cultural setting, the absence of law would be a strange and unnatural omission.

There might even be a place for well executed law-centered science fiction shows such as the mythical "Buck Zeal: Space Lawyer." Yet a series in which a regular character is a lawyer and law makes up a substantial focus of the show is not a prerequisite for dealing with legal issues within a science fiction context.

Science fiction television which presents a well-defined cultural and historical context has the ability to present law and legal issues well. The key is to make the law consistent with the rest of the setting, with the society, with the aliens, and with the technology. Thus, the better defined the science fiction setting, the better the chance that law will be presented well.

Although the lawyer and police shows will continue to present the bulk of legal issues on television series, science fiction, precisely because it presents an altered reality, has the ability to present such issues in fresh and exciting ways.[36] This is its greatest challenge and its most exciting possibility.

13

Situation Comedies

ROBERT M. JARVIS

Situation comedies — or sitcoms as they are typically called — are thirty minute shows that require their characters to solve a different problem in each new episode. As has been pointed out, sitcoms occupy a special place in television:

> American television's signature program form, the half-hour story comedy... plays episodically, usually against a laugh track. Sitcoms have evolved over the years from simple domestic contrivances like *Father Knows Best* and *The Life of Riley* to the sophisticated ensemble playlets of *M*A*S*H*, *Taxi*, and *Cheers*.
>
> Hit sitcoms have extraordinary value, both to their networks and their producers. Single 30-minute series like *I Love Lucy*, *Happy Days*, *All in the Family* and *The Cosby Show* have had the power to carry an entire evening for their networks, and their reruns seemingly go on forever on independent stations. As generally the most sought-after programs in the syndication market, sitcoms tend to fetch the highest prices: *Cosby*, for example, reaped around $1 million an episode.[1]

Since television first began, lawyers have been recurring characters on dozens of situation comedies. This essay traces their evolution from the 1950s to the present.

Sitcom Lawyers of the 1950s

The first situation comedy to include a lawyer among its regular characters was the racially-offensive "Amos 'n' Andy."[2] Like the enormously popular radio series on which it was based, the series featured a fast-talking lawyer named Algonquin J. Calhoun.

> The first appearance of a Black attorney on television, fictionalized or otherwise, was Algonquin J. Calhoun played by veteran actor Johnny Lee in 1951. Lawyer Calhoun was a character in the cast of the infamous *Amos 'n' Andy* television show. Calhoun, America's first Black fictionalized lawyer to appear regularly on major, network television (CBS), was an inept, shyster lawyer who practiced law despite having been disbarred

for malpractice and breach of ethics. Lawyer Calhoun was one of the most offensive characters on a program which has been vilified for presenting insulting and demeaning portrayals of African Americans.... The show was so offensive that the NAACP passed a resolution condemning it and brought suit (unsuccessfully) to enjoin its broadcast. Among the charges set forth in the complaint was that "Negro lawyers are shown as slippery cowards, ignorant of their profession, and without ethics." Although the NAACP's call for boycotting sponsors of the show effectively pressured CBS to take the show off the network's schedule in 1953, the show was syndicated and continued to be seen in reruns until 1966.[3]

One year after "Amos 'n' Andy" debuted, NBC brought another well-liked radio series with a lawyer to television. Although now largely forgotten, "I Married Joan," which starred Jim Backus as domestic court judge Bradley J. Stevens and Joan Davis as his wacky wife Joan,[4] consistently ranked among television's Top 10 programs during its three year run.[5]

Each episode opened with Judge Stevens on the bench.[6] In the course of resolving the case before him, the jurist would explain how he and his wife had handled a similar problem. As he began to relate the story, the courtroom would slowly fade from view and be replaced by the Stevens's home, where the evening's plot would unfold.[7]

While the show's setting offered a marvelous opportunity to tackle any number of serious legal issues, the show's writers—a distinguished group that included Neil Simon and Leon Uris[8]—opted instead for pure farce.

> *I Married Joan* was set somewhere in lobotomy land. I played the part of Judge Bradley J. Stevens who, in a moment of blinding insanity, had married a thoroughly disarranged airline stewardess played by Joan Davis.
>
> She spent the next four years making a complete horse's ass of Brad, perpetrating such horrendous tricks on her poor, befogged spouse as to make her eligible for a stint on Devil's Island—or even Gilligan's! Brad, who hadn't the jurisprudence to judge a dog show, loved every moment of it, as he went about ladling out his own brand of treacly justice—"Whereas, who gets custody of the pony?"[9]

Following the debut of "I Married Joan," two additional lawyer sitcoms reached television during the 1950s. In 1954, CBS presented "Willy," the first lawyer sitcom in which the lawyer was a woman rather than a man. Willa Dodger, played by June Havoc, was a new law school graduate who had decided to return to her hometown of Renfrew, New Hampshire to begin her legal career.[10] As Willy (and the show's writers) soon discovered, however, there wasn't much for a young lawyer to do in a small town. Thus, shortly before it was canceled, the show's locale was moved to New York City, where Willy landed a job as counsel to a vaudeville organization run by Perry Bannister (Hal Peary).[11] As before, however, Willy rarely got involved in serious legal cases.

Although it is probable that "Willy" failed because of poor scripts rather than any overt unwillingness on the part of the public to accept a woman as a lawyer, CBS decided to return to a male lead for its next outing. In 1957, it began airing a show called "Bachelor Father." In it, John Forsythe played Bentley Gregg, a playboy bachelor whose carefree existence was turned upside down when his young niece Kelly moved in with him.

> Bentley Gregg was a wealthy, successful Hollywood attorney, whose clients included many glamorous and available women. He lived with his niece Kelly, his houseboy Peter, and a large shaggy dog named Jasper in posh Beverly Hills. Uncle Bentley had become Kelly's legal guardian after her parents had been killed in an automobile accident when she was 13 years old. Between his large and active law practice, his social life with beautiful women, and the responsibilities of raising a teenage girl, Bentley's time was more than adequately filled. Peter, the helpful but often inscrutable Oriental houseboy, was a jack-of-all-trades who ran the Gregg home and was indispensable to his boss.[12]

"Bachelor Father" quickly proved popular and remained on the air for five seasons.[13] As the show developed, however, less and less attention was paid to Gregg's law practice so that more time could be spent watching Kelly grow up. In the final season, however, a young lawyer named Warren Dorson (Aron Kincaid) was brought in to serve as Gregg's junior partner. Predictably, Dorson and Kelly quickly fell in love with one another.[14]

Sitcom Lawyers of the 1960s

Because of the tremendous popularity of "I Married Joan" and "Bachelor Father," subsequent network comedies adopted their clownish formula. In 1961, for example, NBC introduced the series "Hazel."[15] As in the Ted Key comic strip on which it was based,[16] the show's main character, Hazel Burke (played by Shirley Booth), was a maid who worked for the Baxter family.[17] George Baxter (Don DeFore), Hazel's employer, was a lawyer with the firm of Butterworth, Hatch & Noell.[18]

Like the writers on "Bachelor Father" and "I Married Joan," the writers on "Hazel" played George Baxter strictly for laughs.

> George Baxter was a highly successful corporat[e] lawyer who was always in control of everything at the office, but of almost nothing at home. When he returned from the office at day's end, to his wife, Dorothy, and his young son, Harold, he entered the world of Hazel. Hazel was the maid/housekeeper who ran the Baxter household more efficiently

than George ran his office. She was always right, knew exactly what needed doing, and preempted his authority with alarming, though justified, regularity.[19]

Baxter's helplessness became particularly clear whenever the plot included Harvey Griffin (Howard Smith), a cantankerous businessman who was his most important client.[20] Invariably, Griffin would become upset with Baxter and threaten to fire him. It would then be up to Hazel to save the day by smoothing matters over with one of her homemade brownies.

The portrayal of lawyers as bumblers reached its zenith in 1965, when NBC unveiled "My Mother the Car" and CBS countered with "Green Acres." In the short-lived "My Mother the Car," Jerry Van Dyke played small-town lawyer Dave Crabtree, the only person who could hear the voice of his late mother Gladys (actually Ann Sothern) over the radio of his second-hand automobile (a 1928 Porter).[21] "Universally blasted as one of the feeblest sitcoms of the decade,"[22] the show was canceled after just one year.[23]

"Green Acres," on the other hand, proved wildly popular. The show starred Eddie Albert as Oliver Wendell Douglas,[24] a well-to-do New York City lawyer with the firm of Felton, O'Connell, Clay, Blakely, Harmon, Dillon & Pasteur.[25] Much to the despair of Lisa, his fashionable wife, Douglas had given up his successful practice to become a farmer.[26] Despite the fact that he was a Harvard graduate, throughout the show's six year run Douglas was depicted as a fool.

> Douglas, a Wall Street attorney with a deep-seated penchant for the romance of Jeffersonian democracy, decides one day to give up his New York law practice and penthouse apartment for the ascetic satisfactions of forty acres and a mule. His aristocratic Hungarian émigré wife Lisa (Eva Gabor) protests, "Dahling, I love you, but give me Park Avenue!" Oliver's definition of democracy, however, does not extend to the marriage contract, and the Douglases ride off in their massive pre-energy-crisis Lincoln convertible to start anew in the fresh green breast of Hooterville, U.S.A.
>
> Hoping to fill the frame of a Grant Wood painting, Oliver instead finds himself in the midst of something more in the style of Salvador Dali. Seeking a community of like-minded righteous yeomen, he encounters Mr. Haney (Pat Buttram), a ruthless rural conman who hornswoggles him into buying a ramshackle old farmhouse; Hank Kimball (Alvy Moore), a double-talking county agent whose discourses on plant and animal husbandry rival the lectures of a semiotics professor; and next-door neighbors Fred and Doris Ziffel (Hank Patterson and Barbara Pepper), a childless couple who are raising a young pig named Arnold as if it were their son.
>
> The major problem plaguing the Harvard-educated Oliver in his attempt to drop out of the rat race is that he continues to maintain modern urban man's faith in cause-and-effect logic, a template of reality that

does not apply in the fertile crescent that stretches from Hooterville to Pixley. Determined to spread the gospel of scientific positivism, Oliver reads books on modern American agriculture and spends his money on the items necessary to practice it. At harvest time, however, the lawyer finds he must continue to live off his New York bank account while his poor "backward" neighbors get on as they always have.[27]

Although Douglas was victimized by nearly everyone on the show, no one took advantage of him like the fast-talking junk dealer and horse trader Mr. Haney.

> Oliver Wendell Douglas was a New York lawyer with a fantasy—he wanted to own a farm and have a chance to "feel his hands in the soil." So when Mr. Haney, the country con man, came along with a farm for sale, Oliver snapped it up, sight unseen. That's when his problems began. First, his wife, Lisa, didn't want to leave Manhattan.... And when she finally *did*, their farm in Hooterville turned out to be the worst in the county![28]

Sitcom Lawyers of the 1970s

During television's first two decades, sitcoms were good-natured affairs that paid little attention to the problems of the real world.

> In the early 1960s television became dominated by the "idiot" sitcom. Carrying the lighthearted, noncontroversial style of earlier comedies to its logical conclusion, you arrive at the 1962 prime-time schedule. With shows like "Dennis the Menace," "The Real McCoys," "The Beverly Hillbillies," "Mr. Ed," and "McHale's Navy" dominating the ratings, TV seemed determined to prove itself a vast wasteland.[29]

In 1971, however, sitcom programming underwent a sudden and radical transformation.

> The year 1971 ushered in Norman Lear's *All in the Family* at C.B.S., a show that changed the nature of TV comedy forever. It was the first of the hard-nosed reality comedies, and it was a huge success, particularly in metropolitan areas. As a result, it was especially welcomed by sponsors and advertising agencies, based on the 1970 survey of viewers' spending habits.
>
> Lighthearted situation comedies were virtually eliminated from the television tube. They were replaced by the cynicism of the 70s....
>
> The subject matter of comedy shows also changed. Viewers were offered stories concerned with death, vasectomies, abortion, dope, mastectomies, rape, etc.—subjects never before touched in situation comedy. Reality comedies... took over from the simpler, good-humored domestic comedies of the 50s and 60s.[30]

In keeping with the medium's new emphasis on reality, outlandish characters like George Baxter and Oliver Douglas were quickly replaced by lawyers who were steady, serious, and dependable. Unfortunately, as the networks repeatedly learned, such characters made for poor comedy and even poorer ratings.

The first of this new breed of attorney appeared in 1972, when ABC aired "The Paul Lynde Show." In this series, which lasted just one season, comedian Paul Lynde appeared as Paul Simms, a quiet, respectable lawyer living in Ocean Grove, California with his wife Martha (Elizabeth Allen) and their two daughters.[31] Simms's attempt to be a loving and understanding husband and father were repeatedly tested during the show's run by his new son-in-law, Howie Dickerson (John Calvin), a know-it-all who could not hold a job but who had a special knack for upsetting his father-in-law.[32]

Undaunted by the failure of Lynde's show, in 1973 ABC cast Ken Howard and Blythe Danner in a new series called "Adam's Rib."[33] Like the Spencer Tracy-Katharine Hepburn movie on which it was based, the show revolved around a young assistant district attorney, Adam Bonner, and his wife, Amanda, a junior partner in a law firm.[34] Although the program based many of its stories on Amanda's crusade for women's rights in the hopes of attracting female viewers, the series was unable to find an audience and was canceled after just three months.[35]

In 1975, CBS launched "We'll Get By," a show which starred Paul Sorvino as George Platt, a hardworking attorney who lived with his family in a modest house in the New Jersey suburbs.[36] Despite the fact that it had been created by Alan Alda, the low-key program failed after just two months.[37]

Later in 1975, CBS debuted "Phyllis," one of the many series to be spun off from "The Mary Tyler Moore Show."[38] The program starred Cloris Leachman as Phyllis Lindstrom, Mary's self-centered and high-strung friend and landlady who, following the death of her husband Lars, had moved to San Francisco and taken up residence in the home of her scatterbrained mother-in-law Audrey Dexter (Jane Rose) and Audrey's second husband, Judge Jonathan Dexter (Henry Jones).[39] Despite Judge Dexter's calm and reassuring manner, the show lasted only two seasons.[40]

The last of the reality-based lawyer sitcoms was also the most successful. In 1976 ABC brought out "The Tony Randall Show." Starring Tony Randall as Judge Walter Franklin and Diana Muldaur as Judge Eleanor Hooper (Franklin's love interest), it told the story of a Philadelphia jurist who had begun dating again after two years of widowerhood.[41] Although funnier than its predecessors, the show was canceled in the spring of 1978 after switching both networks (from ABC to CBS) and nights (from Thursdays to Saturdays).[42]

While "All in the Family" was noisily inventing the reality-based sit-com, "The Mary Tyler Moore Show" was quietly pioneering the office sit-com. Earlier television comedies had conspicuously avoided the work-place, preferring instead to focus on the personal lives of their characters. Like "All in the Family," the appearance of "The Mary Tyler Moore Show" caused a major shift in thinking.

> In "The Beverly Hillbillies," Mr. Drysdale and Miss Jane clearly worked at a bank. They never seemed to do any banking, though, aside from occasionally handling the Clampetts' finances. In "Petticoat Junction" Kate Bradley ran the Shady Rest Hotel, but little of her activity ac-tually involved the hotel business.... In "Bewitched" the world of ad-vertising provided many script ideas, but the actual production of ads got short shrift. Most of the comedy emerged from family involvement in Darren's work or from the buffoonery of his glory-seeking boss....
>
> The majority of series continued to present only action-packed or high-status jobs. Most shows also continued to separate the world of work from the personal world, usually by limiting settings to one area or the other in each episode. In those cases where TV did present workplace set-tings, the emphasis was on what the characters did for a living, not on how they did it. For most businessmen and professionals... there was no workplace routine, and the office was just a place to collect messages.
>
> The 1970 premiere of "The Mary Tyler Moore Show" marked a wa-tershed in television's image of the working world. Expanding on the formula developed for "Dick Van Dyke," characters in this show were seen not just at work but doing work. These characters' jobs, including their relationships with co-workers, spilled over into their personal lives. "Mary Tyler Moore" laid the groundwork for a profusion of shows that would follow as TV moved into the workplace with increasing gusto.[43]

Once again, little time was wasted inserting lawyers into the new for-mat. The first sitcom to present attorneys at work was "Sirota's Court." This NBC offering starred Michael Constantine as Matthew J. Sirota, a night court judge in a large metropolitan city.[44] Because he had a sense of humor and took an offbeat approach to judging, most of his colleagues considered Sirota to be something of an oddball.[45] The show's regular cast included Kathleen Miller as Gail Goodman, the idealistic but inept public defender, Fred Willard as Bud Nugent, the egotistical district at-torney, Owen Bush as John Bellson, the court bailiff who believed Sirota possessed the wisdom of Solomon, and Cynthia Harris as Maureen O'-Connor, the court clerk with whom Sirota had an on again-off again sex-ual relationship.[46] Irregularly scheduled during the middle of the 1976–77 season, the show went largely unnoticed and was not renewed.[47]

In 1979, ABC brought out "The Associates," a show that took place in the prestigious Manhattan law firm of Bass & Marshall.[48] Although the series was created by the group responsible for the hit show "Taxi," featured music by B.B. King, starred British character actor Wilfrid Hyde-White (as senior partner Emerson Marshall), had strong network support, and was generally well-received by the critics, it too failed to catch on with the public and was canceled before the end of its first year.[49]

Sitcom Lawyers of the 1980s

Finally, however, in 1984 the office concept produced a smash legal hit: NBC's "Night Court."[50] Set in the Manhattan courtroom of Judge Harold T. Stone (Harry Anderson), an unorthodox boyish jurist with a soft spot for the oddball defendants who paraded through his court and a penchant for bluejeans, magic tricks, and the music of Mel Tormé, "Night Court" pitted lecherous prosecutor Dan Fielding (John Larroquette) against sexy and idealistic public defender Christine Sullivan (Markie Post).[51] The show also featured an unusual bailiff known as "Bull" (Richard Moll) and a harried court clerk named Mac Robinson (Charles Robinson).[52]

Although nearly an exact duplicate of the failed "Sirota's Court," a combination of better casting, scripts, and scheduling allowed "Night Court" to enjoy a long life. By the time the series ended in 1992, its once-unknown cast had become stars and John Larroquette had won four straight Emmys.[53] In stark contrast to earlier lawyer sitcoms, "Night Court" managed to remain funny while tackling a wide array of life's many problems, including alcoholism, mental illness, drug abuse, homelessness, racial prejudice, and greed.[54]

One year after "Night Court's" arrival, two other sitcoms that featured lawyers at work came to the small screen. In "Sara," NBC cast Geena Davis as Sara McKenna, a young, attractive, single attorney who worked in a legal aid office in San Francisco with three other attorneys.[55] Despite extensive promotion by the network, the show folded after just six months.[56] Its brief revival in 1988 led to one of the most scathing reviews ever written about a sitcom.[57]

Six months after "Sara" ended its original run, CBS introduced a similar series called "Foley Square." The show starred Hector Elizondo as Manhattan District Attorney Jesse Steinberg and featured three junior assistant district attorneys: perky Alex Harrigan (Margaret Colin), inexperienced Molly Dobbs (Cathy Silvers), and ambitious and overbearing Carter DeVries (Sanford Jensen).[58] Although many of the show's episodes dealt with criminal law, nearly as much time was spent on Alex's uneven social life.[59] Like "Sara," "Foley Square" struck out with both the public and the critics and was canceled after six months.[60]

At the same time that it began airing "Night Court," NBC inaugurated an even more popular series called "The Cosby Show." Bill Cosby played Dr. Heathcliff Huxtable, a successful obstetrician who lived with his large family in a tastefully-furnished Brooklyn brownstone.[61] Although warm and kindly, Dr. Huxtable often had trouble coping with the incongruities of modern life, particularly where his children were concerned. At such times, Clair (Phylicia Rashad), his beautiful and intelligent attorney-wife, would come to the rescue.

> Clair, a lawyer, is a working mother but one who always finds time for her kids. She stresses education, commitment and personal responsibility to her children. Her loving relationship with her husband is a testament to the institution of marriage. She's a fine role model for youngsters. Yes, she's also wealthy, but maybe that's because of all the above.[62]

In 1986, NBC presented the public with another black lawyer. But as viewers soon learned, "Amen's" Ernest Frye had little in common with Clair Huxtable and more often resembled "Amos 'n' Andy's" Algonquin J. Calhoun.

> *Amen* was a breakthrough of sorts—the first comedy in TV history to be based on religion. Sherman Hemsley, who played pushy, egotistical George Jefferson on *The Jeffersons* for ten years, played a similar character here as an insufferable deacon (and lawyer) whose father had founded the First Community Church of Philadelphia, and who intended to keep it under his thumb. Unfortunately the new minister, Rev. Gregory, had other ideas and every week he quietly deflated the strutting deacon. . . . In the final season, Deacon Frye was appointed a judge, so he could wreak havoc in the courts, too.[63]

Sitcom Lawyers of the 1990s

In 1990, as both "Amen" and "The Cosby Show" were beginning to wind down, NBC introduced a third black sitcom lawyer. "The Fresh Prince of Bel Air" starred Will Smith as a teenage rapper from a tough West Philadelphia neighborhood who had been sent to live in California with the Banks, his snobbish upscale relatives.[64] The head of Will's new family was Philip Banks (James Avery), a successful lawyer who was rich enough to employ a liveried butler.[65] Although Banks was originally intended to be a black George Baxter, by the time the series ended in 1996 he had became a judge and, along the way, evolved into a figure that was not unlike Clair Huxtable.

The [show's] finale has a dramatic and touching moment near the end
of the hour dealing with the notion of fatherhood and the bond that has
formed between Will and his uncle, Philip (James Avery).

Indeed, the growth and development of the Philip Banks character is
emblematic of the maturation of the show. Initially, Uncle Philip, a black
attorney living in Bel Air, was set up to be a target for easy laughs. The
dynamic was the same as that at play in 19th-century minstrel shows,
which mocked blackface characters who tried to use refined language.

As Philip Banks evolved, dimensions of social class and racial awareness were added to the character, with Philip often telling Will in impassioned terms about the obstacles he overcame in moving from his
working-class roots through law school and up to Bel Air.

The power of the final hour comes from Will's struggle to use what he's
learned from Philip, continue his growth and make that most difficult
passage to becoming a man.[66]

After "The Fresh Prince of Bel Air," lawyer sitcoms temporarily fell
out of favor. However, in the fall of 1995 NBC launched "The Home
Court." Similar in concept to its 1950s hit "I Married Joan," "The Home
Court" revolved around the chaotic life of a hapless domestic court judge.
But whereas Bradley J. Stevens had found favor with the public, Sydney
J. Solomon did not.

Objection. Objection, objection, objection.

Where's that gavel? Producers of The Home Court must have used it
to wallop Pamela Reed in the head, then while she was still dizzy forced
a contract under her. How else can one plausibly explain how someone
as talented as Reed got sucked into such a stupid sitcom.

She plays Sydney Solomon, a family court judge (get it? Yeah, it's too
easy, just like the rest of the jokes) who dispenses wise advice from 9–5
then goes home to her own unruly brood.

In the pilot, the most troubling case facing Solomon's court on this
particular day is a couple who wants to give their foster child back because he won't tinkle in the toilet.

This is Chicago, after all, a land where there are no drugs, gangs or
real juvenile crime. A land where a box of Cheerios and a toilet-bowl
game of Battleship can solve everything.

At home, Sydney has bigger problems: her eldest son Mike has dropped
out of college. Without a hearing, she throws him out, no doubt violat-
ing his Constitutional rights. When he takes up residence in his Volvo, she
has him towed. Then comes one of those nice, whiz-bang, aw-shucks
everything's solved endings, and that folks is a TV show.

This judge's ruling would fine producers for digging up four of the
most stereotypical kids to hit TV since The Brady Bunch. As a condition
of parole, Sydney's coworkers would be sent to Sing-Sing. And for community service, The Home Court would only consist of Reed and Meagen
Fay, who plays her sister Greer, a trophy wife content growing herbs.[67]

Although "The Home Court" was not renewed,[68] the genre was clearly back, and in the fall of 1996 viewers were given the opportunity to sample three new lawyer sitcoms. Hoping to win over African-American viewers, the upstart UPN network rolled out "Sparks." The show revolved around two mismatched brothers, Maxie and Greg Sparks (Miguel A. Nunez, Jr. and Terrence Howard), who worked as junior partners in their father's storefront law firm. James Avery, having just finished his long run on "The Fresh Prince of Bel Air," was cast as Alonzo Sparks, the pair's bombastic father, while Robin Givens, boxer Mike Tyson's ex-wife, was Wilma, the firm's brainy associate (as well as the object of both Maxie's and Greg's desires).[69]

The season's other two new lawyer sitcoms both appeared on ABC. Having consistently passed over lawyer sitcoms since its string of flops in the late 1970s, ABC now returned to the category in "Life's Work" and "Common Law."

In "Life's Work," which was set in Baltimore, comedienne Lisa Ann Walter appeared as Lisa Hunter, a wife, mother of two, and fresh-out-of-night-law-school assistant state attorney who found it difficult to keep up with her professional and family responsibilities. Michael O'Keefe co-starred as Lisa's husband Kevin Hunter, a college basketball coach who tried to lend support while pursuing his dream of moving up to a Division I school.[70]

"Common Law" had a much more upscale premise. Comedian (and actual Harvard Law School alumnus) Greg Giraldo appeared as John Alvarez, an offbeat, Harvard-educated attorney who had worked his way up from a poor family to become the only Hispanic associate at Scovell, Powers, Green & Gütenhimmel, a tony Manhattan law firm. Alvarez's live-in girl friend was the gorgeous and wealthy Nancy Slaton (Megyn Price). Because they were associates in the same firm, Alvarez and Slaton were forced to keep their affair secret. The show also featured Gregory Sierra as Alvarez's moralistic father, Luis, who provided a "reality check" for his son.[71]

In short order, "Common Law" and "Life's Work" were canceled; the former after just four weeks,[72] the latter after its first season.[73] "Sparks," meanwhile, was permitted to continue until the end of its second season, when UPN, anxious to expand its appeal beyond its core black audience, decided that the show no longer fit its corporate image.[74]

In the fall of 1997, however, Fox hit paydirt with "Ally McBeal." Produced by David E. Kelley, the creator of such well-regarded television shows as "Picket Fences," "Chicago Hope," and "The Practice," the show's star is a young, single, Harvard-educated lawyer named Ally McBeal (portrayed by Calista Flockhart) whose professional life is only slightly more under control than her personal life. Forced to leave a pres-

tigious Boston law firm to escape unchecked sexual harassment, she reluctantly agrees to go to work for Richard Fish (Greg Germann), an
amoral creep she has known (and loathed) since law school. Upon join-
ing Cage/Fish & Associates, McBeal discovers that the firm's star litigator is none other than Billy Alan Thomas (Gil Bellows), with whom
McBeal had a wrenching breakup while in law school. Although McBeal
still has strong feelings for Thomas, he has since married a gorgeous
lawyer named Georgia (Courtney Thorne-Smith).

Despite uneven writing, "Ally McBeal" quickly became the unqualified
hit of the 1997–98 television season; a midseason review noted that "'Ally
McBeal' is the one new show people are talking about and embracing....
We can start dreading the 'Ally' clones now."[75] Yet despite being hailed
as "sophisticated" and "distinctive,"[76] the show actually represents a
throwback to such earlier series as "Bachelor Father," "Hazel," and
"Green Acres."

> As her name so perfectly suggests, Ally is a slightly off-kilter, upper-
> middle-class Anglo-Saxon — she's imperfection idealized. She went to
> Harvard Law School, and professionally she appears to be a great suc-
> cess. But in fact she's an emotional muddle, confused about her career and
> her love life.... Smart yet also emotional, Ally represents the modern fe-
> male trying to remain true to herself in a harsh male world.
>
> Ally's self-involvement can make the viewer wince... and... her
> predicaments often seem so false.... [Moreover,] Ally's competence at
> work changes capriciously, depending on the needs of the story and the
> jokes. In its story lines as well as in fantasy sequences depicting what
> Ally is thinking, the show edges towards absurdism.... [A] whole episode
> is devoted to the consequences of Ally's argument with a woman over a
> container of Pringles.... [77]

Like Bentley Gregg, Ally is unmarried (but looking) and has a mud-
dled personal life, in large part because of the reappearance of someone
from her recent past; like George Baxter, Ally is professionally accomplished except when the story line demands otherwise; like Oliver Douglas, Ally is a Harvard Law School graduate who finds herself in surreal
situations which serve to remind viewers of her various struggles. And
like all three, Ally's crises often seem contrived and trivial.

Conclusion

As this essay has shown, sitcom lawyers have passed through four dis-
crete phases: from foolish (George Baxter and Oliver Douglas), to hard-
working (Paul Simms and George Platt), to goodhearted (Harry Anderson and Sara McKenna), to respected (Clair Huxtable and Philip Banks).

With the emergence of Ally McBeal, television is now embarking on a fifth phase. So far, however, it looks more recycled than original.

14

Soap Operas

ROD CARVETH

On any weekday afternoon, between 20 to 30 million people are glued to their favorite television soap operas. The magazine racks are littered with periodicals devoted to soap operas, ranging from *Soap Opera Digest* to *Soap Opera People*. There are numerous computer newsgroups and websites devoted to discussing soap operas. Soap operas are the programming genre that is most often videotaped for later viewing.

Until the late 1970s, housewives constituted the largest portion of the soap opera viewing audience. Consequently, this audience was virtually ignored by social scientists, as researchers saw the audience as women who were not part of the "legitimate" working world and who spent their afternoons watching "the troubled people of Ivorytown, Rinsoville, Anacinburg and Crisco Corner."[1]

What little that was known about the soap opera audience largely came from research done on the radio serial audience. Such research concluded that the radio serial served escape and "school of life" functions for its listeners, often taking the place of a good neighbor. Radio serials were also found to increase the self-esteem of female listeners by presenting the family as of the utmost importance and reassuring listeners that real world threats could be overcome.[2] Thus, the typical soap opera devotee was pictured as the bored housewife who tuned into her favorite serial as vicarious participation in the heroine's adventures, or as a form of parasocial interaction.

During the past fifteen years, however, businesspeople, professional athletes, retirees, and college students have been finding time to watch daytime serials. Some college students now arrange their class schedules around serial air times, creating sparsely-attended afternoon classes, while many campus bars hold "soap opera happy hours." Likewise, it is not uncommon to find community television sets—such as those in retirement homes, recreation centers, restaurants, health clubs, and prisons—tuned to soap operas, thereby exposing both the eager and the unwilling to such programming. There are even courses in the psychology or sociology of the soap opera at some colleges.

This shift in the composition of the audience correlates with drastic changes in the content of soap operas. Conceived as a cost-efficient media vehicle to deliver 18-to-49-year-old housewives to household product advertisers, soap operas displayed a relatively fixed format until the mid-1970s.[3] However, as social and economic forces caused more women to work outside of the home, and as network programming discovered teenagers in the daytime serial audience, the nature of soap operas began to change. Slick new show openings were introduced, older characters were dropped in favor of younger ones, and scenes shifted from staid interior settings to exotic exterior locales.

A Closer Look at Current Soap Operas

According to content analysis studies, television's daytime serials differ in form and characterization from most other televised entertainment fare.[4] Soap operas largely take place in white, upper-middle class communities beset with marital and romantic problems. Unlike evening dramas, in which 70% of the speaking characters are male, male and female characters appear with nearly-equal frequency on daytime serials (51% to 49%). Likewise, whereas 12% of prime time dramatic characters are non-white, in soap operas the corresponding figure is just 3%.

Soap opera characters also tend to be concentrated more in the "young adult" category (47% of characters are 20–34 years old). Despite this fact, 75% of the male characters and 60% of the female characters hold professional, technical, or managerial jobs. Almost half (49%) of soap opera characters are single, while 26% are divorced, separated, or re-married, and 9% are widowed. Only 32% of the characters are in their first marriage. The major problem in the soap opera world—roughly half of all problems—concerns romantic or marital turmoil, marked by divorce, infidelity (16% of the male characters on soap operas have fathered illegitimate children), and pregnancy.

To a much greater extent than other types of shows, soap operas are dependent upon talk for plot development. Through verbal interchange, viewers perceive a plethora of actions that are not displayed on screen. Talk becomes the basis for revelation (as actions are disclosed) and concealment (as lies are told). As a result, the soap opera world is continually filled with relationships that are in the process of change. The dramatic conflicts produced by these transitions are what allow soap operas to continue to spin out new storylines.

Many of the events portrayed on soap operas have legal consequences: death, divorce, remarriage, abortion, adoption, the commission of crimes, the repayment of financial debts, disputes regarding paternity, and the sale and distribution of assets all provide regular opportunities for soap opera characters to consult, retain, and rely on lawyers.[5] Nevertheless, attorneys rarely have continuing roles on soap operas; once the immediate crisis has passed, they are usually not seen again until the next predicament. On at least one soap opera, however, CBS's "The Young and the Restless," lawyers do have regular roles.

"The Young and the Restless"

"The Young and the Restless" debuted in 1973 as a replacement for an older soap opera known as "Where the Heart Is." Unlike the rest of CBS's daytime programming, the show was purposely crafted to appeal to a younger audience, relying heavily on stylish sets, an arresting theme song ("Nadia's Theme," composed by Barry DeVorzon and Perry Botkin, Jr.), eye-catching fashions, and "hip" storylines. Set in the medium-sized town of Genoa City, Wisconsin, the show originally was about the Brooks and the Fosters. By the early 1980s, however, the show's storylines had shifted to several new families. Today, viewers are expected to keep track of no less than eight clans: the Abbotts, Chancellors, Dennisons, McNeils, Newmans, Romalottis, Williamses, and Winters.

At the outset, daily episodes were 30 minutes long. Because of the show's enormous popularity, however, its length expanded to one hour in 1980. In its third season, the series received an Emmy for Outstanding Daytime Drama; during the 1980s, it captured this award three more times. By 1988, "The Young and the Restless" had officially become the most popular soap opera in the country, finally overtaking its longtime ABC rival "General Hospital" in the Nielsen ratings.[6]

Lawyers on "The Young and the Restless"

Three lawyers have been seen regularly on "The Young and the Restless" — Mitchell Sherman (played by William Wintersole), a solo practitioner on retainer to Newman Enterprises; John Silva (John Castellanos), another solo practitioner often used by Newman Enterprises; and Christine Williams (Lauralee Bell). While Sherman has represented Victor Newman (the patriarch of the Newman family) in both business and personal matters, Silva, who has also advised Newman in his business affairs, has spent much of his time appearing on behalf of Jill Abbott in her frequent divorce battles. For her part, Williams has handled everything from murder cases to custody disputes.

What is interesting about all three of these lawyers is the ease with which they move from one legal domain to another. Williams is particularly adept at changing specialties: thwarting a slumlord in his attempts to evict elderly tenants from the Rainbow Gardens complex; helping April Lynch beat a murder rap for killing her spouse-abusing husband Robert; aiding Nick Newman in proving his innocence in the shooting of Matt Clark; getting Dr. Timothy Reid to disclose in court that he was biased in his pronouncement that Phyllis and Danny Romalotti belonged together; identifying the real would-be killer of Victor Newman; and, in her spare time, reuniting Jack Abbott with his long-lost wife and son, Luan and Keemo, by locating them in Vietnam.

The experiences of Sherman, Silva, and Williams are typical of soap operas. Rarely are soap opera lawyers specialists. Instead, they are generalists, conveniently able to meet the needs of their clients regardless of what those needs might require in the way of legal expertise.

Sherman, Silva, and Williams are typical of soap opera lawyers in another way: each has an extremely complicated personal life. Soap opera characters in general have incredibly complicated lives and relationships. Thus, it is not surprising that lawyer characters share this complexity. Consider, in this regard, Christine Williams's (or, rather, Christine Blair Romalotti Williams's) background.

Christine (Cricket) Blair came to Genoa City at the behest of her cousin, Skip Blair, who was a photographer at Jabot Cosmetics, and soon became a teen model for Jabot. While working as a model, Cricket was date-raped by boyfriend Derek Stuart. Although she pressed charges against Stuart, his trial ended prematurely when he threw himself out a window to his death. Cricket then became romantically involved with Scott Grainger, who turned out to be her half-brother. This led Cricket to reconcile with her mother, Jessica, a former prostitute dying of AIDS. Jessica subsequently married John Abbott, the head of Jabot Cosmetics, but later died of her disease.

Having abandoned the nickname Cricket, Christine graduated from Genoa City University and Genoa City University Law School, passed the Wisconsin bar exam, and became a lawyer at the local law firm of Whitman, Walker and Wilson. She also found time during law school to date, and then marry, rock star Danny Romalotti.

At the firm, Christine went to work for Michael Baldwin. When Christine accused Baldwin of sexually harassing her, the firm fired Baldwin, prompting him to try to kill her. The plot failed, however, and Baldwin was sent to prison.

On the homefront, Christine's marriage to Danny began to flounder when Danny left to become a star on Broadway. With Christine having remained in Genoa City to work on the Rainbow Gardens case, Danny demanded (and later obtained) a divorce. Heartbroken, Christine turned to private investigator Paul Williams for consolation.

Danny later returned to Genoa City with his new wife, Phyllis, and a son, Daniel. Desperate to win Christine back, Danny asked Phyllis for a divorce, but she refused because of her hatred for Christine. In the meantime, Christine and Paul grew closer together and finally got engaged. On their wedding day, however, Phyllis ran them over, causing Paul to became impotent. Despondent over his condition, Paul broke off the engagement, but later became re-engaged to Christine when his condition improved.

On the night before her wedding to Paul, Christine slept with Danny to "gain closure." Paul walked in on the couple and became furious. As a result, the wedding was called off a second time. Subsequently, Christine helped Danny obtain a divorce by proving that Dr. Timothy Reid, the marriage counselor who had recommended to the courts that Danny and Phyllis stay together, was biased (Phyllis had slept with Reid and then blackmailed him), and convinced Paul to marry her.

In a bizarre twist, Danny and Phyllis remarried after their son Daniel almost died. For a short time, both couples were fairly happy. This state of affairs ended, however, when Danny discovered that Daniel was not his son and that Phyllis had fixed the results of a paternity test. As a result, Danny immediately set out to divorce Phyllis and seek custody of Daniel. Danny turned to Christine to represent him.

While preparing to help Danny, Christine became upset when she learned that Michael Baldwin had been released from prison and become Phyllis's attorney's new paralegal. In the meantime, Paul began to worry that Christine and Danny were starting to get back together. Christine and Danny eventually prevail in court, with Danny not only being granted a divorce, but securing custody of Daniel as well.

Professionalism of Soap Opera Attorneys

Although not all characters have lives as colorful as Christine's, most do. This may account for the fact that, by and large, soap opera attorneys appear to be less successful professionally than their prime time counterparts.

Evening lawyers such as Perry Mason and Ben Matlock rarely (if ever) lose cases. Daytime lawyers, in contrast, frequently do so. During 1995–97, two high-profile trials—Nick Newman's case on "The Young and the Restless" and Ridge Forrester's case on "The Bold and the Beautiful" (a series created in 1987 for CBS by William Bell, the creator of "The Young and the Restless")—resulted in losses for the defense. While things eventually turned out positively for both men, these happy outcomes could in no way be attributed to the skills of their lawyers.

Of course, a failure in the courtroom does allow the plot revolving around the defendant to continue. Courtroom trials only occur once or twice a year on soap operas (whereas murder trials occur almost weekly on prime time programs). Thus, a trial story on a soap opera is a major story arc, one that can get played out over three to six months. Ironically, while trials on soap operas can continue for months, defendants do receive speedy trials, often going to trial within a week or two after arrest.

Daytime lawyers also appear to have fewer scruples than nighttime lawyers. While romantic relationships between lawyers and their clients are discouraged in real life because of the possibility of conflicts of interest, and occur only occasionally on prime time shows (with "Night Court's" Dan Fielding and "L.A. Law's" Arnie Becker being the obvious examples of lawyers willing to cross the line), on soap operas acquiring clients is a form of foreplay. On "The Young and the Restless," for example, when Michael Baldwin is assigned to assist Phyllis Romalotti in her custody fight, they soon become lovers. On the same show, John Silva represents Jill Abbott despite her proclaimed romantic interest in him. On "The Bold and the Beautiful," Connor Davis negotiates a business takeover for client Brooke Logan while also carrying on an affair with her.

Even when new romances don't occur, the flames of old relationships can potentially muddy up attorney-client relations. As noted earlier, Christine Williams has twice represented her ex-husband, first in his divorce case and then in his custody case, and slept with him prior to handling the first of these matters.

Sometimes, lawyers cross more than just ethical lines. For example, on "General Hospital," Justus Ward defended Laura Spencer for the murder of Damian Smith even though he was the one who had actually killed Smith. Spencer was acquitted and Ward went to work as chief legal counsel at ELQ, the international conglomerate owned by the Quartermaine family. (ELQ's founder, Edward Quartermaine, is Ward's grandfather.) Though it could be argued that the intentions of soap opera lawyers are honorable, their behaviors in the course of representing their clients is curious at best.

Soap opera lawyers are different from their evening counterparts in other ways as well. Soap opera lawyers are almost always solo practitioners, who represent individuals rather than companies. Consequently, viewers don't see the demands placed on associates at law firms, the factors that go into the decision to promote an associate to partner, or the ethical compromises that attorneys must sometimes make to keep or obtain a large corporate client (such as a tobacco company or an environmental polluter). Likewise, soap opera lawyers, whose cases often involve either criminal law or family law, tend to spend a lot of their time outside the office conducting their own investigations.

This is not to say that there are no similarities between daytime lawyers and prime time lawyers. Both sets of lawyers are often shown either in the courtroom or huddled with their clients preparing to go to court. Like prime time, lawyers on daytime serials are rarely shown dealing with the business aspects of the law. Fees between clients and lawyers are rarely discussed, nor are expenditures for private investigators or expert witnesses. District attorneys never have to worry about how much money the state has to spend prosecuting a case. Likewise, such mundane lawyer tasks as taking a deposition, conducting legal research, or writing a brief are deemphasized in both prime time and daytime. Finally, both types of lawyers rely on detectives, paralegals, and secretaries, and have relationships with other law enforcement officials, such as court clerks, police officers, and judges.

Conclusion

Ratings for daytime soap operas have been declining in recent years, largely due to competition from other broadcast television and cable television programs. The advent of the cable networks Court TV (which has been called a cross between C-SPAN and a soap opera) and CNN and their relentless coverage of such high-profile murder cases as O.J. Simpson and Louise Woodward has caused many viewers to lose interest in the fiction of daytime serials. Nevertheless, soap operas (and their fictional lawyers) are in no real danger of disappearing. As a genre built on and devoted to romantic turmoil, soap operas will always find a ready group of viewers who cannot wait for the next calamity to unfold.

15

Westerns

FRANCIS M. NEVINS

During the first quarter century of television, Westerns were a staple item of the medium. The first Western series made for television was "The Lone Ranger" (1949–57), which remained on the air through 221 30-minute episodes. Its success inspired numerous other Westerns for children, including "The Cisco Kid" (1950–56, 156 episodes), "The Gene Autry Show" (1950–55, 91 episodes), "The Range Rider" (1950–53, 78 episodes), "The Adventures of Kit Carson" (1951–54, 104 episodes), "The Roy Rogers Show" (1951–57, 100 episodes), "Wild Bill Hickok" (1951–58, 114 episodes), and "Hopalong Cassidy" (1952–54, 40 episodes). All these early series were aimed at a youthful audience.

In the fall of 1955 networks began showing what soon became dubbed "adult" Western series. Among the better-known 30-minute shows were "Gunsmoke" (1955–61, 233 episodes), "The Life and Legend of Wyatt Earp" (1955–61, 266 episodes), "Have Gun Will Travel" (1957–63, 225 episodes), "Trackdown" (1957–59, 72 episodes), "The Rifleman" (1958–63, 168 episodes), "Lawman" (1958–62, 156 episodes), and "Wanted: Dead or Alive" (1958–61, 94 episodes). These were soon joined by such 60-minute adult Western series as "Cheyenne" (1955–62, 107 episodes), "Wagon Train" (1957–63 and 1964–65, 251 episodes), "Maverick" (1957–62, 124 episodes), "Rawhide" (1957–65, 217 episodes), "Sugarfoot" (1957–61, 69 episodes), "Bronco" (1958–62, 68 episodes), "Bonanza" (1959–73, 440 episodes), the expanded version of "Gunsmoke" (1961–75, 403 episodes), and "The Big Valley" (1965–69, 112 episodes). Three adult Western series ran 90 minutes: "The Virginian" (1962–70, 225 episodes), an expanded version of "Wagon Train" (1963–64, 32 episodes), and "Cimarron Strip" (1967–68, 26 episodes).

By the early to middle 1970s, thanks to oversaturation, the Vietnam War, and countless other factors, television Westerns had lost much of their popularity. With the departure of "Bonanza" in 1973 and "Gunsmoke" in 1975, the medium said goodbye to the men and occasionally the women of the frontier. Although there has recently been a small revival of interest with shows like "Dr. Quinn, Medicine Woman" and "The Magnificent

Seven," it seems unlikely that the Western will ever again dominate television the way it once did.

Beginnings

The television Western and the treatment of legal themes within it share the same starting point, namely the fall of 1949 when "The Lone Ranger" made its debut. Within its first few months the series offered superb illustrations of a dichotomy in presentation of legal themes that would characterize virtually all of the first wave of television Westerns.

The first three episodes—"Enter the Lone Ranger," "The Lone Ranger Fights On," and "The Lone Ranger's Triumph"—were all written and directed by George B. Seitz, Jr., the son of the director George B. Seitz, who had produced silent cliffhanger serials for Pathe in the 1920s and ended his career at MGM as director of the Andy Hardy family comedy films. The three episodes form a continuing story, with the first two ending in cliffhangers. The first half of the first episode retold the familiar "origin story"—the ambush of Captain Reid's Texas Ranger patrol and the survival of one man, the captain's younger brother John Reid (Clayton Moore), who is nursed back to health by his boyhood Indian friend Tonto (Jay Silverheels), then assumes the mask and identity of The Lone Ranger. Although his first item of business is to track down the gang that killed his brother and the other Rangers, his ultimate objective is broader. "For every one of those men I'm going to bring a hundred lawbreakers to justice. I'll make the Cavendish gang, and every criminal that I can find for that matter, regret the day those Rangers were killed." But he vows to bring in his quarry not draped over their saddles but alive to stand trial. "If a man must die it's up to the law to decide that, not the person behind the six-shooter." To which Tonto replies: "That right.... Me want law here too, for all." Although never an official representative of the legal system, the masked rider of the plains is as devoted to law-and-order as the most fervent priest to his faith, and we are clearly meant to agree that his cause is right.

Yet whenever a lawyer character appears in a subsequent episode of "The Lone Ranger," he's invariably a swine. In the 1950 episode "Spanish Gold," the adversary figure for the first time in the series is an attorney. James P. Hague (played by Bruce Hamilton) and deputy sheriff Gil Jackson (Kenneth Tobey) commit a cold-blooded murder for which they frame Tug Spencer (Steve Clark). Hague represents Spencer at his trial but, as another character later comments, "Most of the time he didn't seem to know which side was paying him." Hague throws the case so that the old man is convicted and hanged. Later he and the corrupt deputy confer in Hague's office and divide the profits from their crime. "One third for you," Hague says, "the rest for me." When the deputy asks what entitles him to two-thirds, the attorney replies: "If anyone else had defended Tug Spencer, would he have been hanged for a killing you did? That's another third." A minute or so later comes another marvelous exchange between these men.

> Hague: Are you consulting me professionally?
> Deputy: Not me....I want to go on living.

When The Lone Ranger learns of the outrage from the young man who was Spencer's cellmate before his execution, he sets out to bring Hague to justice.

As far as I can determine, no more lawyer characters appear in the series until near its end several years later. In the 1955 episode "The Too Perfect Signature," the masked man and Tonto try to prove that unscrupulous attorney Henry Stacy (Stacy Keach) and his accomplice have been forging deeds to ranchers's land. And in the series's final season, when producer Jack Wrather took over and had the final cycle of 39 segments shot in color and on relatively high budgets, came "Quicksand," one of the show's finest episodes, in which a renegade Indian and his white lawyer accomplice (Denver Pyle) ambush the Ranger and Tonto and leave them to die in a quicksand bog.

In these three episodes we notice an interesting dichotomy. What makes James P. Hague of "Spanish Gold" the vilest of the lawyer villains is precisely that his form of villainy is possible only for a lawyer, whereas in the other episodes the corrupt lawyers could have belonged to any profession or none and the stories would have been exactly the same. This distinction between essential and accidental lawyer chicanery is also found in other television Western series of the first wave.

The first series to reach the small screen after "The Lone Ranger" was "The Cisco Kid," starring Duncan Renaldo as the romantic rogue character familiar to Western fans from the long-running "Cisco Kid" movies and Leo Carrillo as his language-mangling compañero Pancho. The similarities between the series concepts are obvious: two men roaming the old West, frequently mistaken for outlaws, setting things to rights wherever they go. And several of the situations they set to rights involve slimy lawyers.

Among the 26 episodes that made up the first season (1950–51) of the series, three consecutive segments pitted our heroes against a scoundrel with a law license. In "Uncle Disinherits Niece," crooked lawyer Sam Foster (Bill Kennedy) murders a rancher who had threatened to disinherit his niece if she didn't stop seeing her boyfriend. Cisco and Pancho try to clear the young man. In "Phoney Heiress" our heroes try to save a young woman's inherited property from crooked lawyer George Holden (Jack Reynolds), who has hired an impostor to pose as the rightful owner. And in "Water Rights," Cisco and Pancho go up against a banker and his lawyer partner (Tristram Coffin) who are scheming to sabotage the ranchers's water project and then foist their own project on the valley.

Included in the 26 episodes of the second season was "Quicksilver Murder," where the chief adversary is a public prosecutor (Hugh Prosser) who is stealing quicksilver shipments and using chemical means to commit murder when threatened with exposure.

Episodes from later seasons continued on occasion to make use of lawyer characters and themes but without lawyer villains. The third season's "Fear" was an "old dark house" mystery about a dead man's ghost terrorizing the heirs who are required by his will to live on his ranch. One of the ghost's victims is attorney T. Thomas Trimble (John Hamilton), a blustering idiot but certainly no worse. The fourth season's "The Raccoon Story" involved Cisco and Pancho with an old prospector whose will left all his property to his dog. (Apparently no one could find a raccoon who could do what the script required.) In "Not Guilty," a jailed killer's friend plots to abort justice by impersonating the circuit judge (Lyle Talbot). And "New Evidence" contains one of the few courtroom sequences in the first wave of television Westerns but the principal plot device is lifted bodily from the trial sequence in John Ford's 1939 classic "Young Mr. Lincoln."

The first star of feature-length Westerns who recognized that television would shape his genre's future was Gene Autry, who in 1950 formed Flying A Productions for the purpose of making not only a 30-minute television series starring himself ("The Gene Autry Show," 1950–55) but other series with actors he hoped to develop into the next generation of shoot-em-up stars. The first of these to go into production was "The Range Rider" (1950–53), starring Jack (later Jock) Mahoney and Dick Jones as a pair of drifters who go about the old West helping decent folks and fighting bad guys, a certain number of whom are lawyers. In a 1951 episode entitled "Gunslinger in Paradise," the two drifters find the bodies of a man and woman who were left to die of thirst on the desert. It turns out that the killers are a corrupt lawyer (Denver Pyle) and a client of his (Dick Curtis) who will inherit a huge estate in case of the deaths of the couple and their child (Jerry Hunter). In an episode from the second season, "The Fatal Bullet," Mahoney and Jones prove that a man convicted of murder and awaiting execution (Tom London) was framed by his own defense counsel (James Griffith).

"The Adventures of Kit Carson" (1951–54), starring Bill Williams as the California scout and Don Diamond as his perennially lovelorn comic sidekick El Toro, survived for 104 episodes, a few of which included a legal component. "Enemies of the West" (1951) features a sympathetic lawyer (Davison Clark) whom Kit and El Toro are escorting to the state prison with a pardon for a man wrongly convicted of murder. In time we learn that the lawyer agreed to serve as appointed counsel for the defendant despite being the best friend of the judge who was murdered, but this absurdity turns out to have no bearing on the plot.

Most of the attorney characters encountered by Kit and El Toro, however, are cut from darker cloth. In "Ventura Feud" (1951), the lawyer villain (William Tannen) forges a Spanish land grant and uses it as the basis of a suit to dispossess the rightful owners of a huge tract of California land, while in "The Range Master" (1951) an attorney (Kenneth MacDonald) devises a cattle swindle to cheat his rancher client, kills the rancher's foreman, frames the rancher, and then represents him at trial and on appeal, both of which of course he loses.

"The Roy Rogers Show" (1951–57) was the first television shoot-em-up to be set in the contemporary West rather than frontier times but was just as rich in despicable lawyer characters as were series set in the past. Like "The Cisco Kid" and "The Range Rider" and many other early series, episodes of "The Roy Rogers Show" were shot in groups of two, three, or four by the same director using overlapping casts. In the debut episode "Jailbreak," Roy and his real-world wife Dale Evans investigate an attempt on the life of young Tom Lee (Rand Brooks), who's in the Mineral City jail awaiting trial for the murder of the local banker, and soon discover that Tom was framed for the crime by his own attorney (Douglas Evans). Shot back-to-back with this segment but not broadcast until two months later was "The Desert Fugitive," in which Roy and Dale become involved with the twin brother of an escaped convict (Rand Brooks) who was murdered by his lawyer and accomplice in crime (Stephen Chase) after breaking out of prison. Near the end of the first season, in "The Mayor of Ghost Town," Roy and Dale take hands in a title dispute with both an eccentric mining engineer (Hal Price) and a crooked lawyer (Zon Murray) claiming to own a deserted community. As far as I can determine, the only non-corrupt holder of a law license in any of the 100 episodes of this series was the attorney in "Ambush," a 1956 episode, who offers Roy and Dale some information as they hunt for the person who shot and wounded an old prospector. The lawyer's role is so minute that the actor who played the part isn't named in the credits.

Another series set in the new West was "Sky King" (1952, 1956–59), starring Kirby Grant as the aviation-loving owner of the Flying Crown ranch, with Gloria Winters as his niece Penny and, in the early episodes, Ron Hagerthy as his nephew Clipper. In "Designing Woman," the three are returning from an aerial survey when Sky's plane the Songbird is flagged down by a woman (Angela Greene) claiming to be the niece of a local rancher who died mysteriously. She turns out, of course, to be an impostor in the pay of the attorney for the estate (Robert Shayne).

Was there something about the early 1950s that attracted the writers and directors of television Westerns to evil lawyers? "Wild Bill Hickok" (1951–58), starring Guy Madison as the buckskin-clad marshal and gravel-voiced Andy Devine as his sidekick Jingles, pitted its heroes against a fine specimen of the breed in the 1952 episode "Blacksmith Story," where they match wits with a greedy attorney (Robert Livingston) who gets a sadistic blacksmith (Richard Alexander) to beat up ranchers in order to drive them off their property. Near the end of the same year, the relatively short-lived "Hopalong Cassidy" series (1952–54), starring William Boyd in the role he'd made famous in movies between 1935 and 1948, offered a variation on this plot in "Alien Range." This time the victims are immigrant settlers and it's not a blacksmith but a rancher (Glenn Strange) who conspires with the evil lawyer (James Griffith) in the scheme to dispossess them.

But why were attorneys so uniformly presented as villains? It's hard to believe that so many of the writers and directors who worked in this field had grudges against the profession, and in any event these early series were aimed at youngsters who often had only the vaguest notion of what lawyers were or did. My suggestion is that the negative portrayal of lawyers stems from the all-but-invariable tendency of these series to make no distinction between lawful behavior and "doing the right thing." The juvenile-oriented television Western takes place in a land where, as Gene Autry's theme song puts it, "the only law is Right." In this simplistic universe the heroes, who by definition are the good guys, subsume every positive role that a lawyer could possibly perform, leaving nothing for the lawyer characters to be but bad guys. A more diverse and realistic exploration of lawyer characters and legal themes had to await the coming of the so-called adult Western, which freed writers and directors to deal with the chasm that so often separates law and justice.

Foreshadowing the Adult Western

Conventional wisdom has it that the Hoppy-Gene-and-Roy type of Western was displaced almost overnight in the fall of 1955 by the simultaneous debut of "Cheyenne," "Frontier," "Gunsmoke," and "The Life and Legend of Wyatt Earp." A glance at the chronology, however, shows that this is incorrect. On the one hand, the juvenile type of series co-existed with the adult variety for several years: "Annie Oakley," "The Lone Ranger," and "The Roy Rogers Show" continued to air new episodes until the spring of 1957, "Wild Bill Hickok" until the spring of 1958, and "Sky King" and "Adventures of Rin-Tin-Tin" until the spring of 1959. On the other hand, adult Westerns could be seen on the small screen quite a while before "Gunsmoke" and its congeners.

An early foreshadowing of the television Western's future was offered by various 30-minute anthology series like "Ford Theatre" (1952–57), "Schlitz Playhouse of Stars" (1952–59), and "General Electric Theatre" (1953–62) that occasionally featured Western segments, where action and stunts were used (if at all) sparingly, and the emphasis was on dramatic conflict, featuring stars like Dane Clark, Broderick Crawford, and Ronald Reagan, none of whom had ever appealed to juvenile audiences. These programs were soon joined by the longest-running anthology series of them all, "Death Valley Days" (1953–70), which was devoted exclusively to Westerns but without continuing characters or shoot-em-up storylines.

Even those who confined themselves to programs with the same stars every week might have sensed something in the wind before the fall of 1955. "Cowboy G-Men," a 39-episode syndicated series from 1952, with "B" Western hero Russell Hayden and former silent child star Jackie Coogan getting into lots of fights and chases as federal agents operating on the frontier, superficially seemed aimed at fans of Rogers, Autry, and the like. But the scripts (mainly by Buckley Angell or Orville H. Hampton) tended to be quite off-trail, with strong and bizarre roles for women and for excellent actors like Jim Davis and Morris Ankrum and, usually playing psychotic gunmen of a sort never encountered by Hoppy-Gene-or-Roy, a wild-eyed wolf-faced young man named Timothy Carey who a few years later would join director Stanley Kubrick's floating stock company. In "Silver Shotgun," Hayden and Coogan trail a psychotic shotgun killer into the private fiefdom of a dictatorial sheriff (Jim Davis) who makes his own law. In "Chinaman's Chance," the agents defend Chinese gold miners in California who are being outrageously taxed by corrupt officials and terrorized by a racist White Dragon organization. Lawyers were rarely if ever involved in a "Cowboy G-Men" plot but at least two episodes were about judges, and the contrast between them can be seen as a foretaste of the diverse treatment of legal themes in adult Westerns to come. In "Hang the Jury," Hayden and Coogan go after a corrupt judge (Morris Ankrum) who's been conspiring with outlaws so they can collect the rewards for their own capture. And in "Gypsy Traders" they help a federal judge (Gregg Barton) who was run out of town after deciding a case in favor of some gypsies.

Since its formation in 1935 the premier studio specializing in 60-minute Western features had been Republic Pictures, whose executives recognized by the early 1950s that this type of movie was dying and therefore began producing Western series for the small screen. "Stories of the Century" (1954–55, 39 episodes) was something of a cross between the anthology and the single-character series. Each 30-minute segment centered around a genuine Western outlaw but with historic events reshaped so that Jim Davis, as hard-bitten railroad detective Matt Clark, played a major role in bringing the person to justice. The first 30 episodes were directed by William Witney, the Hitchcock of the low-budget action film, and among the soon-to-be prominent actors he cast as badman of the week were Lee Van Cleef (as Jesse James), Fess Parker (as one of the Dalton brothers), Jack Elam (as Black Jack Ketchum), and Jack Kelly (as Clay Allison). Witney's dynamic visual genius makes much of the series still eminently watchable today but the only episode of legal significance is "John Wesley Hardin," a 1954 offering in which Matt Clark and his assistant Frankie Adams (Mary Castle) go after the gunman (Richard Webb) who killed forty people, then became a lawyer and finally resumed a life of crime.

During the same season that saw the debut of "Gunsmoke," Russell Hayden returned as both producer and occasional guest star of a syndicated series that was nowhere near as interesting as "Cowboy G-Men" but seemed likewise split between juvenile and adult elements. "Judge Roy Bean" (1955–56, 39 episodes) starred Edgar Buchanan as the whiskered grouch in a silk hat who called himself "the law west of the Pecos," with Jack Beutel and (every so often) Hayden himself as Texas Rangers who help him keep order. But this can hardly be considered the first television Western series with a protagonist trained in the law: Buchanan's Judge Roy is a jurist purely by his own appointment, and when he bangs his gavel and turns his general store into an improvised courtroom, nothing much of a legal nature happens. The only exception I've discovered is "The Defense Rests," a 1956 episode where the climax takes place in a formal court with Beutel charged with robbery and Buchanan acting as defense counsel.

The 30-Minute Adult Western

In the fall of 1955 not one but two varieties of adult Western series with continuing characters debuted on network television. In many respects the similarities between the two types outweigh the differences, but for simplicity's sake this essay will treat them separately.

Foremost among all 30-minute adult Western series was CBS's "Gunsmoke," starring James Arness as Marshal Matt Dillon, which was a 30-minute show between 1955 and 1961, then expanded to 60 minutes and lasted in that format until the spring of 1975. Most students of television Westerns would probably agree that among 30-minute series only

CBS's "Have Gun Will Travel" (1957–63), with Richard Boone as the black-garbed intellectual gunfighter Paladin, was as consistently excellent as the early "Gunsmoke." But many others also had long runs and are fondly remembered: "The Life and Legend of Wyatt Earp (ABC, 1955–61), with Hugh O'Brian in the title role; "Tales of Wells Fargo" (NBC, 1957–61), starring Dale Robertson as Wells Fargo agent Jim Hardie; "Lawman" (ABC, 1958–62), with John Russell as vaguely Dillonesque Marshal Dan Troop; and "The Rifleman" (ABC, 1958–63), starring Chuck Connors as rancher and single parent Lucas McCain. Among the series that enjoyed respectable two- or three-year runs were "Broken Arrow" (ABC, 1956–58), with John Lupton and Michael Ansara as Indian agent Tom Jeffords and Apache chief Cochise; "Man Without A Gun" (syndicated, 1957–59), starring Rex Reason as frontier newspaper editor Adam MacLean; "The Restless Gun" (NBC, 1957–59), with John Payne as wandering gunslinger Vint Bonner; "Trackdown" (CBS, 1957–59), with Robert Culp as Texas Ranger Hoby Gilman; "The Texan" (CBS, 1958–60), starring Rory Calhoun as Bill Longley; "Wanted: Dead or Alive" (CBS, 1958–61), with Steve McQueen as bounty hunter Josh Randall; "The Deputy" (NBC, 1959–61), starring Henry Fonda as Marshal Simon Fry; "The Rebel" (ABC, 1959–61), with Nick Adams as Confederate veteran Johnny Yuma; and "Shotgun Slade" (syndicated, 1959–61), with Scott Brady playing a cross between a Westerner and a 1950s private eye. The success of the better known series led to a glut of competitors, many of them canceled after one season or less: "Buckskin" (NBC, 1958–59), "The Rough Riders" (ABC, 1958–59), "Hotel de Paree" (CBS, 1959–60), "Johnny Ringo" (CBS, 1959–60), "Man from Blackhawk" (ABC, 1959–60), and the NBC offerings "Tate" and "Wrangler," which were seen during the summer of 1960 but never made it into the fall. Among the commercial failures were at least two gems: "Law of the Plainsman" (NBC, 1959–60), with Michael Ansara as Harvard-educated Apache deputy marshal Sam Buckhart, and Sam Peckinpah's quickly axed cult favorite "The Westerner" (NBC, 1960), starring Brian Keith as drifter Dave Blassingame. Within a few years the 30-minute Western had been displaced by the 60- and 90-minute varieties but there were still some series in the shorter format, including "Branded" (NBC, 1965–66), starring Chuck Connors as disgraced ex-cavalryman Jason McCord; "The Legend of Jesse James" (ABC, 1965–66), with Christopher Jones in the title role; "The Loner" (CBS, 1965–66), with Lloyd Bridges as nomadic Civil War veteran William Colton; "A Man Called Shenandoah" (ABC, 1965–66), with Robert Horton as an amnesic drifter hunting his lost self; and "The Guns of Will Sonnett" (ABC, 1967–69), starring Walter Brennan and Dack Rambo as the father and son of a gunfighter on the run.

It should be noted that the years in which the adult Western flourished happened to coincide with three events in the outside world: 1) the golden age of the Warren Court; 2) the idealized if not idealistic presentation of lawyer protagonists in movies like "Inherit the Wind" and "To Kill A Mockingbird"; and, 3) the heyday of television lawyer series set in the present like "Perry Mason" (CBS, 1957–66) and "The Defenders" (CBS, 1961–65). This conjunction had a profound impact on the way legal themes and lawyer characters were presented in television Westerns.

That the strongest and most enduring of the 30-minute adult Western series were "Gunsmoke" and "Have Gun Will Travel" is due to any number of factors: expert directors, superb scripts (with John Meston, John Dunkel, and the young Sam Peckinpah writing for "Gunsmoke" and Harry Julian Fink and Gene Roddenberry for "Have Gun Will Travel"), haunting background music (much of it by the never-credited Bernard Herrmann), and the powerful performances of James Arness and Richard Boone as protagonists of their respective series. That every episode of "Gunsmoke" during its first few seasons was adapted from a script by John Meston for the earlier "Gunsmoke" radio series, which starred William Conrad as Marshal Dillon, perhaps accounts for the fact that several law-related segments of the series dealt with the same subject, namely the edges of the concept of lawfulness.

In at least three episodes — "The Killer" (1956), "Who Lives by the Sword" (1957), and "There Never Was a Horse" (1959) — Marshal Dillon is pitted against a sociopathic gunman (sometimes wearing a badge) who evades the law by provoking others into drawing first so he can kill them and claim self-defense. But other segments, also adapted from John Meston's radio scripts, offered somewhat different takes on legal themes. In "Bloody Hands" (1957), Dillon turns in his badge after being forced in the name of the law to do something he detests. In "The Bureaucrat" (1957), a Washington politician (John Hoyt) takes over the law enforcement function in Dodge City against Dillon's warnings and soon finds an angry mob rebelling against his dictatorial methods. In "Born to Hang" (1957), Dillon encounters a drifter (Anthony Caruso) who was miraculously saved from being lynched and is planning a legal revenge against the men who tried to hang him. In "Letter of the Law" (1958), Dillon in obedience to a court order tries to evict reformed gunman Brandon Teek (Clifton James) and his wife (Mary Carver) from their home, but when Teek threatens violence, Dillon rides to Wichita to appeal to the court on Teek's behalf. In the rare episode featuring a character who has a law license, that person usually turns out to be no better than the lawyers in the Hoppy-Gene-and-Roy Westerns. In "Print Asper" (1959), Dillon takes a hand when an attorney (Ted Knight), hired by a rancher (J. Pat O'-Malley) to draw up a deed conveying the family property to his sons, phrases the document so that title vests in the attorney himself.

The character of Paladin in "Have Gun Will Travel" had no law degree but his range of intellectual skills and interests was as broad as the prairie and Richard Boone, gifted with perhaps the most magnificent voice in the history of television, could outperform any licensed attorney when the occasion called for oratorical power. "The Five Books of Owen Deaver" (1958) pits Paladin against a moronic sheriff (James Olson) who rules a frontier town by enforcing to the letter every provision in a five-volume statutory code intended for the city of Philadelphia. In "Incident at Borrasca Bend" (1959), Paladin rides into a makeshift town to return a pouch of gold to its owner and suddenly finds himself standing trial for murder in a kangaroo court. The magic of Boone's voice and the imagination of various directors and writers made possible some episodes built around legal problems of the present, such as the violent juvenile offender. In "The Prisoner" (1960), Paladin tries to save a young outlaw (Buzz Martin) who was imprisoned at age 13 and sentenced to hang on his 21st birthday, which as the story unfolds is only a few days off.

Three months later, the theme was revisited in the stunning "Fandango" (1961). Paladin volunteers to help a Civil War comrade (Robert Gist) who is now sheriff of a Western town recapture two youths (Andrew Prine and Jerry Summers) who broke out of jail after being sentenced to hang for a brutal murder. While the two men and their prisoners are on their way back to town, Paladin learns that the victim's brother Lloyd Petty (Karl Swenson) is bent on private vengeance. "He wants to cut the heart out of those boys just like he was an Apache Indian," the gunfighter says after an encounter with Petty on the trail. Director Richard Boone and writer Harry Julian Fink skillfully orchestrate the film to evoke sympathy for the doomed boys—until the jailhouse deathwatch before the hanging at dawn when the sheriff reads from the opening address of the county prosecutor at the youths's trial.

> On the night of August 23, 1876, the defendants James Horton and Robert Olson did with malice aforethought beat Thomas Petty, age 19, to death with clubs, fists and a metal chain, one quarter inch in thickness and four feet in length. The deceased crawled for one mile during a period of five hours before lapsing into a coma. He died two days later of concussion and internal hemorrhages. The defense will contend that this brutal murder began as a fandango; that the defendants meant only to frighten the deceased and that there was no intent to kill. The defense will point out to you the youthfulness of the defendants. They'll play upon your sympathies. They will demand your understanding and indulgence for murder. The defense will point up the background of these boys, one of low mentality and doubtful parentage, the other the only son of an honest widow, lacking a father's firm hand. But I tell you that there is no mitigation for murder. There is no excuse for murder. I tell you that no one,

no matter what his age and no matter what his condition, has the right to kill another human being and ask for our indulgence.

With our reactions split down the middle the film reaches its climax. Lloyd Petty and his gunmen dynamite the jail minutes before the hanging and the explosion blows a hole in the cell wall through which one of the two boys manages to escape. Paladin has a chance to stop the youth but holsters his gun and lets him go.

> Sheriff (injured): You made a mistake.
> Paladin: No. No, I made a judgment.
> Sheriff: He'll kill another man tomorrow, or the day after, or the day after that. It'll happen.
> Paladin: Maybe you're right, Ernie. Maybe.
> Sheriff: Well, I've still got a prisoner and I'm going to do what the law prescribes.

This grim episode ends with bodies littering the half-demolished jail, the unluckier of the young murderers about to be taken to the gallows, and—in a radical innovation for series television—not the slightest assurance that the protagonist's judgment was right.

One of the finest television Western segments built around a legal concept is the 1961 episode "El Paso Stage." On a stagecoach journey to the Texas town of Brackettville, Paladin has a conversation with a young attorney (Jeremy Slate) about a point of contract law.

> Attorney: You see, in this case an employee finds that his job requires him to commit certain legal but immoral transactions so he sues to break the contract and collect all money due him. But his employer contends that any requirement that a job meet individual moral standards was a conditional acceptance and therefore no contract exists. See? To put it simply, can we superimpose our own standards on our business arrangements?
> Paladin: If those standards are usual, common and ordinary, employee wins and collects. [Citing an 1853 Supreme Court case called *McAdams v. United States* that does not seem to exist.]

Later the attorney describes conditions in Brackettville.

> Attorney: They just hired a new marshal last month. Those idiots there, the businessmen, think they can buy peace and order with a six-gun. They've hired a killer.
> Paladin: I take it you don't approve.
> Attorney: We've a few people left with sense. We're fighting it.... With law. I can see you obviously don't agree with that method.
> Paladin: On the contrary. I have the highest regard for the statutes. Including some you won't find in that book there. One of them—survival—if you lose on that count, friend, there's no appeal.

Once the coach reaches Brackettville and Paladin meets saloonkeeper Sam DeWitt (Karl Swenson) and the sadistic marshal Elmo Crane (Buddy Ebsen), this hypothetical becomes real as the gunfighter discovers he's been hired to do something perhaps just barely legal but against his code of ethics.

> Paladin: Mr. DeWitt, The Brackettville Courier a few weeks ago ran an item stating that your son was involved in certain dangerous and reckless activities.
> Sam: Well, he's a good boy but I just want him curbed a bit.
> Paladin: I wrote suggesting a thousand dollars and you wired agreement.
> DeWitt: That's right, and I have the money all counted out here.
> Paladin: I gathered from the article that the boy had been a little wild, a little reckless, but that he had committed no serious crime as yet.
> Crane: Mister, DeWitt hired you to do a simple job. It don't require a lot of explanations. Understand?... We'll arrange for DeWitt's kid to be riding out of town after dark. You grab him and take him over to Laredo. We got friends there who'll sit on him for a while till he cools down a bit.
> Paladin (aghast): Marshal, you want me to kidnap the boy?
> DeWitt: One thousand dollars. Take it or leave it.
> Paladin (counting out money from DeWitt's cashbox): I'll take one, two, three, four, five hundred dollars for my time and trouble in getting here.

Marshal Crane clubs the gunfighter and is ready to shoot him down but DeWitt intervenes, stuffs $25 in Paladin's pocket and orders him to leave town on the next coach. "Easy to make a marshal, DeWitt," Crane growls. "Awful hard to unmake one. Don't meddle in my job again." Paladin, stunned but not cowed, uses the $25 to win $1,000 in one play at DeWitt's crooked roulette wheel, but before he can leave the saloon Crane draws his gun on him. "You tampered with the wheel," DeWitt says. "Put the money back." Paladin crouches and prepares to draw. "He's the marshal," DeWitt reminds him. "If you outdraw him they'll hang you. You can't win." Paladin backs down, holsters his weapon and is followed to the street by the young lawyer from the stagecoach journey.

> Attorney: That took a lot of courage. Moral courage.
> Paladin: No, that was an exercise in the law I told you about. Survival. Survival and patience.

The lawyer then introduces himself as Frank DeWitt, the man Paladin was brought to Brackettville to kidnap.

> Paladin: Your father told me that you were reckless, a troublemaker. I had a different picture in mind.

Attorney: I am a troublemaker. I object to marked decks and watered
whiskey and fear and shotgun justice and Crane and my father and their
kind of clean government!
Paladin: You're reckless all right.

With some time left before the next stage leaves, young DeWitt introduces Paladin to Judge Robbins (Hank Patterson), who explains the legal
situation.

Frank: This document has the effect of removing Crane from office.
Judge: A writ of injunction.
Frank: We've been able to cite five instances of unjustifiable homicide
committed by Crane. We can move in on him now.
Judge: The writ empowers me to appoint someone to relieve him of
his badge and hold him for investigation....
Frank: I thought you might like the job.... We're filing it by telegraph.
If you stay here in the office out of Crane's way till we get back, the judge
can swear you in then.

But Paladin never gets legal authority to act. While he's cloistered in the
judge's office, Crane shoots Frank down on the street, challenges anyone
to say he didn't kill the young lawyer in self-defense, burns the writ, and
shoves Paladin on the four o'clock stage.

That night the gunfighter comes back and corners Sam DeWitt in his
saloon office, where there's another contract negotiation as the saloonkeeper, devastated by the cold-blooded murder of his son, tries to hire
Paladin to "unmake" the marshal with his pistol.

Sam: Can you kill him? I still have the thousand dollars. It's yours.
He tried to kill you. You'll just be protecting yourself.... Two thousand.
Paladin: He wears a badge.
Sam: Three thousand.
Paladin: He ordered me to leave town. The courts would just assume
that I was trying to resist arrest.
Sam: Four thousand. That's every cent I have.
Paladin: And he might outdraw me anyway. The risk alone is worth five.
Sam: I don't have that kind of money.
Paladin: Good night, Mr. DeWitt.
Sam: No, wait! Do you promise you'll kill him?
Paladin: I promise I'll settle my score with him. I promise I'll defend
myself.... Take it or leave it.

As DeWitt is getting the money from his wall safe, Crane comes by
from outside, shoots the saloonkeeper in the back, then climbs into the
darkened office and stalks Paladin, planning to frame him for the murder.
The cat-and-mouse between the two, shot amid the chiaroscuro of the

darkened saloon, climaxes with Paladin luring Crane out of town and over the border into Mexico, where the social contract that gives his badge meaning doesn't apply and where Paladin at last can shoot him down without legal or moral qualms.

No other 30-minute series offered the scope for treatment of legal themes as "Gunsmoke" and "Have Gun Will Travel" but occasional attempts were made. "Jefferson Drum" (NBC, 1958–59), a short-lived series starring Jeff Richards as a frontier newspaper editor, went off the air after 26 unmemorable weeks with "Simon Pitt," in which Drum goes to purchase newsprint in a neighboring town where he's threatened by the local political boss and befriended by the title character, an attorney (Michael Connors). Clearly the segment was intended as the pilot for a new series with a Western lawyer hero (which was never made). But with as many as two dozen Western shows a week on network television, it was inevitable that sooner or later would come a series whose protagonist had a law degree, and indeed a number of attempts at just such a series were aired on one of television's best known Western anthology shows.

Four Star's "Zane Grey Theatre" (CBS, 1956–61) was hosted by one of the production company's owners, Dick Powell, who each week would introduce a story having nothing to do with Zane Grey and featuring actors not usually identified with Westerns. Precisely because it lacked continuing characters, the series had the potential to offer strong stories of all types, including some of legal interest like "Time of Decision" (1957). In the town of Sand Rock, Nevada, farmer Sam Townley (Bill Erwin) comes into the saloon for a drink and is attacked by Ted Curtis (Tommy Cook), son of the area's most powerful rancher. In a fit of rage Ted draws on the unarmed Townley and threatens to shoot him down in cold blood. Townley is forced to kill young Curtis in self-defense but two of the three others in the saloon—Curtis ranch foreman Bart Miller (Mort Mills) and storekeeper Dan Slater (Walter Sande)—charge the hapless farmer with murder. Townley is locked up and clearly has no more chance of acquittal than Tom Robinson was to have a few years later in "To Kill A Mockingbird." There are only two lawyers in Sand Rock and one of them works for the dead man's wealthy father, Jed Curtis (Trevor Bardette). The other, Evan Tapper (Lloyd Bridges), is begged by Townley's wife (Jean Howell) to act as defense counsel even though he's never handled a murder trial before. Knowing what taking on the case will mean to his attempt to build a practice in the community, Tapper refuses to represent the doomed outsider. "If Jed Curtis said the sun wasn't shining you'd try to hide your shadow," a disgusted and despairing Mrs. Townley tells him. Tapper's wife Nancy (Diane Brewster) presses him to reconsider. "Why would you be jeopardizing our future defending a man's life?...I always thought being a lawyer must be a wonderful thing, like being a doctor

or a minister. Someone who'd always be there when you needed help.…
You always told me a man deserved a fair trial, innocent or guilty."

To placate his wife, Tapper drops in at the saloon and questions the
bartender (Regis Toomey), who tells the lawyer what we in the audience
know to be a lie: that he doesn't know what happened. As word spreads
that Tapper may represent Townley, pressure builds on him to turn the
case down. Bart Miller threatens to shoot his nose off. His wife and
daughter are terrorized until Mrs. Tapper begs Evan to stay out of the
case. Jed Curtis offers to give Tapper his lucrative legal business if Tapper doesn't represent Townley. At last Tapper visits the jail to talk to the
farmer himself.

> Tapper: I'm mighty upset about not being able to help you.
> Townley: Don't feel bad. A man does what he's gotta do. Thanks for
> coming by.

After Miller and one of the Curtis goons give Tapper a brutal beating,
the lawyer's wife begs him to move the family out of Sand Rock. "I can't,"
he replies. "I just can't. I don't know if I can tell you why.… We live here.
This is our home. If we start running now, where will we stop?…I'm no
hero, sweetheart, but I've got to stay here and fight. Just something I've
got to do." At this point the storekeeper Slater, moved by Tapper's courage
under fire, secretly visits the attorney and confirms Townsley's self-defense claim. This is how the film ends: not with the optimistic fadeout
television usually demanded (the innocent defendant's acquittal and the
attorney's enshrinement as hero of the town), nor with the implacably
downbeat courtroom climax of "To Kill A Mockingbird," but rather
with a moral decision, rooted not in any idealistic view of the lawyer's
duty but in something much closer to machismo. The only note of hope
at the end is a curiously muted one: "It may not be as lonely as we think."

Eighteen months later the same series presented "Threat of Violence"
(1958), in which gunfighter Clay Culhane (Chris Alcaide) tires of dealing
death, hangs up his weapons, and tries to make a new life for himself as
an attorney but finds his reputation hindering him until he defends a Hispanic (Cesar Romero) whose past record makes him the prime suspect
in a murder case. This segment served as the pilot for Four Star's "Black
Saddle" series (NBC, 1959–60), with Peter Breck replacing Chris Alcaide
as the gunman turned lawyer. Many segments of the series pit Culhane's
earlier career against his present vocation and are structured to assure us
that the legal system offers a way of settling disputes as far above self-
help violence as humankind is above the wild beasts. In "Client: Mc-
Queen" (1959), Culhane, retained by a once wealthy rancher (Basil Ruys-
dael) who was dispossessed of his property by members of his family,
discovers that he's expected to use his gunfighting skills in his client's ser-

vice. Almost exactly a year later, in "Means to an End" (1960), the same storyline recurs as Culhane is hired by a woman (Patricia Donahue) with precisely the same expectation. In "The Apprentice" (1960), the client hires a gunman (Buddy Ebsen) and his protege (Richard Rust) to settle his legal problems the easy way and Culhane tries to persuade the pistoleros to leave town even though the senior of the two is the man who first taught him to kill effectively. As was standard in television Western series with no lawyer character, going outside the law is never justified. In "Change of Venue" (1959), Culhane has to defend a man accused of his girlfriend's murder (Dean Harens) not only in court but against the threats of the dead woman's sister and brother-in-law (Patricia Medina and Willard Sage) to hang the defendant before the trial.

Of course, the series's creators tended to make things easy for themselves by usually having Culhane represent the innocent and expose the guilty (although with more gunplay at the denouements) just as Raymond Burr's Perry Mason was doing every Saturday evening over at CBS. But once in a while the "Black Saddle" storylines were more off-trail. In "Client: Mowery" (1959), a dying rancher (Simon Oakland) who was shot by the town marshal (Russell Johnson) asks Culhane to draft a will that leaves his property either to the marshal or to two outlaws, survivor take all. In "Client: Frome" (1959), Culhane represents a man (Adam Williams) who returned to town after a long period of amnesia only to find that he's been declared legally dead and his wife (Mary La Roche) has remarried. In "Apache Trial" (1959), Culhane finds himself representing a hated Indian agent before a tribal court. And in "Letter of Death" (1960), the frontier lawyer brings and wins a civil suit for false imprisonment and then sets out to prove that his client (Adam Williams) was guilty.

Television Westerns rarely owed anything to the great works of European literature, but Kafka's *The Trial* might well have been the inspiration for a segment of "The Rebel" in which law and outrage are one. In "The Legacy" (1960), Confederate veteran Johnny Yuma (Nick Adams) is arrested, taken to a town he never set foot in, put on trial for the murder of someone he never heard of, quickly convicted, and sentenced to hang. Needless to add that director Bernard McEveety and writer Frank D. Gilroy rationalize the Kafkaesque situation—which turns out to stem from a conspiracy involving the judge (Jon Lormer) and his three sons who are respectively the prosecutor, defense attorney, and sheriff—or that, unlike Joseph K, Yuma survives.

The 60-Minute Adult Western

The 60-minute adult Western began at the same time as its 30-minute counterpart, in the fall of 1955. "Cheyenne" (ABC, 1955–63), starring Clint Walker as trail scout Cheyenne Bodie, marked the entry of the Warner Brothers studio into the television Western market. Two years later came the debut of the long-running "Wagon Train" (NBC, 1957–63, 1964–65). The success of "Cheyenne" led Warners Brothers to launch two more Western series in a somewhat lighter vein: "Maverick" (ABC, 1957–62), starring James Garner as Bret Maverick, gambler, devout coward, and gleeful scammer of the ungodly, and "Sugarfoot" (ABC, 1957–61), with Will Hutchins as bumptious drifter Tom Brewster. The high ratings of those series in turn led Warners Brothers to offer "Bronco" (ABC, 1958–62), starring Ty Hardin as drifter Bronco Layne. Midway through the 1958–59 season came the legendary "Rawhide" (CBS, 1959–66), with Eric Fleming as trail boss Gil Favor and the young Clint Eastwood as his ramrod Rowdy Yates. "Bonanza" (NBC, 1959–73) introduced the family or dynasty Western, with Lorne Greene as Ben Cartwright, patriarch of the Ponderosa, and (originally) Pernell Roberts, Dan Blocker, and Michael Landon as his sons by three different wives. Its 14-year run was topped only by "Gunsmoke," which expanded from 30 to 60 minutes in the fall of 1961 and stayed on the air in that format until 1975, a full two decades after its television debut. Among the other 60-minute series that enjoyed some success were "Laramie" (NBC, 1959–63), "The Outlaws" (ABC, 1960–62), "The Big Valley" (ABC, 1965–69) (with Barbara Stanwyck as matriarch of another dynastic frontier empire), the often wildly amusing "Laredo" (NBC, 1965–67), "The Wild Wild West (CBS, 1965–69) (which attempted to fuse Western action with the James Bond type of thriller), the railroading Western "The Iron Horse" (ABC, 1966–68), and the dynastic "Lancer" (CBS, 1968–70). Hour-long series that fell by the wayside after one year or less include "Stagecoach West" (ABC, 1960–61), "Gunslinger" (CBS, Spring 1961), "The Dakotas" (ABC, Spring 1963), "The Road West" (NBC, 1966–67), "Hondo" (ABC, Fall 1967), "The Legend of Custer" (ABC, Fall 1967), and "The Outcasts" (ABC, 1968–69).

Thus the peak years of the 60-minute Western series coincided roughly with the peak years of its 30-minute counterpart—and also, of course, with the flourishing of the Warren Court, with the release of a number of now classic theatrical films that showed American lawyers and the American legal system at their finest, and with the heyday of such "good lawyer" television series as "Perry Mason" and "The Defenders." As we shall see, 60-minute Westerns were as strongly affected by all three influences as were their shorter and tighter counterparts.

One of the first feature films identified with the Warren Court era was "12 Angry Men" (1957), and within several months its influence began permeating the television Western. An early episode of "Maverick" entitled "Rope of Cards" (1958) puts good-humored gambler Bret Maverick (James Garner) in a situation obviously derived from "12 Angry Men" — he's dragooned onto a jury hearing the case of a young man accused of killing a local rancher and quickly discovers that the jury is packed with the victim's cronies who are predetermined to bring in a verdict of guilty.

Neither Warner Brothers nor any other company making 60-minute television Westerns in the late 1950s and early 1960s offered a series with a lawyer as the central character, but Tom Brewster (Will Hutchins), the protagonist of "Sugarfoot," was perpetually taking correspondence courses in how to be an attorney: "jogging along/With a heart full of song/And a rifle and a volume of the law."

One of the classic "Sugarfoot" episodes, broadcast just a month after "Maverick's" "Rope of Cards," likewise takes off from the premise of "12 Angry Men." The defendant in "Deadlock" (1958) is Calvin Williams (Herbert Heyes), who's been charged by political boss Victor Valla (John Vivyan) with large-scale cattle rustling. Brewster, who has a temporary job sweeping out Valla's saloon, is a newcomer with no knowledge of local affairs and therefore gets dragooned onto the jury, along with a Mexican (Martin Garralaga) and an Indian (Rico Alaniz) who are legally ineligible to serve and nine other men who in one way or another are under Valla's thumb. A neat exchange during the voir dire shows Brewster's naive idealism about legal matters.

> Brewster: Well, according to the law you've gotta believe a man's innocent till he's proved guilty.
> Defense counsel: You understand the law. The question is, will you support it?
> Brewster (taken aback): Doesn't everybody?

The evidence against Williams seems flimsy to say the least, but in his closing argument the puppet prosecutor demands that the jury sentence him to death and confiscate all his property. As the chosen twelve file into a private room, they find that Valla has generously supplied all of them except the Indian with cigars and fine whiskey to lubricate their deliberations. The rush by all his colleagues to an instant verdict of guilty at last tips Brewster to the truth.

> The man is innocent and you know it! You're railroading him!... No one actually stole those cattle. They were deliberately blotted and planted in the Williams herd by Valla himself. This is a frame-up. Valla's trying to destroy Williams and take the ranch. And you're helping him!... You're all in on the same ticket. This jury's rigged from top to bottom. Now

you go out there in that box and present that verdict and I'll repudiate
it. I'll expose the whole rotten frame! All right, try it!

The other jurors, however, have families or roots in the community
and are subject to pressures that the footloose Brewster doesn't face.

> One juror: We do what we have to do.
> Another: You can't fight it. The man's a devil.
> A third: This is his town, Brewster. What he wants, he takes. And
> what he doesn't want, he gets rid of.
> A fourth: Hang this jury, Brewster, and you're writing your own death
> warrant. Now, how are you going to vote?

Brewster manages to persuade the others that the decision should be
made by secret ballot. Result: eleven votes for conviction and one for acquittal. The deadlock is then announced in court. "One clean man in a
colony of lepers!," the defendant Williams cries out. "Eleven of you are
sneaking, stinking bootlicks. But because of one, I don't know who to
hate. To that one, God bless you."

The furious Valla sets out to uncover the identity of the one juror with
integrity by terrorizing each of the twelve in turn until one of them talks.
He cuts off the whisky supply of the alcoholic on the jury, has others
beaten and whipped. In an implausible but characteristic demonstration
of the television Western's idealism, the "stinking bootlicks" behave like
champions and stand together in solidarity, refusing to betray their comrade, while the unheroic Brewster does nothing to help the others.

Finally Valla has one of the recalcitrant jurors (Sam Buffington) shot
in the back on the town's main street, and to Brewster's horror the sheriff refuses to do anything about the cold-blooded murder.

> Brewster: The law's got to be upheld!
> Sheriff: What is the law, Brewster? It's the will of the people. You
> know what this [badge] is supposed to say? It's supposed to say the peo-
> ple of this town want law and order, and they've elected me to see that
> they get it. That I represent their collective power, and that any challenge
> to my authority is a challenge to theirs. This jail has three windows and
> two doors. Find me in this town five men with the courage to guard 'em
> and I'll not only arrest Valla, I'll hang him. Valla'll be dead of old age
> before you find one.
> Brewster: Yeah, I guess so.

Valla continues to pressure the surviving eleven to identify who dead-
locked the jury, but even under torture no one cracks. Finally, as Valla's
henchmen (including a young Dan Blocker, soon to become "Bonanza's"
Hoss Cartwright) are giving Brewster a brutal beating, the other jurors and
the townspeople as a whole take up arms and start shooting their op-
pressors. The uprising climaxes in a violent fistfight between Valla and

Brewster, who at last gets a chance to be macho, and as the episode ends law and order are restored.

The fact that Will Hutchins's character is studying law by correspondence course is irrelevant to most episodes of "Sugarfoot," and in the overtly legal segments he usually operates as a sort of frontier Perry Mason, defending some innocent party and pinning the guilt on the real criminal. In "The Trial of the Canary Kid" (1959), Hutchins portrays both defender and defendant as Brewster's aunt forces him at gunpoint to represent his outlaw cousin and identical double at a murder trial. His client in "The Gaucho" (1959) is a young Latino (Carlos Rivas) who is falsely charged with murder after romancing a young Anglo woman over her father's opposition. In "Vinegarroon" (1960), Brewster himself is convicted of murder and sentenced to hang by the notorious Judge Roy Bean (Frank Ferguson) and tries to save his neck not through any legal ploy but by taking advantage of the judge's fondness for the famous actress Lily Langtry. "Toothy Thompson" (1961) finds him representing a chronic troublemaker (Jack Elam) who's charged with attempting to kill a man investigating political corruption. And in the final episode of the series, "Trouble at Sand Springs" (1961), he's appointed defense counsel for two brothers (former "Lassie" star Tommy Rettig and Craig Hill) accused of murder.

The main reason why "12 Angry Men" proved so useful to television Western series is that, with the action confined to the jury room, no attorney was ever seen. Therefore the film's premise was adaptable not just to series with a lawyer or quasi-lawyer protagonist like "Sugarfoot" but indeed to virtually any series on the air: not just "Maverick" but also the classic cattle-drive series "Rawhide." "Incident of the 13th Man" (1959) offers not one but two stand-ins for Henry Fonda as ramrod Rowdy Yates (Clint Eastwood) and trail cook Wishbone (Paul Brinegar) ride into the town of Blanton so Wishbone can see a dentist and are drafted onto the jury in a murder case where their colleagues are once again dead set on finding the defendant guilty.

Like "12 Angry Men," the 1942 movie "The Ox-Bow Incident," directed by William Wellman and starring Henry Fonda, also had a profound effect on television Westerns. Its belief that the taking of the law into one's own hands (such as by means of a lynch mob or vigilante organization) was never justified became the subject of numerous episodes, including "Maverick's" "Bolt from the Blue" (1960), written and directed by the soon-to-be-famous Robert Altman.

Beauregard Maverick (Roger Moore) catches a sly old man named Eben Bolt (Tim Graham) trying to horsenap his mighty stallion Gumlegs but then they're both captured by a mob of ranchers and townsmen chasing Bolt and his elusive partner Benson January, who have "dehorsed the countryside." Starky (Charles Fredericks) and the rest of the mob take Maverick to be January and are about to lynch both men on the spot when the party is interrupted by a bumptious youth (Will Hutchins) who never gives his name but can only be Tom Brewster from "Sugarfoot."

> Lawyer: Who's their counsel?
> Starky: There ain't gonna be no counsel. We caught 'em, we're gonna hang 'em.
> Lawyer: Without a trial?
> Starky: They're horse thieves and that's trial enough for me.
> Lawyer: Now look, Starky, I am a lawyer and I know the law and the law says....
> Starky: We didn't come here to listen to no speeches, young man.
> Lawyer: They're entitled to a trial even if they're guilty.
> Starky: Who says?
> Lawyer: The law of the land. You seem to forget I am a lawyer.
> Starky: Nobody can forget you bein' a lawyer. You've been runnin' around town for months tryin' to stir up a case for yourself.

When mob member Bradley (Percy Helton) begins to get queasy about lynching the prisoners, Starky decides to resolve the issue democratically.

> Starky: All right, boys, looks like it goes to a vote. All in favor of hangin' say Aye.
> Everyone in the mob except Bradley: Aye!
> Starky: All in favor of a trial....
> Maverick and Bolt (at the top of their lungs): AYE!
> Lawyer: The second bunch of ayes have it.

But before the circuit judge can be sent for there has to be a conference between attorney and client.

> Maverick: Just convince them they've got the wrong man, will you?
> Lawyer (hands over ears): Tuttuttuttuttut! It isn't ethical for me to listen to evidence until I'm hired.
> Maverick: Oh. All right, well, you're hired.
> Lawyer: That'll be one hundred dollars in advance and another hundred if I get you off.
> Bolt (who earlier had noticed that Maverick was carrying a roll of bills): It's a deal! The money's in the saddlebag.
> Lawyer: I'm only going to take a hundred, Mr. January. If you don't hang I'll trust you for the rest.
> Bolt: Mr. Lawyer, I ain't trying to tell you how to run your case, but if you want to win this one for sure, just cut these ropes and let us git!
> Lawyer: You'll get a proper trial, old man. You too, Mr. January.
> Maverick: I'm not January!

> Lawyer: Mr. January, let me decide the proper line of defense. I'm the lawyer.

After the defender of legality has ridden off to find the circuit judge, Maverick takes aside the youngest member of the lynch mob (Arnold Merritt).

> Maverick: Hey, Junior. That lawyer. Is he any good?
> Junior: Hasn't lost a case yet.
> Bolt: That's encouragin'.
> Junior: Hasn't had a case yet. You'll be the first.

When we finally get to meet Judge Hookstratten (Richard Hale), who's just finishing up a trial in town, we wonder whether Maverick might not do better without him. "It is the duty of the law to protect as well as to prosecute. It's our function to work for the accused, look after his interests as well as convict him. Now with these values firmly in mind, I now pronounce the defendant—GUILTY! HANG HIM!" The young lawyer rides into town soon after Hookstratten has left but in time to meet Angelica Garland (Fay Spain), who has just gotten off the stagecoach and has been hunting for the man who had left her waiting at the altar in St. Louis—Benson January. The two catch up with Hookstratten on the trail.

> Lawyer: Your Honor, I am a lawyer and there is a trial you are needed for....
> Hookstratten: What kind?
> Lawyer: Horse stealing.
> Hookstratten (smacking his lips): That's a *hanging* crime!

After arriving just in time to stop the impatient lynch mob from hanging Maverick and Bolt, Altman's version of a "proper trial" gets underway, with no one sworn in, no one cross-examined, and Angelica not only identifying Maverick as Benson January but trying to shoot him where he stands. The mob serves as jury and deliberates for roughly a nanosecond.

> Starky (as jury foreman): Your Honor, we figger we made a mistake about that nice old fella. But January, he's guilty as sin.
> Hookstratten: You're acquitted, old man. January, you're sentenced to hang. That'll be twenty-five dollars.

Bolt, "out of gratitude and due respect for the law," pays the judge's fee out of Maverick's bankroll and, preparing to ride off, happens to mention that it's Sunday.

> Maverick: Sunday! It's Sunday? Why, you can't hang a man on Sunday!
> Starky: You just watch us.

> Lawyer: He's right.... According to law you can't hang a man on
> Sunday.
> Hookstratten (who hanged his last defendant a few hours ago): By
> golly, Counselor is right! You have to wait till after midnight.... That's
> the law, you've got to wait till then. Not a minute before.
> Starky: All right, tie him up, boys, and break out the bottles.

We are still only about halfway through the teleplay, and Altman continues to pile twist upon comic twist and character upon bizarre character much as he would do on the big screen a decade later in "M*A*S*H"
(1970), leaving us with perhaps the only television Western episode that
uses legal themes as the basis for anarchic farce.

One of the feature films from the Warren Court era that proved particularly fruitful for television Westerns was "Witness for the Prosecution" (1958), which was totally different fom "12 Angry Men" except
for one aspect: because nothing in the core of its story required a lawyer
character, its surprise climax could be transposed to virtually any television Western series and indeed was transposed to most. As a teenage
junkie of the genre in the late 1950s and early 1960s I quickly caught on
that, whenever the main character was begged by a friend or a stranger
to prove him innocent of a murder in which he was prime suspect, the
guy would turn out to be guilty. But precisely because these episodes de-
coupled the plot gimmick from the legal environment in which it was
originally played out, they're worth little more than passing mention here.

When the first attempt was made to produce an hour-long Western series with the main character being an attorney in the formal sense, the
venture quickly failed. "Temple Houston" (NBC, 1963–64) starred Jeffrey Hunter as a frontier lawyer and the son of Texas founding father
Sam Houston, with Jack Elam as his gunwise buddy Marshal George
Taggart. The series debuted with "The Twisted Rope" (1963), in which
Houston is hired by Dorrie Chevenix (Collin Wilcox) to defend her half-
brothers (Richard Evans and Anthony Coll), who are charged with the
murder of a lawman and threatened by a lynch mob. Clearly the concept
here is "Perry Mason" out West: the final scenes take place in court, the
prosecutor apes Hamilton Burger by accusing Houston of "prolonging this
trial with a lot of dramatic nonsense," there's a courtroom reconstruc-
tion of the crime scene and even a surprise witness whom Houston gets
to confess on the stand. But two strikingly unusual aspects commend this
otherwise routine Westernization of the "Perry Mason" formula to our
attention. The first is found early in the story when Houston proclaims
to Marshal Taggart that "justice is not necessarily just a brief pause between getting caught and getting hung. It includes a fair trial—with counsel." These lines, written less than five months after the Supreme Court's
landmark decision in *Gideon v. Wainwright*, furnish a superb illustra-

tion of how real-world jurisprudence impacts on the popular culture. The second, more striking aspect of "The Twisted Rope" is that, contrary to the vast majority of lawyer films in the Warren Court years, this one shows the "good lawyer" figure behaving as the sleazy lawyer characters behave again and again in the films of our own post- and anti-Warren Court era. The Chevenix brothers defended by Houston, although innocent of this particular crime, are outlaws who have been abusing their illegitimate half-sister for years, and when Houston makes Dorrie confess on the stand, this sympathetic character is traumatized into mental breakdown. "Winning a case doesn't mean the lawyer has to be happy about it," Houston tells Taggart at the fadeout.

Subsequent episodes of "Temple Houston" tend to fall into the conventional frontier lawyer-detective pattern. In "Find Angel Chavez" (1963), Houston's client is his sidekick Marshal Taggart, who killed a man in a shootout but can't prove it was self-defense because someone stole his adversary's gun after the duel was over. In "Toll the Bell Slowly" (1963), Houston finds that he can't clear his client without first clearing the key witness, who has himself been sentenced to hang for murder. "Gallows in Galilee" (1963) finds Houston appearing before a notorious hanging judge to defend a man charged with murder for a death that in fact was accidental. In "Thy Name Is Woman" (1964), Houston enlists a woman lawyer to help him defend a saloon hostess charged with a murder she insists was self-defense.

As the series evolved, the legal component was kept to a minimum and the stress put on raucous comedy. In "The Law and Big Annie" (1964), Houston finds a huge problem on his hands when his buddy Taggart inherits a four ton elephant. In "The Last Full Moon" (1964), an Indian chief whose son has been accused of horse theft decides to retain Houston as defense counsel rather than follow the usual routine and bribe the local Indian agent to set the youth free.

In retrospect Jeffrey Hunter regretted the whole "Temple Houston" project. "Things went wrong from the start. It was conceived in humor and delivered in dead seriousness. Then about halfway through the season NBC decided to return to the tongue-in-cheek approach. By that time it was too late. The big joke around town was, the series was about a synagogue in Texas."

In one sense the most successful 60-minute series with a lawyer protagonist was "The Big Valley" (ABC, 1965–69), for among the three male leads (two as Barbara Stanwyck's sons and one as her late husband's illegitimate son by another woman) the oldest and least dependent on machismo was Jarrod (Richard Long), whose background as a lawyer served as premise for a substantial number of episodes. To cite just a few from the series's first season, in "My Son, My Son" (1965), Stanwyck as matriarch Victoria Barkley is threatened with a murder charge when she shoots the son of a neighboring rancher (Robert Walker) who was harassing her daughter Audra (Linda Evans); Jarrod clears his mother by exposing the victim's covered-up sociopathic past. In "The Murdered Party" (1965), the patriarch of a Barkley-hating family asks Jarrod to represent his son (Warren Oates) at a murder trial despite the fact that Jarrod's half-brother Heath (Lee Majors) witnessed the killing. "A Time to Kill" (1966) finds Jarrod investigating whether a friend from his law school days (William Shatner) is, as the Secret Service suspects, involved with a counterfeiting ring. And in "Under a Dark Star" (1966), Jarrod tries to help a bitter convict (Albert Salmi) whom he prosecuted but who after nine years in prison has been proved innocent. The legal background of Richard Long's character likewise generated storylines for a number of episodes in subsequent seasons; and because "The Big Valley" survived four years in prime time, in a limited but genuine sense it was the foremost television Western with a lawyer protagonist.

Far less success was enjoyed by "Dundee and The Culhane" (CBS, Fall 1967), starring British actor John Mills as a transplanted barrister and Sean Garrison as his gunwise apprentice. Although the title of each episode followed a common pattern in the "Perry Mason" tradition, the series was not so much a Western lawyer-detective show as a traditional adult Western with 1960s values and often ingenious law-related storylines played out at somewhat irregular trials. "The Vasquez Brief" (1967) finds Dundee and The Culhane using their legal wiles to prevent the summary execution of a land baron's son who's on trial for the brutal acts of his father. In "The Murderer Stallion Brief" (1967), they represent a horse accused of trampling to death the son of the town tyrant. "The 1000 Feet Deep Brief" (1967) sends the legal duo underground to appear for a mine owner whose men blame him for the deaths of seven miners. "The Death of a Warrior Brief" (1967) pits the series's leads against each other in an impromptu court presided over by an old Indian chief with Dundee prosecuting and The Culhane defending a prospector charged with the murder of a member of the tribe. In some episodes Mills and Garrison could easily have been replaced by non-lawyer heroes from almost any other television Western, but the most distinctive segments were generally those with the strongest legal component. The series failed to find an audience and was canceled after thirteen weeks.

The television Western declined in popularity in the 1970s but at least a few of the 60-minute series that survived offered some interesting perspectives on legal or meta-legal themes, especially as the anguish over the civil rights struggle and the Vietnam War penetrated this traditionally escapist medium. As far back as the early 1960s a number of Western series had offered episodes in which the protagonist befriends and saves an innocent tormented black man, but perhaps the finest treatment of the theme and certainly, from the perspective of this essay, one of the richest was the "Gunsmoke" episode "Jesse" (1973). Precisely because James Arness is such a towering embodiment of moral authority, he has only a small role in this gem of moral ambivalence and the true protagonist is Marshal Dillon's good-hearted deputy Festus Haggen (Ken Curtis). In a brawling cowtown Festus happens to meet ex-slave Jesse Dillard (Brock Peters), an old friend he hasn't seen in years, who works as a trail cook for rancher Dave Carpenter (Jim Davis). Like most black characters in episodic television at this time, Jesse is so perfect one almost expects to see him walk on water: generous, compassionate, peace-loving, revered by all who know him, and the finest cook in the West to boot.

But the reunion between Festus and Jesse is ruined by a United States marshal (Regis Cordic) who has a poster offering a $500 reward for the black man's arrest, and it soon develops that Jesse had escaped from prison after being sentenced to ten years for killing a white man who had him whipped. Two hotheaded young drivers (Don Stroud and Robert Pine) to whom Jesse is a father figure ambush and mortally wound the marshal on the trail in an abortive attempt to set the cook free, and the lawman imposes on Festus the obligation to deliver his friend back to the prison where he will surely die. The climax takes place in the aptly-named town of Lovelock, where Festus finds himself in a Hegelian tragic collision: trapped in the hotel by Carpenter and his men, who are determined to release Jesse and spirit him over the border to Mexico even if it means burning the town down. Festus knows that Jesse is morally innocent and desperately wants to free him but also knows he has a legal obligation to return the black man to his unjust prison sentence even if it means a gun battle with the cowhands whose feelings towards Jesse he totally shares.

The tragic dilemma is resolved when Jesse, selflessly thinking not of his own freedom but only of preventing bloodshed, takes a gun smuggled into his room and makes a break, only to be shot in the back by the weaselly hotel clerk (Leonard Stone) who supplied the gun precisely so that he could kill the black man while escaping and claim the $500 reward. Bernard McEveety directs Jesse's death scene so that viewers with any knowledge of art history will be reminded of Michelangelo's Pieta.

One of the last Western series of television's first quarter century, and arguably the most unusual, was "Kung Fu" (ABC, 1972–75), starring David Carradine as half-Chinese Buddhist priest and martial arts expert Kwai Chang Caine. At least once this philosophically inclined shoot-em-up ventured into something like jurisprudence. In "The Book," also known as "Empty Pages of a Dead Book" (1974), Caine and a law-obsessed Texas Ranger named McNelly (Robert Foxworth) are tried and sentenced to death for the accidental killing of a man (James Storm) who was trying to protect his brother (Slim Pickens), a fugitive from Texas justice. "I always thought the law was the most important thing," McNelly tells Caine in their cell. "Now it's going to kill me for something I didn't even do. And it's legal! The trial was legal! The judge did what he thought was right. All together it's the law. I lived by it. I sure don't want to die by it."

Later, the two men break jail but the sheriff is badly injured pursuing them, and Caine convinces McNelly that they must save his life even if it means they'll be recaptured and unjustly hanged. The judge brings about the usual happy ending by reversing himself and ordering Caine and McNelly released.

The 90-Minute Adult Western

The success of 30-minute television Westerns led to the proliferation of 60-minute series whose success in turn led to series that ran a full 90 minutes (including, of course, commercial time). The first of these and the only one to enjoy a long run was "The Virginian" (NBC, 1962–71), which centered on a vast Ponderosa-like spread but without "Bonanza's" family dynasty aspect. James Drury starred as the anonymous foreman of the Shiloh ranch (imagine more than 200 90-minute films where no one could address or refer to the main character by a normal name!) and Doug McClure played his sidekick Trampas, with a huge assortment of regulars weaving in and out of the series over the years. In the first four seasons (1962–66) Shiloh was owned by retired judge Henry Garth (Lee J. Cobb), whose earlier careers occasionally gave rise to an episode of some legal interest. In "It Tolls for Thee" (1962) Garth is kidnapped and tortured by Martin Kalig (Lee Marvin), a sadistic sociopath he had once sentenced to prison. The Virginian and the men from Shiloh ride after him and finally wipe out the gang in an ambush. Judge Garth grabs a gun and comes within a split second of shooting down the cornered Kalig like a mad dog but in a magnificent if implausible display of self-restraint (especially hard to swallow in a Sam Fuller picture) he brings the man in alive to be dealt with according to law.

In "A Time Remembered" (1963) Cobb gets to play frontier Perry Mason. When an opera singer (Yvonne DeCarlo) with whom he'd had an affair shoots and kills her business manager (Paul Comi) and her claim that he was sexually attacking her turns out to be a lie, she's put on trial for murder, with Garth as her lawyer defending her as Mason so often defended innocent clients who were lying to him. The Mason formula blends with the "Witness for the Prosecution" surprise twist when it turns out that DeCarlo's character is guilty but justified: the dead man was making a sexual attack not on DeCarlo but on her young secretary (Melinda Plowman), who is actually her daughter—perhaps by Garth. This heavy-handed soaper gives William Witney no chance to enliven things with the eye-popping action sequences that were his trademark.

"The Virginian's" success led its production company Universal to expand the 60-minute "Wagon Train" to 90 minutes for one season (1963–64), after which it reverted to the tighter hour-length format. A few years later CBS launched "Cimarron Strip" (CBS, 1967–68), a lavishly budgeted 90-minute series more or less on the "Gunsmoke" model, starring Stuart Whitman as hard-bitten marshal Ben Crown, which failed to attract an audience and left the air after one season. At the end of the 1960s "The Virginian" itself ran out of steam and was retooled under a new title, "The Men from Shiloh" (NBC, 1970–71). When it too failed after one season, the 90-minute Western came to an end and only a few hardy perennials of the 60-minute variety, like "Bonanza" and "Gunsmoke," were still in the saddle. The cancelation of "Gunsmoke" at the end of the 1974–75 season, after an astonishing run of twenty years, brought an end to the golden age of the television Western. The few series that came later and the pale imitations of recent vintage are so different from what television offered in its first quarter century that they need not be considered here.

Conclusion

The subject of legal themes and lawyer characters in television Western series could easily fill a book, and the survey attempted here offers only a cross-section that I believe fairly represents the whole. This essay will have accomplished its purpose if it suggests how complex is the skein of similarities and differences in the episodes and series that dealt with the themes of law, lawyers, and justice.

16

Women Lawyers

CHRISTINE ALICE CORCOS

Steven Bochco, who cannot be accused of disliking strong female attorney characters, fought a long battle to get "Civil Wars" on the air. When he first suggested it as a fall series, ABC's reaction was cool. "'They flat out didn't like it.'"[1] The network asked Bochco to "lighten" up the proposed program.

> Creator and co-executive producer William Finkelstein says they looked at every possible avenue, from using a different kind of film and lighting, to changing co-star Mariel Hemingway's hair color from brunette to blond. Her new look is part of the story line of the second episode. Most importantly, four key scenes in the first episode about an emotionally dreary divorce were taken out because the story was too depressing. To lighten the episode, four scenes were inserted that are played mostly for laughs, about a woman's divorce from an Elvis Presley impersonator.[2]

Clearly someone, either at ABC or in the Bochco organization, thought that a blonde lawyer is more attractive to the public[3] and divorce cases that appeal to the sense of the ridiculous are more entertaining than those that carry a serious message, such as the prevalence of violence in domestic dispute cases. Whether this assumption is true is debatable, although it seems clear that when female lawyer shows offer serious subject matter, as in the case of some "Civil Wars" episodes, "Sweet Justice," and "The Client," the public stays away in droves. But co-creator William Finkelstein certainly views the role of women attorneys differently from the vast majority of television watchers; his mother is a divorce lawyer. And on paper the concept seems convincing; as he points out, "'Most people don't know criminals, but divorce is very topical and relatable to everybody—they know people who have either been divorced or thought of getting divorced....'"[4]

Mariel Hemingway was one of the leads in "Civil Wars" and hers was the only major female character, Sydney Guilford. She was one of the partners in the firm, with Charlie Howell, played by Peter Onorati, and Eli Levinson, played by Alan Rosenberg.[5] Apart from her prominence and Barbara Bosson's lack of participation,[6] "Civil Wars" began as a fairly conservative, traditional Bochco drama. It was well-acted and well-scripted, and should have been, if not a hit, at least a respectable plus for the network. But by changing Guilford's hair color, the network both began to trivialize her image as a powerful woman professional and acknowledge the power of the traditionally accepted view of that female professional—a pretty blonde whose brains and ability are nice, but ultimately a liability. These always set the stage for the traditional outcome: that this idealized American woman, who should "have it all," is fated to end up with less of it than her equally attractive but less intellectually gifted sisters, or her less attractive, equally intellectually endowed male colleagues. This image is precisely the one that television perpetuates about women lawyers.

One critic was unconvinced that "Civil Wars" could attract a large audience, precisely because of its subject matter. He thought it likely to appeal primarily to "L.A. Law" addicts.

> The risk involved in "Civil Wars" is two-fold.... With divorce so prevalent in American culture, the legal proceedings involved seem a likely enough subject—but divorce is also almost always painful to those involved. Will there be a vast audience eager to re-experience that pain? Second... "Civil Wars" often looks and sounds like just another episode of "L.A. Law." [D]oes TV need another "L.A. Law?" If ABC believed that, it would have been wiser to stick with "Equal Justice," an excellent series which had a large and talented cast and had already developed a loyal following.[7]

The critical difference between "L.A. Law" and "Civil Wars," which this critic fails to acknowledge, is the emphasis in the latter on a female character who is an equal partner in the firm. Apparently this emphasis is not important enough to justify another television legal drama. Stories featuring a female lawyer simply aren't worth the expenditure of time and effort involved.

Another commentator did take note of that difference, but chose to characterize it as simply an attempt to take advantage of the sexual attractiveness of the female star.

> Mariel Hemingway. What a lawyer: very cool, brainy, reserved, sensitive, beautiful, with legs that don't quit. In the second episode, when her hair is dyed blonde, everybody gets unhinged, even the judge at a trial. "What is it about blonde hair," Syd, the lawyer, asks in a statement that could live in the annals of Clairol commercials, "that makes men descend three levels on the evolutionary scale?"[8]

Although this writer purports to find the show believable as drama and well-made, he focuses on Hemingway's appearance, while dubbing Peter Onorati "[t]he real star... a great lawyer. He's not a slick sleazoid like the early Arnie Becker. Charlie Howell is a glitz-free, hard-working, dedicated lawyer with an interesting face and a good heart."[9] Charlie Howell, not the androgynously named Sydney Guilford, is the "hero." And we hear nary a word about his legs.

Eventually, "Civil Wars" foundered. In a vain attempt to boost ratings, the writers presented Sydney in the buff; media reaction was flustered but the public abandoned the series anyway. It was neither true to traditional views about women lawyers—sex objects without brains—nor courageous enough to emphasize the intelligence that many women lawyers in fact demonstrate.

Such portrayals of women attorneys as incapable, either in their professional or personal spheres, is in fact a very traditional presentation of women in general in television as well as in the movies.[10] Indeed, women attorneys are a much more advantageous target for such portrayals, because law as a body of rules reflects the kind of controlled relationships between men and women that are also evident in non-professional associations. In example after example, female attorney characters are presented as failures because they fall short of traditional, conservative images of women in either the professional or personal sphere. Because they cannot succeed in both, they should make the only choice that validates them as women—the gendered choice to be helpers and caregivers. The other choice, to compete with men, creates social and professional dislocation.

"Civil Wars" as a Test Case

While it rearticulated certain perceived truths about women lawyers, "Civil Wars" also broke nearly every accepted rule about the portrayal of women lawyers on television. That combination dictated the ultimate outcome: its run lasted only from November 20, 1991 to August 10, 1993, with a six month hiatus between March and August of 1993. Unlike "Life's Work,"[11] "Civil Wars" was well-written; unlike "Beauty and the Beast,"[12] it was not heavily romantic—indeed its subject matter was precisely the opposite—what happens when romance ends. Much of the television audience, and the sponsors, will accept a professional woman as a love object; they will not accept her as a heroine. Exploring why this should be so, what the traditional images of female television attorneys have been, how "Civil Wars" differed from these traditional images, and how, since "Civil Wars," we have continued to see traditional images, tells us how far women attorneys in popular culture still have to go before a "woman Perry Mason" appears, or better yet, before a fictional female attorney becomes so recognizable that a male attorney would be designated as the masculine equivalent of that female.

Creators of legal dramas, like David Kelley ("The Practice," "Picket Fences," "Chicago Hope") and Dick Wolf ("Law & Order," "Feds," "New York Undercover") acknowledge that

> [w]hether the show succeeds depends on whether you get your audience to really invest in the characters. And these characters are not like any of the players that we have seen in the O.J. Simpson trial.... [T]he more exposure people get to the law, the more understanding we have of people in law enforcement, the better off we are. At the same time, everyone knows the cops don't catch people in 22 minutes (the length of a TV sitcom). This is basically meant to entertain. It's not for college credit.[13]

Of the two ensemble legal dramas that premiered during the 1996–97 television season, "Feds" crashed and burned while "The Practice" was renewed. "Feds" features a United State Attorney's Office led by an ambitious white woman, Erica Stanton, played by Blair Brown, whose second in command is an ambitious African-American female, Sandra Broome, played by Regina Taylor. A typical Stanton comment: "You can't win cases with sympathy.... We should be 100 percent before we enter a courtroom."[14] Her bluntness is already against her. Additionally, one critic objects to her unattractiveness. "[W]e don't want to get too personal here, but television is, among other things, about stars. Brown, the primary star, looks drawn and haggard. Yes, she's supposed to be the tough, no-nonsense boss, but this is ridiculous."[15] Coupled with her unattractiveness was what was perceived as the novelty of the show:

> "Given the way people feel about the justice system in this country right now, it's time to have a look from the other point of view," [Brown] said, on the heels of the O.J. Simpson trials. "This is not 'Murder One,' this is not about beat cops, this is not a lawyer show. This is about prosecutors. This show you haven't actually seen yet."[16]

The series was indeed something the public hadn't seen yet, and didn't particularly care for.

"The Practice" features as its main character a single white male, who is nearly always right and when he's not, still pulls his irons out of the fire. The women associates in "The Practice" moralize at him, but they do not dominate the conversations, or the firm's practice of law.

Women Television Attorneys of the Past and Present

Traditional female television lawyers have very little success with men or with work, or both, as we can see from a quick survey of series past and present. Does anyone remember the television series "Adam's Rib"?[17] How about "Equal Justice"[18] or "Gabriel's Fire"[19] or "The Antagonists"?[20] Do you remember the "Hill Street Blues" character Joyce Davenport as an attorney or as Frank Furillo's girlfriend? If you had to name a female television character who was a lawyer, would you think of Ava Newton ("Evening Shade") or Clair Huxtable ("The Cosby Show") or even Kate McShane ("Kate McShane")?[21] Marlee Matlin had a short tenure on television in the series "Reasonable Doubts";[22] does anyone reasonably doubt that if her character had been a hearing man this well-written series would have lasted at least a little longer than the few months it was on? "Beauty and the Beast" owes its success to the acting out of the traditional mythical nighttime romance between the beautiful lead character and the fearsome but gentle Vincent; who remembers that Catherine's day job was as a competent district attorney? "Christine Cromwell,"[23] featuring Jaclyn Smith, was simply a clotheshorse show; Cromwell as the well-groomed attorney never seemed to do much lawyering, and spent a great deal of time fending off her much-married socialite mother's attempts to find her a husband.

Is this image of women attorneys at odds with the images of women generally on television? A recent survey suggests that it is not. "In television and movies, male characters are more likely to be shown on the job or talking about work than females. Women were more likely to be talking about romance and dating.... Women's looks provoke a great deal of comment in movies, TV and commercials, while the appearances of men and boys are seldom mentioned."[24] The survey, prepared for the Kaiser Family Foundation and Children Now, found that

> [m]ost of the characters in these samples, particularly the women, could not be categorized as having either a professional or blue collar occupation, that is, they were neither shown on job nor mentioned an occupation. Of the television characters who were presented as having an occupation, over a third of the men (35%) and one-fourth of the women (26%) were cast as professionals (doctor, lawyer, teacher, social worker, entertainer, etc.) or white collar workers (administrators, managers). There were very few characters, 11 percent of the men and 4 percent of the women, in blue collar jobs. The theatrical films had a similar distribution for the women. Men in these movies were also more likely to be seen working—29 percent were professional/white collar workers and 11 percent were blue collar workers.[25]

A bewildering and endless list of female attorneys parades before us.[26] They have certain eccentricities and some original characteristics, but their similarities are more obvious and thought-provoking than their differences. They are usually assistant district attorneys or criminal defense attorneys, the easiest type of legal specialization to write for, because of the story possibilities. They are usually young (just out of law school—the most attractive age for plotlines), beautiful, intelligent, and capable, have unaccountably little taste in and success with men, and their series last less than one season.

During the 1996–97 television season, several new female attorneys made appearances on shows as diverse as the iconoclastic "The Practice" (ABC), the moralistic "Feds" (CBS), and the vaguely decadent (and short-lived) "Orleans" (CBS). "JAG" features a woman attorney whose role is reminiscent of JoAnne Galloway, the Demi Moore character in the movie "A Few Good Men." The plotlines are often as trite as the characters. "The actual mystery isn't much of a mystery, but the big puzzler is how this sexist piece of garbage was created. Parker's character implies that she'll trade sexual favors for information on the case. She and Rabb continually make sexual comments to each other."[27]

"Feds" showed some promise, although the women seemed more concerned with establishing relationships and jockeying for position than in practicing law.

> Although this series will explore the private lives of the characters much more than Law & Order does, the personal issues we get glimpses of seem trite and contrived. One exchange between U.S. Attorney Erica Stanton (Brown) and Sandra Broome (Taylor), about whether Broome is primarily a prosecutor or a black woman, is embarrassingly facile.[28]

Erica Lucas (T'Keyah Crystal Keymah), the daughter on "Cosby," is a lawyer, although what kind of law she practices is unclear. Her professional status complicates her relationship with her close male friend. "Living Single" features Maxine Shaw, a divorce attorney played by Erika Alexander, a character whom the actress sees as "evolving." "At the core, a woman is a woman.... She's caretaker, knowledgeable—but also very confusing at times. And frustrating. And sexy."[29] Clearly, it's preferable that a capable female be sexy. That way she can be appealing without having to rely on her brains, which would be both frightening to men and deprive them of the excuse that she won by seducing the judge or the jury with her looks.[30]

As previously noted, the short-lived "Reasonable Doubts" tried a hearing-impaired assistant district attorney, played by Marlee Matlin, as a lead character. True to form, it followed the usual formula of "opposites attract" by pairing her with a police officer who can overcome any problems posed by her disability because he reads sign language. Like "N.Y.P.D. Blue," which pairs Assistant District Attorney Sylvia Costas with Detective Andy Sipowicz and the formula detective shows, discussed later in this essay, "Reasonable Doubts" contrasts the overly successful professional woman with the more lowly male cop.

Even if these women characters were remotely memorable, they are massively outnumbered by all the male lawyer characters that populate the television screen. For every successful show in which a woman lawyer appears as a lead or strong supporting character there are three or four that die within weeks of their debuts.[31]

Some female lawyer series never even arrive on the small screen, like Terry Louise Fisher's "Bar Girls."[32] Those who cite "L.A. Law" as an example of a show in which women attorneys are portrayed as successful and powerful overlook the fact that all of the women on that show, with the possible exception of Ann Kelsey (Jill Eikenberry), have some personal "defect" that prevents the kind of overwhelming success that male television lawyers routinely achieve, or have some socially laudable reason for foregoing. Grace Van Owen wavers from man to man, uncertain whom she loves and making a fool of herself in the process. After a disastrous marriage and brutal child custody fight, Abby Perkins finds herself in a supportive relationship, but with C. J. Lamb, who is a woman, implying that women who succeed at both careers and love can do so only if one or the other is "non-traditional." It is also interesting to note that Abby is eventually discharged from McKenzie Brackman, causing her to be labelled as a failure when it comes to being a "big time" attorney.

Of Lamb, actress Amanda Donohoe says, "My character is certainly not a run-of-the-mill lawyer, however she is incredibly competent.... The men around her don't know what to do with her; they would rather just go along with her because she's so successful."[33] Lamb is a mystery to the male attorneys around her both because she is good at their game and because she is not susceptible to the only other method they have of neutralizing her, namely sex. However, the fact that she is a lesbian suggests that only women who do not seek a traditional male-female relationship can successfully compete with men in a male-dominated profession.

Women attorneys on television and in films practice law at tremendous personal cost: failed love affairs,[34] soul-searching examinations of whether to continue to practice law,[35] disillusionment and despair at the revelation that a client is guilty, the conscious decision to subordinate a career to a relationship because a man will never accept the reverse. We see male attorneys primarily as professionals, women attorneys primarily in relationships. In addition, these situations set women up to fail.

> In many film and television stories, the mind-body split, and some form of punishment for a woman opting for mind, appears in less obvious, less exaggerated form. Often, the woman lawyer is portrayed as a competent professional, tough, perhaps, but not egregiously so, sharp and competitive, and yet attractive and capable of winning love. But still, something is usually missing—children, or a husband, or both. We see the woman lawyer as incomplete.[36]

This analysis is actually rather generous. In fact, even women attorneys whose careers would be deemed successful if they were men (C. J. Lamb, Sydney Guilford), are not really successes. Because they are women, they are by definition excluded from the possibility of success in law. For a woman lawyer to be truly successful she must be indefinably "better" than her male colleagues without losing her femininity. According to traditional television truths, this combination is impossible, as the history of shows like "Civil Wars" demonstrates.

In many cases the woman attorney attempts to compete with men by playing a man's game; she tries to play by the rules in the courtroom and may succeed in winning only to discover that outside it she is the loser. Whether or not the situation is comedic or dramatic, the woman is rarely completely successful as both a professional and a woman. She must choose one role or the other. Depending on the nature of the television series, her choice is either ridiculed or bemoaned. There are essentially two laws applying to television female attorneys: if they are lawyers in a dramatic series they have limited success with men (Sydney Guilford on "Civil Wars") or they disappear from the series (Rosalind Shays on "L.A. Law"); if they are lawyers in a comedy series they have no success with law (Lisa Hunter on "Life's Work").

Recent articles that have focused on the image of female attorneys in film discuss the overwhelmingly negative messages that these films send. These professional women are for the most part incompetent or conflicted.[37] Such articles examine the film image of the woman attorney first as an example of discrimination against women in the profession, and second as an example of ridicule or disvaluation of the woman as a professional.[38]

Similarly, television series in which we see women lawyer characters as obviously successful and in healthy relationships do not last long: "Adam's Rib" is an example. Clair Huxtable seems to be an exception, but "The Cosby Show" is not primarily about law, nor do we see Clair acting as a lawyer, except infrequently. In one episode she acts as a judge of her son Theo in a "family court" convened by her husband.[39] The parody of the legal system they carry out is not particularly edifying. In several instances she does insist on being treated like a professional woman, as in the episode in which she decides to purchase a piece of art at an auction out of her own savings. Her future son-in-law Elvin comments that he thinks that's a wonderful idea as long as her husband Cliff gives her permission, and she responds firmly that Cliff has no control over her money. Notice, however, that she discusses making this purchase with her husband; we have no parallel examples of his discussing personal purchases "out of his savings" with her. Either his money is their money, or he simply assumes that purchases made from money he regards as his are his concern alone.

Christine Sullivan (Markie Post) on "Night Court" has a stressful personal life brought on by her inability to "know what is good for her," namely a strong and protective male partner; she is incapable of recognizing the judge's love for her, nor would pursuit of that relationship be particularly good for her career. Lesley Williams in "Ransom for a Dead Man," the second "Columbo" pilot, is a murderer;[40] Trish Fairbanks, as Shera Danese in "Columbo and the Murder of a Rock Star," is unethical and grasping. Reggie Love on "The Client" is a recovering alcoholic whose addiction has cost her the custody of her children. Her mother lives with her and harps constantly on the mistakes she makes while trying to help her sort out her personal life. Sydney Solomon (Pamela Reed), the judge on "The Home Court," seems in control of her life—but the show lasted just one season.

After the failure of "Civil Wars," television tried again with "Sweet Justice,"[41] a beautifully made show about two strong women attorneys. It lasted less than one season. Significantly, many of the recent woman lawyer shows that have failed (and that's nearly all of them) feature Southern women as protagonists. Apparently, when women lawyers are the lead characters (as opposed to co-leading or supporting characters) and when they are Southern women who step out of both the subservient woman lawyer and the "Steel Magnolia" mode, the public simply does not like them.

However, in spite of hopeful pronouncements made repeatedly over the years,[42] the evidence is against the interpretation that the image of female television lawyers is changing. Of all of the television shows in which women lawyers play prominent roles, the only successful one has been "L.A. Law." Dramatic shows in which women take center stage, and are good at their jobs, fail miserably: "The Client"[43] (one season), "Civil Wars" (two seasons, precariously), "Sweet Justice" (one season). In addition, none of these shows presents women with satisfying personal lives.

Comedy shows in which women lawyers are important are equally scarce: "Night Court" and "Ally McBeal" are the only hits in which a woman's legal career plays a significant part. "Common Law" lasted less than a season. "Life's Work" was canceled after its second season.

Television Female Attorneys and Male-Female Stereotyping

To a large extent, television attorneys track attorney roles in real life. Likewise, stories about other television professionals mimic real-life pro-

fessional roles and stories. Understandably, television scriptwriters and
television producers, like television studios, create characters and stories
with which the audience is already familiar and comfortable. Those characters that do not resonate with the television audience are not popular
and their shows do not last. Thus, we should not be surprised to see that
the same assumptions and fears that underlie male-female relationships
in real life also characterize male-female relationships in legal dramas.

In addition, television series featuring women attorneys examine the very
confusing questions of personal relationships in a way that those concentrating on male attorneys do not. We find nothing odd in following Sydney Guilford's romantic vissicitudes and puzzling over Grace Van Owen's
truly awful taste in men. Perry Mason's personal life, by contrast, is not
a subject of much concern, although some people have speculated about
his relationship with Della Street. What images we have of Mason's personal life consist of one or two shots of his comfortably-appointed bachelor apartment, some gala events with Della on his arm, and some fish-
ing trips with Paul Drake, during which he invariably trips over a
mysterious murder and takes on a new client.

What do these and other examples tell us about the woman television
professional, and more particularly about the woman television attorney? Does the role of lawyer lend itself more or less powerfully to the
working out of conflicts in this area? I believe—given the role that law
plays in our society—that legal relationships, and by extension, the legal
professionals who create and enforce those relationships, are particularly suited to illuminate some of the social questions that men and women
are currently debating.

First, let us examine the images that women television attorneys currently have in the shows that feature them. After categorizing them, we
can examine the current sociological and biological literature to see if
questions about sex role differences are reflected in these categorizations.

Other Television Shows with Female Attorney Characters

"Civil Wars" is one of the most recent examples of the television series
built around a woman attorney. Does Sydney Guilford break through
the glass ceiling in this show? Or is she just another in a long line of
women attorneys whose commitment to the law, if firm, spells disaster
for their commitment to the traditional female roles of wife and mother,
and if wavering, does a disservice to the cause of women in the profession?

I contend that "Civil Wars," like other lawyer shows, depicts women primarily as incompetents or as harridans, incapable of combining fulfilling personal (heterosexual) relationships with satisfying professional careers. The exaggeration of character flaws is the order of the day; well-balanced attorneys with happy home lives and realistic life expectations need not apply.

Lawyer Shows with Female Leads

Particularly in television shows dealing with the legal system, women are continually portrayed as victims of the system, whether they are attorneys or clients. Such portrayals are ritualized because they send a particular message about the dangers of female power and the institutionalization of male rhetoric in order to dominate women. In dramatic shows about law, such domination is not only expected but required. In situation comedies, male domination may be ridiculed (that is, women may "come out on top") but they do so only when men allow them. The men who lose to these women in the courtroom or at home do so because they are either indulgent (like Lisa's husband on "Life's Work") or patronizing (like her boss) or because they are stupid or incompetent. The case is the man's to lose, not the woman's to win. She never prevails because of her competence, but in spite of it. Any other result would be threatening both to the audience and to the male characters.[44]

Further, while earlier television series and films picture women in dominant roles in legal dramas, beginning in the 1950s films reject the image of successful, ethical, and happy female attorneys. While male television attorneys may be unhappy with the outcomes of their lives, they are unhappy because of substantive problems in which their personal relationships are secondary. Even a series like "Shannon's Deal," in which the main character is spectacularly unhappy in his personal life, shows a male lawyer who achieves a great deal of personal fulfillment through his work. It invariably substitutes for long-term personal relationships. In addition, the use of male characters allows scriptwriters to introduce different "love interests" each week. These new characters add variety to the show in a way that a recurring girlfriend character does not. In addition, men are expected in our society to "play the field," to have a new girlfriend periodically. Women characters who change partners in quick succession would quickly lose the audience's respect.

In her influential book, Susan Faludi explores the problems of producer Barney Rosenzweig in portraying the off-duty life of female police officers in the television series "Cagney & Lacey."

"Cagney's sexual habits were constantly under scrutiny, not only by the network but by the head of programming.... I would say, 'You don't mind when Magnum P.I. has sex,' and he would say, 'That's different.' That Cagney slept with someone cheapened her, he thought." Shephard, CBS's programming chief, says he was worried that she would "come off as promiscuous," which would be a problem because then she wouldn't be "a positive role model." CBS executive Becker explains the anxiety and interference over Cagney's behavior this way: "Well [Lacey], she was married, and so they did have occasion to show her in her home being tender. But [Cagney] was single so that opportunity was not there, so it became more difficult to portray her as being vulnerable." And why did she need to be portrayed as vulnerable? "Because that's the way the vast majority of Americans feel women should be.... I wonder how many men there are in the U.S. today who'd be anxious to marry a hard-boiled female cop."[45]

Such concerns make much more advisable the decision to show male attorneys as ultimately successful because they can, indeed are urged to, divorce their careers from their personal lives.[46] Women attorneys in television are portrayed as "failures" if they cannot reconcile their careers and their personal lives. The long-running series "The Trials of Rosie O'Neill," in which the trials are both personal and professional, emphasizes the main character's neuroses and inability to function as a whole human being. Significantly, this series, which began many episodes with Rosie in her psychiatrist's office, lasted six years. "Civil Wars," which featured a strong female character with a good professional track record and healthy relationships with male colleagues (though not lovers), lasted only two seasons. The failure of "Civil Wars" should not be unexpected. If viewed as an unusual example of a show in which a woman character dominates and is successful and moderately happy, "Civil Wars" is instead right in the mainstream of failed woman lawyer shows. Likewise, the acclaim which has been showered on "Ally McBeal" seems to minimize, if not ignore, her erratic behavior and lack of professionalism.

In dramatic shows the woman's legal career is seen as such an aberration that personal failure is not only predictable but necessary to right the imbalance that the entrance of females into the legal profession creates. The desire of women attorneys to reconcile their two selves, the professional and the private, is seen as overly demanding of male colleagues. If they cannot divorce the two, as male attorneys have been encouraged and rewarded for doing for centuries, they simply cannot function as successful attorneys. But their failure to reconcile the two is also used against them. Women television attorneys cannot win, in real court or in the court of public opinion, any more than can their real-life counterparts. Television shows repeatedly send this ironic and contradictory message through their action and through their rhetoric.

Thus, "Civil Wars" shows us that it is consistent with the traditional message of television series that even successful women must never be too successful, lest they risk losing their lovers, husbands, or friends.[47] No rational woman in a Hollywood film, and few women in real life, would ever put her career ahead of her personal life. Nor can a woman successfully mix the two. Cinematic female lawyers,[48] much more than their male counterparts, fail at this consistently.[49] Clearly, sexual and emotion-dominated relationships for male lawyers are regrettable but severable from their professional lives. Those for women lawyers never are.

In comedic television series such failures are amusing and generally dismissed as unimportant; the show's message is that a woman's legal career does not matter much, anyway. As in the happy-go-lucky world of the screwball comedy film,[50] no one takes a woman's professional career that seriously. Take, for example, "Life's Work." The ambiguous title demonstrates the show's ambivalence about the possibility of reconciling the woman's career as an assistant district attorney with her life as wife, mother, and friend. Her feisty professional persona at the office, in which she alternately does battle with an obnoxious (male) co-worker and attempts to live up to the expectations of a (male) boss who seems not to notice that she is female, contrasts with her inability to deal with housework or child-rearing, except when her extremely supportive, understanding, and industrious husband comes to her rescue.

In one of the show's first episodes, Lisa, the assistant district attorney main character, invites two colleagues to come to her home to work because she has child-care responsibilities for the day. They quickly agree (after all, it is a half-hour show), and the three meet at her home. Before they can get any work done, her badly-brought up children get amusingly in the way. The episode demonstrates quite farcically that wacky, whiny Lisa is more incapable than most women lawyers of separating professional and personal life. In the demanding 1990s, she is in tremendous danger of being left behind in her career because of her inability to present a professional image. As her boss announces the results of the office's current investigation and attributes much of the success to her, she faints dead away, presumably from overwork and stress. A male attorney treated in the same fashion would not lose as much respect from the viewing audience as does Lisa's character; his failure would be viewed as a personal one, not one attributable to gender, especially since he would be surrounded by images of successful male attorneys. In addition, the only other female attorney in the office is man-crazy.

In another episode, Lisa confronts the possibility of pregnancy with dismay, rehearsing bitterly the problems inherent in trying to balance home and career and crying over the likelihood that her newest child will think "the day care lady is its mother." Her husband is suitably supportive and the episode ends with the pregnancy problem resolved and the couple preparing for a romantic evening in a resort hideaway.

Finally, in a third episode, Lisa and her husband are faced with some important decisions about child-care and career choices when he is offered an important new position as a basketball coach at a state university. Luckily, her mother has been fired from her job because she is "too old" (with no comment from her lawyer daughter about age discrimination) and is conveniently available to baby sit. In sitcom land, real life rarely interferes with the happy resolution of life's daily mishaps.

Other episodes are equally disturbing in their suggestion that women attorneys habitually mishandle cases. Lisa violates a gag order during a controversial trial, calls a radio talk show to explain her office's position, and is fired. The District Attorney eventually reinstates her because he is afraid of adverse publicity if he fires a "working mother." Implication: women attorneys cannot follow a judge's orders because they like to talk too much. Lisa asks another attorney to handle a hearing because her daughter is in trouble at school and she needs to leave right away. The "trouble" is her daughter's suspension over "sexual harassment" of another third-grader, possibly serious but not an emergency. Implication: women attorneys allow child-care concerns to interfere with the needs of their clients, in this case the public.

The tall, brunette, androgynously named Alex Harrigan (played by Margaret Colin), in the short-lived series "Foley Square," spends her time coddling her boss and her associates while she carries on faithfully as a good attorney, but she has no successful personal relationships.[51] Although amusing and well-written, that show lasted one season. It was created by Diane English, who was also responsible for "Murphy Brown" and "Love & War." It also included yet another female assistant district attorney, Molly Dobbs (played by Cathy Silvers). At least one critic thought it might have become a hit; comparing it with "Sara," the abortive series about a tall, brunette lawyer starring Geena Davis, Joan Hanauer said:

> Colin is a tall brunette — just as "Sara" was a tall brunette lawyer on NBC last season. Gentlemen may prefer blondes — but on television law offices don't hire them, particularly not the petite variety.... It is hard to tell how a weekly sitcom will develop after having seen only one episode, but there's the tantalizing possibility that "Foley Square" could deal with the same kind of wacky characters and insanity sanely handled that made "Barney Miller" such a delight. The ingredients are there.[52]

Both "Foley Square" and "Sara" were compared to "The Mary Tyler Moore Show," particularly because of their main characters, single professional women trying to "have it all."[53] Why they failed to capture the imaginations of the audience, and why women lawyer shows continue to fail on the small screen, stems primarily from the audience's continued unwillingness to take the idea of a female attorney on television seriously. Maybe it's the hair color: both Alex and Sara were brunettes, and as we know, Sydney was a blonde. Her show lasted a year longer.

More recent legal television dramas making their debut in the second half of the 1996–97 season included "The Practice" and "Feds," both of which feature female lawyer characters. In particular, "The Practice" emphasizes the roles of Camryn Manheim as Ellenor Frutt and Kelli Williams as lawyer Lindsay Dole, two women jockeying for position within the firm. Both try to balance their professional and personal needs, and to a large extent both fail in predictably feminine ways. Frutt is, to be perfectly honest, a frump. In one episode, she makes preparations to meet a man with whom she has corresponded. Like many "over thirty" career women (although it is not clear that this character *is* over thirty), she is choosy about her potential dates. The storyline emphasizes that other women, with less ambition (represented by the paralegal, Rebecca Washington), as well as men find her unacceptably so. Unlike men (including male attorneys) who may legitimately look for the "best deal" they can get in terms of opposite sex attractiveness, she may not. When she points out that her blind date does not meet her standards in terms of physical attractiveness, the paralegal objects to this, implying that as a slightly overweight, older woman, Frutt really has no business rejecting a man because of his looks. By implication as well, the stereotype of the woman as more accepting and less judgmental of physical attractiveness which is rejected in this episode, makes this woman attorney less personally attractive.

In another episode Frutt objects to representing a criminal defendant because she believes he has misrepresented Jewish law and as a practicing Jew she is offended. Her colleagues chide her for unprofessionalism. Ultimately they obtain his acquittal. Yet in another episode, when the head of the firm refuses a settlement offer and is berated for failing to discuss the offer with the client, he holds fast and is vindicated when the opposing side offers an even larger settlement. He is then lauded for his courage and willingness to take risks. Williams, as the slightly fluffy Lindsay Dole (no relation, presumably, to Libby), is an unequally unattractive role model. Her boss shoves her into the spotlight in a high profile case against a tobacco company because he is afraid they will lose, a reality which does not dawn on her until relatively late. More recently, Lindsay has been demonstrating some lawyerly abilities but her romantic fling with the head of the law firm clouds their relationship, and presumably her future career.

Compare these women with the women of "Feds:" "Blair Brown...
as iron-willed U.S. Attorney Erica Stanton, tough boss of the Manhattan Federal Prosecutor's Office who is second to U.S. Attorney General
Janet Reno in authority... Regina Taylor... as Sandra Broome, head of
the civil-rights division; Grace Phillips ("Murder One") as Jessica Graham,
novice prosecutor by day, novelist by night."[54] Compare these descriptions with those of the male characters, who are incomparably more
attractive: "Adrian Pasdar... as sexy prosecutor of corporate offenses
C. Oliver Resor; John Slattery ("Homefront") as lonely, brooding Chief
Assistant U.S. Attorney Michael Mancini...."[55] Similarly, the men of
"The Practice" have enchanting "little boy" qualities to complement their
brains: "Dylan McDermott... stars as Bobby Donnell, iconoclastic defender of underdogs. Supporting cast: Michael Badalucco as sweaty grunt
lawyer Jimmy Berluti; Steve Harris as clever attorney Eugene Young."
The women are "salt-of-the-earth lawyer Ellenor Frutt... blue-chip misfit and novice lawyer Lindsay Dole."[56]

"The Antagonists" is an another example of a heavily sexist and stereotyped lawyer show.

> Ward (Lauren Holly, formerly of "All My Children") is the new kid at
> the district attorney's office. She's hit on by the cops and insulted by an
> arrogant and more experienced male colleague. Scarlett (David Andrews)
> is the town's leading lawyer, an irreverent and brassy sort who drives a
> 'Vette and is intimidatingly skillful in court. We get a sense of this when
> a couple of cops, learning that Ward will be up against him in her first case,
> roll their eyes as sympathetically as if Ward were going into the ring
> against Mike Tyson. This first case involves a drunken-driving arrest that
> escalates into a love-triangle murder, as a very slick woman (Belinda
> Bauer) bamboozles Scarlett. She puts him in such an awkward position
> that he's forced to play some unethical games to secretly guide Ward to
> the guilty party. The mistakes he makes, and the clues she fails to notice,
> make both of the purported hotshots appear to be dunces.[57]

Lawyer Shows with Female Attorney Supporting Characters

Likewise, Christine, the public defender in "Night Court," has a less
than successful marriage, while the judge, with whom she would clearly
be much happier, carries a torch for her and continues to support her
emotionally.

The wife in "Mr. Belvedere" (played by Ilene Graff) is a law student,
then a lawyer, who never does seem to advance in her education or her
career. Apparently she works as a waitress and the fact that she is trained
as an attorney is a gratuitous piece of information superfluous to the

show's purpose, which is to highlight the very particular comedic talents of Christopher Hewett.[58]

Clair Huxtable, the mother on "The Cosby Show," is nominally an attorney, but we rarely see her in a courtroom. We do see a ridiculous episode in which she is up for a partnership and has a demeaning interview with the senior partner. She gets the partnership, but it is hard to take the firm, or her role in it, seriously. According to Susan Faludi, "[t]he wife in the 'Cosby' show may be the first attorney to hold down a full-time job without leaving home; when she does ply her trade, it's only to litigate domestic disputes in the family living room."[59] Clair is an extremely powerful personality, but always as a foil for her husband. Bill Cosby's comedic talents require that the traditional male role be mocked, but no matter how much Cliff Huxtable is ridiculed, he is still a physician, hence a successful, powerful character. He is not expected to be exceptionally capable in the home, except as a father; this is the point of the show, which depicts an idealized, 1980s version of the Cleavers. If this show were a drama we would be entitled to wonder who is raising the children while Clair puts in eighty hour weeks at her law firm in order to make partner and Cliff responds to early morning and late night calls to the hospital while carrying on his private practice.

Similarly, Pam Davidson, a presumably competent attorney in "The Greatest American Hero," is offered a partnership as a bribe. The female judge in "My Two Dads" shows about as much common sense as Margaret in the film "The Bachelor and the Bobby Soxer," ordering two men to pay child support and care for a teenage girl because either one could be the father. She identifies the child's father as "biologically indeterminate." Because the mother was intimate with both, the judge decides to slap both of them with custody. That a paternity test might clear up some of the confusion never seems to enter her mind. Such testing, combined with circumstantial evidence, should have allowed the judge to eliminate one of the two men, rather than so flippantly saddling them both with financial (and emotional) responsibility. But that would have eliminated the show's titillating premise.

On "Matlock," one of Ben Matlock's most consistent adversaries is the competent and intelligent Julie March (Julie Sommars), the district attorney who invariably loses the case because she has charged the wrong person. Julie is a very able attorney and her inability to bring charges against the guilty party the first time around would be inexplicable except for the fact that she is the victim of an updated "Hamilton Burger" syndrome. Her initial appearance on the show makes her seem somewhat unapproachable, consequently unattractive, because we expect women characters who are intended to be likeable to be pliable and conciliatory. Apparently some chemistry resulted between Griffith and Sommars,

since as the years have gone on Julie has become more charming and caring, and has developed an ongoing personal relationship with Ben that has
redeemed her. She still doesn't win any cases against him, however, and
needs his assistance for others. In one episode she takes on a case against
her emotionally exploitive ex-husband; Ben intervenes just in time to prevent him from shaking her confidence to the point that she cannot present
an adequate defense for her client.[60] In another, she succeeds in getting a
conviction, but against an innocent person.

The situation in which a female attorney finds herself in opposition to
someone with whom she has a familial or intimate relationship is fairly
common in television and movies. The plot device seems to heighten the
dramatic tension; in reality it merely denigrates the role of the woman
attorney. It invariably highlights her inability to function when faced with
a conflict between personal and professional relationships. Male attorneys take refuge in the traditional role of single-minded professional, but
screenwriters condemn the female attorney to the cliched emotional tension that arises from a failed love affair or family conflict. Examples on
film include "Class Action," "Primal Fear," and "Naked Lie." On television, series such as "Matlock" often fall back on this kind of manufactured situation. The result is to make women attorneys look less professional and less capable.

Why are such plot devices so common and why do viewers accept
them so readily? Part of the answer lies in the fact that women and men
do tend to approach problems differently. They do juggle competing
concerns in different ways. Indeed, society encourages them to do so.
Women are trained to accommodate, to resolve disputes, to try to understand, traits not normally associated with the attorney. The aggressive
female litigator out to win a case tends to surprise and shock, and to
discourage or disgust, males who otherwise might be sexually attracted
to her.

Male attorneys learn "the game" early, how to fight each other in the
courtroom and play golf afterwards. The male attorney who empathizes
with his client may be a pleasant surprise. However, he never lets his ability to see the other side get in the way of a courtroom victory. Their success
heightens their sexual attractiveness on television just as it does in real life.

The other recurring women attorney characters on "Matlock" are also
successful only because of their relationships with Ben. They are both his
daughters, and both enter into long-term (junior) partnerships with him.
The first, Charlene, disappears inexplicably after a few years; apparently she's gone off to greener pastures in a Northern city. The second, Leanne,
turns up after the end of a disastrous marriage, and Ben takes her in personally and professionally. Of course, "Matlock" is not really intended
to be a realistic portrayal of the workings of a law practice; it is a char-

acter show, a courtroom western, in which the hero rides in every week to save the day by ferreting out the real culprit. Still, it follows the traditional formula in which the woman attorney, although bright, still has a lot to learn from the dominant older male figure.

In the short-lived "The Law and Harry McGraw," a spinoff from "Murder, She Wrote," based on the Harry McGraw detective character, Barbara Babcock plays a sole practitioner, Ellie Maginnis, a widowed lawyer, who is quite good at her job. But she is at most the junior partner in the series, because Harry (played by Jerry Orbach) is clearly the focus of the show. His is the name in the title, and he is a rough and tumble private investigator whose frequent brushes with the law are intended to be charming. Babcock's apparent sole purpose in the show is to get him out of most of his scrapes with his license, if not his dignity, intact, and occasionally to provide him with a meal ticket because he does most of her investigative work. Again, Babcock is the "stay at home" caregiver who patches Harry together after he engages in traditional testosterone-enriched forays into the real world.

Real women attorneys who appear on television have similar problems. Marcia Clark, the lead prosecutor in the O.J. Simpson criminal case, incurred an incredible amount of comment when she appeared in court with her hair styled differently a few weeks into the trial.[61] In addition, her fight with her ex-husband over child custody took center stage for several days while various learned legal commentators discussed the possibility of balancing home and family when one is a divorced female district attorney making $100,000-a-year in a town that regards a salary under seven figures as poverty-line.

Non-Lawyer Shows

Among recent non-legal drama shows featuring female attorneys, the USA Network's "The Big Easy" is prominent, not so much for its popularity as for its softening of the woman lawyer character of Anne Osborne. Unlike Ellen Barkin's film characterization, Susan Walters's portrayal of Anne emphasizes her "pluckiness," her charm, and her repeated insistence on independence from the hero, Remy McSwain. In the film, Anne was clearly both "available" and attracted to the hero, which put her in conflict with other women in the story and brought her ethics into question. The television Anne is "otherwise engaged" (her fiance visits from Washington periodically) and gets along charmingly with the sole other important female character, a police detective named Nadine. Anne's fiance is usually conveniently absent, allowing her to play with romantic fire. This behavior reinforces the traditional message that professional women are only really interested in sex or romance; a female's career is the most recent and convenient means to the conventional end: marriage.

Anne's relationship with Remy is dismayingly sophomoric, relying on double entendres and interrupted embraces. In one episode he tricks her into disrobing by telling her he plans to jump into a bayou to search for clues to the downing of a light plane; he then announces that he wouldn't be so foolhardy as to go swimming with the alligators. Anne takes on investigations herself, following in the footsteps of legal eagles like Perry Mason and Matlock, and disregarding Remy's warnings; invariably her attempts to assert her independence result in danger to both of them. The contrived ending of the filmed "Big Easy" was almost believable, in that we eventually accepted Anne's attraction to Remy and her willingness to assist him in clearing his name.[62] The small screen's Anne engages in foolhardy or demeaning activities in which no sane attorney would engage,[63] and for which no sane client would pay.

Female lawyer characters who are clearly competent are relegated to the dramatic background. Pam Davidson, the capable Connie Sellecca character on "The Greatest American Hero," is the traditional female second banana, helping her man Ralph Hinkley with his various adventures by doling out sage advice with the band-aids and aspirin. We rarely see her acting as an attorney; she is for the most part the "hero's girlfriend," taking a great deal of lip from Bill Maxwell, Robert Culp's chauvinistic and socially-challenged FBI agent (he refers to her constantly as "counselor" in a somewhat demeaning tone of voice), and rescuing both of them periodically. Indeed, her status as a professional woman merely serves to reinforce Ralph's image as an open-minded and thoughtful fellow, in contrast to his friend Bill. It is noteworthy that Ralph is a high school teacher, a less prestigious career than that of lawyer. Pam has had to "settle" for a companion whose social status is lower than hers; in exchange she gains a man who indulgently allows her to practice her profession.

In the episode in which Pam is offered a partnership at her firm, the prize turns out to be a bribe and Ralph has to rescue her from certain death at the hands of the senior partner and his minions. As the episode ends she does get the chance to keep the partnership, the implication being that she really deserves it after all. However, the episode makes clear that she couldn't have coped with her elevation to the partnership without Ralph's assistance.

While "The Greatest American Hero" is a fantasy that indulges in gentle social satire, it significantly presents the man as the hero (albeit a klutzy one) and the woman as the accepting companion. Ralph succeeds in righting wrongs as a suburban vigilante with the assistance of a magic suit given him by aliens. Even though he has lost the instruction booklet, he figures out how it works, a traditional male fantasy. In his endeavors he is assisted by the quick-drawing FBI agent Bill Maxwell. Neither Pam, the female lead character, nor her career, which is rooted in the application of peaceful means to solve problems, is the focus of the show.

Two detective series, "Simon & Simon" and "Magnum, P.I." have recurring female lawyer characters. Both serve primarily as off-again on-again love interests for the hero. On "Simon & Simon," the character Janet Fowler (Jeannie Wilson) is an assistant district attorney who helps her boyfriend A. J. Simon out of various difficulties. At one point they are engaged, but break off the romance, and she disappears from the show. Again, the clever but only moderately successful duo cannot afford the competition presented by an ambitious and competent woman. In addition, both are attractive male characters and tying one of them down to one woman, even a pretty, charming, and successful one, limits the scriptwriters's ability to introduce new and interesting (read sexy) dramatic situations. Television conventions require the male characters to "play the field." Janet does make a re-appearance eventually, but only as a guest in a made-for-television movie when she needs A. J. and Rick's assistance in solving a murder. Magnum's lawyer friend is another female district attorney, again someone who gets him out of trouble, as does Beth Davenport on "The Rockford Files" with Rockford; she is not a dominant love interest on the show.

Beth Davenport (played by Gretchen Corbett), the lawyer girlfriend in the early years of "The Rockford Files," is a very strong character, and her relationship with James Garner (Jim Rockford) seems loving and healthy, although predictably they don't make their partnership permanent. Beth also spends a great deal of time giving Jim good legal advice, which he ignores, and getting him out of jail or saving his professional skin. Eventually she disappears from the show, leaving him (one presumes) heartbroken for a time but ready to chase after other, equally indulgent, but less professionally threatening companions. The Davenport-Rockford romance, like those in "Magnum, P.I." and "Simon & Simon," further represents an example of a professional woman who "settles" for a man with a less socially prominent career.

Made-for-Television Movies

Movies made-for-television combine the best and worst of their parent forms. Like films, they have somewhat more freedom to examine important or controversial issues, particularly if they run on cable networks. Freed from the necessity of charming financial backing out of sponsors week after week, they do not need to present likeable or even admirable characters. Like films they also collapse and oversimplify their messages, concentrating on one or two basic themes which they cheerfully hammer home to a glassy-eyed home-bound audience. Like television they can follow characters through several episodes if they become popular (one good example is the recurring lawyer character played by Walter Matthau in the films "The Incident" and "Against Her Will") without the long lead time and multi-million dollar budgetary gambles of the Hollywood studio, and they can bring many important issues to the screen quickly. Witness the number of docudramas[64] that air only months or even weeks after a given story has hit the headlines.

Particularly in the case of the docudrama focusing on contemporary issues, women lawyer characters could, but rarely do, play pivotal roles. The historical drama presents fewer opportunities for the woman lawyer, because as a general matter women simply did not practice law in great numbers until the 1970s and 1980s.

When the networks have an opportunity to feature strong women attorney characters, they seem reluctant to take it. NBC's 1996 made-for-television movie "The Prosecutors" featured two capable female attorneys (again district attorneys), played by Stockard Channing and Michelle Forbes, both with the ambition to excel in the professional and personal spheres. The creators included Lynda LaPlante, whose series "Prime Suspect" has earned high acclaim on PBS, and Tom Fontana, the producer of the hit series "Homicide: Life on the Street."

> "What we were going for," says Fontana, who wrote the script with LaPlante and "Homicide" producer Julie Martin, "was to build the show around these two characters whose perspective of law would be totally different from each other—Michelle's character being somebody who takes law and molds it into whatever she feels is necessary to get her cause and win the case, and Stockard's character very much by the letter of the law, who believes if you don't stick with the law you'll have anarchy. The fact that they have totally different points of view about how to use the law and the fact that both women have achieved success in the legal system, we thought was really kind of a different perspective."[65]

The perspective was indeed different, creating a realistic picture of women lawyers that more closely mimics what motivates their male counterparts than is normally the case. NBC has so far not indicated any interest in turning this movie into a series.[66]

In the made-for-television movie "The Oldest Living Bridesmaid," Donna Mills plays a successful corporate attorney whose mother and friends remind her constantly that she is over thirty and still unmarried. This character flaw propels her into a romance with a charming younger man whose value as a partner is questionable because he is an artist, not a professional man. The scriptwriters reiterate the message for women aspiring to succeed in both the professional and personal spheres: your success as a lawyer will have an adverse impact on your ability to attract a mate. If you succeed in attracting one he will not fit the traditional formula: older, more successful in a profession, and socially acceptable to all your friends.

Years later, in the film "A Different Kind of Christmas," Shelley Long's ambitious city attorney running for mayor learns her lesson when her son transfers his affections to her father, from whom she is estranged, and a local journalist hoping to kindle a relationship with her shows her that she does not have to be "superwoman" in order to be attractive. Her causes are suitably feminist—she fights an attractive but ruthless shopping mall developer who wants to turn the site for her proposed battered women's shelter into a local version of Rodeo Drive—but she seems unable to translate her caring for others into appropriate concern for her family.

She continues on her heedless way until her son is in a traffic accident. While staying with him at the hospital she finally tells her assistant that she simply cannot make any decisions until her son is out of danger. Once she accepts that only cutting back on her ambition will allow her to be a good mother and companion, she is redeemed. She gets the handsome, successful, supportive suitor (Barry Bostwick), finds a job for her father and welcomes him back into her life, and regains her son's affections.

Her ability to perform as city attorney, it should be pointed out, is heightened by the convenient presence of a housekeeper, who comes complete with an accent. Yet not even with the assistance of another woman who actually raises her son during the day can this woman lawyer succeed. The fact that the average salary for a woman in Shelley Long's character's position is likely to be fairly low, barely enough to pay for a babysitter once in a while, is conveniently ignored. If a woman with the Long character's advantages cannot have both a profession and a successful career as doting mother, says the movie, then no woman can aspire to it.

Women lawyers's professional ambitions regularly lead them astray socially as well. Often women attorneys are rude, grasping, demanding, and thoughtless, traits we are more likely to excuse in men. In "Perry Mason Returns," a young female district attorney takes on the Great Defender with both enthusiasm and foolhardiness, remarking that although he is very experienced, he is old and hasn't been in a courtroom in a very long time (he has just resigned from the bench to defend his longtime secretary and companion, Della Street, on a charge of murder).

We are clearly meant to dislike this woman, who is set up from the beginning by both the screenwriters and her supervisor to lose the case.

Apart from the obvious ugliness of such a remark, which signifies her naiveté and pomposity, we dislike her because she is taking on both the man we know from experience will win and the woman we have known for years as the soul of rectitude and patience. The contrast between the calm professionalism and friendliness of Della Street and the exuberance and overconfidence of the young attorney could not be greater.

Is it at all likely that, faced with the legendary Mason as defense attorney, a moderately intelligent prosecutor would assign a young and inexperienced district attorney? Would he not be more likely to prosecute the case himself? If he is afraid of losing—having looked up Hamilton Burger's won-lost record—why prosecute the case at all, knowing that Della Street is certainly innocent?

In "The Rockford Files: I Still Love L.A.," we meet Jim Rockford's ex-wife Catherine, a successful criminal attorney, who takes on the case of two wealthy young siblings accused of murdering their mother. Rockford immediately identifies the defendants as liars and discovers the truth about their involvement. First he finds a video of the murder that conveniently identifies the children as the killers, and reveals it to the police rather than to his ex-wife, for whom he is working. The defendants change their story, admitting that they killed their mother out of revenge over her failure to protect them from a stepfather involved in satanic rituals. Rockford refuses to believe their story because the former stepfather is a sports hero, and he continues to investigate, even after Catherine fires him from the case. Thus he eventually saves the woman he loves from a horrible professional and personal mistake even though she foolishly pays no attention to his advice.

While the focus of the film is on Rockford and his infallible analysis of the case, his superiority in both psychological investigation and ethics is emphasized through the contrast with Catherine. She is unable to see through her clients's deception; when Rockford makes it clear to her, she is devastated. She then finds it impossible to defend her clients effectively and she tells them she is abandoning them in a very dramatic scene. Apart from the impropriety of her withdrawal from the case so close to trial, she also creates ethical problems for herself in taking the case for both defendants when she was such a close friend of their mother and when, after they make the accusation against their stepfather, they clearly have different interests. The son emerges as the instigator of the crimes, the daughter as the accomplice.

Until Rockford rescues Catherine from the error of her ways, pointing out to her that she is too in love with money and success to remember her true mission as an attorney, she represents the traditional overly-ambitious and unethical lawyer, coupled with the professional woman who has lost touch with her femininity and vulnerability, the qualities most attractive to potential mates. Rockford points out to her that she has changed a great deal since their marriage. The implication is clearly that their relationship failed because she strayed too far from her true ethical and unambitious (i.e., true female) self. Until she recognizes that fact and reforms she cannot be worthy of either a rekindled love or of his professional and personal friendship.

Foreign Television Series

Foreign television shows are not much better. Of them, the one most likely to be familiar to American audiences is "Rumpole of the Bailey," which has in fact rather more female attorney characters, at more stages of professional development, than American television series. The show's two major female attorney characters are Phyllida Erskine-Brown and Liz Probert, the first an extremely ambitious and capable lawyer unhappily married to a vapid and jealous fool, the second an extremely ambitious and capable lawyer moderately happily involved with a young attorney clearly less talented than herself. For these two unruly women success in a profession comes at the price of success in personal life. Compare their lot with that of Phyllida's husband Claude, whose limited talents still allow him to earn a decent living and attract a clever and successful wife, or Rumpole himself, whose career is built on the defense of petty criminals, but whose more successful and loyal friends, including Phyllida and Liz, look out for him, whose marriage is on the whole a happy one,[67] and whose son Nick is productive.

Other female lawyers turn up periodically, but they are hardly cause for celebration. One, Fiona Allways, dissolves into tears her first day on the job when Phyllida criticizes her. Another, Mrs. Heather Whittaker, looks promising: she is an older woman, quietly competent and accepting of the older attorneys's foibles, but she makes only one appearance on the show. Trisha Benbow, an "instructing solicitor," makes several appearances, but her most memorable one is as Claude's unlucky dinner companion in the episode "Rumpole à la Carte," in which she has a hysterical screaming fit in a restaurant upon being served a live mouse.

In short, the palette of female attorneys on "Rumpole of the Bailey" is not particularly edifying, although Phyllida Erskine-Brown, who eventually takes silk[68] and then becomes a judge, has a most satisfactory career.[69]

Escapism and Reality in
Legal Television Drama

Generally speaking, therefore, while much of television, like much of popular culture, is escapist, legal television shows present the world of the female attorney fairly accurately. Unlike romantic fiction, which provides the reader with a world in which she can imagine herself both professionally and personally fulfilled, the television series allows her to imagine herself successful professionally but often not personally. Similarly, the male viewer is reassured to see that in regard to specifically female (that is, gendered) areas of life, the woman television attorney remains "unfulfilled," therefore unhappy.

Reggie's inability to regain custody of her children in "The Client" makes her less of a mother, therefore less of a success in the very arena in which women traditionally triumph over men. The message is clear: women attorneys with the same alcohol problems as men attorneys suffer a disproportionate loss. Alcoholic male lawyers may lose their marriages and children, but so do non-drinking male divorced lawyers. Alcoholic female lawyers lose not only their marriages and children, but their femininity. Images of drunken men often accompany scenes of winning sports teams or bachelor parties; their women may indeed observe their shenanigans somewhat indulgently. Drunken women are unappetizing and pathetic; because they cannot care for anyone else if they cannot care for themselves they are also failures at their primary mission — that of caregiver.

Marginalization of Women Attorneys

Often, the legal role picked for women characters is that of district attorney or assistant district attorney, less often criminal defense attorney or judge. In the gendered world of law, indeed, many women do take the lower paying and less prestigious positions. To that extent these shows are realistic. The television show "Equal Justice" emphasized the youth and inexperience of those prosecutors entrusted with upholding the law; it was based on a real-life attorney acquaintance of creator Thomas Carter.

> "She was a very unlikely assistant district attorney who at 26 or 27 was prosecuting felons.... What was exciting is that I got to go into that world from her point of view. Most people don't realize how young these prosecutors are. They're usually just out of law school, working in urban environments and dealing with tough legal cases. They want to be criminal lawyers, and the best place to get that experience is the D.A.'s office."

Carter followed up his experience in Houston by investigating the challenges faced by female, inner-city assistant prosecutors in New York, Los Angeles and Chicago. "It's definitely tougher for women," said Carter, "because they face a lot of sexism from their partners in prosecution. The legal profession is a people business, not just facts and figures. You've got to stand up there in a courtroom and lead the jury to the verdict you're seeking, usually against a seasoned male attorney. The jury has to feel comfortable with you, and they don't grant you that immediately, as they would with a man. Even female jurors have to overcome their own sexism in thinking that the female attorney is less authoritative. With a woman, the comfort level among the people she's trying to persuade has to be earned." All of which makes for great conflict and, as such, great fodder for dramatic entertainment. "I think it's one of the few times that you can show women exhibiting aggressive behavior," said Patricia Green, "L.A. Law's" supervising producer, "because they're expected to fight hard for what they believe. And they can do it without being less feminine and attractive to viewers."[70]

Female district attorneys include Claire Kincaid (Jill Hennessy) on "Law & Order," Miriam Grasso (Barbara Bosson) on "Murder One," Ava Newton on "Evening Shade," and Lisa Hunter on "Life's Work." Fewer television women attorneys are judges, and when they are they serve in inferior courts—traffic court, municipal court, and family court (Sydney Solomon on "The Home Court," Florence Stanley in "My Two Dads"). In a sense, they are working their way up the legal ladder; the first portrayal of a female associate justice of the United States Supreme Court only came in 1972 in the theatrical film "First Monday in October."

No female lawyer is as colorful as Ben Matlock, as single minded as Jack Shannon or Eddie Dodd, as successful and as bloodless as Perry Mason. No female character on television is as instantly recognizable as representative of the legal profession as are Mason and Matlock. Consequently, television portrayals of women attorneys carry the very clear message that female lawyers are likely to have very little impact on the legal system. The woman lawyer still does not make the rules, nor have she and her sisters achieved the critical mass necessary to change them.

Traditional Roles and Female Television Attorneys

In the world of the male television attorney, child-rearing and marriage take a back seat, much as they seem to do in real-life. Even in dramas such as "I'll Fly Away," in which the widowed attorney father, like

Atticus Finch in "To Kill A Mockingbird," is extremely interested in the day-to-day details of his children's lives, he is conveniently provided with an intelligent nurturing caregiver, with whom he does not have to contemplate marriage. She takes care of his children, leaving him free to pursue relationships as they develop. Admittedly, this series takes place in the 1950s and 1960s, but it demonstrates the social structure that makes the life of the male professional much easier than that of the female, who is traditionally burdened with the bulk of the work associated with maintaining the marriage or other relationship as well as the rearing of the children. Even in the 1990s, women in relationships tend to do more housework than their male companions and more of the child-rearing, even when they both work. Those women lawyers who have children are shown battling with the problems of child care (Lisa Hunter on "Life's Work") or custody (Reggie Love on "The Client," Abby Perkins on "L.A. Law"). Women lawyers who have no children desire them and feel unfulfilled without them (Ann on "L.A. Law," Ally on "Ally McBeal").

Like their real-life counterparts, female television lawyers receive little understanding from their bosses when they seek to balance the competing demands of work and family. As has been noted of real-life women attorneys:

> Upon graduation from law school, if a woman elects to pursue a career in law at full speed, she will find that the work load leaves little time for spouse or children; often she will find herself working 60 or 80 hours a week. This vigorous work schedule may go on for several years before the woman is promoted to a position that does not require the investment of as much time and energy. However, once a woman has reached this point in her career, she may find that she has delayed marriage or childbearing to a point where the chances of either or both of these things occurring in her life are quite slim. If a woman in the legal profession has opted to juggle both family and career, especially at the outset... she will find little empathy from her bosses regarding her divided loyalties.... Or if a woman decides to take time off from her career to start a family, upon her return to work she may find that her status has diminished in the eyes of her employer due to her new responsibilities at home and that she has fallen behind on the career ladder in comparison to her peers. Thus, the choice of a career, as well as the decision to pursue it "full speed", are decisions that greatly impact on a woman's life course.[71]

Relationships

For male television lawyers, seeking and keeping a mate is much less emphasized, therefore much less important, than for female lawyers. The inability of some male television lawyers to obtain female companionship is made light of in some cases (Eli Levinson on "Civil Wars" and "L.A. Law," Arnie Becker on "L.A. Law") precisely because we know that ultimately some woman will agree to accept their company. Eli and Arnie are, after all, successful lawyers in a society which still tends to measure men by their professional success and identify women by the labels it puts on their male companions.

Sydney Guilford, like other single female television lawyers, wants to establish a permanent and supportive relationship with a man, but is frustrated by male competitiveness and jealousy. Like other strong, successful women, Sydney is unlikely to drop everything to gratify an attractive but less self-confident or more traditional and demanding male. This attitude is clearly a mistake on their part, as they will be passed by for more accommodating and less-ambitious women.

Words and Appearance: The Subliminal Message

Legal language sits badly with female characters. We resist hearing a woman character give us the cold, factual analysis that Perry Mason offers. Women are expected to be understanding, empathetic, kind, and supportive, as well as competent. Indeed, competence is often secondary; some man will come along and clean up any unsightly messes.

Because success in law is often a matter of the effective use of language, television women lawyers are paradoxically at even more of a disadvantage. Unlike occupations whose successes derive from physical prowess or dominance, law relies almost wholly on persuasiveness. Thus persuasiveness and the effective use of language as well as wiliness in legal tactics become crucial to male success in the field. Aggression on the field of battle is translated into aggressive tactics in the courtroom. Both biological and social descriptions of male and female behaviors tend therefore to emphasize the fitness of men for this occupation, even though it relies not on physical strength or stamina, the traditional measures of male superiority, but on language and intellect.

Further, the appearance of the woman television attorney sends very clear signals to the viewer about the woman's professionalism and "real self." A real-life counterpart to Grace Van Owen, whose beautiful and sexily low-cut blouses on "L.A. Law" are considered a plus, would certainly send unfortunate signals to opposing counsel as well as to the judge. Van Owen's appearance was clearly at issue for the creators of "Equal Justice," who decided to emphasize professionalism at the expense of glitter.

[T]he roles for women explore the problems of legal professionals. Asked
if he had an agenda for the portrayal of women on "Equal Justice,"
Carter said simply, "Only that they should be taken as seriously as the
men and have the same respect." As a reflection of that seriousness of
purpose, the wardrobe department on "Equal Justice" was advised to
dress the women in suits for court, with muted, conservative colors. "We
wanted them to be attractive," said Carter, "but not glamorous."[72]

Even after Susan Dey left "L.A. Law," however, female attorney
wardrobes continued to be unrealistic. While the character C. J. Lamb
preferred "leather skirts to power suits," according to actress Amanda
Donohoe, she wasn't "stupid. She doesn't go to court and win cases
dressed like that."[73] But attorney Zoey Clemmons (Cecil Hoffmann) was
"much more in the Grace Van Owen mold." "With her," said supervising producer Patricia Green, "we were definitely looking to fill the role of
the romantic heroine."[74]

Conclusion

At the start of the 1997–98 television season, "Ally McBeal," a comedy series featuring a lawyer, made its debut on Fox. Although created
by David Kelley, the man responsible for "N.Y.P.D. Blue" and other well-
produced series, the show represents yet another series that trivializes
female attorneys: Having been forced to leave her previous law firm
because of sexual harassment problems at the hands of a partner, Ally
McBeal joins a new firm that just happens to employ her ex-boyfriend. For
women professionals struggling for recognition and respect, this situation is not a promising start.

The show's gimmick is its use of voiceover to reveal Ally's thoughts; predictably, they center on her emotions. As a comedy the show is amusing;
as a study of the inner life of a woman attorney (as opposed to any other
kind of woman), however, "Ally McBeal" confirms the stereotypes of the
professional woman as insecure in her work, desperate for male attention, overly concerned with her appearance (and the impression she makes
on others), and unable to put aside her emotional reaction to a situation
in order to develop a rational response.

Of course, it is easy to take the position that "Ally McBeal" is only a
television show meant as entertainment. While that is true, it also reinforces
the beliefs we have already seen exemplified in other shows about women
lawyers. Ultimately we are led to believe that the television industry gives
us unflattering portrayals of female attorneys because it believes that is what
is most comfortable for us. Judging by the quick demise of "Civil Wars,"
that may well be true.

17

Young Lawyers

Michael M. Epstein

In the fall of 1996, the fledgling UPN network introduced "Sparks," a situation comedy about a family of African-American attorneys in private practice. The show starred James Avery[1] as a respected former judge who decided to open a firm with his sons, both of whom were relatively new to the profession. Canceled after its second season, "Sparks" failed to generate the wide viewer interest or acclaim of a prime time hit. For the most part, the series offered broad comedy based on the same tired situations that have characterized much of the situation comedy genre for decades. Indeed, whether it was a story of mistaken identity, implausible coincidence, or misunderstanding, "Sparks" proved to be an unremarkable, and largely unfunny, half hour of television.

Yet for all its lack of originality, there was one aspect that set "Sparks" apart from other television comedies. It was a fresh spin on a type of dramatic lawyer program that first became popular in the 1960s and the early 1970s. These antecedent programs were prime time courtroom dramas that paired an older, experienced, father figure lawyer with one or more newcomers to the profession. It is for this reason that I have elsewhere referred to this narrative tradition as the "Mentor-Apprentice Courtroom Drama."[2]

Early incarnations of mentor-apprentice programs, such as "The Defenders," "Harrigan and Son," and "Dundee and The Culhane," explicitly equated good lawyering with manliness. As the 1960s progressed, the mentor-apprentice format became associated with socially relevant programs which pitted young attorneys against the repressive forces of capitalism and social injustice. The most notable of these shows, "Storefront Lawyers" and "The Young Lawyers," featured men and women who shared a sense that they were a team of equals who were ostensibly in rebellion against the status quo. At the same time, as this essay will argue, these shows represented the same traditions of lawyering as manly experience that were established in the pre-youth culture shows. In other words, shows that were essentially meant to subvert patriarchal images of the lawyer actually served to subtly reinforce them.

Origins of the Mentor-Apprentice Genre

The origins of the mentor-apprentice courtroom drama date back to the 1960s. This type of lawyer program paired a young man with his father or with a father figure. Whether it was for dramatic or comic effect, the pairing of a young and old lawyer was always about a mentor leading an inexperienced, if not altogether naive, young man to the greater wisdom that only judicial expertise and temperament can bring. The largely forgotten "Dundee and The Culhane," for example, briefly broadcast on CBS in the fall of 1967, cast John Mills as Dundee, an eminent British attorney who showed his young partner the subtleties of lawyering as they fought corruption in the Old West. In an episode entitled "The 3:10 to Lynchburg Brief," Dundee's first lines to his young partner, The Culhane (Sean Garrison), is a reminder that the "law is the only way to truth." As it turns out, this is the first of several lessons that the experienced lawyer tries to impart on his handsome apprentice. Like others in the series, this episode is essentially about Dundee using his lawyerly skills to teach The Culhane to settle disputes without resorting to violence and to help him develop more meaningful relationships with others, especially the many young women who are attracted to him. In short, it's about Dundee teaching The Culhane to be a better lawyer—and a better man.

The same can be said for the short-lived ABC series "Harrigan and Son," which during the 1960–61 television season paired Pat O'Brien and Roger Perry as father and son attorneys working together as law partners. Although the show conformed to many of the conventional formulas of a thirty-minute situation comedy, including simply-constructed misunderstandings, exaggerated sensitivities, and implausible resolutions, the program's comedy, like the adventure in "Dundee and The Culhane," is predicated upon the instructive, nurturing relationship between the older role model and the professional naif. Harrigan, Jr., fresh out of Harvard Law School, has pretensions of being an excellent lawyer like his father. Hard as he tried to emulate his dad, however, Junior finally recognized that he still had much to learn from his dad's professional—and life—experience. In an untitled episode from 1960, for example, Junior thinks that Harvard Law School wants him to be a guest speaker when it's Senior the school actually wants. Senior, however, is not interested in flying from New York to Boston to deliver an address; he explains to Junior that it is difficult to give a speech that describes the benefit of his "rough and tumble experience." Senior went to night school and has argued before both the Supreme Court and on behalf of prisoners at Sing Sing. For the older Harrigan, it is not enough for a good lawyer to speak about what he does, he must teach by example. Although some of the conflict in this episode involves tensions between elite professionals and working-class values, this clash of class is evocative of the generational differences between working-class parents and their college-educated children, and especially between fathers and sons, that is characteristic of the American post-World War II family experience.

The comic situation develops when Senior turns up missing. Instead of delivering the address at Harvard, Senior is discovered playing chess with some teenage boys at a Boys's Club on the West Side of Manhattan. Senior apparently is more comfortable in a masculine environment where he can nurture and guide young men. The Boys's Club, filled exclusively with young men that venerate the older man, is clearly such a masculine space, just as chess is regarded popularly as a game for men.[3]

Harrigan, Sr.'s involvement with the Boys's Club is more than about helping the boys become men; his actions strongly suggest that he expects these boys to grow up to be lawyers. In addition to likening his chess game to the skills needed to plan a litigation, Senior proudly admits to his son that he has been donating law books to the Boys's Club over the years, as reading for the boys. Senior, in effect, is able to teach both his son and the boys by example. For Junior, the visit to the Boys's Club becomes a moment of poignancy and reassurance—personally and professionally—when one of the boys asserts privately that Senior believes that his son will one day be an even greater lawyer than he. As a result of this passing, if telling, observation, the comically-inspired moment of conflict between father and son is diffused and the scene turns into a group experience of male bonding. In retrospect, a viewer might reflect upon "Harrigan and Son" as one big male bonding experience, from its descriptive title to the fact that, except for the incidental appearance of two unmarried office assistants, everyone in the show was male.

"The Defenders," which appeared on CBS from 1961 to 1965 and is examined in another context elsewhere in this book, is the most significant of the early mentor-apprentice programs. Often cited as a close third in popularity among *all* law shows, after "Perry Mason" and "L.A. Law," "The Defenders" offered viewers a first look at why the mentor-apprentice drama represents an important evolution in television's depictions of lawyers.

The significance of "The Defenders," as well as the mentor-apprentice dramas that followed, lies in its complex depiction of masculine values and ideology as they apply to lawyers. In pursuing a mentor-apprentice relationship in the midst of a culture that, at least in popular consciousness, was becoming more egalitarian, free-spirited, and youth-oriented, the lawyers on these shows acted to reinforce the status quo of patriarchy, just as they seemed at the same time to be trying to subvert that status quo.

Although different in quality, content, and genre from "Dundee and The Culhane" and "Harrigan and Son," "The Defenders" made use of the same father-son formula. The socially provocative courtroom drama teamed up a highly-respected seasoned attorney named Lawrence Preston (E.G. Marshall) with his passionate, fresh-out-of-law school son (Robert Reed). Together, the Prestons took on cases without the line between right and wrong that was so clearly drawn in the "Perry Mason" formula. Cases almost always had to do with some type of policy controversy or a clash of values, issues such as mercy killing or the then-illegal activities of an abortion provider that the law could not mediate with the certainty of a courtroom confession or factual evidence. Indeed, much of the story in "The Defenders" revolved around the differences in approach and opinion between the older attorney and the younger attorney. The elder Preston, like Perry Mason, will agree to represent a client only if he is convinced that the client is telling the truth, that his motives were not economic or vengeful, and that he would do what he did again because of his principles.

In "The Quality of Mercy," for example, the veteran attorney calmly interviews a doctor who euthanized a terminally ill infant, makes a decision about the accused's principles and character, and spends the rest of the time negotiating with the District Attorney (Jack Klugman) for leniency and fair play in the handling of the case and, ultimately, the sentencing. The younger Preston, on the other hand, is less concerned with the nobility of the client; he spends the bulk of the episode trying to come to terms with his passionate feelings, which are both for and against mercy killings. Unlike his dad, the younger man does not enjoy the moral certitude of a Perry Mason. In fact, the son's main role is one of personal discovery outside of the courtroom, whether it's encountering a disabled child during a picnic with his girlfriend or literally coming to blows during an issue-oriented shouting match with the District Attorney in his office. And just as the young attorney increases the tension in the episode, the older Lawrence Preston helps resolve it by showing his son how an expert, caring lawyer can earn respect and dignity for his transgressing client before judge and jury, and even before the hot-under-the-collar District Attorney. By the end of the episode, the father-mentor helps turn his son's enmity with the District Attorney into a warm friendship; the D.A., as it turns out, had been personally vested against mercy killing because he loved a brother with Downs syndrome.

The collegial warmth that Lawrence Preston fosters between the District Attorney and the younger Preston underscores a circulation of masculine space that is far more complex than in "Perry Mason," "Harrigan and Son," or "Dundee and The Culhane." Although women are more of a presence, both in and especially out of the courtroom, the father-son relationship between the two lawyers and the bond between the prosecutor and the neophyte borne of violence very much codes the representation of lawyering as male. Although, unlike his dad, young Preston spends much of his time romancing with his girlfriend, it is during these personal moments that he shares his emotional misgivings about policy or expresses doubt about his role as an attorney. The moments he has with Joanie are always sentimental: a picnic, a walk in the park, holding hands in a domestic setting. And although she's quick to engage the issues involved in the controversy, she also takes on the unconditionally supportive, consoling, and historically-feminized role of a nurturer.

As it happens, however, it is exactly this type of passionate engagement of the issues that the senior Preston teaches his son to cast aside in order to be an effective lawyer. For young Preston, being a good lawyer is all about learning to be a man like his father and, by extension, the District Attorney. It's a bonding experience that exists not only in the courtroom and other spaces inscribed with state power, but also in the masculine space of the smoke-filled sports bar and restaurant where father and son go to unwind or to meet other lawyers.

The Advent of "Social Relevancy" Programming

The representations of lawyering as a masculine experience becomes even more complicated with the spate of mentor-apprentice law programs that briefly graced the airwaves between 1969 and 1971. In tune with an empowered youth culture, programs such as ABC's "The Young Lawyers," CBS's "Storefront Lawyers" (later retitled "Men at Law"), and, to a lesser extent, NBC's "The Lawyers" (which was seen as a recurring installment of "The Bold Ones") used the same pairing of seasoned attorney and neophyte to mediate tensions of justice, state power, and individuality associated with the youth movement of the late 1960s. Part of an orchestrated effort by the national broadcast networks to replace variety shows and rural comedies skewed demographically to older audiences with "social relevancy" programs that would appeal to younger viewers, these courtroom dramas were widely expected to be the "must see TV" among new shows in the fall of 1970.[4]

This was especially the case with CBS which, in the midst of a purge of its three quaint rural comedies — "Green Acres," "Petticoat Junction," and "The Beverly Hillbillies," — saw "Storefront Lawyers," which detailed the lives of three young lawyers in Los Angeles who split their time between a private law firm and a non-profit law clinic, as the type of social relevancy program that would bring younger viewers back to the network. In the late spring of 1970, the Tiffany network took out a dramatically illustrated two-page advertisement in *Variety* in which it called the new show "one of the most vital, most relevant series ever televised."[5] CBS clearly had high hopes for the show: The attorneys on "Storefront Lawyers" were going to "capture the whole spirit of an exciting, significant movement," an oblique reference to the program's youthful appeal.

Unfortunately, the show was never able to earn the type of ratings that would ensure long-term survival in prime time. Although the show performed better than the critics expected, it never made it close to the Nielsen Top 20, despite a favorable 8:00 p.m. Wednesday time slot (opposite "The Courtship of Eddie's Father") and, later, a revamped format.[6]

Variety was more sanguine about "The Young Lawyers," the ABC offering about a Boston neighborhood law office staffed by law students whose pilot had aired with some success in the fall of 1969. *Variety* rated the new series as "fair," though, like "Storefront Lawyers," the show quickly became a ratings disappointment. Ratings were in fact so poor that *Variety* reported that "The Young Lawyers" survived an early cancellation only because ABC's top management "believes in it."[7] Indeed, over the objections of 27 affiliates, ABC resisted moving "The Young Lawyers" from its Wednesday 10:00 p.m. time slot.[8] Stiff competition from "Hawaii Five-0" on CBS and NBC's "four-in-one" mystery crime drama series (which later evolved into "The NBC Mystery Movie"), among the most popular programs with women and men in the 18-to-49 age group, quickly dashed ABC's hopes of turning "The Young Lawyers" into an enduring success. The show was finally taken off the schedule at the end of its first season.

By the end of 1970, relevancy programs had been dubbed by some as the "ideal scapegoat for the season's low yield of new hits and critical acclaim."[9] Despite their earnest attempts to depict empowered youth working to correct social injustice, the new socially relevant shows failed to attract young demographics and, in fact, turned off older viewers. Only "The Mod Squad," a 1969 entry about three under-30 cops, emerged as a ratings hit that year.

In the nearly thirty years since their debut, "Storefront Lawyers" and "The Young Lawyers," like nearly all the social relevancy programs of 1970, have faded into obscurity. Neither program has rerun in syndication nor been released on videotape. Scripts from the series are not in public circulation and no fans or scholars are known to be interested in the programs, despite the recent renewed interest in 1970s culture. Even the shows's stirring instrumental themes are missing from the myriad television theme compilations available for purchase. For this essay, selected episodes were reviewed by special arrangement at the film and video archives of the Library of Congress in Washington, D.C., and at the Museum of Television and Radio in New York.

A New Generation of Lawyers

Upon quick review, "Storefront Lawyers" and "The Young Lawyers" seem vastly different from traditional courtroom dramas like "Perry Mason" and even the early mentor-apprentice shows. At first glance, these mod, young lawyer shows are all about the ascendancy of youth culture and mistrust of the establishment. The young lawyers, through teamwork and tireless effort, are able to find justice for those who are overlooked by the American legal system. Cases would typically involve an issue that pits a well-meaning, principled individual against the state, issues involving people like a young, long-haired doctor being sued for a Good Samaritan rescue, a Latino law student who is framed by a smuggler of migrant workers, the victim of a swindle who turns to vigilantism, or a teenager who seeks the right to demonstrate at a high school. In every case, these are the clients and conflicts that most established lawyers would not take, even as a pro bono matter. In nearly every instance, it is not a matter of a Perry Mason proving the innocence of someone unjustly accused; nor, as was often the case on "The Defenders," is it a self-possessed member of the community who has violated or challenged social convention. No, for the young lawyer teams on "Storefront Lawyers" and "The Young Lawyers," cases and clients revealed a thematic current of racism, class conflict, and anti-establishment sentiment. The people who came to these apprentice lawyers for help were on the margins of society, themselves the victims of social and economic inequality. It is hard to imagine someone like that paying a call on Perry Mason or Lawrence Preston.

In contrast to the more staid image of their respective mentors, both teams of young attorneys were portrayed as free spirits who were egalitarian and liberated from the repressive values of the military-industrial complex. In their crusade for social justice, they expressed such beliefs as all are deserving of equal opportunity in society and under the law, regardless of race, gender, or age. Although each team worked for a mentor lawyer who was inscribed with corporate and social power, the new generation of lawyers, operating out of their own storefronts, seemed to position themselves as outsiders to capitalism who mistrusted those in power. Money did not change hands between these lawyers and their clients; the young attorneys seemed to be telling us that their singular interest was justice. Asking for payment would have implicated them as part of the system they ostensibly were rebelling against.

Role of Women

Even more interesting, for the first time in the courtroom genre the role of lawyer was no longer seen as an exclusively masculine domain, for both "The Young Lawyers" and "Storefront Lawyers" included a woman as one of the young attorneys. These women were competent, attractive, and (usually) comfortable with their role as young lawyers.

Pat Walters (Judy Pace), a hard-working third-year student at an elite law school, is an inquisitive and sensitive member of "The Young Lawyers." Although the only black apprentice lawyer in any of the shows of the period, she is depicted as a woman of privilege, the daughter of a wealthy dentist from San Francisco. Her blackness is largely symbolic, less a matter of ethnic identity and more a plot convenience that makes the lawyers seem more credible when dealing with racial issues and non-white clients. She is dressed in expensive clothes, keeps a second job, and drives her own car.

Debra Sullivan (Sheila Larken), one of the "Storefront Lawyers," enjoys the same type of financial and social independence that Pat Walters has. Sullivan is an aggressive and articulate member of her legal team, all of whom are associates at an affluent law office. Presumably, Sullivan receives the same high salary that her male colleagues are paid.

Both of these women seem to be natural leaders, filled with zeal and energy as they run—literally—to and from meetings and court appointments. Apart from the mentoring lawyer, no one tells them how to behave or what they can and can't do. In theory, they have every opportunity that their male counterparts have as professionals in and out of the courtroom.

Still, as women who are subordinate to the leading male young lawyer and, of course, the always male older lawyer, they act to enforce the patriarchal status quo of the law, while also trying to challenge it. In "The Young Lawyers," the leading young attorney is Aaron Silverman (Zalman King); in "Storefront Lawyers," it is David Hansen (Robert Foxworth). These two young men get the lion's share of responsibility in court and attention from the mentor. Thus, one sees strong-minded, liberated women dressed in brightly colored mini-skirts and snug blouses relegated to the role of supporter or spectator in the courtroom, where the story is essentially about the young male lawyer learning how to be like the fatherly older lawyer.

The upbeat title sequence to "Storefront Lawyers" is emblematic of the program's ambivalent depiction of women lawyers. The sequence begins with several cuts that intersperse aerial shots of Los Angeles freeways, pedestrians, police on motorcycles, and the Los Angeles County courthouse (including close-ups of a statue representing justice on the building's facade). A bass drum solo reminiscent of the driving beat that opens "Hawaii Five-0" accompanies these rapidly revealed images.[10] As the horns begin blaring the main theme — flashing images of the three young attorneys — are added into the montage. The three attorneys are running along the street in front of the courthouse. They are holding hands; David Hansen, a blue-eyed blond in a conservative business suit, is on the right, holding a small leather portfolio in his free hand as if it were a football. On the far left is Gabriel Kaye (David Arkin), running with a broad smile but laden with a heavy briefcase that makes him lag behind the other two. He has dark, curly hair and features and complexion that one might generally associate with Mediterranean ancestry or more specifically, as is the case here, with being Jewish. Kaye is also in a jacket and tie, though his outfit is more brightly colored and less conservatively tailored than Hansen's business suit.

Rounding out the team — and team is clearly what the three hand-holding lawyers evoke — is Sullivan. She is wearing a short blue mini-dress that drapes well above the knee and is smiling with an expression approaching rapture as she runs between the two men. Unlike her male companions, both of her hands are being held. Indeed, in order to foster the type of closely knit, hand-holding fellowship among this lawyer team, she must be positioned between the two men. Otherwise, the two young men would have to be holding each other's hand, an image suggesting homosexuality that is nearly as taboo today as it certainly was on 1960s network television. Sullivan's presence in the center of this trio establishes from the outset that the three lawyers are more than just co-workers — they care about each other and derive pleasure from their work together — even ecstasy.

Yet a close examination of the shots in the opening montage reveals a hierarchy of legal responsibility for our three young attorneys that is consistent with notions of the good lawyer as manly. As the name of the show's star, Robert Foxworth, appears as a supertitle, the interspersed shots of Los Angeles city scenes are replaced by two longer shots of Foxworth running alone into the main entrance of a skyscraper in the corporate enclave of Century City and inside a courtroom, where he is presumably addressing a jury. From the outset, Foxworth's character (David Hansen) is associated with the trappings of corporate power and professional accomplishment. That he is alone among the three young lawyers in ability is made even more evident as the montage begins to intersperse shots of Sheila Larken as Debra Sullivan. Unlike Foxworth, Larken is not seen in the halls of commerce or justice; she is behind the wheel of a convertible automobile that is cruising on a Los Angeles street.

Placing Larken in the driver's seat of a sports car is an empowering image for her character, but only to an extent. Few would argue against the premise that the car in America has long been a symbol of power, both economic and mechanical, and masculinity. Whether it's the enduring images of "cruising for dates" or drag racing, the driving of a powerful car has traditionally been a male pleasure in popular culture. Although much of this tradition has eroded in the last thirty years, in the 1960s it was still much more common to see a young woman draped across the hood of a car than behind the wheel of one in a car commercial. The decision to show Larken driving was likely the result of the producers's desire to depict her character as strong and independent, which Debra Sullivan is, for the most part. What's missing, of course, is any suggestion that the source of her power is related to her professional skills as a lawyer. Sullivan, as it turns out, is daydreaming in the car and the camera zooms in for a freeze frame close-up just as she opens her mouth in an alluring pose. While Foxworth's Hansen is on his feet and doing his job, Larken's body (even before the freeze frame) barely moves; it's the car that is doing all the work.

The third lawyer of the team, Gabriel Kaye (David Arkin), occupies a middle ground when it comes to representations of masculinity and professional leadership. As Arkin's name is emblazoned across the screen, viewers see two shots of Arkin close up in an office. Arkin is not on the move. He is not in court, although he in depicted as functional in a workplace environment. As a character, Gabriel Kaye is less able — both as a man and as a lawyer — than David Hansen. Although as a man he occupies a more privileged position in the courtroom than Debra Sullivan, he is clearly a supporting player that aspires to the leadership — and manliness — of Hansen. In many ways, Gabriel Kaye represents a tradition of sidekicks to a strongly masculine character that are less comfortable with their masculinity. Whether it's Sergeant Enright to Rock Hudson's McMillan on "McMillan and Wife" or Martin Pawley to John Wayne's Ethan in "The Searchers," these second bananas take on a comic dimension as they struggle to assert their manhood with women and on the job. And so is the case with lawyer Kaye, who is depicted as someone who is nervous in court and anxious around women, except for Sullivan.[11]

Hansen's primacy as leading man and leading lawyer is reinforced at the end of the opening sequence. The final shot is a 360-degree track shot of the three lawyers posing in front of a fountain in Century City. Foxworth is pointing at something in the distance. As the camera pans around him, Arkin and Larken are looking at Foxworth. The camera stops and freeze frames just as Foxworth places his hand in his pockets. Larken is frozen in full feminine profile as she looks at Foxworth. Arkin, further in the background, is in three-quarter profile. Although this sequence is on one level a moment of leisure that may help foster a sense of team bonding for our three characters (consider, for example, the opening of the ensemble comedy "Friends"), it acts also to reinforce Hansen's aloofness from his friends. Hansen never returns his colleagues's glances. His eyes remain fixed on someone or something distant.[12]

The hierarchy of lawyerliness that is suggested in the opening credits of "Storefront Lawyers" plays out in the episodes themselves. Sullivan helps prepare clients, witnesses, and the issues to be argued in the case with as much energy and competence as her male colleagues, perhaps even more. But when it comes to making the case in court, the older attorney-mentor (Barry Morse) turns to the leading young attorney, David Hansen. Here is a typical exchange from "A Man's Castle," the program's premiere episode: "Well, David, are you ready?" "Ready. Let's go to court!" And together David and his two peers run off to the Los Angeles County courthouse across the street. Outside the courtroom, the mentoring lawyer treats his trio of young lawyers as three team members worthy of equal respect. When it comes time to argue the case in court, however, the mentor relies on David, the leading male member of the team, to argue the case. Only in rare instances does Gabriel Kaye take a leadership role before a judge.

In "The Young Lawyers," the ambivalence of women lawyers is addressed directly in the program's narrative. As the only woman on the apprentice legal team, Pat Walters must often do battle with those who cannot accept women as lawyers. In the series's pilot, for example, Pat, then known as Ann, is frequently reminded by mentor-lawyer Michael Cannon that her femininity is inconsistent with what it takes to be a good lawyer. When, early on in the pilot, Walters suggests that she could babysit for a friend's child at the office, Cannon rebukes her, even though Walters is trying to accommodate *his* schedule at the last minute. "Don't bring children to the office," says Cannon sternly. When Walters asks why not, Cannon replies tellingly, "Because we're lawyers not social workers." Cannon's sentiments are immediately echoed by Walters's non-lawyer boyfriend, who initiates a moment of male bonding and condescension. "That's what I've been telling her all along," says the young man.

This sequence with Cannon, Walters, and her boyfriend is made all the more powerful by the scene's setting. As the sequence begins, Walters, in a black leotard with white tights, is teaching ballet to a class consisting exclusively of young girls. Her boyfriend is photographing her as she and the young students dance to some recorded music. As a photographer, the boyfriend is relegated to a role that is supportive of Walters and the girls in what is clearly feminine space. As soon as lawyer Cannon enters the studio, the flow of the activity is interrupted. The girls disperse, the music is switched off, and, perhaps most significantly, she places a shawl over her skin-tight outfit. Walters is no longer comfortable as a woman, either physically or in her activities, once in the presence of Cannon. For Walters, being a lawyer ends up being a struggle to suppress her womanhood. Michael Cannon sums up her predicament when he tells Walters not to babysit even though she had previously committed to do so. "It's a question of who you are," he says as he exits the studio. Left with an ultimatum to either show up to work by herself or stop working as a lawyer, Walters rejoins the young legal team and assumes the same lawyerly demeanor of her male colleagues.

Still, for Pat Walters, as for Debra Sullivan on "Storefront Lawyers," being a woman lawyer does mean taking a back seat to men, especially in the courtroom. These women have defined roles as both characters and lawyers. Their strengths lie largely in passion, intuition, and conscience. In "The Young Lawyers" pilot, Walters seems genuinely disturbed when a witness comes forward to identify two young clients as armed robbers. At a meeting in which the young attorneys meet with Cannon to discuss the facts of the case, Walters wonders out loud why the witness, a stranger who claims to have been beaten by the defendants, would want to lie. "What kind of person lies about two human beings?" The moment is almost like a soliloquy. She is not addressing the comment to her male colleagues, nor do they have the chance to respond. The episode immediately cuts to a sequence in which Walters pursues the witness, an elderly taxi driver. As a passenger in the back seat of the taxi, Walters eyes a photograph of the witness and a young woman in his wallet. Acting entirely upon intuition, Walters decides that this photo will somehow be the key to solving the case and exonerating her clients, even though there is no reason for her—or viewers—to interpret the photo as significant. As the story progresses, Walters's hunch about the photo is correct. Incredibly, the photo leads Walters to uncover evidence that the taxi driver was having an affair with his son's wife. The son, a Vietnam vet with emotional problems, brutally beat his father when the affair was discovered. Walters's involvement in the case, however, is limited to her preliminary investigation and intuitive conclusions. When it comes to confronting the father and son, male lawyers Aaron Silverman and David Barrett are in charge. It is ultimately their efforts, in and out of court, that lead the taxi driver to admit under oath that he lied about being robbed by the two young men in order to protect his son. In the final courtroom sequence, Walters has been relegated to the sidelines, a passive observer to the work of her male colleagues.

In later episodes of "The Young Lawyers," Pat Walters is depicted as more active in the courtroom. In defense of a young doctor being sued for a Good Samaritan rescue, Walters takes center stage in court, conducting a cross-examination of two non-party witnesses and introducing evidence that the doctor was not drunk at the time of the rescue. Still, compared to the leading role that Aaron Silverman assumes in arguing the case, Walters's involvement is brief and inconsequential. Silverman first argues that the case should be dismissed as frivolous. When that tactic fails, he is given the opportunity to cross-examine a party witness, the plaintiff, and does such an excellent job that the opposing side decides to drop the case. Both the plaintiff and opposing counsel are so impressed with Silverman's ability that they congratulate his mentoring attorney for finding someone who has "got great potential." With the expression and intonation of a father proud of his son, the prominent older attorney responds by saying that we should be thankful for young men like him. Silverman, in the eyes of his father-mentor, has lived up to his name. He has proven himself to be a silver-tongued man. Walters, on the other hand, has once again been relegated to the periphery as a spectator.

The lawyering skills of Debra Sullivan on "Storefront Lawyers" are also defined and limited by her gender. Even more so than Pat Walters, Sullivan is reduced to a role that is supportive of, and secondary to, the male lawyers on her team. Sullivan is usually positioned by the client's side in the courtroom. She functions, for the most part, as the person whom clients can go to for reassurance about a case or comfort in general. Although she has strong opinions and verbal skills, she is never given the type of meaningful leadership position before a judge or a jury that David Hansen, and to a lesser extent Gabriel Kaye, enjoy.

Sullivan performs the same role for clients outside the courtroom. In "First We Get Rid of the Principal," it is Sullivan's repeated expressions of social conscience that convince her colleagues to take on the case of an activist teen expelled from high school. After the lawyers meet with one of the boy's teachers, Hansen is ready to reject the case because there's nothing he thinks he can do "from a legal standpoint." Sullivan, on the other hand, is not ready to give up on the case. She makes it clear then and several times later in the episode that she is moved by the plight of the boy in trouble, who has had a difficult upbringing. She intercedes with Hansen by suggesting that "we ought to try and find out" if there is a case and wins his assent with a smile. After Hansen fails to convince a juvenile court that the boy should not be sent to a reformatory, it is Sullivan who approaches the boy's timid mother in an effort to convince her to appeal the court's decision to a judge in state superior court. Even with his mother as a character witness, the boy loses the appeal before the superior court judge. Hansen was right; the child did not have a legal case. Still, because the principal was impressed with the dignity of the mother, he decides to drop the case and permit the adolescent to return to school. Sullivan's social conscience triumphs where the law—and Hansen's skilled courtroom advocacy—cannot. Sullivan's function as conscience and moralizer is equally evident in the sequences in which she interacts with attorneys outside her team.

As an associate at a prominent Los Angeles law firm, Sullivan's attention seems focused exclusively on her work at the storefront, whereas her male colleagues appear better focused. In one episode, entitled "Survivors Will Be Prosecuted," a senior partner is trying to find Hansen, who evidently is about to work all night preparing a tax brief for a corporate client. Similarly, in "First We Get Rid of the Principal," Hansen refers to a project he's completing for an oil company, and Kaye makes a connection between a storefront case and a labor representation he's involved with for the firm.

On the other hand, in "Survivors Will Be Prosecuted," Sullivan has to endure a senior partner's complaint that the storefront practice is preventing associates from pursuing profitable client work. As it turns out, she's come to see the partner to ask for help in getting a judge to reduce bail for a Latino law student wrongfully charged with a felony. The partner is at first unsympathetic and dismissive. He makes a quick, general judgment about the quality of law student volunteers that one could interpret as racist. Sullivan makes the issue personal by responding, "You wouldn't say that about him if you knew him." Ultimately, Sullivan, with some support from Kaye, changes the partner's mind. Although he won't intercede with the judge, he decides to write a $10,000 check to cover the bail.

In "A Man's Castle," the episode where the storefront lawyers are defending a victim turned vigilante, Sullivan raises eyebrows when she states that murder is a psychotic act. While the other attorneys in the scene seem content to argue within the law, Sullivan's compassion leads her to confrontation with the law. Is she suggesting that the law is too quick to judge murderers responsible for their misdeeds? Her emotional investment in her clients is so complete that at times she seems almost to fear the consequences of the law on her clients. Hansen is excited—even strident—in his approach to this case; Sullivan seems upset. At a dinner meeting with the client's wife, Sullivan is barely able to tell the woman that her husband may face the death penalty.

Role of the Mentor

For all their independence and anti-establishment sensibilities, the young attorneys of both "The Young Lawyers" and "Storefront Lawyers" relied on their mentors as legal role models and financial sponsors. At least that was the way the shows had originally been conceived. With all the emphasis on empowered, socially-aware youth, it's no wonder that both series struggled with the paternalistic relationship implicit in the mentor-apprentice formula. As it turned out, both programs had their original mentors replaced.

For reasons that are not entirely clear, Jason Evers, the actor who played the senior attorney in the pilot of "The Young Lawyers," was replaced by Lee J. Cobb, who appeared as David Barrett. As Michael Cannon, Evers at times seemed severe and distant. Recall, for example, the scene in which he seeks out Ann Walters at the ballet studio and gives her an ultimatum. Cobb is much more relaxed as a mentor and more supportive. Where Evers was confrontational and authoritarian, Cobb was patient and gentle, even to Walters. Essentially a kinder, hipper father figure (and one perhaps more palatable to young viewers's tastes in 1970), Cobb's character still spent the bulk of his time as a role model to Aaron Silverman.

The mentor problem on "Storefront Lawyers" was evident within weeks of its debut on September 9, 1970. Although the show's original mentor, played by Barry Morse, initially was depicted as an active adviser and supporter of David Hansen, the mentor role was diminished to such an extent that Morse soon disappeared from the series. The reasons for his absenteeism have nothing to do with Morse's character, a prominent law firm partner, and everything to do with a fundamental flaw in the program's mentor-apprentice format. As explained earlier, the young attorneys split their time between a dingy, inner-city storefront law office, which they operated on their own, and an opulent law firm suite in downtown Los Angeles, where the mentor was based. Although the original design of the series had the young attorneys running to the office suite whenever they needed their mentor's guidance, the newly opened storefront was their domain alone, a place set aside for the people marginalized from the establishment because they were young, poor, or a person of color. As the storefront took on greater prominence in the episodes, scenes with the mentor became increasingly scarce. Perhaps as a result of the network's desire to lure younger viewers, the storefront lawyers effectively worked without a mentor for a short period in the fall of 1970.[13]

As a mentor-apprentice show without a mentor, "Storefront Lawyers" quickly proved to be a failed experiment in demographic engineering. Within six weeks of the show's premiere, Variety reported that CBS was considering moving the show's lawyers out of the storefront and back to a law firm. In order to "heighten the show's appeal with over-35 viewers," CBS also stated that the role of a senior partner might be reestablished.[14] Three weeks later, CBS formally announced that the show's setting would be moved to a prestigious law office in the skyscrapers of Century City. The three young attorneys would now be under the close supervision of an experienced partner named Devlin McNeil (Gerald S. O'Loughlin).[15]

As a result of all these format changes, the program became even more beholden to the paternalistic mentor-apprentice format than it had been before. The relationship between McNeil and Hansen became the focus of the last ten episodes, and the roles of Debra Sullivan and Gabriel Kaye were de-emphasized.[16] Revamped into a show that showcased a relationship of male bonding between a young man and a "highly respected"[17] father figure role model, the once youth-relevant program was given a title that more accurately represented what it had become, and, to an extent, what it always had been. On January 13, 1971, "Storefront Lawyers" became "Men at Law."

Conclusion

Decades later, it is easy to look back at "The Young Lawyers" and "Storefront Lawyers" and say that they were nothing more than experiments in subversive, youth-oriented programming that failed because they privileged the relationship between two male lawyers and reinforced hegemonic values of patriarchy. Ironically, these "now relevant"[18] programs from 1970–71 represent the end of the tradition in which the courtroom was depicted as a masculine space where good lawyers were also good men. In the fall of 1975, Anne Meara made television history when she starred in "Kate McShane,"[19] the first prime time courtroom drama about a woman attorney.[20] Although the series was short-lived, "Kate McShane" marks the beginning of the modern era of lawyer representations on television.

Americans have come a long way from the time when programs such as "The Young Lawyers" and "Storefront Lawyers" could be viewed as socially relevant. Indeed, as the 20th century draws to an end, a profession that once referred to supreme court justices as "brethren" has more women lawyers on the bench, in government, on Wall Street, and in law school than ever before. Although men still occupy the lead positions in American prime time courtroom drama, the day may yet come when viewers will be able to tune into a mentor-apprentice courtroom drama that focuses more fully on the lawyering experience of women. Art does, after all, often imitate life.

Epilogue

RONALD D. ROTUNDA

Even without televised commercials, it is hard to watch much television without seeing lawyers in action. Sometimes the lawyers are bad, sometimes they are heroic, but they are nearly as pervasive as television itself. Other than shows about police dramas or medical doctors, no other profession is featured nearly as often in the storyline—not the clergy, nor the military, nor other professions.

Empirical evidence demonstrates that the primary way that most people learn about lawyers is through watching television. Yet when people turn to television, they do not rely on the news, C-SPAN, or lawyers's commercials for their view of lawyers. Instead, they turn to *fictionalized* portrayals of lawyers like the ones discussed in this book.[1]

When people are asked to name the lawyer that they most admire, they frequently cite Ben Matlock. Many people apparently think that Matlock is a real person. And because Matlock fights for justice, many of the people who watch "Matlock" think more highly of lawyers. Yet despite having Ben Matlock among their numbers, lawyers will never win popularity contests. Even television does not have that much power.

It is hardly surprising that lawyers would like to be more well-liked. So too would car mechanics, tax collectors, undertakers, and politicians. There is one important difference, however, between lawyers and other professionals. We will never be widely loved as long as we are really doing our jobs. Our quest for universal popularity is therefore as futile as the quest for the holy grail.

Surveys illustrate the dilemma that lawyers face. When people are asked what they dislike most about lawyers, they routinely answer that lawyers are "too interested in money" (31%), file "too many unnecessary lawsuits" (27%), and "manipulate the legal system without regard for right or wrong" (26%).[2] By the same token, people praise lawyers for "putting clients" first (46%) and protecting people's rights (25%).[3]

People dislike lawyers because we are guns for hire who manipulate the legal system, but they like us because we fight for our clients, protect their rights, and cut through bureaucratic red tape. When we fight zealously for our clients, file lawsuits, and cut through red tape we are doing

good, but when we fight zealously for our clients, file lawsuits, and manipulate the legal system, we are doing bad. We receive accolades and
denunciations for doing the same thing.

Individuals want a Rambo-type litigator on their side but want the op-
ponent's lawyer to be Mr. Milquetoast, understanding and supportive of
their (the adversary's) position. The general public wants lawyers to be less
aggressive, to compromise more, but they also know that if Rosa Parks
is suing because she objects to a law forcing blacks to sit at the back of
the bus, the last thing she needs is a lawyer who will compromise and
find her a seat in the middle of the bus.

As one astute commentator of the legal profession has noted, lawyers
are "simultaneously praised and blamed for the very same actions."[4] The
popular culture dislikes lawyers because we "manipulate the legal system in the interests" of our clients, but the popular culture also likes us
because our "first priority" is our clients, whom we represent with zeal.

> We expect lawyers to fulfill both desires, and so they are a constant irri-
> tating reminder that we are neither a peaceable kingdom of harmony
> and order, nor a land of undiluted individual autonomy, but somewhere
> disorientingly in between. Lawyers, in the very exercise of their profes-
> sion, are the necessary bearers of that bleak winter's tale, and we hate
> them for it.[5]

If, as this volume of essays has shown, television is ambivalent in its
treatment of lawyers, it is because society is ambivalent in its treatment
of lawyers. The little black box of television to some extent molds, but to
a much greater extent reflects, the equivocalness that the popular culture
has for lawyers.

We should not be surprised that medical doctors rate more highly in public opinion polls than lawyers do, because doctors simply represent the patient. There is no doctor fighting zealously for the disease. Not so for
lawyers. Our legal system gives everyone their day in court, and some of
these litigants are viewed less favorably than ugly diseases. Lawyers are
the messengers who are blamed for the bad message.[6]

Litigation is what economists call a "zero-sum" game. In order for
one side to win, the other must lose. When lawyers represent clients in
non-litigative matters, clients are much more positive about their experiences with lawyers.[7] In litigation, however, at least one side (often called
the loser) will be unhappy. Even if the other party (often called the winner) believes that he or she has been ultimately vindicated, it is not unusual
for that party to complain that justice did not come easily but had to be
fought for. When winners and losers are disgruntled, their lawyers are
like magnets for their complaints. People want to see their lawyers about
as much as the dinosaurs wanted to see giant meteors hit the earth.

It is true that one of Shakespeare's characters, Dick the Butcher, says that we must "kill all the lawyers,"[8] but Dick was an unsavory character, and in context he meant that the only way for his revolution to succeed was to kill those who represented the law. Luke's Gospel does refer to lawyers in a disparaging way, but the corresponding sections of the Gospel of Matthew only complains about the scribes and Pharisees.[9] Lawyers are not necessarily Pharisees.

Carl Sandburg wrote years ago:

> The knack of a mason outlasts a moon.
> The hands of a plasterer hold a room together,
> That land of a farmer wishes him back again.
> Singers of songs and dreamers of plays
> Build a house no wind blows over.
> The lawyers—tell me why a hearse horse snickers
> hauling a lawyer's bones.[10]

But why should we pay attention to what horses think?

Several years ago, Harry Blackmun told me that if he had his life to live over again, he would like to be a medical doctor. I related this conversation to a friend of mine and said that I found Blackmun's remarks surprising. At the time, after all, he was a justice of the United States Supreme Court. One would think that he was at the pinnacle of his career. Why would anyone want to trade that to become a doctor? My friend remarked, "People often want to be doctors so that they can help people." I replied, but that is what lawyers do. We mend no bones. We build no bridges. We design no buildings. We paint no pictures except, perhaps, for our own amusement. There is little that we do that the human eye can see or the human hand can feel. But, if we are doing our jobs properly, we take up other people's burdens and relieve their stress. We make possible living a peaceful life in a peaceful state.[11]

Notes

Notes for Chapter 1
The Defenders

1. For a discussion of "point of view," see M. H. Abrams, *A Glossary of Literary Terms* 142–45 (4th ed. 1981). Raymond Williams compares "point of view" to "alignment" in *Marxism and Literature* 199 (1977).

2. Reginald Rose, "Law, Drama and Criticism," in 3 *Television Quarterly* 26 (Fall 1964).

3. Barbara Ehrenreich, "Legacies of the 1960s: New Rights and New Lefts," in *Sights on the Sixties* 230–32 (Barbara L. Tischler ed. 1992).

4. A useful survey is Allen J. Matusow, *The Unraveling of America: A History of Liberalism in the 1960s* (1984). James P. Young, *Reconsidering American Liberalism: The Troubled Odyssey of the Liberal Idea* (1996) ambitiously traces liberalism from the Puritans to the 1990s.

5. Partial collections of episodes are available for viewing at the Museum of Broadcast Communications in Chicago and the Museum of Television and Radio in New York City. A full set is available at the Center for Film and Theater Research at the University of Wisconsin in Madison. In October 1997, Showtime revived "The Defenders" by airing the first of several planned made-for-television movies, with E.G. Marshall in the starring role and Beau Bridges and Martha Plimpton as his son and granddaughter, both of whom are attorneys. See further Howard Rosenberg, "New 'Defenders' Lacks Depth of Old," *Los Angeles Times*, October 11, 1997, at 21.

6. James L. Baughman, *The Republic of Mass Culture: Journalism, Filmmaking, and Broadcasting in America since 1941* 95 (1992).

7. Useful treatments of "12 Angry Men" can be found in Paul Bergman and Michael Asimow, *Reel Justice: The Courtroom Goes to the Movies* 265–69 (1996), and Thomas J. Harris, *Courtroom's Finest Hour in American Cinema* 1–21 (1987).

8. Quoted in Mark T. Alvey, *Series Drama and the "Semi-Anthology": Sixties Television in Transition*, Ph.D. Dissertation, University of Texas at Austin (1995).

9. Quoted in Edith Efron, "The Eternal Conflict Between Good and Evil," in *TV Guide: The First 25 Years* 61 (Jay S. Harris ed. 1978).

10. Id. at 60.

11. Alvey, supra note 8, at 207.

12. Id. at 208–14.

13. Muriel G. Cantor, *Prime-Time Television: Content and Control* 26–27 (1980).

14. Alvey, supra note 8, at 213.

15. Harris, supra note 7, at 60.

16. Id.

17. Alvey, supra note 8, at 215. After the sixth draft, incidentally, scripts for "The Defenders" were sent to a legal expert for review. An attempt to achieve legal "accuracy" also became a part of later lawyer shows on prime time, such as "L.A. Law." See in this regard two articles by Charles B. Rosenberg, attorney and legal adviser to "L.A. Law": "An L.A. Lawyer Replies," 98 *Yale Law Journal* 1625 (1989), and "Inside L.A. Law," 74 *American Bar Association Journal*, November 1988, at 56.

18. Two brief pieces surveying lawyer programming on prime time television are David R. Papke, "Prime-Time Lawyers," *IU Law-Indianapolis*, Spring 1995, at 2, and "Fictional Lawyers and Television Justice, 1949–1996," in *Just Images II*, a publication of the American Bar Association Division for Public Education, May 8, 1996.

19. Useful articles on "Perry Mason" include Patricia Kane, "Perry Mason: Modern Culture Hero," in *Heroes of Popular Culture* 125–33 (Ray B. Browne, Marshall Fishwick, and Michael T. Marsden eds. 1972); David R. Papke, "Erle Stanley Gardner and His Amazing Perry Mason Machine," *Juris Doctor*, August/September 1973, at 26; Anita Sokolsky, "The Case of the Juridical Junkie: Perry Mason and the Dilemma of Confession," 2 *Yale Journal of Law & the Humanities* 189 (1990).

20. Rose, supra note 2, at 21.

21. Id. at 24.

22. Id. at 25.

23. Quoted in Alvey, supra note 8, at 235.

24. Quoted in Efron, supra note 9, at 60.

25. Cantor, supra note 13, at 27.

26. David Levine, "John Randolph on the Blacklistings," in *TV Book* 267–70 (Judy Fireman ed. 1977).

27. Tim Brooks and Earle Marsh, *The Complete Directory to Prime Time Network and Cable TV Shows 1946–Present* 253 (6th ed. 1995).

28. Val Adams, "TV Sponsors Quit Disputed Drama," *New York Times*, April 9, 1962, at 58.

29. 1 Horace Newcomb, *Encyclopedia of Television* 470 (1997).

30. John Fiske, *Television Culture* 95–99 (1987).

31. Harris Dienstfrey, "Doctors, Lawyers & Other TV Heroes," in *Television: The Critical View* 75 (Horace Newcomb ed. 1976).

32. Not surprisingly, the identical sensibility also manifests in Rose's "12 Angry Men."

33. Hal Himmelstein, *Television Myth and the American Mind* 180 (1984). The same tendency to market liberal sensitivies, Horace Newcomb argues, continued later in time in "The Trials of Rosie O'Neill" (CBS, 1990–92). See "The Lawyer in the History of American Television—An Overview," in *The Lawyer and Popular Culture* 43 (David L. Gunn ed. 1993).

34. Fiske, supra note 30, at 309–26.

35. John Fiske disdains discussion of television's impact, but he does discuss the ways television prefers and promotes certain types of meanings. Television, in his language, has an "effectivity" in society as a whole. Fiske, supra note 30, at 20. In Todd Gitlin's words, "The executives who sit uneasily at the commanding heights of the cul-

ture industry, desperately holding on to their tenuous positions, are not so much managers of the popular mind as orchestrators of its projects and desires." "Television's Screen: Hegemony in Transition," in *American Media and Mass Culture: Left Perspectives* 243 (Donald Lazure ed. 1987).

Notes for Chapter 2
Hill Street Blues

1. Robert J. Thompson, *Television's Second Golden Age: From Hill Street Blues to ER* 65 (1996).

2. Id. at 59.

3. Thompson describes the audio-visual style as "like nothing else before it on prime time," describing "[o]verlapping conversations in a style that would be compared to the movies of Robert Altman," little use of music, "a sense of urgency and realism" and the look of a documentary. Id. at 68.

4. Id. at 66.

5. Donna Lemaster and Joel W. Tscherne, "Hill Street Blues, An Episode Guide," available at <http://www.xnet.com/~djk/HillStreetBlues_2.shtml>. This comprehensive guide to "Hill Street Blues" is the source for all of the titles and descriptions of individual episodes that follow. Another internet source for the episode descriptions and titles can be found at <ftp://src.doc.ic.ac.uk/public.media/tv/co.../drama/HillStreetBlues/Hill-StreetBlues.ds>. The internet site <http://us.imdb.com/M/title-exact?title=%22Hill+Street+Blues%22> lists the principal actors, episode titles, air dates, and important guest stars.

6. Other notable characters included partners Officers Robert (Bobby) Hill (Michael Warren) and Andrew (Andy) Renko (Charles Haid), Detective Henry Goldblume (Joe Spano, the sensitive cop), Detective Neal Washington (Taurean Blacque), Officer Lucy Bates (Betty Thomas), Officer Joe Coffey (Ed Marinaro), Lt. Norman Buntz (Dennis Franz, who plays a similar character on "N.Y.P.D. Blue"), and Lt. Ray Calletano (Rene Enriquez). Sgt. Stanislaus Jablonski (Robert Prosky) took over for Sgt. Esterhaus after the latter's real-life death in 1984. Fay Furillo (Barbara Bosson), Furillo's ex-wife, and Grace Gardner (Barbara Babcock), Sgt. Esterhaus's lover, were continuing civilian characters. The show featured few recurring characters involved on the other side of the criminal justice equation—the accused, offenders, and victims—with the exception of Jesus Martinez (Trinidad Silva), who appeared regularly as a gang leader, sometime informant, and foil for Furillo, greeting the Captain as "hey Frankie."

7. Thompson, supra note 1, at 69. Other commentators, however, recall "Hill Street Blues" as modern-age heroes, despite or because of their flaws. "Hill Street Blues ... [has] shown the police to be as gallant as any heroes in history. It is just that they have become 1980's heroes—less macho, more compassionate, and more upscale. Today, we prefer a 'groovier sort of policeman,' critic Mark Crispin Miller wrote in a prescient 1981 article, 'hip, streetwise, yet caring,' likeably rebellious without losing his authoritative air." Steven D. Stark, "Perry Mason Meets Sonny Crockett: The History of Lawyers and the Police as Television Heroes," 42 *University of Miami Law Review* 229, 270 (1987).

8. Michael Pollan, "Can Hill Street Blues Save NBC?," *Channels*, March–April 1983, at 331, quoted in Stark, supra note 7, at 276. "The Blues have some patience for civil liberties, but it has worn thin. When Captain Furillo has had it up to here with looters, rapists, con-artists, lawyers, and liberal politicians, he's apt to take a sarcastic swipe at the public defender. 'Now, whose civil rights have we violated today, counselor?'"

9. Id.

10. Decorously clothed in pajamas, mind you. Shows like "N.Y.P.D. Blue" were still years away.

11. See, e.g., Episode 40, "Officer of the Year," broadcast October 28, 1982 (Davenport must cross-examine Officer Bates and, setting aside her personal feelings for Bates, destroys her on the stand).

12. See, e.g., Episode 36, "Trial by Fury," broadcast September 30, 1982 (Davenport is frustrated by media coverage that biases a trial against her high-profile client).

13. See, e.g., Episode 60, "The Long Law of the Arm," broadcast October 27, 1983 (defending an immigrant cabdriver), Episode 81, "Watt a Way to Go," broadcast October 4, 1984 (defending a defendant on death row), and Episode 134, "More Skinned Against Than Skinning," broadcast December 23, 1986 (defending a store owner who displays Nazi items).

14. See, e.g., Episode 67, "The Russians are Coming," broadcast December 15, 1983 (somewhat unrealistically, the judge and victim cooperate with Davenport to keep the defendant, a mentally disabled man, out of jail), and Episode 85, "Ewe and Me, Babe," broadcast November 8, 1984 (Davenport tries to reform her client, who is a young prostitute).

15. See, e.g., Episode 128, "Bald Ambition," broadcast October 30, 1986 (Assistant District Attorney Bernstein saves Davenport from a prisoner and confesses that he is in love with her), and Episode 135, "She's So Fein," broadcast January 6, 1987 (in which Davenport is held hostage by a client).

16. Episode 127, "The Best Defense," broadcast October 16, 1986.

17. Episode 29, "Of Mouse and Man," broadcast February 11, 1982.

18. See, e.g., Episode 20, "The Last White Man on East Ferry Avenue," broadcast February 11, 1982.

19. See, e.g., Episode 69, "Nichols from Heaven," broadcast January 19, 1984 (Davenport protects a woman and children from an abusive husband with the help of Officers Bates and Coffey), Episode 140, "Sorry Wrong Number," broadcast March 3, 1987 (Davenport and two Hill Street Station officers try to reconcile lovers), Episode 143, "Days of Swine and Roses," broadcast March 31, 1987 (Davenport tries to protect a family which includes a mentally disturbed man).

20. See, e.g., Episode 35, "Invasion of the Third World Body Snatcher," broadcast May 13, 1982 (Davenport's "nice" client is accused of rape).

21. See, e.g., Episode 32, "Some Like it Hot-Wired," broadcast March 18, 1982 (Davenport walks out of court in the middle of a case).

22. See Episode 93, "Dr. Hoof and Mouth," broadcast January 24, 1985.

23. See Episode 94, "Davenport in a Storm," broadcast January 31, 1985 (prosecuting white teenagers for the death of an African-American athlete).

24. See Episode 100, "Queen for a Day," broadcast April 11, 1985.

25. Originally not married, Davenport and Furillo married during the third season in Episode 54, "Eugene's Comedy Empire Strikes Back," broadcast March 3, 1983. It is impossible to imagine Perry Mason in a similar situation.

Notes for Chapter 3
L.A. Law

1. Stephen Gillers, "Taking L.A. Law More Seriously," 98 *Yale Law Journal* 1607 (1989). See also Robert E. Rosen, "Ethical Soap: L.A. Law and the Privileging of Character," 43 *University of Miami Law Review* 1229 (1989), and Charles B. Rosenberg, "An L.A. Lawyer Replies," 98 *Yale Law Journal* 1625 (1989).

2. Besides occasional viewing of "L.A. Law" during its run and other television watching, the author conducted research at the Museum of Television and Radio in New York City. The museum's "L.A. Law" collection includes a symposium on the show produced by the museum in 1996 for its seminar series. In addition to many of the cast members, the symposium included Bill Finkelstein, the New York lawyer and producer who wrote for the show.

3. I have called attention to the triangulated shape to show how serendipitously the triadic function of courts described by Martin Shapiro is represented in this shape. Here, western courts are seen as agents of dispute resolution with the court attempting to join opposing parties behind a judicially-determined resolution.

4. Although it appears on occasion in post-modernism, the Greek portico, like the Chippendale curlicues atop the AT&T building in Manhattan, seems more superficial than integral to contemporary court architecture.

5. Magali S. Larson, Behind the Postmodern Facade (1993).

6. See *Court House: A Photographic Document* (Richard Page ed. 1978), and *Courthouses and Courtrooms: Selected Readings* (James J. Alfini and Glenn R. Winters eds. 1972).

7. See National Center for State Courts, *Twenty Years of Courthouse Design Revisited* (1993), and American Bar Association/American Institute of Architects, *The American Courthouse: Planning and Design for the Judicial Process* (1973).

8. National Center for State Courts, supra note 7, at 213.

9. "The Practice" received a tryout from ABC in the spring of 1997 in the "N.Y.P.D. Blue" time slot. The show stars Dylan McDermott as Bobby Donnell, the head of a small Boston law firm who must fight eviction from his low-rent office at the same time that he fights for his clients. The show features the traditional struggle of the underdog against the forces of power and influence and relies on the storybook rewards of lives saved and trusts kept over the financial rewards more central to McKenzie, Brackman, Chaney, and Kuzak.

10. John Fiske, *Television Culture* 21 (1987).

11. Id. at 38–39.

12. See David Bordwell et al., *The Classical Hollywood Cinema: Film Style and Mode of Production to 1960* (1985).

13. Dianne L. Brooks, *The Law of Daytime: Television Soap Operas and Legal Narratives* (forthcoming).

14. There is even considerable difference between "Chicago Hope" and "ER" with reference to the levels of detail portrayed in the room.

15. See Brooks, supra note 13, and Julie D'Acci, *Defining Women: Television and the Case of "Cagney & Lacey"* (1994).

16. With its attention to the day progressing and vivid closeups, "Law & Order" combines the emotional intensity of daytime television with production values more

characteristic of prime time. In this show, the courtroom takes second place to the pores on a witness's face or the sweat beading on counsel's forehead. In yet another concession to the realities of justice, the "parts" of the New York City trial court system come to the screen as venues with no architectural distinction. They are dirty, crowded versions of Los Angeles courtrooms. In this regard, the literary form is far more prominent than was true in either "L.A. Law" or the O.J. Simpson trial.

Notes for Chapter 4
Law & Order

1. Robert P. Laurence, "New York Law-Man Likes to Shoot from the Grit," *San Diego Union-Tribune*, November 18, 1996, at E1.

2. Aaron Barnhart, "TV Law: 'The Practice' Speaks up for the Defense—'Law & Order' for the Prosecution," *Kansas City Star*, March 2, 1997, at K1.

3. The exclusion of its characters's personal lives changed during the 1997–98 season, with the opening episode showing detective Rey Curtis (Benjamin Bratt) dealing with the news that his wife has multiple sclerosis.

4. Bill Carter, "Tracking Down Viewers Till They're Captured; Stars Come and Go, but NBC's 'Law & Order' Plugs Away," *New York Times*, February 19, 1997, at C11.

5. Id.

6. In a recent essay on prime time shows about crime, Judith Grant argues that they are almost uniformly characterized by precisely the self-evidence of crime that "Law & Order" is intent on disrupting: police dramas, she argues, decontextualize and thus simplify crime, pretending "that crime's causes and definitions are self-evident, that criminals are easily recognizable and the punishments that we should give to them obvious." See Judith Grant, "Prime Time Crime: Television Portrayals of Law Enforcement," 15 *Journal of American Culture* 58 (1992).

7. For definitions of these and other abuse excuses see Alan Dershowitz, *The Abuse Excuse and Other Cop-Outs, Sob Stories, and Evasions of Responsibility* 321–41 (1994).

8. Mimi White, "Ideological Analysis and Television," in *Channels of Discourse Reassembled: Television and Contemporary Criticism* 179 (1992).

9. Pierre Bourdieu, "The Force of Law: Toward a Sociology of the Juridical Field," 38 *Hastings Law Journal* 817 (1987).

10. Barnhart, supra note 2.

11. Susan Rutberg, "Confronting the 'Abuse Excuse,'" *The Recorder*, July 16, 1997, at 5.

12. For a discussion of the Gilchrist case, and a reference to the show's representation of the case in "Rage," see Paul Harris, *Black Rage Confronts the Law* 193 (1997). All Harris says about "Law & Order" is that it "negatively portrayed the black rage defense."

13. Paul Langner, "Gilchrist Called 'Psychotic' by Defense," *Boston Globe*, March 31, 1989, at 17.

14. Doris S. Wong, "Gilchrist Convicted of First-degree Murder," *Boston Globe*, April 18, 1989, at 1.

Notes for Chapter 5
Matlock

1. Although this question does not rise to the same level of philosophical importance, it brings to mind Bishop Berkeley's question regarding the sound made by a tree falling in the forest when no one is there to hear it. See George Berkeley, *Three Dialogues Between Hylas and Philonous* (1713).

2. *TV Guide*, June 28, 1997, at 10.

3. Atlanta superstation WTBS regularly airs "Matlock" episodes.

4. *TV Guide*, January 25, 1997, at 193, 200. *TV Guide* called Griffith "inimitable" and Matlock himself "wily." Interestingly, "Matlock" and "Diagnosis Murder" tied for 63rd place in the final 1994–95 ratings. See "Prime-Time Box Scores," *Entertainment Weekly*, June 2, 1995, available at LEXIS, News Library, Entwkl file.

5. It is not entirely clear whether Matlock actually had two daughters practicing with him or whether the creators renamed an only daughter. When Linda Purl left the series, Charlene Matlock became a lawyer in Philadelphia; when Brynn Thayer joined the cast, Leanne Matlock came to Atlanta after being a prosecutor in Philadelphia. Steven Lance, *Written out of Television* 275 (1996).

6. Preliminary discussions to bring original "Matlock" episodes to WTBS did not lead to a tenth season. Lisa de Moraes, " 'Matlock' May Stay Alive on New Network," *The Hollywood Reporter*, May 5, 1995, available at LEXIS, News Library, Thr file.

7. Because "Matlock" ran at 8:00 p.m. during its first five years, it never benefitted from a strong lead-in show. If anything, it provided the foundation for NBC's other series: only one of the five shows in the network's 9:00 p.m. hour was canceled at the end of the season. "Matlock" competed against several popular "family hour" series during this period, including "Who's the Boss?," "Growing Pains," "Roseanne," and "The Wonder Years." Fortunately, it ran on Tuesday throughout those five years, avoiding both the slot-shifting that impedes audience building and competition from "N.F.L. Monday Night Football."

8. Although John Rubinstein played an attorney, his private detective father, played by Jack Warden, was the star. "The Mississippi," starring Ralph Waite, was ranked seventeenth in one text but not in a competing source. Compare Alex McNeil, *Total Television: The Comprehensive Guide to Programming From 1948 to the Present* 1156 (4th ed. 1996) with Tim Brooks and Earle Marsh, *The Complete Directory to Prime Time Network and Cable TV Shows 1946–Present* 1269 (6th ed. 1995).

9. Emmy awards went to several series featuring attorneys as well as to mini-series and specials. Robert Cummings was 1954's Best Actor in a Single Performance for his role in Studio One's showing of "12 Angry Men"; that show also received Best Direction and Best Written Dramatic Material awards. The following year Lloyd Nolan won the same award for his role in "The Caine Mutiny Court Martial," presented by Ford Star Jubilee; its director and adapter also received awards. "Perry Mason" cast members garnered the first awards for a dramatic series. Raymond Burr won two awards and Barbara Hale won one during the late 1950s and early 1960s. During the 1960s, "The Defenders" received multiple awards four times, and Carl Betz earned the Best Actor award once for "Judd for the Defense." "The Andersonville Trial," presented by Hollywood Television Theatre, won two awards for 1970–71, and "The Lawyers" won a

directorial achievement award in 1971–72. "The Law" won for Outstanding Special, while "IBM Presents Clarence Darrow" won for Outstanding Writing in a Special in 1974–75; the "John Adams, Lawyer" episode of "The Adams Chronicles" earned two awards the following year. In 1978–79, Rob Liebman was named Best Actor for "Kaz." An awards drought ended in 1986–87, when "L.A. Law" won at least one award in six consecutive years. "Night Court," a comedy series, also won an award in more than one year. Winners during the 1990s included "The Trials of Rosie O'Neill," "Equal Justice," and "I'll Fly Away" (which earned awards for each of its two seasons).

10. "James Stewart starred as Billy Jim Hawkins, a plain ol' country lawyer from Beauville, West Virginia, in this hour-long crime show. Veteran character actor Strother Martin costarred as his cousin, R.J. Hawkins, who occasionally did some investigating for Billy Jim." McNeil, supra note 8, at 365. Perhaps Hawkins wasn't as wily as Ben Matlock; in any event this series lasted only a year.

11. Id. at 1158–60 (compiling ratings data for the 1949–50 through 1994–95 seasons).

12. During that season, "Matlock" had an overall ranking of seventeenth.

13. Aficionados could engage in a five-hour viewing overload on Tuesday, September 23, 1997. Beginning at 7:00 p.m. (EDT) they could watch "Law & Order" (A & E); "JAG" (CBS); "Michael Hayes" (CBS); "The Practice" (ABC); and "Law & Order" (A & E).

14. "JAG" attorneys do much of their own investigating; courtroom scenes are absent in many episodes.

15. Both Nancy Drew and the Hardy Boys became television series in 1977. Interestingly, the father of the Hardy boys was a private investigator, while Nancy Drew's was an attorney. See also Margaret C. Albert, "Jessica is Nancy Drew Grown Up," in *The Fine Art of Murder* 323 (Ed Gorman et al. eds. 1993).

16. Although there were periods in which more than one attorney or detective show finished in the Top 20, these series paled in significance to the popularity of Westerns in the late 1950s. In 1958–59 alone, seven of the Top 10 shows, and eleven of the Top 20, were Westerns.

17. As our fascination with the Olympics proves, amateurism is particularly attractive in certain contexts. Indeed, the popularity of forms for do-it-yourself wills indicates that even amateur lawyering has its proponents.

18. A typical "Matlock" episode reunited a girl and her accused father just in time for Christmas. The murder occurred at a Christmas party, at which all of the male guests were dressed as Santa Claus. Matlock unmasked (both literally and figuratively) the real killer using a clue made famous by Sherlock Holmes, a dog that didn't bark.

19. Nevertheless, television executives regularly revive series, in part because of the difficulty of coming up with fresh ideas. See further Sharon Waxman, "Networks Rewind to Hits of the '70s," *Fort Lauderdale Sun-Sentinel*, January 28, 1998, at 4E (noting that the 1998–99 television season is expected to bring back "Fantasy Island," "The Love Boat," and "The Mary Tyler Moore Show").

20. Each had his failures. Franz also appeared in "Bay City Blues," "Beverly Hills Buntz," "Chicago Story," and "Nasty Boys." In all but the first, he played either a policeman or a former policeman. Waterston played a science professor turned amateur detective in "Q.E.D."

21. Helmond's characters appeared in "Soap," "Who's the Boss?," "Coach," and "Everybody Loves Raymond."

22. Although "The New Andy Griffith Show" returned him to the South, it did so as the retooled 1971 version of "Headmaster," and audiences never returned. "Headmaster" had the unenviable task of competing against "The Partridge Family" for family viewers.

23. In contrast, consider the role of Trapper John McIntyre, originated for television's "M*A*S*H" by Wayne Rogers and reprised in that medium's "Trapper John, M.D." by Pernell Roberts. The first series was a comedy; the second a drama. Ed Asner successfully transplanted his Lou Grant character into a dramatic spin-off of the same name after "The Mary Tyler Moore Show," a comedy, ended its long run.

24. See generally Lance, supra note 5.

25. William Katt, who played Paul Drake, Jr., was actually the son of Barbara Hale (Della Street) and not of William Hopper (Paul Drake).

26. "The Andy Griffith Show" produced both "Gomer Pyle, U.S.M.C." and "Mayberry, R.F.D."

27. Several books celebrate "The Andy Griffith Show." See, e.g., Ken Beck and Jim Clark, *The Andy Griffith Show Book* (rev. ed. 1995), and Richard Kelly, *The Andy Griffith Show* (1981).

28. Jack Klugman starred in "The Odd Couple" and "Quincy, M.E."; Dick Van Dyke in "The Dick Van Dyke Show" and "Diagnosis Murder"; and Tom Bosley in "Happy Days" and "Father Dowling Mysteries." Bosley also appeared on "The Dean Martin Show," "The Debbie Reynolds Show," "Murder, She Wrote," "The Sandy Duncan Show," narrated "That's Hollywood," and provided a voice for the cartoon show "Wait 'Til Your Father Gets Home." Van Dyke appeared in several less successful series between his two hits.

29. Other comedic icons made less successful attempts to become detectives. Both "The Cosby Mysteries" (featuring Bill Cosby as a criminologist) and "Lanigan's Rabbi" (in which Art Carney played a police chief) were one-season ventures. Cosby's much earlier Emmy-winning role in "I Spy" was overshadowed by "The Cosby Show," an eight-year blockbuster; in returning to comedy in "Cosby," he even brought Phylicia Rashad back to play his wife.

30. Bosley did play a police chief on "Murder, She Wrote." Although Carroll O'Connor followed a twelve-year stint as bigoted Archie Bunker on "All in the Family" and "Archie Bunker's Place" with six years playing a Mississippi sheriff on "In the Heat of the Night," he is not included in the main text because he was not an amateur in his later series.

31. "No Time for Sergeants" was the fourth highest grossing movie released in 1958. It was the only one of that year's top five that failed to receive an Academy Award nomination. Susan Sackett, *The Hollywood Reporter Book of Box Office Hits* 134–39 (rev. ed. 1996).

32. See Peter Applebome, *Dixie Rising: How the South is Shaping American Values, Politics, and Culture* (1996).

33. New Southern franchises include the Atlanta Thrashers (NHL), Carolina Hurricanes (NHL), Carolina Panthers (NFL), Charlotte Hornets (NBA), Florida Marlins (MLB), Florida Panthers (NHL), Jacksonville Jaguars (NFL), Miami Heat (NBA),

Nashville Predators (NHL), Orlando Magic (NBA), Tampa Bay Devil Rays (MLB), Tampa Bay Lightning (NHL), and Tennessee Oilers (NFL).

34. Other shows do have such themes. In "I'll Fly Away," for example, the early days of the civil rights movement in Mississippi provide the show's backdrop (even though the series was actually filmed in Atlanta). Fran W. Golden, *TVacations* 103 (1996). Although "Matlock" was set in Atlanta, it was shot initially in Los Angeles and ultimately in Wilmington, North Carolina. Id. at 112.

35. After the depression-era "The Waltons" and the rowdy "The Dukes of Hazzard," audiences welcomed a Southerner who could afford to buy a new suit, even if he preferred to wear the old model. If he failed to use expressions such as "might could" or "shouldn't ought to," at least he had a drawl.

36. Griffith had played such a character in "No Time for Sergeants," where, as Will Stockdale, a Georgia farm boy, he threw the Air Force into an uproar with his warm naviété and questioning ways.

37. Atlanta boasted a metropolitan area population of 2,233,000 in 1980 and 2,960,000 in 1990. Miami could exceed that figure only by including Fort Lauderdale; neither Charlotte nor Nashville was even remotely close. Bureau of the Census, Economics and Statistics Administration, U.S. Department of Commerce, *Statistical Abstract of the United States 1996* 40–42, 44–46.

38. When the first black investigator left the show, he was replaced by another black investigator. When the first female attorney left, she was replaced by a second, who in turn was replaced by a third.

39. W. J. Cash, The Mind of the South 128 (1991 ed.).

40. See *United States v. Virginia*, 518 U.S. 515 (1996).

41. See *Hishon v. King & Spalding*, 467 U.S. 69 (1984).

42. Despite *TV Guide's* failure to list "Matlock" in its memorable episode listing, the episode in which Michelle buys him a new suit is one of which I am particularly fond.

43. After "Matlock" ended, Griffith won a Grammy award for an album of Gospel music.

44. See Curtis Wilke, "Southern Style: National Clout with a Smile," *Fort Lauderdale Sun-Sentinel*, January 19, 1997, at G1, quoting Senator Thad Cochran (R.-Miss.): "Some of the traits that have enabled Southerners to do well in office include the warmth of their personalities. Southerners are good at dealing with people. They have the ability to tell a good story and to be a good listener." Id. at G2.

45. "The Perry Mason Mysteries" ran between 1985 and 1993. "L.A. Law" also ran during this time period (1986–94), but resemblances between it and "Matlock" were superficial at best.

46. Joan Hess, "Southern Fried," in Gorman, supra note 15, at 44, 45. The author continues, "Bigotry's no longer an acceptable motive; we leave that kind of tackiness to sanctimonious northerners and Hollywood producers. We're much more inclined to poison an eccentric old aunt for the family silver or take an ax to a spouse in order to avoid the social stigma of divorce (not to mention the legal fees and the problematic issue of who gets the season football tickets)." Id.

47. Bruce Babcock received an Emmy for music composition—dramatic underscore for his work on "Matlock." "Primetime Emmy Award Winners," August 30, 1992 (UPI), available at LEXIS, News Library, Arcnws file. Nevertheless, the series is omitted

from the leading text discussing television music. See Jon Burlingame, *TV's Greatest Hits* (1996). Burlingame does cite Babcock for his work on "Murder, She Wrote."

48. Consider this statement: "It's straight out of a 'Perry Mason' or 'Matlock' script book and does well to borrow on the strengths of those traditions. Not surprisingly, it comes from executive producer Dean Hargrove." Rick Sherwood, "MacShayne," *The Hollywood Reporter*, April 28, 1994, available at LEXIS, News Library, Thr file. Silverman and Hargrove collaborated on "Perry Mason," "Matlock," "Jake and the Fatman," and "Diagnosis Murder." A similar comment concerned "The Client": "The TV version... is no genre bender—many weeks the plots could be transplants from Matlock or In the Heat of the Night." "Legal Aid; After Mistrials, Grisham's 'Client' Shows New Appeal," *Entertainment Weekly*, November 10, 1995, available at LEXIS, News Library, Entwkl file.

49. By the middle of the 1993–94 season, "Matlock" was "ABC's oldest-skewing show, strongest in adults 55-plus. Among women 55-plus, 'Matlock' is the No. 5-ranked show....Among men in that age bracket, 'Matlock' is No. 11." Its audience share among women aged 18–49 exceeded its share for men in that same age group. Lisa de Moraes, "More 'Matlock' on ABC Docket," *The Hollywood Reporter*, February 10, 1994, available at LEXIS, News Library, Entwkl file. When ABC picked up "Matlock" in 1992, it ranked third for viewers aged 50 and up. Lisa de Moraes, "Ad Executives Question ABC's 'Matlock' Ad," *The Hollywood Reporter*, March 4, 1992, available at LEXIS, News Library, Entwkl file.

50. In addition to a successful motion picture series starring William Powell and Myrna Loy, audiences could watch the Peter Lawford and Phyllis Kirk version of "The Thin Man" on television between 1957 and 1959. "Mr. and Mrs. North" appeared on television from 1952 through 1954. Recent variations on this genre include "McMillan and Wife" (1971–77) and "Hart to Hart" (1979–84).

51. "Perry Mason" initially held evidentiary hearings rather than jury trials and saved the cost of jurors. McNeil, supra note 8, at 652.

Notes for Chapter 6
Murder One

1. One commentator made the comparison this way: "Perry Mason probably wouldn't have had the patience to plead a case on 'Murder One.' The glib defense attorney of 1950s TV used to plow through one trial a week, winning them all with a combination of legalistic prowess and theatrical flair. But in Steve Bochco's 1995 series 'Murder One,' the entire 22-week run will be devoted to the progression of a single murder trial." Joe Mandese, "Increasing Friction between Fact and Fiction in Burgeoning Genre," *Advertising Age*, November 21, 1994, at 12.

After analyzing the first season's statistics, the producers apparently decided that viewers had a difficult time staying with one case the whole season, so they decided to focus on three different cases during the second season. See, e.g., Jeffrey Ressner, "All New Trials by Fire: Murder One's Latest Defense Tactics Include a Sexier Star and More Straightforward Cases," *Time*, October 21, 1996, at 82.

2. Ken Tucker, "Murder One," *Entertainment Weekly*, September 15, 1995, at 92.

3. Ken Tucker, "Anatomy of a 'Murder'—Steven Bochco Makes a Case for His Ratings-Challenged Show," *Entertainment Weekly*, May 10, 1996, at 61.

4. "Murder One" was canceled after its second season. Tom Shales, " 'Murder One': The Final Verdict; Canceled Crime Drama Won't Win on Appeal," *Washington Post*, May 24, 1997, at C01. Although the program was critically acclaimed, it was unable to attract enough of a regular audience. Part of the show's problem had to do with scheduling. During part of its first season, "Murder One" was shown opposite NBC's "ER"; during its second season, it had to battle NBC's "Seinfeld." Keith Marder, " 'Murder One' Wins its Case as a Three-Part Miniseries," *Los Angeles Daily News*, May 24, 1997, at L18.

5. See Kate O'Hare, " 'Murder One' Changes Format, Lead Actor," *Los Angeles Daily News*, October 6, 1996, at L1 (following a single trial for an entire season was "a revolutionary concept for television").

6. Cheryl Heuton, "Bochco Show Gets '95 Go," *Mediaweek*, September 19, 1994, at 5.

7. Id. In another interview, Bochco said: "Not only the O.J. Simpson trial but the Menendez trial and all the trials you see on Court TV have gone a long way toward educating the viewing public about the complexities of trial preparation and the trial itself....These trials have made people more sophisticated about what to expect, and that's good for us." Steve Coe, "Laying Down the Law in Prime Time," *Broadcasting and Cable*, September 4, 1995, at 15.

8. Elayne Rapping, "Land of the Good-Guy Prosecutors," *The Progressive*, May 1, 1996, at 38.

9. Steve Marshall, "Poll Finds 56% Dislike Verdict," *USA Today*, October 4, 1995, at A2. Although numerical estimates are not available, the case was being watched around the world. See Anne Swardson, "There's No Place Safe From O.J.; Trial Seen as Window on American Culture," *Washington Post*, January 29, 1995, at A4.

10. See Kate Stith-Cabranes, "The Criminal Jury in Our Time," 3 *Virginia Journal of Social Policy and Law* 133, 133–35 (1995). For examples of the reaction to the O.J. Simpson verdict, see "Trial Writes a New Chapter for Criminal Justice," *USA Today*, October 18, 1996, at 6A, and Tony Mauro, "OJ Trial Could Spell Change to Justice System," *USA Today*, October 5, 1995, at 1A.

11. As Robert Payant, a former judge and president of the National Judicial College, put it: "People have talked about the need for reforming the jury system, but that's usually when a verdict is returned they don't think is correct." "Trial Writes a New Chapter for Criminal Justice," *USA Today*, October 18, 1996, at 6A.

12. "Murder One, Chapter One" (ABC television broadcast, September 19, 1995).

13. "Murder One, Chapter Two" (ABC television broadcast, September 26, 1995).

14. "Murder One, Chapter One" (ABC television broadcast, September 19, 1995).

15. "Murder One, Chapter Two" (ABC television broadcast, September 26, 1995).

16. "Murder One, Chapter Three" (ABC television broadcast, October 3, 1995).

17. "Murder One, Chapter Thirteen" (ABC television broadcast, February 12, 1996).

18. "Murder One, Chapter Eleven" (ABC television broadcast, January 22, 1996).

19. "Murder One, Chapter Seven" (ABC television broadcast, November 9, 1995).

20. "Murder One, Chapter Fourteen" (ABC television broadcast, February 19, 1996).

21. "Murder One, Chapter Thirteen" (ABC television broadcast, February 12, 1996).

22. "Murder One, Chapter Sixteen" (ABC television broadcast, March 11, 1996).

23. "Murder One, Chapter Fifteen" (ABC television broadcast, March 4, 1996).

24. "Murder One, Chapter Sixteen" (ABC television broadcast, March 11, 1996).

25. "Murder One, Chapter Fourteen" (ABC television broadcast, February 19, 1996).

26. "Murder One, Chapter Sixteen" (ABC television broadcast, March 11, 1996).

27. "Murder One, Chapter Seventeen" (ABC television broadcast, March 18, 1996).

28. Id.

29. "Murder One, Chapter Eighteen" (ABC television broadcast, April 1, 1996) (quoted from <http://www.geocities.com/Hollywood/1120/m1trans.html>).

30. Id.

31. Id.

32. "Murder One, Chapter Nineteen" (ABC television broadcast, April 8, 1996) (quoted from <http://www.geocities.com/Hollywood/1120/m1trans.html>).

33. Id.

34. "Murder One, Chapter Twenty" (ABC television broadcast, April 22, 1996).

35. Id.

36. "Murder One, Chapter Twenty-One" (ABC television broadcast, April 23, 1996).

37. "Murder One, Chapter Two" (ABC television broadcast, September 26, 1995).

38. "Murder One, Chapter Three" (ABC television broadcast, October 3, 1995).

39. Id.

40. "Murder One, Chapter Eighteen" (ABC television broadcast, April 1, 1996).

41. The Jury Project of the University of Chicago Law School surveyed judges in 3,576 cases, and found agreement 75.4% of the time. See Harry Kalven, Jr. and Hans Zeisel, *The American Jury* 56 (1966).

42. "Murder One, Chapter Twenty" (ABC television broadcast, April 22, 1996) (quoted from <http://www.geocities.com/Hollywood/1120/m1trans.html>).

43. "Murder One, Chapter Twenty-One" (ABC television broadcast, April 23, 1996).

44. "Murder One, Chapter Three" (ABC television broadcast, October 3, 1995).

45. Id.

46. Id.

47. Id. (quoted from <http://www.geocities.com/Hollywood/1120/m1trans.html>).

48. Id.

49. This is essentially the theory advanced by Professor Alan Dershowitz in his book about the O.J. Simpson trial, *Reasonable Doubts* (1996). Another commentator, in response to the O.J. Simpson civil verdict, has suggested that the mishandling of the criminal case justified the not guilty verdict. See R. Bruce Dold, "An Amazing State of Affairs: O.J. Got What He Deserved in Both Trials and That's All the More Reason Why We Shouldn't Lose Faith in our Jury System," *Chicago Tribune*, February 7, 1997, at 27.

50. "Murder One, Chapter One" (ABC television broadcast, September 19, 1995).

51. "Where Prosecutors Went Wrong, According to Experts," *USA Today*, October 18, 1996, at 6A.

52. Two psychologists who study jury behavior have noted: "Today the nation is littered with so-called jury experts who claim an ability to select favorable juries through scientific techniques.... It is almost unusual now to come across an important case, criminal or civil, in which the jury is selected without the help of an expert." Saul M. Kassin and Lawrence S. Wrightsman, *The American Jury on Trial: Psychological Perspectives* 57 (1988). See also Cathy E. Bennett and Robert B. Hirschhorn, *Bennett's Guide to Jury Selection and Trial Dynamics in Civil and Criminal Litigation* § 1.1 (1993) (noting that jury consultation is a "booming field" that "has grown to sizable proportions, drawing people from a variety of backgrounds, including psychology, counseling and sociology, acting and communication.").

53. See Bennett & Hirschhorn, supra note 52, at § 1.1.

54. "Murder One, Chapter Six" (ABC television broadcast, November 2, 1995) (quoted from <http://www.geocities.com/Hollywood/1120/m1trans.html>).

55. One scholar put it this way: "The siren call of the jury-selection expert, therefore, is a simple and seductive one: I'll get you the right jurors and that way you'll win your case regardless of the evidence against you." John Guinther, *The Jury in America* 56 (1988).

56. "Murder One, Chapter Six" (ABC television broadcast, November 2, 1995) (quoted from <http://www.geocities.com/Hollywood/1120/m1trans.html>).

57. Guinther, supra note 55, at 58.

58. After reviewing the studies, one scholar concluded: "It seems probable, therefore, on the issue of bias, that voir dire questioning—particularly when conducted by lawyers—can lead to identifying overtly prejudiced jurors, and that the procedure should ordinarily catch out those who have already formed an opinion of the case. That, in itself, is no small accomplishment." Id.

59. "Murder One, Chapter Nine" (ABC television broadcast, January 8, 1996) and "Murder One, Chapter Ten" (ABC television broadcast, January 15, 1996).

60. See *Batson v. Kentucky*, 476 U.S. 79 (1986). For a more complete explanation of *Batson* and its history and implications, see Michael W. Kirk, "Sixth And Fourteenth Amendments—The Swain Song of the Racially Discriminatory Use of Peremptory Challenges," 77 *Journal of Criminal Law* 821 (1986). See also Kenneth J. Melilli, "Batson in Practice: What We Have Learned About Batson and Peremptory Challenges," 71 *Notre Dame Law Review* 447 (1996).

61. "Murder One, Chapter Ten" (ABC television broadcast, January 15, 1996) (quoted from <http://www.geocities.com/Hollywood/1120/m1trans.html>).

62. For examples of scholarly criticism, see, e.g., Jeffrey Abramson, *We, the Jury: The Jury System and the Ideal of Democracy* 9–12 (1994); Akhil R. Amar, "Reinventing Juries: Ten Suggested Reforms," 28 *University of California at Davis Law Review* 1169, 1182–83 (1995); Albert W. Alschuler, "The Supreme Court and the Jury: Voir Dire, Preemptory Challenges and the Review of Jury Verdicts," 56 *University of Chicago Law Review* 153 (1989). Some members of the judiciary have advocated the complete abolition of preemptory challenges. See *Georgia v. McCollum*, 505 U.S. 42, 60–62 (1992) (Thomas, J., concurring); *J.E.B. v. Alabama ex rel. T.B.*, 511 U.S. 127, 146–51 (1994)

(O'Connor, J., concurring); *J.E.B.*, 511 U.S. at 156–63 (1994) (Scalia, J., dissenting); *Batson*, 476 U.S. at 107 (Marshall, J., concurring).

63. "Murder One, Chapter Nine" (ABC television broadcast, January 8, 1996).

64. The quote is from the question put to Ms. Milligan by Mr. Hoffman, to which she replied, "Of course I would." Id. (quoted from <http://www.geocities.com/Hollywood/1120/m1trans.html>).

65. There was a substitution in characters from the consultant first interviewed in Chapter 6, which aired on November 2, 1995. The new character was Lorraine Vitalli, who was introduced as the partner of the original jury consultant, Margaret Stratton. Ms. Stratton had to discontinue working on the case for "medical reasons." "Murder One, Chapter Eight" (ABC television broadcast, November 16, 1995).

66. This appears to be a reference to lawyer folklore about the role of religion as an indication of a prospective juror's predisposition or bias. See Bennett & Hirschhorn, supra note 52, at §§ 15.30–15.55 (describing "basic biases" of religion), and Robert A. Wenke, *The Art of Jury Selection* 79 (2d ed. 1989).

67. "Murder One, Chapter Nine" (ABC television broadcast, January 8, 1996) (quoted from <http://www.geocities.com/Hollywood/1120/m1trans.html>).

68. There is some empirical evidence to show that criminal defense lawyers's use of preemptory challenges can make a difference in the deliberations of the jury. See Hans Zeisel and Shari Diamond, "The Effect of Preemptory Challenges on Jury and Verdict: An Experiment in a Federal District Court," 30 *Stanford Law Review* 491 (1978).

69. A former superior court judge has identified "[w]ives, children and parents of policemen" as ideal jurors for the prosecution. See Wenke, supra note 66, at 72. It follows that a retired police officer would be even better, but probably was not mentioned because it is so unlikely that the defense would allow such a person to remain on the jury.

70. "Murder One, Chapter Nine" (ABC television broadcast, January 8, 1996).

71. Id.

72. See, e.g., Laura G. Dooley, "Our Juries, Our Selves: The Power, Perception and Politics of the Civil Jury," 80 *Cornell Law Review* 325, 339–40 (1995) (noting that juries are often described as being irrational, emotional, and inflamed by passion).

73. See, e.g., Lou Cannon, "It Wasn't the Jurors' Fault," *Washington Post*, October 8, 1995, at C07, and Nell Henderson, "Ex-Juror's Comments Put Race Center Stage in Simpson Trial," *Washington Post*, April 8, 1995, at A03. A poll following the verdict found that 34% of those surveyed thought race "determined" the verdict, and another 38% thought that race was a factor as it related to the evidence. Only 22% of those surveyed thought that race had no influence on the jury. Steve Marshall, "Poll Finds 56% Dislike Verdict," *USA Today*, October 4, 1995, at A2.

74. "Murder One, Chapter Seventeen" (ABC television broadcast, March 18, 1996).

75. Id. (quoted from <http://www.geocities.com/Hollywood/1120/m1trans.html>).

76. "In total, therefore, a highly significant 90% of the crucial trial events recalled [by jurors surveyed in the Pound study] was directly evidentiary or demeanor-related." Guinther, supra note 55, at 64. See also Kassin & Wrightsman, supra note 52, at 61 ("controlled studies of individual juror bias, as reviewed earlier, suggest that the vast majority of verdicts are determined by the evidence… [and that] jury verdicts are more readily predictable from the strength of the evidence than from the characteristics of individual jurors.").

77. See Harry Kalven, Jr., "The Dignity of the Civil Jury," 50 *Virginia Law Review* 1055, 1065–66 (1964).

78. "Murder One, Chapter Nineteen" (ABC television broadcast, April 8, 1996).

79. See Lorraine Adams and Serge F. Kovaleski, "The Best Defense Money Could Buy; Well-Heeled Simpson Legal Team Seemed One Step Ahead All Along," *Washington Post*, October 8, 1995, at A01 (quoting Dershowitz as saying "money meant everything in this case," and Uelmen as saying "I think the resources made the difference."). Most Americans agreed. In response to a CNN poll asking whether Simpson's wealth played a role in his getting a not guilty verdict, 73% of those surveyed felt "Simpson would have been convicted had he not been rich." Steve Marshall, "Poll Finds 56% Dislike Verdict," *USA Today*, October 4, 1995, at A2.

80. "Was Justice Served?," *Wall Street Journal*, October 4, 1995, at A14.

81. "Murder One, Chapter Twenty" (ABC television broadcast, April 22, 1996).

82. "Murder One, Chapter Two" (ABC television broadcast, September 26, 1995) (quoted from <http://www.geocities.com/Hollywood/1120/m1trans.html>).

83. "Murder One, Chapter Twenty-One" (ABC television broadcast, April 23, 1996). Portalegre's response is one of the most chilling lines from the show: "You should know, Mr. Hoffman, that, uh, killing that girl was not difficult for me. On the contrary, I took pleasure in it." Id.

84. "Murder One, Chapter Fifteen" (ABC television broadcast, March 4, 1996).

85. "Murder One, Chapter Two" (ABC television broadcast, September 26, 1995).

86. Rita J. Simon, *The Jury: Its Role in American Society* 117 (1980) (reviewing various studies). Professor Simon concludes: "The results show that when ordinary citizens become jurors, they assume a special role in which they apply different standards of proof, more vigorous reasoning, and greater detachment." Id.

87. Kassin & Wrightsman, supra note 52, at 48.

88. Id.

89. Mock jury research has shown "that pretrial publicity had a dramatic effect on their verdicts. Although only 55 percent of those in the neutral-news condition voted that the defendant was guilty, that number increased to 78 percent in the prejudicial-news condition. In a subsequent study... the percentage of guilty votes increased from 35 to 69 percent. Additional research has corroborated the finding that pretrial publicity can violate the ideal of a fair trial." Id. at 48–49.

90. "Murder One, Chapter Six" (ABC television broadcast, November 2, 1995).

91. "Murder One, Chapter Four" (ABC television broadcast, October 12, 1995).

92. See Peter Johnson and Alan Bash, "At NBC, Fallout After Simpson's Pullout," *USA Today*, October 12, 1995, at 1D, and John Carmody, "The TV Column," *Washington Post*, October 12, 1995, at C06. See also Robert Bianco, "Viewers Didn't Lose Much When O.J. Cancelled," *Pittsburgh Post-Gazette*, October 12, 1995, at A11.

93. The jury in the O.J. Simpson civil case awarded the plaintiffs $33.5 million in damages, finding Simpson's lack of credibility on the witness stand a significant factor. See Gale Holland and Jonathan T. Lovitt, "Jurors Detail the Thinking That Went Into Their Ruling," *USA Today*, February 11, 1997, at A1.

94. "Murder One, Chapter Eight" (ABC television broadcast, November 16, 1995) (quoted from <http://www.geocities.com/Hollywood/1120/m1trans.html>).

95. Id.

Notes for Chapter 7
N.Y.P.D. Blue

1. Robert J. Thompson, *Television's Second Golden Age: From Hill Street Blues to ER* 59 (1996).

2. Todd Gitlin, *Inside Prime Time* 273 (1983).

3. Id. at 305.

4. Id. at 324.

5. See further Mark Christensen and Cameron Stauth, *The Sweeps: Behind the Scenes in Network TV* (1984).

6. Gitlin, supra note 2, at 25: "Maximum audiences attract maximum dollars for advertisers, and advertiser dollars are, after all, the network's objective. (Network executives recite the points so predictably, so confidently, they sound like vulgar Marxists.)"

7. As has been noted elsewhere, probably the most often repeated adage in the television business is, "'If I knew what would work, I'd be the richest man in town.'" Christensen & Stauth, supra note 5, at 34.

8. See David Milch and Bill Clark, *True Blue: The Real Stories Behind N.Y.P.D. Blue* 9–84 (1995).

9. Quoted in "Scotland on Sunday: Police and Thieves," *Spectrum Section*, January 28, 1996, at 7.

10. Milch & Clark, supra note 8, at 82–84.

11. I am completely sympathetic to Steven Bochco's stand, when the "N.Y.P.D. Blue" series began, against the campaign of the American Family Association to "combat filth in television" (especially sexual language and nude scenes) by forcing ABC to drop the program, or, "that failing," to organize a boycott of companies advertising on the show. See further Milch & Clark, supra note 8, at 65–85. My objection to the repeated use of "scumbags" and "assholes," by Simone and other detectives, is not that the words are "filthy" — why pretend that police don't use them? — but that they help stir up viewers to cheer on the detectives in the violence against detainees that the words sometimes presage.

12. Of course, the Public Defender is not a widely admired figure these days. Elayne Rapping, in "Land of Good-Guy Prosecutors," *The Progressive*, May 1996, at 38, remarks that her son is a public defender, but that the staff attorneys in his office wear buttons that say, "'Don't tell my mother I'm a public defender, she thinks I play the piano in a whorehouse.'"

13. Amnesty International USA, *United States of America: Police Brutality and Excessive Force in the New York City Police Department*, June 1996, at 1.

14. Id. at 2.

15. Id. at 1.

16. Id. at 1–2.

17. Id. at 2, 11.

18. Id. at 13–14.

19. Erik Barnouw's indispensable history, *Tube of Plenty: The Evolution of American Television* (1990), recalls Newton Minow's famous 1961 speech in which, describing television at its worst, he depicted a "'vast wasteland'" of "'blood and thunder,

mayhem, violence, sadism, murder, western bad men, western good men, private eyes, gangsters, more violence....'" The "Western" has given way to the urban police show, but violence isn't less conspicuous on television a generation after Minow's critique.

20. Barnouw, supra note 19, at 132.

21. See August Strindberg, "There Are Crimes and Crimes: A Comedy," in *Eight Famous Plays* 167–231 (Edwin Bjorkman and N. Erichsen trans. 1949).

22. See Robert Sherrill, "A Year in Corporate Crime," *Nation*, April 17, 1997, at 11.

23. Id.

24. Id. at 12.

25. Id.

26. Id. at 17.

27. Id.

28. Gitlin, supra note 2, at 266.

29. Barnouw, supra note 19, at 366.

30. Arthur Koestler, *Darkness at Noon* 210 (Daphne Hardy trans. 1977).

31. Gunnar Myrdal, with the assistance of Richard Sterner and Arnold Rose, notes in *An American Dilemma: The Negro Problem and Modern Democracy* (1994): "The belief in a peculiar 'hircine odor' of Negroes, like similar beliefs concerning other races, touches a personal sphere and is useful to justify the denial of social intercourse and the use of public conveniences which would imply close contact, such as restaurants, theaters, and public conveyances. It is remarkable that it does not hinder the utilization of Negroes in even the most intimate household work and personal services." The passage in Myrdal's magisterial work occurs in Chapter 4 (page 107), "Racial Beliefs," in a section called "Specific Rationalization Needs."

32. Bernard Manning, Assistant Attorney General of the Criminal Division, Commonwealth of Massachusetts, wrote in the preface to *Enforcing the Criminal Law* (1975): "Through *Mapp*, *Gideon*, and *Miranda*, the Court has placed the law enforcement community on notice that it will no longer tolerate activities that violate the rule of fundamental fairness articulated by the law of the land. The nation's highest court has consistently said that those who have been sworn to uphold the law must not profane its principles even to accomplish a legitimate result."

More recently, Judge David Bazelon, in *Questioning Authority: Justice and Criminal Law* (1988), while observing that "In the courts we see a loosening of the elementary prophylactic role of *Miranda v. Arizona*," notes that "*Miranda's* success as an instrument of education is marked by the fact that every television viewer is familiar with the required litany of station-house rights," and that *Miranda* "reflected the equality principle. Those most likely to suffer coercive police practices behind closed station-house doors are the poor and uneducated perpetrators of street crime....By insisting that the disadvantaged be informed of [their rights to be silent and to retain a lawyer], by demanding that all subjects be treated with dignity,... *Miranda* promised genuine equal justice before the law." Id. at 289, 152, 151.

33. Tom Fontana received an Emmy for this episode for "Outstanding Individual Achievement in Writing in a Drama Series." See Don Franks, *Entertainment Awards: A Music, Cinema, Theatre and Broadcasting Reference, 1928 Through 1993* 129 (1996).

Notes for Chapter 9
Perry Mason

1. Miller wins the honor of having appeared in more episodes, 57, than any other non-regular in the series. See "The Perry Mason TV Series," available at <http://www.oz.net/~daveb/perry.htm>. In addition to the episodes of the "classic" series, there are thirty made-for-television films based on the "return" of Perry Mason in 1985. These episodes, like those in the original series, are in wide circulation through syndication and are often played on cable television. Except in passing, this essay will not discuss these later episodes.

2. For a view of "camp" as applied to the dramas of the 1950s, see Barbara Klinger, *Melodrama and Meaning: History, Culture, and the Films of Douglas Sirk* (1994).

3. See further Norman L. Rosenberg, "Gideon's Trumpet: Sounding the Retreat from Legal Realism," in *Recasting America: Culture and Politics in the Age of Cold War* 107–24 (Lary May ed. 1989).

4. The discussion of the Perry Mason films is based on my own research of legal-reelist texts, some of which appears in Norman Rosenberg, "Hollywood on Trials: Courts and Films, 1930–1960," 12 *Law and History Review* 341 (1994), and Dennis Bounds, *Perry Mason: The Authorship and Reproduction of a Popular Hero* chapter 3 (1996).

5. Many years later, Bette Davis actually got to play the Perry Mason role; during a brief period when Raymond Burr was laid up with a back injury, several "guest attorneys," including one played by Davis, filled in for him.

6. See further Norman L. Rosenberg, "Young Mr. Lincoln: The Lawyer as Super-Hero," 15 *Legal Studies Forum* 215 (1991).

7. See further Anthony Chase, "Law and Popular Culture: A Review of Mass Media Portrayals of American Attorneys," 1986 *American Bar Foundation Research Journal* 281, and Norman Rosenberg, "Law Noir," in *Legal Reelism: Movies as Legal Texts* (John Denvir ed. 1996).

8. See Dorothy B. Hughes, *Erle Stanley Gardner: The Case of the Real Perry Mason* (1978).

9. See David R. Papke, "Peace Between the Sexes: Law and Gender in Kramer vs. Kramer," 30 *University of San Francisco Law Review* 1199 (1996).

10. Bounds, supra note 4, at chapter 5.

11. "The Big Sleep" (1945, 1946) is the classic example of a film noir whose narrative is so intricately knotted that not even Raymond Chandler, the author of the novel on which the screenplay was based, could help the film's director and screenwriter straighten out the story!

Notes for Chapter 10
Picket Fences

1. 1 Alexis de Tocqueville, *Democracy in America* 290 (Knopf ed. 1945).

2. The major regular cast members were: Tom Skerritt (Sheriff Jimmy Brock); Kathy Baker (Dr. Jill Brock); Holly Marie Combs (Kimberly Brock); Justin Shenkarow (Matthew Brock); Adam Wylie (Zachary Brock); Costas Mandylor (Deputy Kenny Lacos); Lauren Holly (Deputy Maxine Stewart); Ray Walston (Judge Henry Bone); Fyvush Finkel (Douglas Wambaugh); Kelly Connell (Coroner Carter Pike); Don Cheadle (District Attorney John Littleton); Jason Beghe (District Attorney Petrovek); Zelda Rubenstein (Ginny Weedon); Denis Arndt (Franklin Dell); Marlee Matlin (Mayor Laurie Bey); Michael Keenan (Mayor Bill Pugen); Leigh Taylor Young (Mayor Rachel Harris); Robert Cornthwaite (Mayor Howard Buss); Richard Masur (Mayor Ed Lawson); Dabbs Grier (Reverend Henry Novotny); Roy Dotrice (Father Gary Barrett); Roy Brocksmith (Principal Michael Oslo); Cristine Rose (Lydia Brock); Amy Aquino (Dr. Joanna "Joey" Diamond); Ann Guilbert (Myriam Wambaugh, 1992–94); Erica Yohn (Myriam Wambaugh, 1995–96); Bojesse Christopher (Billy O'Connell); and Elisabeth Moss (Cynthia Parks). Special guest stars included Adam Arkin, James Coburn, Alan Dershowitz, Louise Fletcher, Louis Gossett, Jr., James Earl Jones, Richard Kiley, Della Reese, Paul Winfield, Teresa Wright, and Efrem Zimbalist, Jr. Former New York City Mayor Ed Koch, sportscaster Pat O'Brien, and host Harry Smith appeared in cameos.

3. "Picket Fences" won the following Emmy Awards: *1992–93*: Outstanding drama series; Outstanding lead actor—drama series (Tom Skerritt); Outstanding lead actress—drama series (Kathy Baker). *1993–94*: Outstanding drama series; Outstanding supporting actress—drama series (Leigh Taylor Young); Outstanding supporting actor—drama series (Fyvush Finkel); Outstanding guest actor—drama series (Richard Kiley); Outstanding costuming—series (Shelly Levine and Loree Parral). *1994–95*: Outstanding lead actress—drama series (Kathy Baker); Outstanding supporting actor—drama series (Ray Walston); Outstanding guest actor—drama series (Paul Winfield); Outstanding costuming—series (Shelly Levine and Loree Parral). *1995–96*: Outstanding lead actress—drama series (Kathy Baker); Outstanding supporting actor—drama series (Ray Walston).

4. See, e.g., John J. Cound et al., *Civil Procedure* 1299 (7th ed. 1997), and David Luban, "Are Criminal Defenders Different?," 91 *Michigan Law Review* 1729, 1744 (1993).

5. The question has produced the sort of controversy that provided grist for many of the best "Picket Fences" episodes. Some researchers and commentators assert that exposure to media violence has a harmful effect on the behavior of some juveniles. Others argue that media violence does not affect juvenile behavior, that an effect has not been proved, or that violence in our society is a product of other factors, such as poverty, racial divisions, and poor parenting. Compare, e.g., Steven P. Shelov et al., "Media Violence," 95 *Pediatrics* 949 (June 1995) ("Over 1000 studies... attest to a causal connection between media violence and aggressive behavior in some children") with Jonathan L. Freedman, "Violence in the Mass Media and Violence in Society: The Link is Unproven," 12 *Harvard Mental Health Letter* 4 (May 1996). See also, e.g., *Television in Society* 105–72 (Arthur A. Berger ed. 1987), and Scott Stossel, "The Man Who Counts the Killings," *Atlantic Monthly*, May 1997, at 86.

6. See, e.g., Bob Smizek, "Ruling on Kids Supremely Wrong," *Pittsburgh Post-Gazette*, June 29, 1995, at D1; John Rosemond, "Children's Rights? What Rights?," *Buffalo News*, January 22, 1995, at 3; James J. Kilpatrick, "Regarding Drug Testing of Children," *Tampa Tribune*, December 29, 1994, at 11.

7. See Howard N. Snyder et al., *Juvenile Offenders and Victims: 1996 Update on Violence* 14 (1996); "U.S. Reports Sharp Drop in Youth Violent Crime," *New York Times*, October 3, 1997, at A13 (9.2% decline in 1996); Fox Butterfield, "After a Decade, Juvenile Crime Begins to Drop," *New York Times*, August 9, 1996, at A1 (2.9% decline in 1995).

8. See Fox Butterfield, "Experts on Crime Warn of a 'Ticking Time Bomb,'" *New York Times*, January 6, 1996, at 6.

9. See, e.g., Telecommunications Act of 1996, § 551(a), P.L. 104-104, 110 Stat. 56, 139–40 (Parental Choice in Television Programming; Findings). See also, e.g., Willard D. Rowland, Jr., *The Politics of TV Violence* (1983); Brian Lowry, "The Times Poll: TV on Decline, But Few Back U.S. Regulation," *Los Angeles Times*, September 21, 1997, at A1; Richard T. Cooper, "A New Kind of TV Guide," *Los Angeles Times*, July 15, 1997, at E1; Gloria Goodale, "Battles Over Media Violence Move To a New Frontier: The Internet," *Christian Science Monitor*, November 18, 1996, at 10; "79 Percent in Poll Believe TV Violence Spurs Real Mayhem," *Washington Post*, December 19, 1993, at A12.

10. See, e.g., Lawrie Mifflin, "Deal on Making Ratings for TV Specify Content," *New York Times*, July 10, 1997, at A1. The wisdom and constitutionality of any such congressional mandate remain open questions. See, e.g., Harry T. Edwards and Mitchell N. Berman, "Regulating Violence on Television," 89 *Northwestern University Law Review* 1487 (1995), and "Television and Violence: A Symposium," 22 *Hofstra Law Review* 773 (1994).

11. Juvenile curfews have proliferated in the 1990s. See, e.g., U.S. Department of Justice, Office of Juvenile Justice and Delinquency Prevention, *Curfew: An Answer to Juvenile Delinquency and Victimization* 1 (April 1996), and John Pionke, "Conference Survey Finds Cities Moving to Youth Curfews," *U.S. Mayor*, December 11, 1995, at 18–19. The Supreme Court has not determined the constitutionality of juvenile curfews, and lower court holdings have been mixed. See, e.g., *Qutb v. Strauss*, 11 F.3d 488 (5th Cir. 1993), cert. denied, 511 U.S. 1127 (1994) (upholding Dallas's curfew), and *Hutchins v. District of Columbia*, 942 F. Supp. 665 (D.D.C. 1996) (striking down D.C.'s curfew).

The embrace of uniforms by many public school districts is described in Michel Marriott, "Uniforms: Public Schools Stand Up and Salute," *New York Times*, February 4, 1996, at 45; Margaret A. Jacobs, "Court Lets Public School Require Uniforms," *Wall Street Journal*, December 5, 1995, at B1; Kathryn Wexler, "Sizing Up a Uniform Answer To Address Problems at School," *Washington Post*, November 8, 1995, at A3; Louise Lee, "Sales of Uniforms Are Looking Sharp As More Public-School Kids Wear Them," *Wall Street Journal*, August 22, 1995, at B1. President Clinton endorsed school uniforms in his 1996 State of the Union address: "[I]f it means that teenagers will stop killing each other over designer jackets, then our public schools should be able to require their students to wear school uniforms." "President's State of the Union Message," *FDCH Political Transcripts*, January 23, 1996.

In *Vernonia School District 47J v. Acton*, 515 U.S. 646 (1995), the Supreme Court upheld random urinalysis drug testing of students participating in the defendant district's school athletics programs. Some school districts have sought to extend drug testing beyond interscholastic athletes. See, e.g., Charles Strouse, "Students in Dade Face Drug Testing," *Fort Lauderdale Sun-Sentinel*, September 25, 1997, at 1B, and Allan Turner,

"Defending His Rights: Student Risking All to Oppose Drug Testing," *Houston Chronicle*, February 2, 1997, at 1.

12. See 32 *Weekly Compilation of Presidential Documents* 2111 (October 19, 1996).

13. See Snyder, supra note 7, at 5 (1993 survey reported that 3% of students carried a weapon to school at least once during a six-month period), and *Kids These Days: What Americans Really Think About the Next Generation* 18 (1997).

14. The fifteen-year-old was convicted and sentenced to concurrent sentences of life imprisonment for murder, twenty-five years each for burglary and robbery, and three years for possession of a firearm. The Florida District Court of Appeal affirmed the conviction. See *Zamora v. State*, 361 So. 2d 776 (Fla. Dist. Ct. App. 1978). The state courts denied the motion to vacate the judgment on the ground that the prisoner had received ineffective assistance of counsel because the television intoxication defense did not exist in law. See *Zamora v. State*, 422 So. 2d 325 (Fla. Dist. Ct. App. 1982). The prisoner later unsuccessfully sought federal habeas corpus relief on this ground. See *Zamora v. Dugger*, 834 F.2d 956, 959–60 (11th Cir. 1987), aff'g *Zamora v. Wainwright*, 637 F. Supp. 439, 440–43 (S.D. Fla. 1986). The federal district court had earlier dismissed a civil damage action by the juvenile and his parents alleging that the three major networks had breached their duty to use ordinary care to prevent the juvenile from being "impermissibly stimulated, incited and instigated" to duplicate the atrocities he viewed on television. See *Zamora v. CBS*, 480 F. Supp. 199, 200 (S.D. Fla. 1979).

In various forms, the television intoxication defense has periodically resurfaced in later years. See, e.g., "Reject Tired 'Pulp Fiction' Excuse, Hold Teen Responsible For Actions," *Fort Lauderdale Sun-Sentinel*, May 3, 1996, at 2A, and Dorothy J. Gaiter, "Lawyer Says 9-Year Old Bank Robber Was Influenced By TV Crime," *New York Times*, March 2, 1981, at B3.

15. Hillary R. Clinton, *It Takes a Village* (1995). See also, e.g., S. Robert Lichter et al., *Watching America* 185–90 (1991), and George Gerbner, "Trial By Television: Are We At the Point of No Return?," 63 *Judicature* 416, 419 (1980).

16. Wambaugh might have had an effective rejoinder. Canada may suffer from less violence than the United States, but at least one study has indicated that televised violence has significantly increased the rate of violence in Canadian society, first among children and later among adults who had been introduced to violent television as children. See "Children, Television and Violence," 9 *Pediatric Report's Child Health Newsletter* 52 (September 1992).

A 1981 study found that Japanese television portrays violence differently than American television does. For one thing, in Japan "the 'bad guys' commit most of the violence, with the 'good guys' suffering the consequences—the exact opposite of American programming. In this context, violence is seen as wrong, a villainous activity with real and painful consequences, rather than as justifiable." American Academy of Pediatrics, Committee on Communications, "Media Violence," 95 *Pediatrics* 949 (June 1995). Not only that, but Japanese television portrays violence more realistically, with greater emphasis on physical suffering. Id. Network standards rarely permit American television to show, for example, a bullet's true effect on the human body. See Richard A. Blum and Richard D. Lindheim, *Prime Time: Network Television Programming* 177 (1987).

17. See, e.g., American Academy of Pediatrics, Committee on Community Health Services, "Health Needs of Homeless Children and Families," 98 *Pediatrics* 789 (October 1996).

18. See, e.g., *In re T.A.C.P.*, 609 So. 2d 588 (Fla. 1992) (denying petition by parents of anencephalic newborn to permit transplant of the newborn's organs; because the newborn's heart was beating and she was still breathing, she was not yet dead under state law). Cf. *Donaldson v. Lungren*, 4 Cal. Rptr. 2d 59 (Ct. App. 1992) (plaintiff had no constitutional right to pre-mortem cryogenic suspension of his body, or to a suicide assisted by persons who would help him achieve that state).

19. The scene was written and played with such characteristic realism that viewers could readily imagine a mayor and a town counsel making this offer and expecting to enforce it. The agreement, however, would likely have violated Teacher's constitutional right to interstate travel. See generally Ronald D. Rotunda and John E. Nowak, *Treatise on Constitutional Law* § 18.38 (2d ed. 1992 & Supp. 1997).

20. The question has provoked ongoing debate. See, e.g., William H. Simon, "The Ethics of Criminal Defense," 91 *Michigan Law Review* 1703 (1993); David Luban, "Are Criminal Defenders Different?," id. at 1729; William H. Simon, "Reply: Further Reflections on Libertarian Criminal Defense," id. at 1767; John B. Mitchell, "The Ethics of the Criminal Defense Attorney—New Answers to Old Questions," 32 *Stanford Law Review* 293 (1980); A.S. Cutler, "Is a Lawyer Bound To Support an Unjust Cause? A Problem of Ethics," 38 *American Bar Association Journal* 300 (1952). See also, e.g., *United States v. Wade*, 388 U.S. 218, 257–58 (1967) (Harlan, White, and Stewart, JJ., dissenting in part and concurring in part) ("[A]bsent a voluntary plea of guilty, we ... insist that [defense counsel] defend his client whether he is innocent or guilty. ... [A]s part of our modified adversary system and as part of the duty imposed on the most honorable defense counsel, we countenance or require conduct which in many instances has little, if any, relation to the search for truth.").

See generally ABA Model Rules of Professional Conduct Rule 1.1 (Competence); Rule 3.1 (Meritorious Claims and Contentions); Rule 3.3 (Candor Toward the Tribunal); Rule 3.4 (Fairness to Opposing Party and Counsel); Rule 3.5 (Impartiality and Decorum of the Tribunal). Cf. *In re Armani*, 371 N.Y.S.2d 563 (Hamilton Co. Ct. (1975) (recommending attorneys's fee awards in amounts exceeding the statutory hourly limit to two appointed counsel who, after the client had told them the location of the bodies of victims murdered by the client, had failed to reveal the location to the victims's families who asked for the lawyers's help during investigation); *People v. Belge*, 372 N.Y.S.2d 798 (Onondaga Co. Ct. 1975), aff'd, 376 N.Y.S.2d 771 (App. Div.), aff'd, 359 N.E.2d 377 (N.Y. 1976) (dismissing indictment that charged one of the two silent appointed counsel with failing to give a dead person a decent burial and failing to report a person's death without medical attendance).

21. See, e.g., Dusty Saunders, "Linda Ellerbee's V-Chip Stance Overlooks Most Important Issue," *Rocky Mountain News*, August 23, 1995, at 14D, and Ed Siegel, "It Doesn't Take a Law to Curb TV Violence," *Boston Globe*, October 22, 1993, at 49.

22. See Stephen Budiansky et al., "How Lawyers Abuse the Law," *U.S. News and World Report*, January 30, 1995, at 50. See also, e.g., Peter A. Joy, "Clients Are Consumers, Too," 82 *American Bar Association Journal* 120 (April 1996) (discussing a 1993 Gallup Poll which placed lawyers among the lowest ranked occupations, along

with television talk show hosts, car salespersons, and advertising people), and Gary A. Hengstler, "Vox Populi: The Public Perception of Lawyers: ABA Poll," 79 *American Bar Association Journal* 60 (September 1993) (discussing a 1993 American Bar Association survey of the general public which indicated that "the more a person knows about the legal profession and the more he or she is in direct personal contact with lawyers, the lower an individual's opinion of them"; among respondents from the general public, lawyers received a 40% favorable rating, considerably less than teachers's 84%, pharmacists's 81%, police officers's 79%, doctors's 71%, accountants's 60%, and bankers's 56%; the only other professions with less than majority favorable ratings were stockbrokers (28%) and politicians (21%)).

23. See, e.g., Steven D. Stark, "Perry Mason Meets Sonny Crockett: The History of Lawyers and the Police as Television Heroes," 42 *University of Miami Law Review* 229, 230–231 (1987), and Charles Winick and Mariann P. Winick, "Courtroom Drama on Television," 24 *Journal of Communication* 67 (Autumn 1974).

24. See Thom Weidlich, "A Cynical Age Sees Few Heroes in Its Lawyers," *National Law Journal*, November 29, 1993, at S26.

25. With respect to the Latham prosecution, see *Minnick v. Mississippi*, 498 U.S. 146 (1990), and *Brewer v. Williams*, 430 U.S. 387 (1977).

26. Television courtroom dramas began examining public policy questions as early as "The Defenders," which appeared on CBS from 1961 to 1965. At a time when most entertainment series avoided controversy, "The Defenders" occasionally treated such issues as abortion, mercy killing, and government restrictions on the right to travel to hostile nations. One notable episode treated the entertainment industry's own practice of blacklisting persons who held particularly unpopular views. See Tim Brooks and Earle Marsh, *The Complete Directory to Prime Time Network and Cable TV Shows 1946–Present* 252–53 (6th ed. 1995).

27. See Douglas E. Abrams, "Winning Isn't Everything in Youth Leagues," *Wisconsin State Journal*, May 5, 1997, at 7A.

28. Bernard J. Ward, "The Federal Judges: Indispensable Teachers," 61 *Texas Law Review* 43, 46 (1982).

29. See, e.g., Eugene V. Rostow, *The Sovereign Prerogative* 167–68 (1962) ("The discussion of problems and the declaration of broad principles by the courts is a vital element in the community experience through which American policy is made. The Supreme Court is, among other things, an educational body, and the Justices are inevitably teachers in a vital national seminar."). See also, e.g., Alexander M. Bickel, *The Least Dangerous Branch* 26 (1962) ("[T]he courts... are... a great and highly effective educational institution....No other branch of the American government is nearly so well equipped to conduct" the seminar Rostow described); Lee C. Bollinger, *Images of a Free Press* 42 (1991) (the Supreme Court "can perform a deeply educative role in society, affecting behavior far beyond the strictly legal domain"); Robert Bork, *The Tempting of America* 249 (1990) (quoting Rostow with approval); Paul A. Freund, *The Supreme Court of the United States* 115 (1972) ("judicial review... is an educative and formative influence that... may have consequences beyond its immediate application for the mind of a people"); Richard Funston, *A Vital National Seminar: The Supreme Court in American Political Life* 216–17 (1978) ("[T]he Supreme Court is engaged in an educative dia-

log with the American people."); Alexander Meiklejohn, *Free Speech and Its Relation to Self-Government* 58 (1948) ("The Supreme Court... is and must be one of our most effective teachers."); Christopher J. Eisgruber, "Is the Supreme Court an Educative Institution?," 67 *New York University Law Review* 961, 962 & n.2 (1992) (citing a sampling of the "astonishing range of thinkers" who have endorsed some version of Rostow's view); Irving R. Kaufman, "Helping the Public Understand and Accept Judicial Decisions," 63 *American Bar Association Journal* 1567, 1567 (1977) ("Judges often play the role of teacher or leader in shaping the public's view.").

30. See William H. Rehnquist, "Act Well Your Part: Therein All Honor Lies," 7 *Pepperdine Law Review* 227, 227–28 (1980), reprinted in 9 Human Rights 42, 42–43 (Spring 1980) ("[T]he Supreme Court does not 'teach' in the normal sense of that word at all. In many cases we hand down decisions which we believe are required by some Act of Congress or some provision of the Constitution for which we, as citizens, might have very little sympathy and would not choose to make a rule of law if it were left solely to us.").

31. See, e.g., Eliot E. Slotnick, "Television News and the Supreme Court: A Case Study," 77 *Judicature* 22 (July–August 1993) (most Americans perceive television as their main information source).

32. See Larry A. Viskochil, "Foreword," in Lloyd DeGrane, *Tuned In: Television in American Life* (1991).

33. See Jeff Greenfield, *Television: The First Fifty Years* 13 (1977) (citing congressional report), and Daniel Goleman, "How Viewers Grow Addicted to Television," *New York Times*, October 16, 1990, at C1 (citing A.C. Neilsen & Co. report).

34. See American Academy of Pediatrics, Committee on Communications, "Children, Adolescents, and Television," 96 *Pediatrics* 786 (October 1995) (citing A.C. Neilsen & Co. data).

35. See Newton N. Minow, *Equal Time* 101 (1964), and Newton N. Minow, "Television Values and the Values of Our Children," 6 *Journal of Art and Entertainment Law* 193, 195 (1996).

36. See "Children, Adolescents, and Television," supra note 34.

Notes for Chapter 11
Rumpole of the Bailey

1. See generally Janice A. Radway, *Reading the Romance* (1984).

2. Now I recognize that many readers will resist my statement that America is an unjust society. It is a point which I cannot document here, but I would rhetorically ask these doubters to think for a few minutes about the life chances of a minority child born in poverty in the inner-city as compared to those of a white suburbanite child of upper middle class parents. Do we really believe that the poor minority child has an equal opportunity to make good on America's promise of "life, liberty, and the pursuit of happiness"?

3. See Theresa G. Phelps, "The Margins of Maycomb: A Rereading of 'To Kill A Mockingbird,'" 45 *Alabama Law Review* 511 (1994).

4. It is interesting to note that both characters seem to have less appeal to non-lawyers; "To Kill A Mockingbird" has been debated at length in the pages of legal journals, but has been mostly ignored by literature professors. So too my informal poll indicates that non-lawyers are much less attracted to Rumpole than practitioners.

5. See generally Dan T. Carter, *Scottsboro: A Tragedy of the American South* (1969).

6. Michael Asimow, "When Lawyers Were Heroes," 30 *University of San Francisco Law Review* 1131, 1138 (1996).

7. See Monroe H. Freeman, "Atticus Finch—Right and Wrong," 45 *Alabama Law Review* 473 (1994).

8. See John Denvir, "Capra's Constitution" in *Legal Reelism: Movies as Legal Texts* (John Denvir ed. 1996).

9. See Carolyn P. Blum, "Images of Lawyering and Political Activism in In the Name of the Father," 30 *University of San Francisco Law Review* 1065 (1996).

Notes for Chapter 12
Science Fiction

1. The television and cable rights for "Buck Zeal: Space Lawyer" are available from the author at very reasonable rates.

2. In the late 1930s, a transformation in science fiction began to take place, spearheaded by John W. Campbell and the authors he featured in his magazine, *Astounding Stories* (later changed to *Astounding Science Fiction*).

> Stories should not be about machines and great ideas, but about how those machines or great ideas affected individuals and society as a whole. There should be no scientific lectures clumsily placed in the story: authors should present the background and the scientific information seamlessly woven into their stories. The science that sf writers should concern themselves with need not be just physics and engineering, but could include sociology, psychology (and, notoriously with Campbell, parapsychology), and even—as in Asimov's "Foundation" series, developed in close co-operation with Campbell—historical science fiction. Indeed, one of the main themes of sf should be future historical change; Campbell himself said that sf was the history that had not yet happened.

Edward James, *Science Fiction in the 20th Century* 57 (1994).

3. Quoted from "The Lurker's Guide to Babylon 5" at <http://www.midwinter.com/lurk/synops/010.html>.

4. See James, supra note 2, at 11.

5. See Frederik Pohl and C.M. Kornbluth, *Gladiator-at-Law* (1955).

6. See Melinda M. Snodgrass, *Circuit* (1986).

7. See Joe Patrouch, "Legal Rights for Germs?," *Analog*, November 1977, at 167, and Dennis L. Cox, "University Medical Versus Diplococcus Pneumoniae," *Analog*, May 1978, at 153.

8. See Clifford D. Simak, "New Folks' Home," *Analog*, July 1963, at 69.

9. See Jeff Mathews, "To Keep and Bear Arms: A Brief History of Self-Defense in the United States," *Analog*, March 1978, at 152.

10. See Hayford Peirce, "The Reluctant Torturer," *Analog*, September 1983, at 64.

11. See Lord St. Davids, "In the High Court of Justice," *Analog*, October 1975, at 155.

12. "It's been pointed out that TV-SF is generally 20–30 years behind print SF....In the 1960s or so, along came the New Wave of SF, which eschewed hardware for stories about the human condition set against a SF background. And the fanzines and prozines and techno-loving pundits of hard-SF declared it heresy, said it wasn't SF, this is crap. And eventually they were steamrolled, and print SF grew up a little. Now the argument has come to settle here. Well, fine. So be it." J. Michael Straczynski, creator of "Babylon 5," quoted at <http://www.midwinter.com/lurk/guide/010.html>.

13. For example, in "The Champion," an episode of "V," Lydia (June Chadwick), a regular cast member, is convicted of murder. See <http://www.enqueue.com/v/v-episodeguide.html>. Similarly, in "Takeover," an episode of "Space Precinct," two regulars are subjected to an internal affairs investigation after being accused of murder. See <http://www.intersource.com/~mmiller/sf/sp/sp_epgd.html>.

14. An example might be a show like "Sliders," in which the audience follows a group of people as they jump from one to another parallel realities while trying to find a way to get back to their own. This plot device allows the writers to create an alternate reality each week. Some of the plots are ripe with legal issues. For example, in "Season Greedings," runaway consumerism has led to a contractual recognition of virtual slavery for shoppers who cannot pay their debts. Perhaps because none of the main characters in "Sliders" is a lawyer, the show finds an extra-legal way to resolve the situation. For general information about the alternate earths in the series, see <http://www.brillig.com/sliders/alternate-earths.html>.

15. When lawyer characters have been included in particular episodes, they have generally shared qualities of aggressive verbal combativeness and an adversarial outlook which make them familiar to contemporary viewers. For example, in the "Star Trek" episode called "Court Martial," a lawyer is brought in to defend Captain Kirk (William Shatner), who is accused of wrongfully causing the death of a subordinate. The lawyer, Samuel T. Cogley (Elisha Cook, Jr.), distrusts computers and other technologies and quotes the Code of Hammurabi as precedent. In a "Star Trek: The Next Generation" episode entitled "The Measure of a Man," the judge who must decide "Whether the android, Commander Data, is a free being or a slave machine," is Phillipa Louvois (Amanda McBroom). She is described by Picard as someone who "always enjoyed the adversarial process more than getting at the truth."

16. "Quantum Leap" was able to solve this problem by having the show's star Dr. Sam Beckett (Scott Bakula) "jump" into the body of a lawyer in the episode "So Help Me God."

17. See <http://www.midwinter.com/lurk/synops/010.html>.

18. As with any other aspect of the physical world, context can affect the perceived qualities of an item. Thus, a block of granite will "weigh" less on a world with less gravity although its "mass" will be the same.

19. A wonderful example of this comes to us from the tort law of causation. Causation might be thought to be an aspect of the natural world, but in reality it is inextricably

tied to policy choices about responsibility which humans make for human reasons.

A good illustration of this point can be found in the famous case of *Summers v. Tice*, 199 P.2d 1 (Cal. 1948). Two hunters negligently shot in the direction of a third, who was struck in the eye. Under traditional legal rules of causation, the injured hunter, being unable to prove which shot had injured him, would have lost against both hunters. Instead, the California Supreme Court shifted the burden of proof on this issue to the defendants.

What is striking about the case is that the court frankly acknowledged that it had acted not out of some natural truth about causation but because shifting the burden to the defendants was perceived as being fairer than the alternative.

> When we consider the relative position of the parties and the results that would flow if plaintiff was required to pin the injury on one of the defendants only, a requirement that the burden of proof on that subject be shifted to defendants becomes manifest. They are both wrongdoers both negligent toward plaintiff. They brought about a situation where the negligence of one of them injured the plaintiff, hence it should rest with them each to absolve himself if he can. The injured party has been placed by defendants in the unfair position of pointing to which defendant caused the harm. If one can escape the other may also and plaintiff is remediless.

Id. at 4.

20. *Brown v. Board of Education*, 347 U.S. 483 (1954), is one such example.

21. A recent book by Professor Anthony Chase, *Law and History: The Evolution of the American Legal System* (1997), explores the connection between economics and law and makes the case that economic shifts cause corresponding shifts in the law.

22. Of course, there is nothing to preclude a science fiction series from being set in modern society. An example is "Alien Nation," a police show based on the movie of the same name. Its premise is that a spaceship full of alien slaves lands near Los Angeles and the former slaves are given political asylum. The series follows two cops, one human and one "newcomer," as they attempt to understand and accept one another. In the process, a number of contemporary issues are explored.

> *Alien Nation* was a cop show with a difference. Like *Cagney and Lacey* [sic], it chose to deal with the people element. No matter how outlandish the situations may have seemed, the unique cast of characters helped to root them in reality, making it all completely believable. This is true whether you're talking about the investigation of a prostitution ring or a Newcomer *male* giving birth to a child. Each episode served to further develop the Newcomer race via George Francisco, and took just as much time delving into the background of Matt Sikes. It is probably safe to say that the Sikes/Francisco combination was television science fiction's most potent relationship since Captain James T. Kirk and Mr. Spock.

Edward Gross, Marc Shapiro, and Carr D'Angelo, *Newcomers Among Us: The Alien Nation Companion* 3 (1991).

23. Paul R Joseph and Sharon Carton, "Perry Mason in Space: A Call for More

Inventive Lawyers in Television Science Fiction Series," in *Imaginative Futures: Proceedings of the 1993 Science Fiction Research Association Conference* (1994) [hereinafter cited as Perry Mason in Space].

24. In a later series, "Star Trek: Deep Space Nine," the Cardassian empire underwent an interesting change of fortune. A coup, engineered covertly by an alien shape-shifting race called "The Dominion," transforms Cardassia into a vassal state.

25. For example, the method of pleading under the writ system disappeared relatively recently.

26. See <http://www.midwinter.com/lurk/find/GEnie/jms94-08-15/2849.html>.

27. "*Babylon 5* is a unique environment. There are only two basic types of people (speaking only of humans for now) around: those employed by EA or the station (conflict of interest), or travelers, who won't be around long enough for a prolonged trial. So in that kind of situation, the Ombuds arose… a 2258 version of a Circuit Court Judge." J. Michael Straczynski, creator of "Babylon 5," quoted at <http://www.midwinter.com/lurk/find/GEnie/jms94-08-15/2849.html>.

28. Paul R Joseph and Sharon F. Carton, "The Law of the Federation: Images of Law, Lawyers, and the Legal System in 'Star Trek: The Next Generation,'" 24 *University of Toledo Law Review* 43 (1992) [hereinafter cited as The Law of the Federation]. International law aspects of the series are considered in Michael P. Scharf and Lawrence D. Roberts, "Interstellar Relations of the Federation: International Law and 'Star Trek: The Next Generation,'" 25 *University of Toledo Law Review* 577 (1994).

29. The Law of the Federation, supra note 28, at 52.

30. "SeaQuest DSV," for example, was a series about a powerful underwater submarine. In order to make the technology believable, the series had to be set in the future, specifically the 21st century. To provide a suitable setting, a "future history" of earth was created, including the United Earth Organization (UEO), a kind of United Nations of the near future, for which the SeaQuest works as its chief peacekeeping and law enforcement resource. Some tantalizing legal snippets are included, such as the idea that genetic engineering was abused and then outlawed. The setting is fraught with legal possibilities but they are not really exploited. There is always a sense, when watching this show, of missed opportunities. For a further look at the show, see the "SeaQuest DSV Frequently Asked Questions" site at <http://www.vis-con.com/ seaquest/text/story1.html>.

31. Perry Mason in Space, supra note 23, at 308–09.

32. The Law of the Federation, supra note 28, at 67–84.

33. See <http://www.geocities.com/Hollywood/Lot/9053/kingisback.html>. Similarly, in a "Star Trek: The Next Generation" episode called "Justice," we are introduced to an alien culture where death is the sole penalty for any transgression. In another episode of "Sliders," "Time Again and World," President J. Edgar Hoover "abridges" the Constitution and incarcerates "political prisoners," such as Robert Kennedy and Martin Luther King, Jr., at Alcatraz. See <http://www.geocities.com/Hollywood/Lot/9053/timeagain.html>.

34. See <http://www.midwinter.com/lurk/find/Answers/answ110.html>.

35. J. Michael Straczynski, creator of "Babylon 5," answering questions on-line at <http://www.midwinter.com/lurk/find/Usenet/jms94-01-usenet/49.html>.

36. In the "Encounter at Farpoint" episode of "Star Trek: The Next Generation," the Omnipotent Q (John de Lancie) puts the human race on trial in a barbarous earth

courtroom from the "post atomic horror" year 2079. The following exchange takes place between Q and Captain Picard.

> Q: Legal trickery is not permitted. This is a court of fact.
> Picard: I recognize this "court" system as the one that agreed with that line from Shakespeare, "kill all the lawyers."
> Q: Which was done.
> Picard: Leading to the rule "guilty until proven innocent."
> Q: Of course, bringing the innocent to trial would be unfair.

Notes for Chapter 13
Situation Comedies

1. Lester L. Brown, *Les Brown's Encyclopedia of Television* 510–11 (3d ed. 1992). See also Bill Carter, "News Magazine Caught Between 'Third Rock' And a Hard Place," *New York Times*, October 2, 1996, at B3 (reporting on NBC's decision to squeeze a one-hour news show into a fifteen minute slot so as to not delay the starting time of its hit sit-com "Third Rock From the Sun"). Today, the commercial importance of sitcoms is at an all-time high, and the 1996–97 television season included more new sitcoms than any other season in recent memory. Yet because of the increased demand, many of these shows arrived with large gaps in their storylines, plots, and characters. For a further discussion, see Bill Carter, "Back to the Storyboard for Sitcoms," *New York Times*, August 29, 1996, at B1 (describing the numerous problems that forced CBS to delay releasing its most prominent new sitcom, "Ink," about a divorced couple working for the same newspaper), and Elizabeth Jensen, "Television: Surfeit of Sitcoms May Be No Laughing Matter," *Wall Street Journal*, September 4, 1996, at B1.

2. Although extensive research strongly suggests that "Amos 'n' Andy" was the first situation comedy to include a lawyer, it is impossible to be completely certain. Because the early days of television left behind little in the way of permanent records, it is possi-ble — although not very probable — that another comedy was the first to feature a lawyer. See generally Jeff Kisseloff, *The Box: An Oral History of Television, 1920–1961* (1995), and Michael Ritchie, *Please Stand By: A Prehistory of Television* (1994).

3. Ric S. Sheffield, "Constructing a Social History of African American Lawyers Through Popular Culture: Film, Television, and Lawyer Calhoun," 17 *Journal of the Legal Profession* 45, 46–47 (1992) (footnotes omitted).

Despite its offensive nature, in 1997 "Amos 'n' Andy" made a limited comeback when twenty of its episodes were packaged on videocassette and quickly sold more than 40,000 copies. Overlooking its past objections to the show, the NAACP issued no con-demnation of the re-releases. See Lynn Elber, " 'Amos 'n' Andy' Resurfaces," *Fort Laud-erdale Sun-Sentinel*, July 10, 1997, at 9A.

4. Alex McNeil, *Total Television: A Comprehensive Guide to Programming From 1948 to the Present* 403 (4th ed. 1996), and Tim Brooks and Earle Marsh, *The Com-plete Directory to Prime Time Network and Cable TV Shows 1946–Present* 494 (6th ed. 1995).

5. Jim and Henny Backus, *Forgive Us Our Digressions: An Autobiography* 160 (1988).

6. Brooks & Marsh, supra note 4, at 494.

7. Id.

8. Backus & Backus, supra note 5, at 154. Simon, of course, later became celebrated as a playwright while Uris achieved fame as a novelist. See further 2 *Who's Who in America* (Harriet Tiger et al. eds. 50th ed. 1996) 3866 (Simon) and 4256 (Uris).

9. Backus & Backus, supra note 5, at 153–54. The typical "I Married Joan" episode was fast-paced, heavy on physical comedy, and replete with sight gags.

> Joan Stevens has done it again! Thinking her husband's new golf clubs will make the perfect gardening tools, she uses them as hoes... and breaks every single one! Now he's decided he wants to go golfing! Thinking fast, she locks the door of the closet where he keeps the clubs, and throws the key out the window. "The door is stuck, dear. We'll have to call a carpenter. It shouldn't take him more than a month to fix it." "But I want to go golfing *now*," Judge Stevens moans. Just then, the doorbell rings; it's the mailman. "I was passing by, and this key hit me on the head," he says... and Joan's in trouble *again*.

John Javna, *The TV Theme Song Sing-Along Songbook* 46 (1984). See also Backus & Backus, supra note 5, at 152–53 ("Ours was what is known as in the trade as a 'physical' show. We never had a quiet scene where we sat in the living room while I read the paper and she calmly knitted.... There was a registered nurse on the set at all times, and she saw plenty of service.").

10. Brooks & Marsh, supra note 4, at 1137.

11. Id.

12. Id. at 71.

13. Id.

14. Id.

15. McNeil, supra note 4, at 366.

16. Id. Key's comic strip was a regular feature of *The Saturday Evening Post*. Id.

17. Id.

18. 1 Vincent Terrace, *The Complete Encyclopedia of Television Programs 1947–1979* 416 (2d rev. ed. 1979).

19. Brooks & Marsh, supra note 4, at 446.

20. McNeil, supra note 4, at 366.

21. Brooks & Marsh, supra note 4, at 717.

22. McNeil, supra note 4, at 580.

23. Id. The show's cancelation sent Van Dyke's career into a long slump from which he did not recover until 1989, when he was cast as Assistant Coach Luther Van Dam in the hit series "Coach." For a description of "Coach," which starred Craig T. Nelson as football coach Hayden Fox and Shelley Fabares as his newswoman wife Christine Armstrong, see Brooks & Marsh, supra note 4, at 198–99.

24. Id. at 418. Douglas's name, of course, was a take-off on United States Supreme Court justices Oliver Wendell Holmes, Jr., and William O. Douglas. The judicial careers

of the two are compared—and found to be strikingly similar—in Melvin I. Urofsky, "William O. Douglas as a Common Law Judge," 41 *Duke Law Journal* 133 (1991).

25. Melissa F. Stoeltje, " 'Green Acres' Quiz Will Show If You Know A Hoot About Sitcom," *Houston Chronicle*, April 13, 1993, at 3 (Houston).

26. McNeil, supra note 4, at 343.

27. David Marc and Robert J. Thompson, *Prime Time, Prime Movers: From I Love Lucy to L.A. Law—America's Greatest TV Shows and the People Who Created Them* 35–36 (1995).

28. Javna, supra note 9, at 6. For descriptions of the farm's many problems, see Brooks & Marsh, supra note 4, at 418 ("The farm… was in horrible shape. It had not been worked in years, the house was run-down, unfurnished, and in desperate need of major repairs."), and David Story, *America on the Rerun: TV Shows That Never Die* 161 (1993) ("First of all the bathtub, the kitchen sink, and the stove are all missing. Then there's the matter of no electricity and no telephone.").

To get the farm back in order, Douglas hired a handyman named Eb Dawson (Tom Lester), as well as Alf and Ralph Monroe (Sid Melton and Mary Grace Canfield), a brother-and-sister carpenter team. Brooks & Marsh, supra note 4, at 418. Once again, the gullible Douglas was taken in: neither Dawson nor the Monroes knew the first thing about their respective jobs. But as in all other matters, Douglas failed to see their shortcomings and kept them on. Id.

29. S. Robert Lichter et al., *Prime Time: How TV Portrays American Culture* 15 (1994).

30. Sherwood Schwartz, *Inside Gilligan's Island: A Three-Hour Tour Through the Making of a Television Classic* 258–59 (1994).

31. Brooks & Marsh, supra note 4, at 803–04.

32. Id. at 804.

33. Id. at 12.

34. Id.

35. Id.

36. Id. at 1117.

37. Id.

38. Id. at 822. "The Mary Tyler Moore Show" is discussed further infra text accompanying note 43.

39. Id.

40. Id.

41. McNeil, supra note 4, at 857. There is some disagreement over exactly which court Franklin and Hooper served on. McNeil maintains that they were members of the Superior Court. Id. His chief competitors, however, contend that the two presided over the Court of Common Pleas. Brooks & Marsh, supra note 4, at 1054. While the Superior Court is one of Pennsylvania's two intermediate appellate courts (the other being the Commonwealth Court), the Court of Common Pleas is the state's main trial court. *Directory of State Court Clerks and County Courthouses—1996 Edition* 220 (Robert S. Want ed. 1995). A third source sides with Brooks & Marsh. See Rick Mitz, *The Great TV Sitcom Book* 392 (1983).

42. McNeil, supra note 4, at 857.

43. Lichter, supra note 29, at 184–85.

44. Brooks & Marsh, supra note 4, at 938.

45. Id.

46. Id.

47. McNeil, supra note 4, at 758.

48. Id. at 65.

49. Brooks & Marsh, supra note 4, at 64.

50. McNeil, supra note 4, at 602.

51. Brooks & Marsh, supra note 4, at 750–51.

52. Id.

53. The show's success is described further in Susan Sackett, *Prime-Time Hits: Television's Most Popular Network Programs, 1950 to the Present* 310–11 (1993). In a magnificent display of good sportsmanship, Larroquette graciously withdrew his name from future consideration after winning his fourth Emmy. See Matt Roush, "Larroquette Bows Out of Emmy Balloting," *USA Today*, July 12, 1989, at 3D.

54. Brooks & Marsh, supra note 4, at 751.

55. Id. at 901–02.

56. Id. at 901.

57. See David Friedman, "Say It Isn't So, 'Sara,'" *Newsday*, June 1, 1988, §II, at 15:

> IT'S NOT OFTEN you get to see the same bomb explode twice. You can tonight, though, when NBC drops "Sara" on us for the second time….
>
> You remember "Sara." It was going to be the "The Mary Tyler Moore Show" of the '80s. It was going to remind us how hip it is to be single and female in a world of dull married men. It was going to prove that "Family Ties" isn't the only good idea inside creator Gary David Goldberg's head. It was going to be television's first yuppie sitcom. It was going to make a star out of Geena Davis. It was going to end world hunger.
>
> OK, so I'm exaggerating. But not by much. "Sara" didn't merely arrive on the TV scene in January, 1985. It was blown there by a gale force of hype rarely matched before or since. Like "Miami Vice" and "Hill Street Blues," etc., "Sara" was going to be one more way in which Brandon Tartikoff, the Boy Wonder of Television, had made it hip to watch the tube again. Especially the part of the tube programmed by NBC.
>
> It didn't happen, though. And as tonight's "encore presentation" proves all too well, it didn't happen on merit. "Sara" is boring television. Even worse, it's not very funny—a major flaw, to say the least, on a show billed as a comedy. Thanks to the writers strike, and the scheduling chaos it has created, we're getting a chance to learn that lesson twice.
>
> For those with short memories, Sara McKenna (Davis) is a "guileless attorney with a feel for the underdog" (NBC's words, not mine) living in San Francisco. There, she's surrounded by supposedly lovable flakes, many of them played by actors and actresses who've gone on to bigger and better things— Bronson Pinchot, for example.
>
> Nowadays, Pinchot's making millions playing a displaced shepherd on ABC's "Perfect Strangers." On "Sara," he's setting back the gay liberation movement a good 20 years.
>
> But Pinchot isn't the only performer slumming on "Sara." There's also Alfre Woodard, a two-time Emmy winner ("Hill Street Blues," "L.A. Law")

whose considerable talents are squandered in a part that asks her to play the one role Woodard can't pull off—someone funny.

I'd like to say that Mark Hudson, later to become Joan Rivers' musical sidekick on Fox, was another talented performer wasting his time on "Sara." But that would imply Hudson has a talent to waste. Even in TV, where Willard Scott is said to have talent, you've got to draw the line somewhere. Still, it's upon Geena Davis' broad shoulders that falls the burden of carrying "Sara." And, sad to say, she's simply not up to it. You may remember Davis as the wonderfully ditsy production assistant on "Buffalo Bill," or in a similar role in "Tootsie." This is a woman with a large gift for small comic roles. Trouble is, "Sara" is a large role with small comic gifts.

58. Brooks & Marsh, supra note 4, at 364.

59. Id.

60. Id.

61. Id. at 215–16.

62. Ron Miller, "From Mom to Momsters: Have Today's Bad TV Moms Eclipsed the Good Ones of Yesteryear?," *Chicago Tribune*, May 14, 1989, at C18. Clair Huxtable's effortless ability to excel as both a lawyer and a mother greatly angered some viewers.

> She's supposed to be a hot-shot lawyer, but when does this woman work? Ever see Clair buried under legal briefs? Ever heard her discuss the latest judicial appointment? Wondered why she has so much time to banter with her family? It's because her career is a prop, like the refrigerator and the bed, only it's used less often.

Cynthia Crossen, "Hall of Shame; Stereotypes and Working Women," *Working Woman*, November 1991, at 115.

63. Brooks & Marsh, supra note 4, at 38.

64. Id. at 375.

65. Id.

66. David Zurawik, " 'Prince' Gears Up for Season Finale," *Cleveland Plain Dealer*, May 20, 1996, at 9D.

67. Sandy Smith, " 'Home Court' Loses Comedy Advantages," *Tennessean*, September 30, 1995, at 5D.

68. See David Bianculli, "Best Bets," *Fort Worth Star-Telegram*, June 22, 1996, at 10 (Life & Arts).

69. Tom Jicha, "Fall Preview," *Fort Lauderdale Sun-Sentinel*, September 8–14, 1996, at 3 (TV Book).

70. Id. at 4.

71. Id. at 13.

72. See Greg Braxton, "Latino Groups Decry ABC's Pulling of 'Common Law,' " *Los Angeles Times*, October 18, 1996, at F2.

73. See Mike Hughes, "Canceled 'Life's Work' Shows New Episode," *Idaho Statesman*, May 27, 1997, at 4D.

74. See Greg Braxton, " 'Sparks' Fly at UPN in Midseason Brouhaha," *New York Post*, January 18, 1998, at 73.

75. Caryn James, " 'Must See,' 'Must Not': Switching Channels at Midseason," *New York Times*, January 15, 1998, at B1.

76. See Tom Jicha, "Winning on Appeal," *Fort Lauderdale Sun-Sentinel*, September 8, 1997, at 1D.

77. James Collins, "Woman of the Year: Confused and Lovable? Or a Simpering Drag? Taking Sides on Fox's Surprising New Hit," *Time*, November 10, 1997, at 117.

Notes for Chapter 14
Soap Operas

1. James Thurber, *The Beast in Me and Other Animals* 43 (1948).

2. See further W. Warner & W. Henry, "The Radio Daytime Serials: A Symbolic Analysis," 37 *Genetic Psychology Monographs* 3 (1948), and H. Herzog, "On Borrowed Experience: An Analysis of Listening to Daytime Sketches," 9 *Studies in Philosophy and Social Science* 65 (1941).

3. Muriel Cantor and Suzanne Pingree, *The Soap Opera* (1983).

4. For a further look at the design, structure, nature, and effects of soap operas, see, e.g., *Staying Tuned: Contemporary Soap Opera Criticism* (Suzanne Frentz ed. 1991), and Mary Cassata and Thomas Skill, *Life on Daytime Television: Tuning-In American Serial Drama* (1983). See also Rod Carveth and Alison Alexander, "Soap Opera Viewing Motivations and the Cultivation Process," 29 *Journal of Broadcasting & Electronic Media* 259 (1985).

5. See further Dianne L. Brooks, *The Law of Daytime: Television Soap Operas and Legal Narratives* (forthcoming).

6. For a further look at the show, see Mary Cassata and Barbara Irwin, *The Young and the Restless: Most Memorable Moments* (1996).

Notes for Chapter 16
Women Lawyers

1. Jefferson Graham, " 'Civil Wars' Adopts a Lighter Strategy," *USA Today*, November 19, 1991, at 3D.

2. Id.

3. Hemingway attributed the change to aesthetic reasons. She had dyed her hair brown for the film "Falling From Grace." " 'I thought, well, this would be a good thing for this project.... You know it kind of makes her darker, serious. Well, it turned out that the whole pilot was almost too dark, it was darkly photographed, my hair was dark, the subject was dark, everything was dark.' " Later in the interview, however, she said, " 'They wanted me blonde again...', giving her reputation another playful knock when she adds, 'No pretense. Don't even try to be smart[,] Hemingway.' " James Endrst, "Hemingway Courted Onto TV Screen By Bochco's New Drama 'Civil Wars': Hemingway Takes to Prime Time," *Hartford Courant*, November 18, 1991, at B1.

4. Graham, supra note 1.

5. After the demise of "Civil Wars," Rosenberg and Debi Mazar, the receptionist, turned up on "L.A. Law."

6. Bosson was Mrs. Steven Bochco, and has been featured prominently in several Bochco series, including "L.A. Law" (the fuming Faye Furillo) and "Murder One" (the waspish prosecutor Miriam Grasso). See Susan King, "Television; Say, Isn't That... ? Through the Years and Several Series, Producer Steven Bochco Has Built Up a Stock Company of Actors He Knows He Can Count On," *Los Angeles Times*, September 14, 1997, at 82.

7. John Voorhees, "If You Liked 'War of the Roses,' You'll Love 'Civil Wars,'" *Seattle Times*, November 18, 1991, at C6.

8. Marvin Kitman, "A Divorce From Self-Indulgence," *Newsday*, November 18, 1991, at 51.

9. Id.

10. Some recent law review articles that have surveyed the role of women attorneys on film and television include: Diane M. Glass, "Portia in Primetime: Women Lawyers, Television and L.A. Law," 2 *Yale Journal of Law and Feminism* 371 (1990); Louise E. Graham and Geraldine Maschio, "A False Public Sentiment: Narrative and Visual Images of Women Lawyers in Film," 84 *Kentucky Law Journal* 1027 (1996); Judith Mayne, "L.A. Law and Prime-Time Feminism," 10 *Discourse* 30 (Spring/Summer 1988); Carolyn L. Miller, Note, "What a Waste. Beautiful, Sexy Gal. Hell of a Lawyer.": Film and the Female Attorney," 4 *Columbia Journal of Gender and the Law* 203 (1994); Carole Shapiro, "Women Lawyers in Celluloid: Why Hollywood Skirts the Issue," 25 *University of Toledo Law Review* 955 (1994); Ric S. Sheffield, "On Film: A Social History of Women Lawyers in Popular Culture 1930 to 1990," 14 *Loyola of Los Angeles Entertainment Law Journal* 73 (1993); Elaine Weiss, "Who's Missing in This Picture?," *Barrister*, Winter 1989, at 5.

11. This situation comedy ran on ABC during 1996–97 and was renewed for 1997 but only aired for a few weeks. See Jenny Hontz, "CBS Tags Walter For 'Late Bloomer' Pilot," *Daily Variety*, October 1, 1997, at 4.

12. But note the criticism that "Beauty and the Beast" took when it aired on The Family Channel.

Remember beastly Vincent and beautiful Catherine's lovely wedding scene during the CBS run of Beauty and the Beast? No? Well, sure, that's because it never happened. But executives at the Family Channel are thinking the ceremony should have taken place—and maybe it's not too late for Vincent "to do the right thing" by making an "honest woman" of Catherine. The Family Channel is carrying reruns of Beauty and the Beast, the fantasy series that was cut down by CBS after its Jan. 24 airing and before all of its third-season episodes aired. What has the Family Channel nervous is the notion that Vincent impregnated Catherine without the benefit of marriage (we're talking out-of-wedlock concerns, here, not out-of-species). To remedy this shocking situation, the cable service is considering the addition of a marriage scene.

Mark Dawidziak, "Wedding Plans for Beauty, Beast?," *Orlando Sentinel Tribune*, October 20, 1990, at E6.

13. Kinney Littlefield, "For the Love of Justice," *Orange County Register*, March 2, 1997, at F06.

14. Lon Grahnke, "A Lean, Mean 'Feds'; Prosecutors Team with FBI in New CBS Crime Drama," *Chicago Sun-Times*, March 5, 1997, at 49.

15. Tom Walter, "'Feds' Has Makings of a Hit, But It's Flat," *Nashville Commercial Appeal*, March 5, 1997, at C4.

16. Patricia Brennan, "It's the Law, Again: Series Focus on Attorneys, Prosecutors," *Washington Post*, March 2, 1997, at Y07.

17. "Adam's Rib," based on the 1949 film starring Spencer Tracy and Katharine Hepburn, aired on ABC during the 1973–74 season and starred Ken Howard and Blythe Danner. In 1994, CBS tried to revive the idea with the husband and wife team of Cotter Smith and Mel Harris. It does not seem to have been broadcast. See Brian Lowry, "Smith & Harris Sign for 'Adam's Rib' Pilot," *Daily Variety*, October 19, 1994, at 1.

18. This ABC series, which aired during 1990–91, featured Sarah Jessica Parker as prosecutor Jo Ann Harris, Jon Tenney as public defender Peter Bauer, and Debrah Farentino as prosecutor Julie Janovich. See Tim Brooks and Earle Marsh, *The Complete Directory to Prime Time Network and Cable TV Shows 1946–Present* 317 (6th ed. 1995).

19. "Gabriel's Fire," a beautifully-made drama on ABC, starred the incomparable James Earl Jones as a recently released ex-convict and Laila Robins as Victoria Heller, who was smart, beautiful, and righteous. It bombed early in the 1990–91 season, was refurbished and replotted as "Pros and Cons" (dropping Robins and adding the durable Richard Crenna as a private eye), and promptly flopped again. See Brooks & Marsh, supra note 18, at 383–84.

20. The main characters on this show were prosecutor Kate Ward (played by Lauren Holly) and her flame, defense attorney Jack Scarlett (David Andrews). The show flopped on CBS at the end of the 1990–91 season, during a period that produced "Shannon's Deal," "The Trials of Rosie O'Neill," "Gabriel's Fire," and "Eddie Dodd." Also running during that period were "Matlock," "L.A. Law," "Law & Order," and "Equal Justice." Rick Kogan, "Hapless 'Antagonists:' As Another Lawyer Series Premieres, Viewers May Be Tempted to Sue," *Chicago Tribune*, March 26, 1991, at C5.

21. "Kate McShane," which lasted for just two months at the start of the 1975–76 season, starred Anne Meara as McShane and Charles Haid ("Hill Street Blues") as her brother, a Jesuit priest. "Kate was lovable but always became emotionally involved with her clients and had to be bailed out by her ex-cop pop and Jesuit little brother." See Gregory N. Joseph, "Media Image of Women Still Needs Fine-Tuning," *San Diego Union-Tribune*, January 27, 1987, at D1.

22. This series ran on NBC for two years beginning in 1991 and starred Matlin as Tess Kaufman, an assistant district attorney, and Mark Harmon as Dicky Cobb, her police officer sidekick. Howard Rosenberg, "Television's Criminal Tendencies," *Los Angeles Times*, September 26, 1991, at F1. At least one commentator objected to the attention paid to Matlin's hearing impairment.

"Reasonable Doubts" not only doesn't work, it symbolizes the all-too-typical misguided network thinking. It would have been a far classier and possibly more effective move for the show's producers to underplay Matlin's impairment. Yet, instead of being incidental, her lack of hearing is made her character's central focus as well as that of Harmon. Matters likewise are helped little by the fact that Harmon is woefully underqualified to pull off a convincingly intense Chicago police detective. He has minimal acting range. Matlin fares far better as the fiercely independent assistant district attorney, who is paired oh-so-reluctantly with Harmon's character because he knows sign language.

Ray Richmond, "NBC Series 'Reasonable Doubts' Misuses Its Star Power," *Orange County Register*, September 26, 1991, at G03.

23. This show ran for one season (1989–90) as part of "ABC Saturday Mystery Movie" series.

24. Maureen Downey, "Media's View of Women Limited," *Cincinnati Enquirer*, May 2, 1997, at E03.

25. Nancy Signorelli, "A Content Analysis: Reflections of Girls in the Media," available at <http://www.kff.org/archive/media/general/gender/gender.html>.

26. For a list of female television and film attorneys and their portrayal, see Mona Harrington, *Women Lawyers: Rewriting the Rules* 151–72 (1993). Harrington also considers many of the shows mentioned in this essay, pointing out the often frustratingly clear message that intelligent, professional women lawyers cannot expect personal happiness.

27. Sandy Smith, " 'JAG' is Gunning For Ratings," *The Tennessean*, September 23, 1995, at 3D. Andrea Parker played the woman attorney in one episode and was then replaced by Tracey Needham.

28. Walter, supra note 15.

29. Drew Jubera, "Women on TV: You've Come a Long Way, Lady; Smart, Sexy Stars and a 'Sisterhood' of Writers, Producers Celebrate a New Age of Realistic Roles," *Atlanta Journal and Constitution*, May 12, 1996, at 08L.

30. The charge that women lawyers are very likely to rely on "feminine wiles" to succeed has been made for decades. See generally Christine A. Corcos, "Portia Goes to Parliament," 75 *Denver Law Review* 307 (1998), and Christine A. Corcos, "Lawyers for Marianne," 12 *Georgia State University Law Review* 435 (1996).

31. For a quick rundown of female lawyer characters on television, see Deborah S. Seibel, "Outrageous Lawyers: A Crop of Television Lawyers Takes On the Real World," *Chicago Tribune*, April 28, 1991, at 11.

32. "Bar Girls? Images of Women Lawyers on TV Slowly Improving, Panel Says," 76 *American Bar Association Journal*, April 1990, at 41.

33. Seibel, supra note 31.

34. Grace Van Owen ("L.A. Law") and Joyce Davenport ("Hill Street Blues") are notable examples.

35. On "L.A. Law," district attorney Grace Van Owen leaves the prosecutor's office for a more lucrative private practice after much soul-searching, and in the final 1996 episode of "Law & Order" Claire Kincaid returns to talk to her law school professor

about leaving the profession. The character departs the series through a well-timed car accident; while the producers report that she is not dead, neither is she alive enough to return to the show, leaving her, as a woman attorney, once again in limbo.

36. Harrington, supra note 26, at 157.

37. "Female attorneys in film have been presented as an oxymoron; they have two identities—"female" and "attorney"—which cannot logically coexist. Initially, these characters are introduced as successful and bright legal practitioners; however, their personal lives are empty, which in the film's sexual economy means they are unmarried." Miller, supra note 10, at 205. See also Amelia Jones, " 'She Was Bad News:' Male Paranoia and the Contemporary New Woman," 25/26 Camera Obscura 297 (1991), which analyzes the image of the prosecutors Carolyn Pohlhemus and "Mac" in the movie "Presumed Innocent." Jones believes the film presents both as failures in reconciling gender and profession, Pohlhemus because of her blatant sexuality and "Mac" because her disability and her male nickname are clearly intended to render her both capable as an attorney and sexless as a person.

38. On Hollywood's treatment of the woman who attempts to break down gender stereotypes, see Kathleen Rowe, The Unruly Woman: Gender and the Genres of Laughter (1995).

39. The new "Cosby" series on CBS also features a continuing female character as a lawyer, this time as the main character's daughter.

40. Interestingly, the judge shown presiding over a case Williams is defending in this episode is female. The number of female judges portrayed in films and on television is hopelessly out of proportion to their occurrence in real life and always has been. For a discussion of other "Columbo" characters and themes, see Christine A. Corcos, "Columbo Goes to Law School, Or Some Thoughts on Television and the Teaching of Law," 13 Loyola of Los Angeles Entertainment Law Journal 499 (1993).

41. The show aired on NBC during the 1994–95 season. See Brooks & Marsh, supra note 18, at 1004.

42. The critic Stephanie B. Goldberg maintains, "While Clair Huxtable... of 'The Cosby Show' is a latter-day June Cleaver, and flaky Christine Sullivan... of 'Night Court' could double for Lucy Ricardo, the formidable trio of the hit 'L.A. Law'—Ann Kelsey... Grace Van Owen... and Abby Perkins—manage to be strong, sexy and supremely competent as lawyers, certainly a new twist for prime-time television." See "Bar Girls?," supra note 32. Similarly, both Diane Glass, in her 1990 case note, and Carole Shapiro, in her 1995 article, indicate that they think portrayals are either getting more positive or have the potential to be more positive, based on the images of television characters like those on "L.A. Law." See supra note 10.

43. Reggie's image in the film version of "The Client" was not flattering, however. For one thing, the eponymous character of the title, an eleven-year-old boy, had to explain to her that the Bill of Rights applies to children.

44. Note that in cases in which a female defense attorney does prevail, as in "Jagged Edge" and "Guilty as Sin," her win is the "wrong" result, because it results in the acquittal of a guilty person. This further demonstrates her inability, because it shows her incapable of divining whether a client is worthy of her representation. She is not superior to the male attorney; in fact she is inferior, because she allows herself to be manipulated sexually by the male client. In such cases the double standard acts to condemn women

attorneys just as it condemns other women; they cannot be trusted to leave their feelings outside the office door. In order to right the wrong they have done society by enabling a murderer to go free, these women end up killing their clients (admittedly in self-defense). Both sacrifice some part of their careers, probably irreparably.

In "Witness for the Prosecution," Sir Wilfrid Robarts, although fooled by his client, is saved from having to deal with the consequences by another character. He then can enter the legal lists once more as her attorney. The law continues to give his life meaning as he prepares yet another courtroom triumph. In "Jagged Edge" and "Guilty as Sin," the client's betrayal of the lawyer's trust is based primarily on sexual manipulation. The betrayal in "Witness for the Prosecution," while carried out by a woman and a man in combination, is intellectual. In "The Verdict," the betrayal is both professional and sexual, and the betrayer is a female attorney.

45. Susan Faludi, *Backlash: The Undeclared War Against American Women* 150–51 (1991). The message that women cannot expect to have it all is likewise a large part of Faludi's argument.

46. Other professional males also are excused for their inability to do both. Consider the words of Jake Gittes's police officer friend at the end of the film "Chinatown" as Gittes surveys the dead body of his lover. "Forget it, Jake. It's Chinatown." It's just the way things are: Women are interchangeable; move on, and find another.

47. This kind of criticism continues. In particular, women are criticized for their dress. "In the 1987 film 'Suspect,' a defense attorney shows up for a murder trial in a shortie black-leather jacket. But then, she is played by Cher, and that's Hollywood. In reality, women lawyers are often subjected to either of two equally undesirable juror perceptions: too mannish or not commanding enough." Kristin Tillotson, "Women Lawyers Get Harsher Criticism," *Star Tribune*, August 8, 1993, at 3E.

48. Female lawyers appear in the following (not an exhaustive list) films: "The Judge," "The Bachelor and the Bobby Soxer," "Adam's Rib," "Jagged Edge," "The Accused," "A Few Good Men," "Suspect," "Criminal Justice," "Defenseless," "Guilty as Sin," "Wild Orchid," and "Hostile Witness."

49. When Michael Douglas realizes in "Fatal Attraction" that he is involved with a dangerous woman (Alex Forrest, played by Glenn Close), he breaks off the relationship. He thus acknowledges that he should not have sinned, but that being a man he is constantly exposed to temptation. He demands forgiveness, it is granted ("Boys will be boys"), and blame for the continually deteriorating situation then shifts to the woman.

Notice that Dan Gallagher's (Douglas's character) ultimate response to her threats is to defend his home and family as Doris Attinger (Judy Holliday) tries to do in "Adam's Rib"; that is, he acts, but his act is excusable whereas the woman's is not. Her stalking is unacceptable. However, we have numerous examples of male stalking in films after a woman breaks off an affair. More often than not, the male succeeds in winning back the woman. A woman's "no" in these cases is much less "truthful," and hence less powerful, than a man's.

Susan Faludi points out that originally the Glenn Close character was much more attractive, the Michael Douglas character less so. After Douglas objected to what he perceived to be the unheroic nature of the male lead, it was sweetened. See Faludi, supra note 45, at 119. In the contemporaneous film "Broadcast News," Holly Hunter's character (Jane Craig) puts her career ahead of a relationship with either of the two men who admire her. They continue with their personal as well as professional lives, finding women to replace her, while she goes on alone.

50. On the screwball comedy genre, see generally Joy G. Boyum, "Columbia's Screwball Comedies: Wine, Women, and Wisecracks," in *Columbia Pictures* 89 (1991). A more detailed study is Wes D. Gehring, *Screwball Comedy: A Genre of Madcap Romance* (1986). Screwball comedy films that use the law as a backdrop for the action include: "Adam's Rib," "Mr. and Mrs. Smith" (where, as in "The Awful Truth" and "We're Not Married," a couple discovers they are not legally married), "The Talk of the Town" (a Supreme Court nominee assists an escaping prisoner), and "My Favorite Wife" (a variation of the Enoch Arden story in which wife Irene Dunne returns from seven years on a desert island just as her lawyer-husband Cary Grant has her declared legally dead and marries another woman). Interestingly, the director of "The Awful Truth" was Leo McCarey, a failed lawyer. Gehring, id. at 85–86.

51. In the initial episode she advertises for a date in the personals.

52. Joan Hanauer, "TV World; New Mary Tyler Moore Show Looks Good," December 9, 1985, BC Cycle, available at LEXIS, News Library, Arcnws file.

53. See generally Hanauer, supra note 52, and Tom Shales, "The Trials of 'Sara': A Disappointing Start for NBC Sitcom," *Washington Post*, January 23, 1985, at D1.

54. Littlefield, supra note 13.

55. Id.

56. Id.

57. Kogan, supra note 20.

58. See further Rick Marin, " 'Belvedere' Joke May Be On Us; Is It a Put-On?," *Washington Times*, September 8, 1989, at E1.

59. Faludi, supra note 45, at 153.

60. Why a district attorney is allowed to appear as a defense attorney, even in another jurisdiction, is a problem the scriptwriters leave for us to ponder.

61. Kendall Hamilton, "Marcia Clark Goes Straight," *Newsweek*, April 24, 1995, at 72.

62. Some critics, however, object that the character portrays a stereotypically sexually repressed woman with very poor judgment. See, for example, Shapiro, supra note 10.

63. Compare Anne's (and other small screen lawyers's) private investigations sua sponte with his associate's warnings to Alan Dershowitz in the film "Reversal of Fortune" when he decides to meet with a particularly smarmy witness. She reminds him that he is not Perry Mason; he disregards her warnings and heroically gets the needed information.

64. Within weeks of their arrest, the two accused cadets in the case of the murder of a young Texas girl were featured in "Love's Deadly Triangle: The Texas Cadet Murder." "In the Line of Duty: Assault in Waco" was on NBC's upcoming schedule before the final attack on the Branch Davidian compound. See Ken P. Perkins, "Responsible TV Channel 5 Deals With the Hard Questions in Blacking Out 'Texas Cadet Murder,'" *Fort Worth Star-Telegram*, February 10, 1997, at 3 (Life & Arts). Although Fox announced that it was working on a version of the Nicole Brown Simpson-Ronald Goldman murders in July 1994, it at least waited until the O.J. Simpson jury was sequestered before airing its retelling of the story. See David Zurawik, "Docudrama Becomes a Rush To On-Air Judgment," *Baltimore Sun*, February 10, 1997, at 1D.

65. Diane Werts, "Glued to the Tube/A Case for Prosecutors/Hey, NBC, This Has the Makings of a Series," *Newsday*, December 2, 1996, at B21.

66. "What do they want? It's not enough to feature two tough, smart women in a brainy character-study suspenser? To let 'em be such frank dames as TV rarely gives us? To vividly explore their motivations, weaknesses, fears, pride, vanity, heroism and the essential nature of trust? Not to mention the situational ethics of American due process." Werts, supra note 65.

67. We do sense, however, that Hilda Rumpole, the daughter of a judge, would probably have enjoyed a career as a lawyer, although that option was undoubtedly not open to her.

68. In the British legal system, "taking silk" means becoming a Queen's Counsel (or in the case of a male monarch, a King's Counsel).

69. Among other foreign series featuring women lawyers, the Canadian series "Street Legal" and the Scottish series "The Advocates" offer several unremarkable female lawyer characters.

70. Seibel, supra note 31.

71. Florence L. Denmark, "The Thirty-Something Woman: To Career or Not to Career," in *Gender Issues Across the Life Cycle* 71, 72 (Barbara R. Wainrib ed. 1992).

72. Seibel, supra note 31.

73. Id.

74. Id.

Notes for Chapter 17
Young Lawyers

1. Avery also played a respected judge on the NBC situation comedy "The Fresh Prince of Bel Air," which aired from 1990–96.

2. Much of the material contained in this essay is excerpted from a more comprehensive study of prime time lawyer images set forth in "Detectives, Therapists, Fathers, and Hired Guns: A Cross-Examination of Lawyer Images on Television," my unpublished University of Michigan doctoral dissertation.

3. Chess, essentially a medieval war game, has long been associated with men's leisure and as a measure of power. Consider, for example, the film "Searching for Bobby Fischer" (1993), in which chess is a metaphor for the relationship between a father and his adolescent son.

4. See *Variety*, March 11, 1970, at 36. See also, "Eye's Got It (Youth) On Mind," *Variety*, June 10, 1970, at 50.

5. See *Variety*, June 17, 1970, at 32–33.

6. See *Variety*, November 18, 1970, at 42. Indeed, one of its best outings was for the week ending November 1, 1970, when it was ranked last in the Nielsen Top 40. See "Web's Top 40: 'Safe Zone,'" *Variety*, November 11, 1970, at 28.

7. "Networks in Juggling Act as '2d Season' Takes Shape," *Variety*, November 11, 1970, at 28.

8. See "ABC-TV's Duffy Claims Full Credit For Primetime Cutback in January; Cites Bottom-Line Values For Affils," *Variety*, December 23, 1970, at 27.

9. See "TV Webs In Image Recession," *Variety*, December 30, 1970, at 23, 30. See also *Variety*, November 18, 1970, at 64.

10. Similarities between the visual images and musical accompaniment in the opening sequences of "Hawaii Five-0" and "Storefront Lawyers" are more than coincidence. "Storefront Lawyers" was produced for CBS by Leonard Freeman, who also produced and created "Hawaii Five-0." The Ventures, a popular instrumental group of the period best known today for the musical theme to "Hawaii Five-0," performed the theme to "Storefront Lawyers."

11. In "First We Get Rid of the Principal," Kaye reluctantly solicits assistance from Della Levy, a woman who is romantically interested in him. Over a candlelit dinner at her apartment, Levy can't keep her hands off him. Kaye, clearly uncomfortable by her strong advances, tries to steer the conversation back to the purpose of his visit. After Levy agrees to help, she resumes her seduction.

12. The title sequence to "The Young Lawyers" places each lawyer in a freeze frame as he or she descends the steps of a courthouse. There is little differentiation among the shots of the actors except that Judy Pace, like Sheila Larken, poses with her mouth open.

13. See, e.g., the episode entitled "The Emancipation of Bessie Gray."

14. See "CBS 'Lawyers' May Leave Store," *Variety*, October 14, 1970, at 40.

15. See "Here Comes De-Relevance," *Variety*, November 4, 1970, at 29.

16. See Les Brown, *The New York Times Encyclopedia of Television* 415 (1977).

17. In the promotional trailer for the revamped series, Robert Foxworth introduced O'Loughlin's new character as "highly respected attorney Devlin McNeil."

18. "Now relevance" is a term that was widely used in the trade press to describe the social relevance programs of 1970. See, e.g., *Variety*, October 21, 1970, at 36.

19. In "Kate McShane," Meara played an aggressive crusader who passionately represented her clients. The show did not, however, completely break with the mentor-apprentice tradition. Meara's character regularly relied on the advice and support of her father (a cop) and her brother (a law professor and priest).

20. In 1954, June Havoc starred in "Willy," a short-lived CBS situation comedy about a small town lawyer who lived with her parents. Although Willy occasionally handled minor cases, the comedic plots made fun of the fact that she was lawyer. In the show's premiere episode, Willy naively tries to claim that she's the attorney for a malfeasing dog.

Notes for
Epilogue

1. See further American Bar Association Commission on Advertising, *Lawyer Advertising at the Crossroads: Professional Policy Considerations* 66 (1995).

2. See Randall Samborn, "Anti-Lawyer Attitude Up, But NLJ/West Poll Also Shows More People Are Using Attorneys," *National Law Journal*, August 9, 1993, at 1, col. 1.

3. Id.

4. Robert C. Post, "On the Popular Image of the Lawyer: Reflections in a Dark Glass," 75 *California Law Review* 379, 380 (1987).

5. Id. at 386.

6. Id. at 388–89.

7. See Barbara A. Curran, *The Legal Needs of the Public: A Final Report of a National Survey* 262–63 (1977).

8. William Shakespeare, *Henry VI*, Part II, act 4, scene 2, line 68.

9. Compare Luke, chapter 11, verses 46 and 52, with Matthew, chapter 23, verse 13.

10. Karl Llewellyn, *The Bramble Bush: Of Our Law and Its Study* 142 (1960) (quoting Carl Sandburg, *The Lawyers Know Too Much* (1951)).

11. This paragraph is paraphrased from the remarks of the famous lawyer John W. Davis, as quoted in Martin Mayer, *The Lawyers* 3 (1967).

Contributors

DOUGLAS E. ABRAMS is an Associate Professor of Law at the University of Missouri (Columbia). He holds a B.A. from Wesleyan University and a J.D. from Columbia University. Professor Abrams wishes to thank Tracey E. George, Chris P. Guthrie, and Scott A. Robbins for their assistance with his essay.

JOHN BRIGHAM is a Professor of Political Science at the University of Massachusetts (Amherst). He holds a B.A. from the University of California (Berkeley), an M.A. from the University of Wisconsin (Madison), and a Ph.D. from the University of California (Santa Barbara).

ROD CARVETH is an Associate Professor of Mass Communication at the University of Bridgeport. He holds a B.A. from Yale University and an M.A. and a Ph.D. from the University of Massachusetts (Amherst).

CHRISTINE ALICE CORCOS is an Associate Professor of Law at Louisiana State University (Baton Rouge). She holds a B.A. and an M.A. from Michigan State University, an A.M.L.S. from the University of Michigan, and a J.D. from Case Western Reserve University. Professor Corcos wishes to thank Jill Kuswa and Madeline Hebert for their assistance with her essay.

JOHN DENVIR is a Professor of Law at the University of San Francisco. He holds a B.S. from Holy Cross College, a J.D. from New York University, and an LL.M. from Harvard University.

WALTER A. EFFROSS is an Associate Professor of Law at American University (Washington, D.C.). He holds an A.B. from Princeton University and a J.D. from Harvard University.

MICHAEL M. EPSTEIN is a Visiting Assistant Professor of Communications at Syracuse University. He holds a B.A. and a J.D. from Columbia University and a Ph.D. from the University of Michigan.

SUSAN BETH FARMER is an Assistant Professor of Law at Pennsylvania State University (Carlisle). She holds a B.A. from Wellesley College and a J.D. from Vanderbilt University. Professor Farmer wishes to thank Tara Wempe and Joanna Toft for their assistance with her essay.

ROBERT M. JARVIS is a Professor of Law at Nova Southeastern University (Fort Lauderdale). He holds a B.A. from Northwestern University, a J.D. from the University of Pennsylvania, and an LL.M. from New York University.

PAUL R JOSEPH is a Professor of Law at Nova Southeastern University (Fort Lauderdale). He holds a B.A. from Goddard College, a J.D. from the University of California (Davis), and an LL.M. from Temple University. Professor Joseph wishes to thank his wife Lynn Wolf and Randy Ginsburg for their assistance with his essay.

DAWN KEETLEY is an Assistant Professor of English at North Carolina State University (Raleigh). She holds a B.A. from the University of South Alabama, an M.A. from Pennsylvania State University, and a Ph.D. from the University of Wisconsin (Madison).

FRANCIS M. NEVINS is a Professor of Law at St. Louis University. He holds an A.B. from St. Peter's College and a J.D. from New York University. Professor Nevins wishes to thank Boyd Magers, Thomas Carr, Paul Landres, Joseph H. Lewis, William Witney, Will Hutchins, and Glenn Mosley for their assistance with his essay.

DAVID RAY PAPKE is the R. Bruce Townsend Professor of Law at Indiana University (Indianapolis) and a Professor of Liberal Arts at Indiana University-Purdue University (Indianapolis). He holds an A.B. from Harvard University, an M.A. and a J.D. from Yale University, and a Ph.D. from the University of Michigan.

GAIL LEVIN RICHMOND is a Professor of Law at Nova Southeastern University (Fort Lauderdale). She holds an A.B. and an M.B.A. from the University of Michigan and a J.D. from Duke University.

NORMAN ROSENBERG is the DeWitt Wallace Professor of History at Macalester College (St. Paul). He holds a B.A. and an M.A. from the University of Nebraska (Lincoln) and a Ph.D. from the State University of New York (Stony Brook). Professor Rosenberg wishes to thank his wife Emily for her assistance with his essay.

RONALD D. ROTUNDA is the Albert E. Jenner, Jr. Professor of Law at the University of Illinois (Champaign). He holds an A.B. and a J.D. from Harvard University. Professor Rotunda wishes to thank Sandra Pulley, the Stuart N. Greenberger Research Assistant in Legal Ethics, for her assistance with his essay.

RICHARD CLARK STERNE is a Professor of English Emeritus at Simmons College (Boston). He holds an A.B. from Columbia University and an A.M. and a Ph.D. from Harvard University. Professor Sterne wishes to thank his wife Ruth and his son Lawrence for their assistance with his essay.

JEFFREY E. THOMAS is an Assistant Professor of Law at the University of Missouri (Kansas City). He holds a B.A. from Loyola Marymount University and a J.D. from the University of California (Berkeley).

General Index

Series Index